TAKING STOCK

THE MODERN JEWISH EXPERIENCE

Deborah Dash Moore and Marsha L. Rozenblit, *editors*
Paula Hyman, founding *coeditor*

TAKING STOCK

Cultures of Enumeration in Contemporary Jewish Life

Edited by Michal Kravel-Tovi and
Deborah Dash Moore

Indiana University Press

Bloomington and Indianapolis

This book is a publication of

Indiana University Press
Office of Scholarly Publishing
Herman B Wells Library 350
1320 East 10th Street
Bloomington, Indiana 47405 USA

iupress.indiana.edu

The paper used in this publication meets the minimum requirements of the American National Standard for Information Sciences—Permanence of Paper for Printed Library Materials, ANSI Z39.48-1992.

Manufactured in the United States of America

Cataloging information is available from the Library of Congress.

ISBN 978-0-253-02047-5 (cloth)
ISBN 978-0-253-02054-3 (paperback)
ISBN 978-0-253-02057-4 (ebook)

1 2 3 4 5 21 20 19 18 17 16

For Yoel, Eviatar, and Shaul Tovi—the three who count most in my life

For my fourth grandchild, Oren Jacob Moore, who brings with his arrival the joys of taking stock

Contents

Acknowledgments

THIS VOLUME has been long in the making, and it is a great pleasure for us to have a chance to thank several people who have contributed to it in various ways. It began as an idea for a workshop on the social life of Jewish numbers developed by Michal Kravel-Tovi as her public contribution as Mandell L. Berman Postdoctoral Research Fellow in Contemporary American Jewish Life. As Director of the Frankel Center for Judaic Studies of the University of Michigan, Deborah Dash Moore brainstormed together with Michal to give shape and substance to the proposed workshop, held on March 18–20, 2012. Both of us recognized that numbers have long occupied Jewish imagination and practice, mediating and shaping the ways in which Jews have constructed and narrated themselves and their worlds. It seemed worthwhile to examine in greater depth how Jews have produced numerical accounts of themselves and then employed these accounts to negotiate their relationships with both God and meaningful social others. To this end, we convened an international workshop and invited diverse scholars to both write formal papers and present comments. Over several days, the Frankel Center seminar table reverberated with lively discussions and sharp analyses, along with respectful disagreements and personal stories. Invigorated, we agreed that the papers deserved to reach a wider audience. However, we recognized that we would have to narrow the focus for publication, so we decided to emphasize such key issues as the Israeli-Palestinian conflict, actualization of the Zionist dream, meanings ascribed to numbers in the Holocaust, and the embrace of numbers by American Jews to interpret political and religious notions of continuity.

The workshop and this volume benefited from the contribution of all of the scholars who participated. In addition to those in *Taking Stock,* workshop participants and their topics included: Robert Kawashima (University of Florida), "Calculating Sacred Time: On the 'Archeology' of the Ancient Jewish Calendar"; Gwynn Kessler (Swarthmore College), "Rabbinic Numerology: Making Lists, Counting Numbers, and Creating Worlds"; Ian Lustick (University of Pennsylvania), "Numbers and the Production of Quantification: Israeli Investigations"; Noam Pianko (University of Washington), "Is Counting Counterproductive? Toward a Jewish Collectivity Beyond Numbers"; and Seth Schwartz (Columbia University), "Why Do Historical Demography of Ancient Jews?"; Ruth Behar, Karla Goldman, Rachel Neis, Sammy Smooha, and Geneviève Zubrzycki, all affiliated with the University of Michigan at the time of the workshop, contributed formal as well as informal comments in their capacity as respondents. We are grateful to all of these scholars as well as to the support of the Frankel Center for Judaic Studies, and especially Cheri Thompson, its business manager, for hosting the workshop.

At Indiana University Press, Dee Mortensen proved to be a superb editor. We benefited from her editorial suggestions as well as from the extraordinarily careful reading done by both external reviewers. Their thoughtful criticisms immeasurably improved the volume. We particularly want to thank Lila Corwin Berman for her generous and provocative comments. We appreciate Marsha Rozenblit's enthusiastic endorsement of the volume as a worthy contribution to the Modern Jewish Experience Series. We are grateful for the careful attention to copyediting and production details of Frances Andersen at Newgen North America. We also want to thank Thalia Thereza Assan at Tel Aviv University for her extraordinary work on the index of this volume.

Deborah has enjoyed working with Michal on this path-breaking volume. Her high standards, clarity of vision, and willingness to share occasionally difficult tasks have been exemplary.

Michal is grateful to the financial support of Mandell L. Berman as well as to the academic and emotional generosity of Deborah Dash Moore. Deborah has unique ways to engage with others' ideas both openly and critically. Throughout the joint work on this volume, Deborah has provided ongoing support and mentorship and has modeled such a strong sense of professionalism and intellectual wisdom. It has been a true privilege to co-edit this book with her.

TAKING STOCK

Introduction

Counting in Jewish

Michal Kravel-Tovi

Delivered through rapid, hip-hop beats and intense lyrics, Hadag Nachash's "The Numbers Song" provides a critical, numerical account of what matters to young Israeli Jews. It begins by counting states ("one or two") in the land that stretches between the sea and the Jordan River and ends with the sacred icon of six million. In between, it offers a more intimate account of the numerical texture of personal experience ("three years and four months is the time I gave to the IDF";[1] "nine times I have been too close to a terror attack"), while detailing the harsh arithmetic that underwrites everyday life in Israel ("a quarter of a million are unemployed"; "the government cut off 12 percent of child benefits"). Fast-paced and abrasive in content, the song echoes in form the pervasive flow of statistical data in Jewish public spheres, while simultaneously mocking, through its poetics, the overwhelming presence of numbers in Jewish life. However, as critical a reflection on numbers as this song provides, its lyrics also disclose their inescapable grip: "Me too," the chorus admits, "like all Jews, is obsessed with numbers 24/7, twelve months a year."

Hadag Nachash is not alone in its use of numbers as a structuring device for popular narration of Jewish-Israeli culture. In the late Yossi Banai's famous song, "Sfirat Melai" (generally translated as either "stocktaking" or "counting stock"), the famous Israeli singer-actor relied on numbers to tell an insightful story about Jewish life in Israel. Playfully toying with the numerical associations of the Passover song "Who Knows One?," Banai introduces some twists into a familiar numerical tradition. Instead of counting Jewish motifs and teachings alone, as is done in the Haggadah (e.g., the number of the tablets of the covenant or the number of the tribes of Israel), Banai's song weaves together older Jewish numbers with more contemporary ones. Look, he teasingly lays out, at just how many numbers Israel has managed to accumulate in its national and political stockpiles: "One state, two seas, one lake and malaria as well . . . one nation, full of uniqueness, one headache and three pills, six days and seven nights . . . a huge immigration following two thousand years of diaspora . . . one moment of security and then thirty days of illness, one day of victory, one day of downfall, half-a-dozen veteran major-generals, two ministers without a portfolio . . . five wars . . . three tired soldiers at the post, seventy kids laughing in the bomb-shelter, three prisoners of Zion and another serving his sixth month of a life sentence." In the chorus that ends each of Banai's ironic lists, he insistently returns to the text of the traditional song, as if to sarcastically assure his audience that Israel still has "one God in heaven and earth."

To the extent that building upon traditional Jewish numbers entailed a degree of flexibility on the part of Yossi Banai, it is not surprising that, after his passing, his colleagues playfully continued to riff on his contribution. A few years after Banai's death, at an event in his honor, the famous actress Tiki Dayan performed "Sfirat Melai," but dramatically changed one line. Rather than singing "One prisoner in his sixth month of a life sentence," she shifted the song's energetic tone and, singing slowly, emphasized each and every word: "One captive in his fifth year." It was May 2011, and no further context was required; everyone in her audience understood that Dayan was referring to Gilad Shalit, an Israeli soldier who was abducted in 2006 and had since been held captive in Gaza by Hamas. That this moment created what the daily Ynet news service described as an "intense sadness" among the audience can be easily grasped.[2] After all, Shalit stood at the center of an affectively loaded media campaign that not only advocated for his release but also encouraged the public to care personally about his return home. That the individual person of Gilad Shalit could be abstracted into a powerful number—an especially significant "one," listed among the national stock—can also be easily understood. The campaign for his release had largely been organized in numerical terms. From the outset, his captivity was discursively constructed as a temporal experience of waiting, one that foregrounded the amount of time in which he had been held. Live clocks, on webpages or roadsides, could often be seen counting the time passed since his abduction. Commemorations or concerts publicly marked special dates (i.e., "round" numbers such as 1,000 days or five years of captivity).

When Shalit was released in October 2011, numbers again occupied the public imagination, dampening an otherwise euphoric national mood that greeted Shalit upon his return. In keeping with previous prisoner exchanges in the history of Israel, the Shalit deal seemed sorely uneven in terms of numbers. "One Israeli captive for 1,027 Palestinians," the headlines called out in bitterness and frustration about the obvious lack of numerical reciprocity in this transaction. The release of *so many* Palestinian prisoners, who, as the media continuously reported, were imprisoned because of an association with terrorist groups and actions against Israeli citizens, in exchange for *only one* captive was portrayed as too high and risky a price for a state to pay for any *one* of its citizens. What was, however, being recognized in these bold headlines is the extent to which

Jewish morality extends beyond mere numbers. By staking out positions on the uniquely high value that the Jewish state is assumed to place on the sanctity of life, all sides acknowledged and even celebrated the incommensurable system of calculations that supposedly makes Israel morally exceptional. To paraphrase the title of this introduction, one could say that what was celebrated was the extent to which Jews "count in Jewish."

As evidenced in this threefold intertextual (or, perhaps, "internumerical") description, numbers have become normalized in many representational practices in Jewish-Israeli public culture. If we turn our attention to American Jewry, another leading Jewish community that engages us in this volume, we can easily identify a similarly profound cultural investment in quantified forms of knowledge and representation. Take, for example, the 2013 book *And Every Single One Was Someone*—a provocative textual monument of Holocaust memory that consists of 1,250 pages in which the single word "Jew" is printed six million times. If one searches the pages of this book with Amazon's "Surprise Me!" search option, the reader will always encounter the same structure and content; no surprises here. With no names of victims or places, no dates of births or deaths, this book attempts to both totalize and communicate the enormity of the Holocaust by maintaining the solidity of a numerical icon. In other words, the book presents a graphic minimalism whose emotional and moral, though debated, effects lie precisely in its repetitive, aggregate, and intentionally crude numerical nature.

Beyond the irreplaceable, "sacred" number of six million, many other, more mundane numbers saturate American Jewish public spheres, including the number of people who fast on Yom Kippur, the number of synagogues and Jewish federations, the rate of Jewish intermarriage, and the number of "Birthright Israel" participants. To the extent that these and other numbers have become ubiquitous features of American Jewish public culture, the very engagement of Jews with numbers—sometimes described as an obsession—has also received growing public attention within communal conversations. Take, for example, *Contact*'s special issues dedicated to the numerically related topics of Jewish demography and Jewish social research[3] or *Sh'ma*'s special issue on counting Jews.[4] In the following introductory note, the editors of *Sh'ma* stress the need for such a communal conversation:

> Numbers count. And while our people have always been relatively few, how many is too few Jews? Since the days of King David, our numbers have been a source of contention. Today is no different. When does a preoccupation with the number of Arabs, or Ultra-Orthodox or Russian Jews in Israel cross the line separating legitimate political consideration from rank racism or ethnocentrism? . . . This month, Sh'ma explores these questions in the context of demography and more: we ask about how, and whether, numbers ought to

determine policy: Who are we as we count ourselves? How do we count on the world's stage as Jews?[5]

Taken together, these different vignettes illustrate myriad ways in and through which Jews rely heavily on numbers in the process of shaping and representing their collective life. Indeed, numerical figures dominate countless communal, public, and institutional domains in which Jews act and speak in the name of Jewish collectivity. Both ideas and ideals about numbers inform public discussions that animate and divide Jewish politics. Essentially, conceptions of numbers underwrite policy and public discourse about such key issues as the Israeli-Palestinian conflict, the relationship between the Jewish nation-state and the Jewish diaspora, the extent of anti-Semitism in the world, and many others. Additionally, quantified modes of thinking govern the production of knowledge undertaken by Jewish communities, research institutions, and think tanks throughout the world. Such modes also inform grassroots and institutionally mediated cultural productions aimed at Jewish commemoration, preservation, and innovation. But scholars have yet to pursue a critically informed, in-depth investigation of the cultures of enumeration that have permeated modern and contemporary Jewish life. We aim to initiate this investigation in *Taking Stock*.

The Social Life of Jewish Numbers

The chapters in this book began their social lives as papers presented and discussed at "The Social Life of Jewish Numbers" workshop, organized by the co-editors of this volume and held at the University of Michigan's Frankel Center for Judaic Studies (March 2012). All papers were individually solicited and originally written for the workshop. Our strategy was to invite scholars to both acknowledge and reflect on the pervasive presence of numbers in Jewish life as this presence has emerged within a diverse range of overlapping settings: national, religious, communal, institutional, and scientific in nature. We asked workshop participants to consider what we tentatively called "Jewish numbers" as highly constructed artifacts that emerge, and sometimes endure, through a complex array of performative modalities and social relations, including their production, presentation, consumption, and negotiation. We also asked participants to think through the vast range of practices (i.e., measuring, counting, collecting, comparing, and narrating) that coalesce to shape the ways in which Jewish groups, polities, and institutions immerse themselves in the cultural work of enumeration.

While the analytical potential of the "social life of Jewish numbers" framework was initially exploratory in nature, a few solid premises shaped this collaborative project from the outset. We proposed an expansive approach to numerical cultures. We shared an understanding that numbers matter; that is, they count and are counted upon as anchors of significance and power in multiple ways and across various contexts. We aimed to move beyond the explicitly politicized rubric of Jewish statistics and to demonstrate instead a richer array of cultural engagements of Jews with numbers. Undoubtedly, the rubric of Jewish statistics might be the first topic to come to mind in connection with such a project, and rightly so. Numerical thinking and demographic consciousness assume prominence in some of the most burning issues that confront Israel as a Zionist, Jewish state. The Israeli occupation of the West Bank, the contours of the Law of Return (Israel's repatriation law), and the state's conversion policies—all these implicate questions and anxieties regarding Jewish demography. However, while some of the chapters in this volume speak to politicized processes and repercussions of counting Jews, the volume also attempts to move beyond domains usually or more intuitively associated with numbers, such as science making, nation building, and production of the political imagination. By bringing together in one place diverse case studies, the volume articulates unexpected connections among cultures of enumeration that might otherwise appear unrelated. In so doing, the volume encourages a thematic breadth that, we hope, will ultimately enrich our understanding of the hold that numbers have over Jewish public life.

This expansive framework of numerical cultures emerged out of inductive premises. Indeed, we initiated our project based on questions—rather than assumptions and shared agreements—about the roles of numbers in modern and contemporary Jewish life. Going beyond the influential yet abstract and sweeping argument of Alain Badiou that, "we know very well what numbers are for: they serve, strictly speaking, for everything, they provide a norm for All,"[6] the contributors to this volume ask what numbers are for. Their careful, original analyses in response to this question inquire into the particular, historically situated contexts and culturally contingent manifestations of numbers in order to better understand the modes and effects of their deployment. The chapters emerged not only as a way to demonstrate and analyze what numbers "do" for Jews but also what becomes enumerable for them. The authors ask: How and to what ends do Jews introduce numbers into their public and institutional lives and, ultimately, form relationships with them? What is the nature of these deep relationships that Jews have developed with certain numbers? And what are the modalities and practices that constitute them?

The potential value of asking these questions is even greater in light of the fact that they have rarely been addressed—or even raised—in the interdisciplinary rubric of Jewish studies. Hence, a third motivation for this project derives from an attempt to initiate a scholarly conversation in a field that has thus far been ignored. Whereas a substantial scholarly literature on the modern uses of numbers has both historicized and theorized their varied forms and contexts, within Jewish studies similar research trajectories have hardly been explored. With the exception of a few excellent pieces on Jewish social science, there is a dearth of literature on Jewish histories and cultures of enumeration. This research lacuna can be explained, at least in part, by the influence that quantitatively based scholarship holds over numerical engagements of Jews. As a consequence of this epistemological bias, counting practices and numbers have been primarily understood, respectively, as a method and an end goal. Acknowledging this limited and, so often, uncritical treatment of numbers in the social scientific study of Jews, *Taking Stock* opens up alternative research agendas, ones that frame numbers and processes of quantification as analytic objects requiring critical investigation in their own right. In identifying this lacuna, and taking a step toward addressing it, the book offers a fresh perspective on the modern Jewish experience. We hope that we may thus encourage more research in this vein—research that would add to our understanding of "what numbers are for."

Integral to our premises and goals was the attempt to assemble a diverse group of contributors who stand in different relationships to both Jewish studies and critical scholarly engagement with numbers. Since we wanted to create a meta-discussion on Jews and numbers, we had less to gain from social scientists whose scholarly work focuses specifically on counting Jews and quantifying their lives. Instead, we sought to include scholars who work on Jews in areas that seemed to be conducive to productive perspectives on numerical cultures as well as scholars who work on social histories of numbers outside of the academic framework of Jewish studies. In other words, we invited scholars who focus on Jews to think about their work through the prism of numbers and scholars who focus on numbers to think through case studies that emphasize the embeddedness of numbers in Jewish histories. The intentional gap between "scholars of numbers" and "scholars of Jews" helped provoke mutually valuable discussions in unanticipated ways. The broad range of disciplinary orientations (including anthropology, history, science and technology studies, and religious studies) augmented the rich, open, and critical approaches we seek to advance in this volume.

Ongoing conversations at the workshop made apparent that Jews do not only count (a lot) but that they do it, so to speak, "in Jewish." Building on an analogue with Jonathan Boyarin's *Thinking in Jewish,* the idea of "counting in Jewish" suggests a grounded understanding of the phenomenology, semiotics, and politics of Jewish counting.[7] Even if Jews employ in their practices of enumeration what came to be an almost universal, or Western hegemonic arithmetic logic, their counting is particularly Jewish in the sense that it is deeply situated in Jewish historical experiences and cultural sensibilities. The reasons for which, and the cultural formats through which, Jews immerse themselves in counting should be understood within these different Jewish sociocultural matrixes. This grounded approach to counting resonated as the scholarly voices raised in the seminar room at the University of Michigan were oftentimes registered, heard, and reacted upon "in Jewish." When workshop participants, most of whom are Jewish scholars, introduced personal narratives, experiences, and perspectives, discussion of numbers was inevitably held or anchored "in Jewish"—a fact that attests to the inescapability and power of the very phenomenon we all gathered to critically explore.

The Promise of Numbers

The difficulty involved in attempting to account for the sheer volume and breadth of studies on numbers surely requires an acknowledgment of the inherent limitations of such an account: it is impossible to exhaustively survey the numerous trajectories and explorations that scholars have undertaken in the study of numbers. Nevertheless, the abundance of scholarship itself seems to disclose the extent to which numbers are a ubiquitous and multidimensional phenomenon. As scholars increasingly attend to numerical matters, both as fresh points of entry into the study of social life and as objects of investigation, they demonstrate numbers' analytical potential. The following review illustrates this promise of numbers and thus serves as a backdrop against which this volume calls for further investigation of numbers among scholars interested in modern and contemporary Jewish social life.

Unsurprisingly, much academic work on numbers starts with their pervasiveness in contemporary social life. Scholars have detailed the ways in which numbers have been employed in ancient, medieval, and other premodern eras in a variety of contexts of administration and regulation:[8] for example, in census accounts (mostly for the purpose of taxation and military conscription) and within exchange and kinship relationships.[9] At the same time, scholars have argued that the modern preoccupation with enumeration is unique and unprecedented, closely associated with the emergence of urban and industrial mass societies, of the modern state (i.e., administrative bureaucracy, professional expertise), and of the social sciences. Part and parcel of this linkage between numbers and modernity is the understanding that numbers dominate, if not "colonize,"[10] modern societies. In particular, scholars have paid attention to the ways in which numbers are so indispensably (almost invisibly or "naturally") put on display in public, to the fact that modern people inhabit and internalize worlds populated with numbers, and to the fact that numeracy is as central and diffused a skill as literacy. "Obsession," "passion," "fetishism," and "enchantment" are some of the expressions that recur in the vocabulary that defines the nature of the trust that modern people place in numbers.

The ideologies that underwrite the strengths of numbers—that is, their association with "objectivity," "universality," "efficiency," and "synoptic vision"— engage scholars in their attempt to historicize the appeal of numbers. How, why, and under what conditions, scholars have asked, have numbers become such an object of sustained trust? How and why have numbers come to occupy privileged spaces of influence in their capacities as a language, a mode of knowledge, and a source of action? The answers given to these questions illuminate important political and social work that numbers do for people and polities. At the same time, these answers do not ignore the price that individuals and societies pay for their trust in numbers. Far from concentrating merely on the manipulative potential of numbers, scholars point also to their destructive effects as they make people both calculable objects and calculating subjects. Interestingly, the very features that have made numbers such effective artifacts of modern social life are also considered by scholars to contribute to the abuse of individuals and collectives as people immerse themselves (or are immersed by others) in processes and logics of quantification. Numbers, for example, can be misused in population data systems in ways that threaten human rights,[11] can result in structural violence,[12] or, perhaps less dramatically, frustrate their practitioners by oversimplifying a complex lived experience.[13]

While a limited number of studies concern themselves with numbers in their broadest and most diversified applications,[14] or with their most fundamental materializations in social situations,[15] most scholars limit themselves to more confined realms of enumeration, usually financial, political, and religious. Even if numbers, as stated elsewhere,[16] travel and spread easily across various domains, a thematic and more bounded review would do better justice to the literature. What follows lays out the above-mentioned three key thematic clusters that have emerged in the scholarship on numbers. Although these clusters do not necessarily materialize in this volume, I briefly gesture toward some compelling directions they take in the general literature on numbers. In illuminating how this volume fits into a broader scholarly enterprise, I hope that this review may also precipitate similar interest among Jewish studies scholars. Following the brief threefold review of the scholarship on numbers, I will then concisely examine the extant literature of numbers in Jewish contexts.

Accounting, Money, and Financial Numbers

Academic scholarship has recognized the co-constitutive relationships and connections between numbers and money. Numbers have played critical roles in the monetization, industrialization, and capitalization of social life as well as in cultures of auditing and accounting that emerged in concert with these large-scale historical processes.[17] As the anthropologist Caitlin Zaloom summarizes: "From the invention of number-based accounting practices such as double-entry bookkeeping, numbers have been a cornerstone of economic calculation, providing the essential tools for rationalized action."[18] At the same time, exchange of money provides the immediate context in which mathematical logics and numerical practices have been developed, circulated, and embraced in everyday life.[19] In this vein, one could consider the historical accounts of Patricia Cline Cohen and Michael Zakim on the spread of numeracy and the emergence of capitalism, respectively, in early and nineteenth-century America.[20] Or, one could consider the growing ethnographic accounts of how financial institutions represent—and ultimately, live with—numbers.[21]

Scientific Knowledge, Government, and Political Numbers

Numerous studies in the social history of quantification in both the natural and social sciences have shown the degree to which this history is intimately tied to the history of modern power and politics, primarily under the rubric of the modern state.[22] As Theodore Porter acknowledges in the opening of *Trust in Numbers*, though his initial intention was to study the modern history of social quantification in relation to academic disciplines, he found himself paying more attention to professions and bureaucracies.[23] Following Michel Foucault's theories of modern forms of power, the intersection of the scientific and the administrative (i.e., the statistical and the political) has been almost universally recognized as the starting point for academic work on science—and numbers—making.[24] If numbers, as Foucault and many others suggest, play a mutually constitutive role in the production of "the social," then, the argument goes, we must also consider how the domain of politics is numerically constituted, and conversely how the domain of numbers is politically constituted.[25]

There has been a great deal of work on the social histories of the scientific development of quantification.[26] These social histories show the processes by which numbers acquired connotations of scientific impartiality, transparency, neutrality, and, ultimately, objectivity.[27] Perceived as resistant to biases of conjecture, numbers promise certainty and order within the growing chaos of modern life.[28] Ironically, because of their technical, scientific, and de-politicized aura,[29] numbers have become a potent discursive tool in politics—a firm anchor with which to ground political debate and decisions.[30]

Unsurprisingly, much scholarship on the political numbers of the state centers on the national census.[31] Such an investigation has been applied to the state in its varied instances, including the national,[32] the socialist,[33] the postsocialist,[34] and the colonial.[35] If we apply what Talal Asad has written about national statistics in the colonial state—about its being a "strong language"[36]—we might say more broadly that numbers seem to possess the power to transform modes of life writ large. In their constitutive and prescriptive capacities, numbers make by way of objectification and classification the realities and abstractions they seemingly describe: they create the "population," the mass public, the "unified nation," the "average, normative" individual, the "crisis," and the "social problem."[37] In so doing, they also establish understandings, affects, norms, and forms of power that are implicated in shaping the modern experience.

Church, Religion, and Theological Numbers

To the degree that finance, science, and the state—domains most extensively associated in modernity with numbers—are imbued with "sacredness," it should come as no surprise that numbers can also be associated with explicitly religious spheres. However, scholars display less interest in religious numbers than in financial and political ones. In their call to thicken this line of inquiry, and question the assumption that the field of numbers is inherently disenchanted, Jane Guyer and others argue that "any radical secularization of the study of numbers—as technique alone—is necessarily incomplete for anthropologists."[38] To complete what is often missing in discussions of numbers, Guyer and colleagues remind us of the manifold instances of enumeration within texts and contexts we easily define as "religious," "spiritual," or "sacred." For example, numerology occupies a vibrant place in many religious traditions; both the mathematical and economic imagination originated in devotional and theological contexts; the religions of "The Book" draw on biblical references of calculation and measurement; and the notion of accounting is embedded in religiously informed moral and spiritual frameworks.

This timely call to attend to religious enumeration in its own right might be read as a response to the fact that most scholars who introduce religion to be considered in the study of numbers, do so as part of their broader interest in overtly politicized religious realms. Indeed, case studies are often situated in Christian contexts, an unsurprising bias given the emphasis in the literature on science and state making in Western and colonial contexts. This rubric includes resistance to census taking based on religious belief,[39] statistical spectacles in politicized frameworks of religious conversion,[40] as well as the centrality of numbers in the realization of global Christianity—the mission of saving countless souls.[41]

Jews and Numbers

Though few in number, studies of quantification in modern and contemporary Jewish life carry much weight, demonstrating just how much we gain, both empirically and analytically, by exploring the engagement of Jews with numbers. By pointing to the "promise of numbers," some of the work briefly reviewed here served as a significant springboard for this collaborative project. In particular, this volume departs from important scholarship that explores key historical moments in which Jews have come to be concerned with counting themselves and quantifying their lives. This scholarship sheds light on the ways in which political numbers have come to structure and reflect national and ideological agendas within Jewish contexts.

In his pioneering work on Jewish social sciences in nineteenth- and twentieth-century central Europe, Mitchell Hart illustrates how and why Jews mobilized statistical language in order to understand and address the "Jewish problem."[42] Not only did statistics provide Jewish scientists with a discursive means through which to enter a European scientific community, but it also gave them scientific tools to position themselves in relation to ideological issues they confronted as Jews. Zionists, more than any other ideological group, argues Hart, drew on statistics to reinforce and advocate their political agenda: to prove that Jews were a unified nation or a "folk," rather than merely a religion, and thus both required and were entitled to national sovereignty.

The institutional intersection of Zionist, national ideologies, and statistical projects has also been explored in relation to developments in prestate Palestine.[43] Etan Bloom, for example, argues that the political radicalism of early twentieth-century Zionism lies in its enthusiasm for enumeration, an attitude that represents a clear break from biblical and rabbinical resistance, or at least ambivalence about counting Jews.[44] By focusing on the undertakings of the prominent social scientist and activist Arthur Ruppin, Bloom demonstrates the centrality of demographic statistics for the legitimation of Zionism as a "modern" political force. Relatedly, Arie Krampf illustrates how statistics entwined in 1930s Palestine with an emergent national economy: an ideologically laden economy which drew on Zionist doctrines about mass immigration and productivization of Jews.[45] Anat Leibler's early work demonstrates the mutually constitutive role of the Central Bureau of Statistics and newly emerging political institutes of the state. The first census of the Israeli state, Leibler argues, became a governmental event through which the Zionist state consolidated its selective politics of inclusion.[46]

Statistics also inform the communal dynamics of American Jews. In her suggestive account of the shifting American Jewish public sphere throughout the twentieth century, Lila Corwin Berman demonstrates how Jewish leaders and organizations harnessed the social sciences (sociology in particular) to explain and demystify Jewishness for both Jewish and non-Jewish Americans.[47] Their moral prescriptions (i.e., about intermarriage, assimilation, and other emotionally laden issues) stemmed from fertile soils of empiricism and sociological reason. As Berman writes: "Rabbis were quick to learn the power of numbers, often citing the same statistics about divorce and religious endogamy that were used in popular magazines. Attempting, it seemed, to tie their own normative authority to the new cultural authority carried by sociology, survey, and statistics, postwar rabbis learned to explain Jewish endogamy in a new language."[48] Other sociohistorical accounts of Jewish organizations conform with Berman's work. In particular, Naomi W. Cohen's research on the American Jewish Committee, Stuart

Svonkin's book on Jewish antiprejudice organizations, and Shaul Kelner's more recent scholarship on the cultivation of young Jewish leadership, all trace the central role of knowledge processes in the making and remaking of the Jewish professional world over the twentieth century.[49]

Taking Stock

Following the workshop, the notion of *Taking Stock* emerged as a rich framework with which to think through contemporary cultures of enumeration. Needless to say, we do not aim to produce a grand narrative about Jews—or "the Jews"— and numbers; the notion of taking stock is not intended to cover or exhaust all possible relationships Jews have developed with numbers. Rather, it offers a set of lenses into some of the features, contexts, and implications that characterize contemporary instances of Jewish counting. From these examples we can consider social forms, religious traditions, and national sensibilities that shape the collective lives of Jews who live with numbers.

The expression "taking stock" captures two main layers of meaning to analyze how numbers operate in the public life of modern and contemporary Jewish collectives. By drawing on both layers, the chapters in this volume demonstrate different processes and contexts in which numbers create a mechanism of taking stock.

The first and most obvious meaning that resonates with this notion is that of an inventory: the creation of a quantified, itemized representation of amassed goods, materials, and artifacts available "in stock." Because inventories are intimately linked with the marketplace and are sustained by models of accounting, the term "taking stock" implies an array of economically informed understandings about commodified resources and possessions. In these contexts, inventory technology secures the ongoing cycle of supply and demand by recording and categorizing stocked goods, forecasting future needs, and advancing replenishment, thereby fostering institutional memory, knowledge, and planning.

In line with the notion of inventory, one might say that Jews engage numerically with what they have "in stock": both their available or amassed human resources (e.g., living and yet-to-be-born Jews) and cultural, material resources (e.g., Jewish objects, artifacts, traditions, and social institutions). Notions of scarcity, surplus, and replenishment reverberate through such engagements. Similarly, one might frame the myriad investments of Jews in numerical representations of their national losses (e.g., the number of Jews killed during the Holocaust and other national tragedies) as an engagement with those absent-yet-present Jews: those who are simultaneously "out of stock" as human resources and "in stock" as iconic, symbolic resources of commemoration.

As Jews produce numbers, they also inescapably construct and objectify the categories of identity that "store" these numbers. By creating a numerically informed stock, Jews introduce new vocabularies and regimes of value through which a portrait of the Jewish world is drawn. Like the work of inventorying, Jewish cultures of taking stock discussed here govern institutionally mediated memory and planning processes of collective Jewish life. Put simply, through numerical engagements with their histories, contemporary realities, and projected futures, Jews aim to assess "how they are doing." This intimate connection between inventory and counting helps us recognize not only how Jews, like other modern subjects, are fond of neatly quantified forms of knowledge, but also the ways in which they engage themselves in assessing their collective stock.

In *Keepers of Accounts: The Practice of Inventory in Modern Jewish Life,* Jeffrey Shandler takes Jewish inventories (whether demographic, folkloristic, linguistic, or otherwise) as defining cultural practices of modern Jewish experience.[50] Through list making of Jewish items, Shandler argues, Jews keep track and take stock of modern Jewish phenomena; more importantly, they also realize their Jewishness in a "modern" fashion. As Jews employ a tool whose features— standardized, modularized, and systematic in nature—are deemed distinctively modern, they also negotiate their encounters with modernity. Two points made by Shandler in his analysis of modern Jewish inventory particularly relate to how this volume considers Jewish enumeration as mechanisms of stocktaking.

Shandler first points out that inventories are performative, discursive, and conceptual projects. As such, they constitute the very categories, items, and elements they register. Books, persons, movies, or jokes become "Jewish" as they are included in "Jewish" lists; their Jewishness is constructivist rather than essential. Something new is made through the practice of inventory: new ways of imagining the collective (as if that collective can assume in real life the unified existence that it takes on paper), new comforts and validations about the existence of such collectible items, and new rubrics to organize relationships among the items. Like the cultural practices of inventory described in Shandler's analysis, cultural practices of enumeration described in this volume evince creative and constitutive qualities. After all, like inventories, numbers are produced through an invention of organizing rubrics and endorsement of particular assumptions of what should be enumerated and what is measurable. Like inventories, numbers solidify the things they reference and help instantiate the very realities they measure. As will be exemplified throughout this volume, the numbers that emerge out of Jewish instances of enumeration construct these phenomena and categories as worthy of taking stock. One might consider in this regard chapter 2 by Carol Kidron on how the enlistment of names in Yad Vashem's Shoah Victims' Names Recovery Project constitutes people as "victims"; chapter 4 by Mitchell Hart on how, in the course of statistical debates about Jewish criminality, the category of "the social" emerged as a powerful explanatory framework against the "racial" framework that loomed large at the time; chapter 5 by Anat Leibler on how Jewish scientific endeavors of demography in 1940s Palestine created intra-Jewish ethnic divisions despite Zionist ideologies of a "unified" Jewish existence; and, finally, chapter 6 by Michal Kravel-Tovi on how discursive practices regarding growing rates of Jewish intermarriage construct what might otherwise be considered as a thriving reality of American Jewish life in terms of a cultural, even existential, "crisis."

Shandler's second point refers to the possible role of inventory as a technique of cultural salvage that, by its very undertaking, redeems dispersed items from potential obliviousness or disappearance. Interestingly, instances of enumeration in this volume are often entangled within, and triggered by, anxieties about crisis. Thus one might consider chapter 7 by Josh Friedman on the institutional, numerically informed salvage of Yiddish books in the wake of declining populations of reader-consumers for whom they were originally intended; chapter 3 by Yael Zerubavel on how numerical commemorative toponyms encode the Jewish-Israeli landscape with memories of historical events that might otherwise be forgotten; finally, one can think of the "census for the Holocaust dead," as analyzed by Carol Kidron, as an institutional project of counting and collecting that works against the daunting semiotic emptiness of the six million icon. The object of salvage around which this institutionalized culture of enumeration revolves is the number itself.

Beyond the immediate world of inventories, tidy spreadsheets, and dusty stockrooms, colloquial usages of the expression "taking stock" index its rich capacity as a device for reflection and self-understanding. This is the second layer of meaning on which we draw, and it is not unconnected to the first. As Jewish individuals, groups, and institutions engage in numerical calculations in accounting for what "they have," they also undergo careful processes of appraisal and evaluation that come with such stocktaking. They ask themselves: How are we doing? What have we become? and Where are we heading? In other words, in assessing the sum total and quality of their possessions, in quantifying and inventorying "who they are," Jews simultaneously grapple with questions about their values, concerns, and prospects as well as their nature as a social and political category.

Although these reflexive processes of collective assessment are informed by logics of bookkeeping and are, therefore, associated with the celebrated notion of precision, several authors in this volume show how the importance of numbers—as mechanisms of stocktaking—might lie elsewhere. Rather than presuming to demonstrate a scientific power, this volume reveals how the central roles that numbers play in processes of stocktaking rely also on their symbolic, discursive, and affective effects. Matters of precision are often simply not at stake. Take, for example, the numerical icon of "the six million" whose social life engages Oren Stier in chapter 1 of this volume. As Stier shows, the iconic power of this figure derives from something beyond actual and presumably precise counting; rather, it stems from the continuous cultural work invested in this number as an approximation and estimation that quantifies what is, ironically, often perceived as the unquantifiable horrors of the Holocaust. While the exactness of the number cannot be guaranteed, Jews define themselves as a community of memory in relation to this singular statistic. In chapter 3 on numerical commemoration in Israeli public space, Yael Zerubavel shows that numerical toponyms sometimes reference historically questionable events. In spite of this historical contestation—a clear vulnerability of commemorative practice—the numerical semiotic signs persist. In chapter 2 on Yad Vashem's Shoah Victims' Names Recovery Project, Carol Kidron demonstrates the filling of the testimony pages in the institution's database by potential "witnesses" as a moral act of commemoration that outweighs concerns over possible inaccuracies. Another illustrative case presents hyperbolic reckoning on Passover-related undertakings, described and analyzed by Vanessa Ochs in chapter 8 of this volume. As Ochs shows, various forms of numeric exaggeration are deployed in mostly American Jewish discourses so as to project celebratory visions of Jewish well-being and thus facilitate an optimistic account of the collective stock. In this case study, hyperbolic imprecision—not to be mistaken with lies—enables Jews to look collectively in the public mirror and take pleasure (or relief) in what they see. Josh Friedman's chapter (chapter 7) on the institutional salvage of Yiddish books by the Yiddish Book Center provides another example of how the powerful effects of numbers as central devices of stocktaking are not grounded in any presumption of scientific validity or meticulously achieved accuracy. As Friedman writes, these qualities are almost entirely beside the point. Rather, numerical descriptions regarding how many Yiddish books were actually "saved" or put on display for the public emerge from this chapter as holding out something else; as affectively laden abstractions, they enable creation of the "magic of Yiddish" at the Book Center. Mitchell Hart's chapter (chapter 4) on Jewish social scientific debates about the causes of the distinct statistical features of Jewish criminality also bears mentioning in this regard. As Hart shows, even when numbers are fully trusted as fundamental tools of precision and objectivity, what matters in the reflexive processes of accounting for deviant behavior among Jews (e.g., why Jews are overrepresented in white-collar crimes) is the explanatory framework and interpretive filter through which numbers are made able to tell their truths.

The Organization of This Volume

The notion of taking stock structures this volume, placing the research chapters into three thematic parts. Each part focuses on cultures of enumeration that unfold in relation to a particular category: the Jewish dead, the Jewish living, and Jewish material artifacts.

The first part, "Counting the Dead: Iconic Numbers and Collective Memory," examines practices and logics of enumeration in domains of national commemoration. Opening the volume with this part, allowing the dead to precede the living, speaks not only to the centrality of grief, memory, and commemoration in Jewish life; it also calls attention to the foundational significance of past traumas, losses, and absences in any numerical engagement of Jews with what they have "in stock." The three chapters that make up this part analyze in different yet related ways the cultural investment in the quantification of national memory.

The part opens with Oren Stier's study of the processes of iconization that have rendered the figure of six million a sacred symbol and one of the most condensed and accessible icons of Shoah memory. But, as Carol Kidron reveals in the second chapter of this part, this iconic number runs the risk of becoming an empty signifier. Grounded in an ethnographic study of the memory work at the Shoah Victims' Names Recovery Project, Kidron unpacks Yad Vashem's attempt to "breathe life" into this iconic number. The interplay between numbers and names also concerns Yael Zerubavel, the third author of this part. Her chapter focuses on the Jewish-Israeli tradition of numerically based place names that have inscribed national commemoration into Israeli-Jewish public spaces.

The second part, "Counting the Living: Putting the 'Jewish' in Social Science," explores numerically informed social-scientific understandings and undertakings that Jews and Jewish institutions have developed to come to terms with Jewish identity, community, state formation, and anti-Semitism. The authors in this part explore frameworks through which Jewish social scientists attend to the social "here and now" and its implications for future understandings, policies, and social arrangements. Drawing on case studies of Jewish social scientists in nineteenth-century Germany, Israel in the 1940s, and the American Jewish community in the 1990s, the three chapters in this part highlight how statistics have shaped key processes through which Jews take stock. Covering such diverse topics as intermarriage, Jewish criminology, and Mizrahi fertility, these chapters demonstrate the power of scientific cultures of enumeration to shape the categories and discourses that enable Jews to regulate their social reality.

This part starts with Mitchell Hart's historical account of debates over Jews and crime in nineteenth- and early twentieth-century Germany. In the second chapter of this part, Anat Leibler traces the "political demography" of the demographer Roberto Bachi in the decade before the establishment of the state of Israel. In the last chapter in this part, Michal Kravel-Tovi illustrates how American Jewish sociodemographic statistics have been framed by both a rigorous, "dry" scientific language of enumeration and an emotional, "wet" language about the gloomy prospects of American Jewish survival in the context of what, in the 1990s, came to be called the "continuity crisis."

The third part, "Counting Objects: Material Subjects and the Social Lives of Enumerated Things," brings to the fore the material connotations so integral to notions of inventory and stock. The two chapters that comprise this part center on Jewish material cultures that have become objects of counting and tell the story of the quantifying gazes and descriptions that have constituted them as such. These chapters focus on realms of cultural, institutional, and religious production that unfold in and through practices of enumeration.

In the first chapter of this part, Josh Friedman analyzes how the "thin" descriptive power of numbers is elaborated within the institutional dynamics of the Yiddish Book Center and the institution's efforts to "rescue" the world's Yiddish books. In the second chapter in this part, Vanessa Ochs employs the concept of hyperbole to describe discursive practices that surround the quantitatively based, public celebration of Passover-related consumption.

In the postscript, Theodore Porter reflects on intersections of scholarship in Jewish studies with historical and cultural interpretations of numbers, measurement, and statistics. He argues that while numbers of things, especially of persons, objects, deaths, and births are almost always at issue, this book offers particularly interesting analyses of numbers, affection, and meaning.

Emerging Themes

In what follows I draw together some conceptual themes that animate this volume in order to reflect on the critical roles that Jewish cultures of enumeration play in collective, public, and institutional processes of stocktaking. As these themes will apply to some chapters more than others, I want to avoid forcing a thematic unity on the clearly diverse directions taken by the authors of this volume. At the same time, I offer these conceptual themes with the hope that they might contribute productive vantage points from which to read the following chapters and also provide possible analytical tools for thinking through other cultures of enumeration, within as well as outside of Jewish contexts.

Enumerated Units and Aggregated Wholes

To the extent that practices of enumeration rely on the grouping of individual items into aggregated wholes, they raise questions about the relationships that unfold—through counting—between the amassed "units" and the emerging whole. Who gets to count, or is counted on, in creating the group, and what forms of exclusion arise in the course of this process as some items are not deemed important enough for inclusion? Is it the coalesced whole or the constitutive "units" that are given precedence over the other? And what is the value of those units as parts of a whole? Several scholars have attended to these questions, largely by pointing to the capacity of numbers to generalize, abstract, and hence flatten and even dehumanize individuals.[51] The notion of taking stock lends itself particularly well to thinking through such effects, as it resonates with possible commodifying and standardizing connotations about individuals as resources in a stock.

Given particular Jewish sensibilities about Nazi dehumanization and its notorious links to logics of quantification—simply put, the turning of individuals into sheer numbers tattooed on their forearms—it is not surprising that several authors in this volume take this paradigmatic objectification of Jews as their point of departure for the investigation of Jewish cultures of enumeration. Oren Stier (in chapter 1), for example, unpacks the collecting projects of six million items for their inevitable recapitulation of Nazi objectification of Jews, and Yael Zerubavel (in chapter 3) speaks to the disturbing replacement of names of fallen individuals by the numerical, collective representations of death tolls of particular events, an act that brings to mind erasure of personal identities. In drawing these connections, these authors point to the inherent ambivalences that underwrite and complicate any post-Holocaust Jewish undertaking of enumeration.

Indeed, other instances of Jewish enumeration emerge in this volume as double edged in nature; that is, they often entail unsettling relationships between the distinct units that have been counted and the group that is only made coherent through these units' enumeration. These accounts invite us to think more expansively about the strengths and weaknesses entailed in how numbers, as mechanisms of taking stock, amass individual items into aggregated wholes. Two examples of these double-edged dynamics will suffice here. From Carol Kidron's chapter (chapter 2) we learn of a dialectic relationship between the recovery of individual names of Holocaust victims and the recovery of the semiotic power of the symbol of six million. While the representation of the absent individual names, narratives, and faces of each victim is justified as a moral corrective to Nazi dehumanization, Kidron shows how it also, or even primarily, works as a means for the completion and re-invigoration of the empty signifier of six million. Hence, the somewhat bureaucratic, reductionist manner in which individual biographies have been solicited and displayed in Yad Vashem's Shoah Victims' Names Recovery Project speaks to the fact that their importance lies more in enlivening and solidifying the whole than in turning numbers into individuals. In Josh Friedman's chapter (chapter 7) on the Yiddish Book Center, enumeration simultaneously enhances and impedes the institutional mission of "saving" both physical Yiddish books and their cultural values and potentials. This institutional endeavor succeeds in impressing and mobilizing its American Jewish public precisely due to the thin, numerical description of Yiddish books, one that elides distinctions among books and renders each of them a "treasure" regardless of the books' biographic trajectory or literary value. At the same time, books are at risk of being looked at as "just numbers," and the institution faces suspicions that it cares more for numbers than for books. "At some moments," writes Friedman, "thin description is too thin."

In many of the cultures of enumeration described in this volume, numbers create egalitarian relationships among the units that constitute the whole regardless of the size and circumstances of that whole: each Jewish criminal, Jewish newborn, intermarried Jew, Jewish victim, memorialized Jewish dead, Jewish Mizrahi woman, or Jewish participant in a Passover ritual "counts" the same and each is potentially "useful" or harmful for the whole as the others gathered together under the same rubric. Within that enumerated whole, they all carry the same value. However, with the framework of taking stock, I want to draw attention to how the size, or more broadly, the assessed circumstances and "shape" of the stock (e.g., how large and secure it is, or, alternatively, how endangered it might be) can, in fact, dictate the value given to each Jew. Such a direction becomes particularly relevant for crisis-laden situations in which people, societies, and institutions so often come to engage in the work of taking stock. In order to better ground my call for such a perspective, it is instructive to read afresh the parable with which Jonathan Boyarin ends his chapter, "Waiting for a Jew":

> Two Jews can afford to be fastidious about the dress, comportment, and erudition of a third. It gives them something to gossip about and identify against. Ten healthy Jews can have a similar luxury: an eleventh means competition for the ritual honors. It's nine Jews who are the most tolerant, as I learned one forlorn shabbes at Eighth street. It was almost ten o'clock, and there was no minyan. Since everyone seemed content to wait patiently, I assumed that someone else had promised to come, and asked, "Who are we waiting for?"
> "A yid," our oldest member replied without hesitation.
> Eventually a Jew came along.[52]

The tenth Jew—the one who the other Jews at the Eighth Street synagogue in lower Manhattan were waiting for, the one who was fortunate enough to complete the minyan (prayer quorum), is invested with a particular qualitative value. The eleventh Jew will likely be redundant. Taking my cue from this anecdote, I suggest, for example, that in the context of the growing scarcity of living Holocaust survivors, scholars should pay attention to the potential value that might one day not too far in the future be invested in the "last" or "oldest" living victim, or at least in the last victim to be listed in the "census of the dead." Similarly, we might consider the affective and moral value that could be granted to the Yiddish books attributed to the (supposedly) last elderly native Yiddish-speaking Jew. To go beyond the instances of enumeration discussed in this volume, one can also consider the value placed on the Jewish rituals conducted by the "last Jews in Afghanistan"[53] and those in other Jewishly endangered places. As Shaylih Muehlmann suggests in her discussion of "countdown" in the context of ecological crisis in Mexico's Colorado River delta, the value of items in a countdown might be distributed unevenly in such a way that those at the bottom (e.g., the last speakers of a language) count more.[54]

Abstractions and Their Concretization

The ability of numbers to facilitate processes of taking stock can be linked to what scholars of quantification have recognized as numbers' dual work of abstraction and concretization. On the one hand, numbers (particularly but not exclusively statistics) are part of a complex abstraction that references a social world lying outside of the numbers themselves; on the other hand, numbers capture in specific ways concepts and constructs that might otherwise remain too abstract and vague. Thus, Holocaust victims were not simply "overwhelmingly many," or "uncountable," but were estimated to be six million. Or, to draw on a very different example, there are not just "so many Haggadot" but (if we want to be precise), there are two million ArtScroll copies. As Silvana Patriarca, in her account of statistics in nineteenth-century Italy, writes: "Applied to society, quantifying procedures, while making comparison easier, give a concrete body to abstract entities and ideas, and make concrete things more abstract."[55] This interaction between the work of abstraction and that of concretization that numbers perform appears in several chapters in this volume. For example, Michal Kravel-Tovi demonstrates in chapter 6 that the notion of Jewish cultural assimilation in the United States was both abstracted and concretized in the 1990s by grounding it in a certain number (i.e., 52 percent of recent Jews intermarried) that indexed in a tangible manner generalized patterns of reality.

Sometimes, however, the concrete numerical representation captures too much: too many items, too vast a phenomenon, too large a quantity. "At a certain point," writes Engelke, "large numbers simply do not convey anything *because* they are so large."[56] If some phenomena are described by numbers that are alarmingly too small or too rapidly dwindling, large numbers also create their own challenges. Several chapters in this volume speak to what Engelke describes, or to what might be described, to paraphrase both Joshua Cole's *Power of Large Numbers* and Arjun Appadurai's *Fear of Small Numbers*,[57] as "the fear of large numbers": namely, the fear of living with numbers that are simply too large, and thus also too abstract and incomprehensible. This fear invites us to explore further relationships between the abstract and concrete nature of numbers and complexities that these relationships might create for numerical processes of taking stock.

Several chapters in this volume depict vulnerabilities implicit in numbers that seem too large. In their size, their power seems unsustainable. These chapters pay attention to aesthetic and performative mechanisms employed in attempts to make numbers more tangible. Numbers, or the actual processes of counting and collecting, are put on display in Yad Vashem (chapter 2) and at the Yiddish Book Center (chapter 7); in each of these institutional domains, their overwhelming scale is experienced in a visual and sensorial manner. Such mechanisms of putting numbers and counting on display can have their own complications. As Oren Stier writes (in chapter 1) in relation to the Whitwell Middle School paper clips project, "the technical challenge of actually counting to six million objects limits our ability to fully comprehend the victimhood of the Holocaust in a concrete, rather than abstract, manner."

Affective Temporalities

Numbers seem to inform processes of taking stock because of the ways in which they foreground perceptions of time and forge affective links. The idea that numbers contribute to the social organization of time or to processes embedded in temporal logics should not be foreign to students of quantification. After all, time is a highly calculable feature in human societies.[58] Political and monetary numbers can be compared across time and allow for planning of future policies, while theological numbers articulate cosmological understandings about the beginning and end of times. Connections between numbers and affection seem less intuitive or familiar, although some scholars recognize how numbers—in spite of their aura of "coldness" and "dryness"—might in fact be processed in affective and sensorial, rather than cognitive and rational, modes.[59] Interestingly, when we examine some expressions used by scholars to describe relationships that modern subjects and cultures have with numbers, we can easily see that affectively laden discourses, such as "delight," "fetish," and "enchantment," are so often employed.

Many of the chapters collected here point not only to the processes by which numbers carry time and contribute to affective discourses but also to the processes by which these two axes—the temporal and the affective—are interconnected. Numbers bring time into play: they introduce the past into present spaces, through pedagogies and practices of commemoration, while they also fashion arenas of forgetting within the present. Numbers are integral to other processes of integration that revolve around passing down culture and identity from past generations to present and future ones; and they feed imagination of the future as well as planning or correcting its course. Numbers spark intense emotions about temporal possibilities. Sadness, awe, reminiscence, anxiety, hope, and desire unfold within the following chapters. This list of emotions includes affective references to time, such as urgency, pessimism, and optimism.

Due to statistical, demographic exercises of prediction, the protagonist of Anat Leibler's chapter (chapter 5), Roberto Bachi, can "provide a new way of understanding the present in terms of the future," while advocating for a sense of urgency in how his understanding should be translated into state-sponsored policy.

Similarly, a sense of urgency created in the aftermath of the 1990s National Jewish Population Survey was anchored in the synergetic workings of scientific and affective discourses. As Michal Kravel-Tovi demonstrates (in chapter 6), the processes of "dampening" numbers accompany a darkening of the future and a push for immediate intervention in the identity work of the contemporary American Jewish community. Vanessa Ochs's and Josh Friedman's chapters (chapters 8 and 7) further attest to how affective temporalities work in the American Jewish context. Ochs argues that thanks to hyperbolic numerical descriptions, American Jews can extricate themselves from the pessimistic tone with which they usually envision their future and instead envision an optimist possibility. Josh Friedman shows the extent to which the formation of a potential Yiddish future relies on an affective economy of desire and anticipation produced by the Yiddish Book Center. Its numbers, in this case, are employed in the creation of possible, promising links between ancestors and future generations.

* * *

This volume opens a wide engagement with numbers in the Jewish past and present. As it takes stock of the rich implications of "counting in Jewish," it invites others to consider the numbers swirling around in songs and stories, lists, and censuses for their meanings and influence. Both ordinary numbers and powerful iconic ones deserve our attention and analysis for the claims that they make on politics, culture, society, and economy. The contributors to *Taking Stock* point to new directions in answering the underlying question of "what numbers are for." How Jews count and are counted has much to teach us about modern Jewish experiences.

Notes

I am grateful to Deborah Dash Moore and Mitchell Hart for their helpful comments on earlier drafts of this chapter and to Joshua B. Friedman for his thorough editing of it.

1. IDF is an acronym for the Israeli Defense Forces.
2. See http://www.ynet.co.il/articles/0,7340,L-4013589,00.html.
3. *Contact: The Journal of Jewish Life Network* / Steinhardt Foundation 5, no. 3 (2003); and *Contact: The Journal of Jewish Life Network* / Steinhardt Foundation 8, no. 4 (2006).
4. *Sh'ma: A Journal of Jewish Responsibility*, 41, no. 673 (2010).
5. Ibid., 1.
6. Alain Badiou, *Number and Numbers* (Cambridge: Polity, 2008), 1.
7. See Jonathan Boyarin, *Thinking in Jewish* (Chicago: University of Chicago Press, 1996).
8. William Seltzer and Margo Anderson, "The Dark Side of Numbers: The Role of Population Data Systems in Human Rights Abuses," *Social Research* 68, no. 2 (2001): 481–515; and Theodore M. Porter, *The Rise of Statistical Thinking, 1820–1900* (Princeton, NJ: Princeton University Press, 1986), 17.

9. Biblical references to census taking reveal ambivalent attitudes about counting; in particular, we can see an engagement with counting Jews existing alongside the array of prohibitions, restrictions, and punishments associated with the act of counting.

10. Daniel Seabra Lopes, "Making Oneself at Home with Numbers: Financial Reporting from an Ethnographic Perspective," *Social Anthropology* 19, no. 4 (2011): 463.

11. Seltzer and Anderson, "Dark Side."

12. Akhil Gupta, *Red Tape: Bureaucracy, Structural Violence, and Poverty in India* (Durham, NC: Duke University Press, 2012), 159.

13. Shaylih Muehlmann, "Rhizomes and Other Uncountables," *American Ethnologist* 39, no. 2 (2012): 339–352; and Julia Paley, "Making Democracy Count: Opinion Polls and Market Surveys in the Chilean Political Transition," *Cultural Anthropology* 16, no. 2 (2001): 135–164.

14. See, for example, Thomas Crump, *The Anthropology of Numbers* (Cambridge: Cambridge University Press, 1990).

15. For example, Hendrik Vollmer, "How to Do More with Numbers: Elementary Stakes, Framing, Keying, and the Three-Dimensional Character of Numerical Signs," *Accounting, Organizations and Society* 32, no. 6 (2007): 577–600.

16. Ibid., 580.

17. Crump, *Anthropology of Numbers;* and Mariana Kawall and Leal Ferreira, "When 1 + 1 ≠ 2: Making Mathematics in Central Brazil," *American Ethnologist* 24, no. 1 (1997): 132–147.

18. Caitlin Zaloom, "Trading Technologies and Interpretation," *Financial Markets* 30, no. 2 (2003): 2.

19. Jane I. Guyer et al., "Introduction: Numbers as Inventive Frontier," *Anthropological Theory* 10, no. 1–2 (2010): 49.

20. Patricia Cline Cohen, *A Calculating People: The Spread of Numeracy in Early America* (New York: Routledge, 1999); and Michael Zakim, "Statistics-for-Profit," in *Measuring Everything* [in Hebrew] (Be'er Sheva, Israel: Ben-Gurion University Press, 2010); see also Peter Miller, "Governing by Numbers: Why Calculative Practices Matter," *Social Research* 68, no. 2 (2001): 379–396.

21. Seabra Lopes, "Making Oneself at Home"; Gerhard Anders, "The Normativity of Numbers: World Bank and IMF Conditionality," *PoLAR: Political and Legal Anthropology Review* 31, no. 2 (2008): 188–202; and Caitlin Zaloom, "Ambiguous Numbers: Trading Technologies and Interpretation in Financial Markets," *American Ethnologist* 30, no. 2 (2003): 1–15.

22. U. Kalpagam, "The Colonial State and Statistical Knowledge," *History of the Human Sciences* 13, no. 2 (2000): 37–55; Bruce Curtis, *The Politics of Population: State Formation, Statistics, and the Census of Canada, 1840–1875* (Toronto: University of Toronto Press, 2002); and Joshua Cole, *The Power of Large Numbers: Population, Politics, and Gender in Nineteenth-Century France* (Ithaca, NY: Cornell University Press, 2000).

23. Theodore M. Porter, *Trust in Numbers: The Pursuit of Objectivity in Science and Public Life* (Princeton, NJ: Princeton University Press, 1995), x.

24. Michel Foucault, *History of Sexuality* (New York: Pantheon, 1978); Michel Foucault, "Governmentality," in *The Anthropology of the State: A Reader*, ed. Aradhana Sharma and Akhil Gupta (Malden, MA: Blackwell, 2006), 131–142; and Ian Hacking, "Biopower and the Avalanche of Printed Numbers," *Humanities in Society* 5, no. 3–4 (1982): 279–295.

25. Cole, *Power of Large Numbers;* and Nikolas Rose, *Numbers, Powers of Freedom: Reframing Political Thought* (Cambridge: Cambridge University Press, 1999), 197–232.

26. Stephen Stigler, *The History of Statistics: The Measurement of Uncertainty before 1900* (Cambridge, MA: Belknap, 1990); Porter, *Rise of Statistical Thinking;* Ian Hacking, *The Taming of Chance* (Cambridge: Cambridge University Press, 1990); Zohreh Bayatrizi, "Counting the Dead and Regulating the Living: Early Modern Statistics and the Formation of the Sociological

Imagination (1662–1897)," *British Journal of Sociology* 60, no. 3 (2009): 603–621; and Theodore M. Porter, "Statistical and Social Facts from Quetelet to Durkheim," *Sociological Perspectives* 38, no. 1 (1995): 15–26.

27. Porter, *Trust in Numbers*.

28. See also Cohen, *Calculating People*, 1.

29. Rose, *Numbers*.

30. Numbers, obviously, foster not only trust but also suspicion—primarily in relationship to the possibility of their manipulation in the service of political interests.

31. William Alonso and Paul Starr, eds., *The Politics of Numbers* (New York: Russell Sage Foundation, 1987); Margo J. Anderson and Stephen E. Fienberg, *Who Counts? The Politics of Census-Taking in Contemporary America* (New York: Russell Sage Foundation, 1999); David I. Kertzer and Dominique Arel, eds., *Census and Identity: The Politics of Race, Ethnicity, and Language in National Censuses* (Cambridge: Cambridge University Press, 2002); and Melissa Nobles, *Shades of Citizenship: Race and the Census in Modern Politics* (Stanford, CA: Stanford University Press, 2000).

32. Anat Leibler and Daniel Breslau, "The Uncounted: Citizenship and Exclusion in the Israeli Census of 1948," *Ethnic and Racial Studies* 28, no. 5 (2005): 880–902; Anat Leibler, "Statisticians' Ambition: Governmentality, Modernity and National Legibility," *Israel Studies* 9, no. 2 (2004): 121–149; and Silvana Patriarca, *Numbers and Nationhood: Writing Statistics in Nineteenth-Century Italy* (Cambridge: Cambridge University Press, 1996).

33. Susan Greenhalgh, "Planned Births, Unplanned Persons: 'Population' in the Making of Chinese Modernity," *American Ethnologist* 30, no. 2 (2003): 196–215.

34. Alain Blum, "Social History as the History of Measuring Populations: A Post-1987 Renewal," *Kritika: Explorations in Russian and Eurasian History* 2, no. 2 (2001): 279–294; and Inna Leykin, "'Population Prescriptions': State, Morality, and Population Politics in Contemporary Russia" (Ph.D. diss., Brown University, 2013).

35. Benedict Anderson, *Imagined Communities: Reflections on the Origin and Spread of Nationalism* (London: Verso, 2006); Arjun Appadurai, "Number in the Colonial Imagination," in *Orientalism and the Postcolonial Predicament: Perspectives on South Asia,* ed. Carol A. Breckenridge and Peter van der Veer (Philadelphia: University of Pennsylvania Press, 1993), 314–339; Talal Asad, "Ethnographic Representation, Statistics, and Modern Power," *Social Research* 61, no. 1 (1994): 55–88; Bernard Cohn, *Colonialism and Its Forms of Knowledge: The British in India* (Princeton, NJ: Princeton University Press, 1996); Kalpagam, "Colonial State"; Sumit Guha, "The Politics of Identity and Enumeration in India c. 1600–1900," *Comparative Studies in Society and History* 45, no. 1 (2003): 148–167; and Sudipta Kaviraj, *The Imaginary Institution of India: Politics and Ideas* (New York: Columbia University Press, 2010).

36. Asad, "Ethnographic Representation," 78.

37. Curtis, *Politics of Population;* Rose, *Numbers;* and Sarah Igo, *The Averaged American: Surveys, Citizens, and the Making of a Mass Public* (Cambridge, MA: Harvard University Press, 2007).

38. Guyer et al., "Introduction," 40.

39. Cohen, *Calculating People*, 35.

40. Patricia Spyer, "Serial Conversion / Conversion to Seriality: Religion, State, and Number in Aru, Eastern Indonesia," in *Conversion to Modernities: The Globalization of Christianity,* ed. Peter van der Veer (New York: Routledge, 1996), 171–198; and Brian Peterson, "Quantifying Conversion: A Note on the Colonial Census and Religious Change in Postwar Southern Mali," *History in Africa* 29 (2002): 381–392.

41. Matthew Engelke, "Number and the Imagination of Global Christianity; or, Mediation and Immediacy in the Work of Alain Badiou," *South Atlantic Quarterly* 109, no. 4 (2010): 811–829.

42. Mitchell B. Hart, *Social Science and the Politics of Modern Jewish Identity* (Stanford, CA: Stanford University Press, 2000).

43. Sometimes people who were central in the institutionalization of Jewish statistics in Europe were also central to its institutionalization in prestate Palestine. Arthur Ruppin is such an individual.

44. Etan Bloom, "Zionist Statistics in Light of Jewish Thought," in *The Limits of Quantification: Critical Perspectives on Measuring and Grading People, Their Behaviours and Achievements* [in Hebrew], ed. Yohai Hakak, Lea Kacen, and Michal Krumer-Nevo (Be'er Sheva, Israel: Bialik Institute, 2012), 132–172.

45. Arie Krampf, "The Metaphysics of the Fact: The Social Measurement in Historical and Comparative Perspective," in *The Limits of Quantification: Critical Perspectives on Measuring and Grading People, Their Behaviours and Achievements* [in Hebrew], ed. Yohai Hakak, Lea Kacen, and Michal Krumer-Nevo (Be'er Sheva, Israel: Bialik Institute, 2012), 103–131.

46. Leibler, "Statisticians' Ambition"; Leibler and Breslau, "Uncounted."

47. Lila Corwin Berman, *Speaking of Jews: Rabbis, Intellectuals, and the Creation of an American Public Identity* (Berkeley: University of California Press, 2009).

48. Ibid., 69.

49. Naomi W. Cohen, *Not Free to Desist: The American Jewish Committee, 1906–1966* (Philadelphia: Jewish Publication Society, 1972); Stuart Svonkin, *Jews against Prejudice: American Jews and the Fight for Civil Liberties* (New York: Columbia University Press, 1999); and Shaul Kelner, "In Its Own Image: Independent Philanthropy and the Cultivation of Young Jewish Leadership," in *The New Jewish Leaders: Reshaping the American Jewish Landscape,* ed. Jack Wertheimer (Hanover, NH: University Press of New England, 2011), 261–321.

50. Jeffrey Shandler, *Keepers of Accounts: The Practice of Inventory in Modern Jewish Life,* vol. 17, *David W. Belin Lecture in American Jewish Affairs* (Ann Arbor: Frankel Center for Judaic Studies, University of Michigan, 2010).

51. See Cole, *Power of Large Numbers;* Engelke, "Number," 813; Porter, *Trust in Numbers,* 7; and Muehlmann, "Rhizomes."

52. Boyarin, *Thinking in Jewish,* 33.

53. See Jessica Donati and Mirwais Harooni, "Last Jew in Afghanistan Faces Ruin as Kebabs Fail to Sell," Reuters, November 12, 2013, http://www.reuters.com/article/2013/11/12/us-afghanistan-jews-idUSBRE9AB0A120131112.

54. Muehlmann, "Rhizomes."

55. Patriarca, *Numbers and Nationhood,* 9.

56. Engelke, "Number," 818.

57. Cole, *Power of Large Numbers;* and Arjun Appadurai, *Fear of Small Numbers: An Essay on the Geography of Anger* (Durham, NC: Duke University Press, 2006).

58. See Crump's chapter on numbers and time in his *Anthropology of Numbers.*

59. See, for example, Zaloom, "Ambiguous Numbers."

PART I

COUNTING THE DEAD:
ICONIC NUMBERS AND COLLECTIVE MEMORY

1 Six Million

The Numerical Icon of the Holocaust

Oren Baruch Stier

> In every computation there are question marks. . . . However elaborate or cumbersome these computations may be, their purposes are simple. The primary goal is a single number that in a quintessential manner expresses the Holocaust as a whole.
>
> Raul Hilberg, "The Statistic"

THAT "SIX MILLION" is a definitive number for Jews is no secret. As one of several key cultural icons of the Holocaust, representing, in encapsulated, economic language the entirety of the Shoah, the number six million signifies powerfully in post-Holocaust culture. Originating in an attempt to count the dead, the presumably authoritative number also conjures an accounting for mass murder, in all possible senses of the word—explaining, justifying, avenging. Beginning with its historic contextualization, I ask therefore not only how we count the victims of the Holocaust but who counts, why, and to what end. Ranging across some key moments in the social life of this powerful number, in Europe, Israel, and the United States, I discuss some of the number's symbolic meanings and applications; I make no attempt, however, at a comprehensive historicization of the figure, which would be impossible. Rather I outline here some of the number's iconic meanings and uses.

These applications of six million as a symbolic figure touch on other symbolic numerals that function as historiographic or ideological alternatives to that iconic figure. Indeed, if thought of as the culmination of a counting sequence, the number six million is arrived at beginning with the first victim—the number "one"—resulting in a historical (ac)counting of and for the total number of Jewish victims of the Shoah. Furthermore, the subtle but not inconsequential shift from six million to *the* six million—from a number reached by counting to an expression signifying all Jewish victims of the Holocaust as one collective—can be seen as an additional representation and stage of the number's iconization.

The essence of my argument is that what matters—what ultimately counts—concerning this key figure of six million is its iconic power, which is derived from something beyond counting and even beyond symbolism. Indeed, actually counting to six million is a grand undertaking: if I were to count at an average rate of one digit per second, it would still take over sixty-nine days to reach the number six million, without breaks or stops. This chapter is therefore about the transformation of a number—usually assumed, like all numbers, to be precise, exact, scientific, even though, as many numbers turn out to be, its sources are more political and bureaucratic than scientific. This number thus becomes a symbol that points beyond itself and, moreover, becomes iconic, understood as an embodiment beyond symbolism. That transformation hinges on recognizing that the number is an approximation—rounded, round—but its power derives from seeing that approximation as a distillation of a truth transcending numeric precision and thereby intensifies its connection to and representation of the Holocaust. By this process, six million becomes an iconic representation and an incarnation of social apprehensions of the Shoah.

Iconic and Numeric Power

Icons derive their power from their inherent ability to encapsulate complex narratives and meanings in simplified, condensed form. The classic Eastern Orthodox Christian icon (from the Greek, *eikon,* for "image") is an object of veneration with a didactic function. Expressing a hidden spiritual reality and assisting in the instruction of the faithful in that reality,[1] the icon is an incarnation of divine mystery. In general, a religious icon stands in for what adherents believe to be true and significant; in contemporary usage, a "pop icon" or "screen icon" represents the epitome of that individual's artistic genre. But icons are typically thought of as material artifacts, not abstract numerals. As Dominik Bartmanski and Jeffrey C. Alexander have argued, "Objects become icons when they have not only material force but also symbolic power." Iconicity, they continue, is central to social life and the organization of reality:

> Icons allow members of societies (1) to experience a sense of participation in something fundamental whose fuller meaning eludes their comprehension and (2) to enjoy the possibility for control despite being unable to access directly the script that lies beneath. Icons are cultural constructions that provide believer-friendly epiphanies and customer-friendly images. . . . Icons provide an aesthetic contact with encoded meanings whose depth is beyond direct ratiocination. Iconicity consists in retrieving, activating, and articulating the depth of the signified by introducing it to the realm of immediate sensory experience, connecting discursive meaning with the perceptual and the palpable.[2]

Icons are mediators that connect people to the deeper realities to which they refer, permitting identification with those inaccessible meanings through a symbolic code the icons establish. As iconicity is culturally constructed, icons exist in a range of cultural forms not limited to the material realm—not necessarily concrete, physical—reflecting a variety of cultural symbols—including numbers—that provide access to transcendent meaning, as implied by Bartmanski and Alexander. But icons are more than mere representations of things, more than simple symbols; in connecting people to deeper, otherwise inaccessible meanings, icons serve as representatives of those meanings as well. In their representational aspects, icons are commemorative and look to the past; as representatives of complex realities, icons operate in the present and offer a framework for social engagement. Functionally, an icon acts as a kind of short circuit, allowing quick, noncognitive access to the larger, hidden reality to which it refers. In the case of the representation and remembrance of the Shoah, then, a Holocaust icon would be an object, symbol, word, image, concept, or, in this instance, number that serves as shorthand for and an embodiment of the Holocaust as a whole. As such an embodiment, six million serves as an icon of the Holocaust.

A familiar and infamous number, six million sums up, authoritatively and succinctly, Jewish losses in the Holocaust. Its strength as an authoritative figure derives from its political power, which lies not only in its enumerative function or presumed objectivity but also arises out of the social-cultural institutions that use it. As Nikolas Rose suggests, "Numbers, like other 'inscription devices,' actually constitute the domains they appear to represent; they render them representable in a docile form—a form amenable to the application of calculation and deliberation. Hence it is not just that the domain of numbers is politically composed, but also that the domain of politics is made up numerically."[3] In this particular case, we are speaking not only about the political power of the state and its invocation of numbers but also reflecting on legal, social, and cultural institutions and their utilizations of the figure. We are also reflecting on the ways in which the number six million itself constitutes and determines the discourses of Holocaust remembrance and representation that in turn rely upon it.

The continuing importance of six million as a significant number in various spheres also points to persistent questions and anxieties about the role the Holocaust plays in contemporary Western and Jewish cultures. As Rose argues, societies turn to numbers when political authority is contested; secure communities have less need for numeric validation:

> When the authority of authority is secure, when authoritative judgments carry inherent authority, when the legitimacy of their authority is not subject to skeptical scrutiny and challenge, experts have little need of numbers. But

where mistrust of authority flourishes, where experts are the target of suspicion and their claims are greeted with skepticism by politicians, disputed by professional rivals, distrusted by public opinion, where decisions are contested and discretion is criticized, the allure of numbers increases. . . . Numbers are resorted to in order to settle or diminish conflicts in a contested space of weak authority.[4]

While there is little debate in the public sphere today about whether six million is the number representing Jewish murders under the Nazi regime, that consensus masks a continuing difficulty scholars face in arriving at an absolute and precise tally of Jewish victims; so long as that final accounting remains tantalizingly out of reach, the number six million stands as an attractive figure instrumental, but not completely successful, in reducing conflict about the enumeration of victimization. In the absence of a strong governmental authority authorizing Holocaust memory, Jewish groups invest in this number to reinforce the importance of the Shoah to them, while others rely on a different number to support alternative political-cultural claims. The communal investment in six million also serves to keep at bay those fringe elements such as Holocaust deniers who would challenge that number's veracity.

A numerical icon, then, is a political number that has an iconic component, providing access to the less accessible depths to which any icon refers. Beyond simple enumeration and the implications of objectivity and authority, numerical icons serve to summarize complex sociocultural processes and represent them for "believers," just as a traditional icon would, only in numeric form. An example might be the number "18" in Jewish life: derived from the numerological value (*gematria*) of the Hebrew letters *chet* and *yud*, spelling the word *chai*, "life," the number "18" and its multiples can be employed in a variety of ways to communicate communal fellowship and wishes for good luck and success, as in the custom of gift-giving and charity donating in $18 increments. Six million, therefore, is a numerical icon of the Holocaust that, when invoked, signifies the symbolic presence of the Shoah in its totality and the Holocaust memorial consumers' access to it.

Origins

The number six million, as a representation of the total number of Jewish Holocaust victims, appears to have originated in the International Military Tribunal of major Nazi war criminals held in Nuremberg from November 14, 1945, to October 1, 1946. That is, it originated in a legal setting, in the course of prosecution of Nazi leaders and documentation of evidence against them; it is a "perpetrator's" number, not a "victim's" number, which has nonetheless come to be appropriated memorially and representationally. In an affidavit dated November 26, 1945, SS

Sturmbannführer (SS-Major) Dr. Wilhelm Höttl, deputy group leader in Office VI (the "international" office of the Sicherheitsdienst [SD; Security Service]) of the Reich Security Main Office (Reichssicherheitshauptamt, or RSHA), testified concerning a conversation he had had with Adolf Eichmann in Höttl's apartment in Budapest in August 1944 in which Eichmann asked Höttl for information on the military situation. According to Höttl, Eichmann

> expressed his conviction that Germany had lost the war and that he personally had no further chance. He knew that he would be considered one of the main war criminals by the United Nations, since he had millions of Jewish lives on his conscience. I asked him how many that was, to which he answered that, although the number was a great Reich secret, he would tell me since I, as a historian too, would be interested and that probably he would not return anyhow from his command in Romania. He had, shortly before that, made a report to Himmler, as the latter wanted to know the exact number of Jews who had been killed.[5]

In citing Höttl's affidavit and reading it into evidence at the Nuremberg trials, Major William F. Walsh, one of a number of assistant trial counsels, had already revealed this "exact number" in another translated quotation from Höttl's affidavit: "Approximately 4 million Jews had been killed in the various concentration camps, while an additional 2 million met death in other ways, the major part of which were shot by operational squads [Einsatzkommandos] of the Security Police during the campaign against Russia."[6] Höttl goes on to suggest that he thinks the figure to be about right, and that there is no reason to doubt Eichmann, especially since in his position he surely had access to correct figures. However, "Himmler was not satisfied with the report, since in his opinion the number of killed Jews had to be greater than 6 million . . . [and would therefore] send a man from his Statistics Office to Eichmann so that he could compile a new report based on materials provided by Eichmann, wherein the exact number should be calculated."[7]

The number appears again in the prosecution's summation on the morning of July 26, 1946, in which Justice Robert H. Jackson, chief of counsel for the United States, presented his closing argument for the prosecution, outlining five groups of crimes supporting the conspiracy charge against the defendants; the fifth being "Persecution and Extermination of Jews and Christians":

> Adolf Eichmann, the sinister figure who had charge of the extermination program, has estimated that the anti-Jewish activities resulted in the killing of 6 million Jews. Of these, 4 million were killed in extermination institutions, and 2 million were killed by Einsatzgruppen, mobile units of the Security Police and SD which pursued Jews in the ghettos and in their homes and slaughtered them by gas wagons, by mass shooting in antitank ditches and by

every device which Nazi ingenuity could conceive. So thorough and uncompromising was this program that the Jews of Europe as a race no longer exist, thus fulfilling the diabolic "prophecy" of Adolf Hitler at the beginning of the war ([referring to document] 2738-PS).[8]

The six million figure originates in the International Military Tribunal (IMT) in a sworn statement by a witness entered into evidence in a ground-breaking and monumental set of legal proceedings committed to historical documentation.[9] What is especially fascinating about the origins of the six million figure in this context, however, is that its basis is not sworn trial testimony but, rather, hearsay, in legal terms; and that, probably because of its alleged source and despite the fact that other total figures were cited, it quickly became *the* figure used to tally Jewish victims. Ironically, because the number is sourced in the Nazi leadership, it carries within itself a certain authenticity. But even more interesting is the fact that it was about right: in 2007, for example, the Division of the Senior Historian at the United States Holocaust Memorial Museum (USHMM) developed a series of authoritative estimates (dependent on means of counting) of between 5.65 million and 5.93 million, based on published accounts as well as on Soviet documents available only since 1991.[10]

Raul Hilberg, however, the late dean of Holocaust historiography (though himself trained as a political scientist), estimated 5.1 million Jewish victims, a number that did not change in the third edition of his monumental work, *The Destruction of the European Jews,* indicating, one might presume, that he was satisfied with his extensive scientific investigation into this figure.[11] *The Columbia Guide to the Holocaust* likewise provides a number of "more than" five million in its definition of the Holocaust.[12] Other estimates have ranged upward from there, but none has gone higher than six million. Eichmann himself was finally asked the question in 1961, in Jerusalem, and his answer then was five million.[13] It may be, as Hilberg notes in his essay "The Statistic" (which discusses methods of arriving at the number of Jewish victims under the subtitles "adding," "subtracting," and "recapitulation"), that "exactness is impossible"—an assertion that might disturb people, particularly those whose association with the figure is primarily political, social, or cultural, who are not regularly engaged with the scholarly and scientific assessment of the numbers and who may expect precision.

So, while the figure of six million appears to be an upper limit for these calculations and is not the number agreed upon by all scholars, it nonetheless is the tally that has endured for nearly seventy years in the public consciousness. It is both a ceiling on the calculation of the total number of Jewish Holocaust victims and a lasting approximation of that number that has assumed a life of its own, thus exceeding the merely symbolic. In contrast to Hilberg's figure, which, perhaps because it is not round, cannot easily assume a symbolic function, and also against an alternative round number such as "five million," which has never gained much traction as an agreed-upon representative tally (perhaps because it would be regarded as an underestimate), the number six million has attained iconic status. Interestingly, Hilberg himself alludes, if not to numeric symbolism outright, then at least to the significance of arriving at a "single number" that, essentially, summarizes the Holocaust—the significance of an iconic number that, in its simplicity and singularity, represents a complex truth. Ironically—because of this quest for numeric singularity—his essay was published in a collection titled *Unanswered Questions,* whose editor convened a colloquium of noted historians because "the time had come for summing up the 'state of the question,'" and who expressed the hope that, were his volume to help "account for [the mystery of Nazism], in the fullest sense of the term—that is, to work out possible explications for the questions it raises—it will have fulfilled its aim."[14] The volume is in fact permeated with answers, like Hilberg's, to the questions it poses, literally accounting for the Holocaust and thus accentuating the irony of its title.

Quantified Revenge

Tom Segev and Berel Lang recount a fascinating and disturbing episode in the immediate postwar era. The episode sheds light on the symbolic potential of the six million figure while also depicting its deep resonance in a portion of the survivor community; the episode is all the more fascinating because it indicates an awareness of the six million figure and its power prior to the presentation of the International Military Tribunal evidence at Nuremberg. Abba Kovner, Holocaust survivor and Vilna partisan leader, "a living symbol of Jewish resistance to the Nazis, a spiritual and moral authority," met in Lublin in February 1945 with a group of survivors, all former members of Zionist youth movements. They formed the "Revenge Group" (Irgun ha-Nakam), adopting "the [Hebrew] acronym DIN (Judgment), based on the first letters *of Dam Yisrael Noter* (the blood of Israel avenges)," delaying *Aliyah* in order to extract revenge from their tormentors.[15] Owing to the collective nature of Jewish suffering at the hands of the Nazis, the group's aim was collective revenge; their "Plan A proposed placing members of the Group among the sewage and water plant workers in four German cities—Hamburg, Frankfurt, Munich, and Nuremberg. . . . to poison the cities' water supply."[16] Kovner then traveled to Palestine in 1945, hoping to secure support for this mad plan to "murder six million Germans."[17] Indeed, Segev suggests that the desire for vengeance consumed Holocaust survivors and cites an unpublished study of Aliyat Hanoar (Youth Aliya, or immigration) graduates that found that, "years later, eight out of ten young survivors recalled that at war's end they longed for vengeance: no other emotion was so widespread among them—not agony nor anxiety, happiness nor hope."[18] Kovner later described the feeling as interfering with the ability to get on with normal life, "to get up in the morning and work as if accounts with the Germans had been settled." Segev suggests, therefore, that the plan for revenge was "an accounting between two nations. To be true revenge it had to precisely equal the dimensions of the crime. Kovner therefore set six million German citizens as his goal. He thought in apocalyptic terms: revenge was a holy obligation that would redeem and purify the Jewish people."[19] In a literalistic and chilling application of "eye for an eye" retribution, Kovner would exact revenge *exactly,* reifying the six million figure and transforming it into a blueprint for action, expressing the desire for revenge in the language of numeric precision. In this case, the six million figure was more than a symbolic number; as the basis for a plan of vengeance, it loomed as the ultimate goal of a plan of action.

Thankfully, this settling of accounts was not to be. Kovner's plan found little support among the organized Yishuv leadership; David Ben-Gurion took little time to dissuade one of Kovner's associates from the plan:

> "Revenge in history is a very important thing indeed, but if we could bring back six million Jews, rather than kill six million Germans—this would be even more important.". . . The revenge fantasies of the Holocaust survivors belonged, like the Holocaust itself, to a different, very foreign world. The death of millions of Germans could not advance the Zionist struggle. On the contrary . . . the revenge operation was likely to harm the Jewish Agency's efforts to create goodwill and support for its major goal—the establishment of the state.[20]

It is interesting to note that though Ben-Gurion rejected Kovner's audacious proposal, his own "positively oriented revenge" was also numerically based; in both ways, we see how the number six million had quickly become the basis for immediate post-Holocaust social accounting.

In this calculus, the state of Israel was conceptualized as a response to the six million victims, though not in the guise of an avenging angel come to settle a score. To stretch the implications of the Kovner plan a bit further, I would suggest it also failed because it was too literal: a one-for-one exchange as the antithesis of symbolism. Any nascent Israeli approach to represent and symbolize the six million would have to be more rhetorical and political, collective and national; any impulse to revenge would need to be redirected toward a successful national birth. Indeed, the continuing influence of the past on the present in a national context is a key component of Segev's argument and the reason for his book's title: "Just as the Holocaust imposed a posthumous collective identity on its six million victims, so too it formed the collective identity of this new country—not just for the survivors who came after the war but for all Israelis, then and now."[21] It is due to the collectivization of the six million victims and the continuing impact of that composite persona that Segev can conceive of a "seventh" million in postwar Israel, which depends on, and thus serves to further enhance, the iconic value of the six million.

The Six Million

What is the "posthumous collective identity" Segev identifies? It has taken various forms: the six million have been described as victims, martyrs (whether they knew it or not), "lambs to the slaughter," and, more recently, as resisters, often of a spiritual kind; they have even been posited as Zionists, retroactively, through a proposal to grant Holocaust victims honorary Israeli citizenship.[22] All of these characterizations serve to engender a posthumous coherence, defining a group that coalesces in the postwar period despite the fact that, before and during the war, no such coherence had occurred. This by-product reflects not only the desire for a single number that expresses the outcome of a process of counting/accounting (tallying and also explaining) but also of a social process that is simultaneously grappling with issues of meaning, an end product of which is a community of memory that defines itself, in part, in reference to that singular statistic. The rhetorical-political application of the figure of six million abounds in Israel in the 1950s, especially in debates over German reparations (one more area in which suffering and loss are quantified). But it arguably reached its peak in 1961 in Attorney General Gideon Hausner's opening statement in the Eichmann trial:

> As I stand before you, judges of Israel to lead the prosecution of Adolf Eichmann, I am not standing alone. With me are six million accusers. But they cannot rise to their feet to point an accusing finger toward the glass booth and cry out at the man sitting there, "I accuse." For their ashes are piled up on the hills of Auschwitz and the fields of Treblinka, washed by the rivers of Poland, and their graves are scattered the length and breadth of Europe. Their blood cries out, but their voices cannot be heard. I, therefore, will be their spokesman and will pronounce, in their names, this awesome indictment.[23]

Hausner, the sole accuser, here purports to embody all six million of the victims that cannot speak, thereby pointing a collective, singular finger at Eichmann; though the dead are dispersed throughout Europe, they are constituted as one (dead) body politic. Hausner's rhetorical flourish recalls Primo Levi's articulation of the "drowned," the "true witnesses" who cannot speak because they were murdered, and for whom the writer and memoirist must try to speak vicariously, despite the impossibility of really doing so.[24] Even Hausner's echo of God's accusation against Cain in Genesis 4:10, usually rendered as "the voice of your brother's blood cries out to me from the ground," very subtly supports the rhetorical reduction of six million victims into one. Daniel Mendelsohn points out that the grammar of the Hebrew original is contradictory, because "voice" is singular while "blood" and "cry out" are rendered in the plural, a problem most translators simply ignore;[25] a more accurate translation might read "the voice of your brother's bloods—they cry out to me [God] from the ground." The grammatical implication in the biblical case would be that the multitude of "bloods" and "cries" coalesce—congeal—into one singular voice. Hausner reverses the grammar (singular "blood" and plural "voices") so that the biblical allusion complicates his language, but it nonetheless culminates in his sole speaking voice on behalf of and indeed embodying the inaudible dead. The rhetorical flourish embodied in Hausner's famous accusation, as he personally stands in for the victims, points also to a potential conversion of the number indicating a multitude of victims into a condensed expression of their ultimate unity as a symbolic phrase: "*the* six million."

In the United States—to present a comparative framework for analysis—due to the absence of a Jewish nationalistic platform, there has been less *identification* with the six million victims. Nonetheless, the figure also became iconic, perhaps owing to the geographic distance from the events of World War II and the concomitant necessity of defining "the Holocaust" in accessible, human terms: "six million" as an iconic representation and representative of the Shoah becomes even more socially necessary in a country less directly affected by Jewish losses, offering a convenient handle on the magnitude of those losses for a population needing more mediation and explication. Hasia R. Diner's groundbreaking book, *We Remember with Reverence and Love,* for example, proves, contrary to previously accepted scholarly opinion, that the Holocaust was indeed discussed and present in American Jewish consciousness from the immediate postwar era all the way through the Eichmann trial, Hannah Arendt's book on it, and the Six-Day War. Diner's research also implies that there was no debate over the figure of six million—that it was already a given in memorial discourse. While preparing this chapter, I lost count of the times Diner or those she cites invoke the six million in the course of analysis, and it is clear that, in multiple ways, the number was immediately seized upon within the Jewish community as a vehicle for remembrance. A key component of this memorial construction is the definite article, "the," of the six million. At some point in its evolution as an iconic number, six million as an expression of counting (and accounting for) the total number of Jews murdered in the Holocaust also became something more: a figure preceded by a definite article that indicates its specificity, particularity, and additional iconic power as a representation of a collective.[26]

Among her many examples, Diner offers two compelling ones of the iconic use of the six million. One links back to the Israeli memorial-political context in which, in the late 1940s, the Jewish National Fund (JNF) proposed planting six million trees in a Martyr's Forest in the hills around Jerusalem. In a JNF letter sent from the New York office, the JNF attempted to engage American Jewry in an arboreal commemoration of "six million Jews who perished in Europe."[27] Donors received certificates that thanked them for their assistance in establishing "a living monument to the 6,000,000 martyrs."[28]

The second example dates to 1952: the American Jewish Congress had convened and charged a committee to compose a ceremonial Passover text. The result, the "Seder Ritual of Remembrance for the Six million Jews Who Perished at the Hands of the Nazis and for the Heroes of the Ghetto Uprisings," simultaneously looks backward and forward. First, it inserts the six million into the grand mythic-historical sweep of Jewish religious experience and persecution, resistance and martyrdom, referring to Hitler, without naming him, as "a tyrant more wicked than the Pharaoh who enslaved our fathers in Egypt" and noting, "On the first day of Passover the remnants in the ghetto of Warsaw rose up against the adversary, even as in the days of Judah the Maccabee." But also, while connecting to past motifs of redemption, the text, through this insertion, links the six million to the promise of redemption and a future messianic age through communal singing of "Ani Ma'amin" (musical score provided). This Jewish affirmation of patient belief in the coming of the Messiah, the twelfth of Maimonides's thirteen articles of faith, was set to music and reportedly sung by Holocaust victims even on the way to the gas chambers.[29]

Even more fascinating is the fact that the number six million was further compressed into the number "six" in the developing commemoration of the Holocaust. This is evidenced most notably in Diner's analysis of the Warsaw ghetto uprising as a symbol and as a basis for early American Holocaust commemoration, which began even before World War II ended, becoming "the prism through which American Jews performed the memory of the six million."[30] Indeed, as we can observe in the seder ritual, the Warsaw ghetto uprising brought Holocaust remembrance and Passover together (it helped that the uprising began during Pesach in 1943), leading into countrywide public programs following the holiday sponsored by a wide variety of groups, all commemorating the uprising. The typical program for these ceremonies varied little and still dominates the format of Holocaust commemoration ceremonies to this day; it regularly included "the lighting of six candles often by Jews who had lived through the catastrophe."[31] This now ubiquitous performance not only introduced a new ritual-cultural mechanism for Holocaust remembrance but also translated the already iconic figure six million, meant to represent and embody the totality of Jewish Holocaust victims, despite its abstract nature, into a more concrete, performative figure that transcended the implied narrative focus of a Warsaw ghetto uprising commemoration on armed resistance: "The widespread use of the number six in conjunction with Warsaw ghetto memorial programs made it clear that the victims as a collectivity, rather than heroes and fighters, served as the real subject of the commemorations."[32] It is significant, I think, that the number six is much easier to imagine, perform, and concretize than six million, so that, if six million is an icon in its own right, "six," used in this manner, is a potent distillation of that icon. From this reduction of an almost unimaginable number into something more manageable and actively mediative, it is only a small step to the six points of a Magen David, a hexagonal floor tile, or other renditions of the number six that some might cite as evidence for its symbolic importance. Particularly in the case of the six-pointed so-called Star of David, which has come to be regarded as the paradigmatic Jewish symbol that has its own independent relationship to the Holocaust, a connection can be established between the reduction of Holocaust millions into one symbolic number and the ubiquitous symbol for Jews and Jewishness. Of course, the number six and the Magen David do not refer on their own, without interpretation and elaboration, to the six million murdered. Rather, what this relationship shows is how, once the iconic significance of the number six in relation to the six million has been established—as in commemorative performances in which survivors light six candles to represent the six million dead—conceptual and material associations to the number six can be and are made to enhance the number's iconicity.

Counting to Six Million (or Not)

These examples clearly show the affective relationships some postwar Jews developed with the number six million. In chapter 7 of this volume, Josh Friedman engages a parallel phenomenon in the significant emotional attachments people have created with other very large numbers: "1.5 million," "over a million," or simply "countless" volumes collected at the Yiddish Book Center. His example also raises an important relevant issue of concretizing such a number through collecting, linking salvage and salvation. The Whitwell, Tennessee, Middle School paper clips project offers a comparison in the context of a re-embodiment of the six million figure. In this case, a parent proposed in 1998 that middle school students in this rural, nearly all-white town near Chattanooga begin learning about diversity; a course about the Holocaust was soon introduced. As a way for the class to grasp the notion of six million, the students began collecting paper clips, since they had "learned from the Internet—inaccurately—that non-Jewish Norwegians subtly protested the rounding up and deportation of their Jewish neighbors by wearing paper clips, which Norwegians mythologize—also inaccurately—as their own invention."[33] Ironically, the students were collecting items that are themselves banal symbols of bureaucracy in order to try to represent the quantified evil of the Shoah, itself the culmination of modern bureaucracy.[34]

While the project got off to a slow start, after receiving some international publicity and the involvement of journalists Peter and Dagmar Schroeder (who also helped the project secure a railway boxcar of the type used to transport Jews during the Shoah), the students eventually collected over twenty-five million paper clips by the time their Children's Holocaust Memorial opened on November 9, 2001. The stream of incoming paper clips continues; to date, over thirty million have been collected.[35] While many were quick to dismiss the project as simplistic and undeserving of serious attention, scholars such as Daniel Magilow, as well as numerous viewers of the film documenting the enterprise, disagreed. Magilow, in his insightful article, "Counting to Six Million: Collecting Projects and Holocaust Memorialization," uses the Whitwell example as a springboard to argue that projects like it, which collect six million of an item as a vehicle for teaching about the Holocaust, collectively represent a new memorial form that emphasizes play and process over work and final product. "In this new mode of memorialization, two obsessions have converged. The obsessive childhood tendency to gather, arrange, and play with stamps, coins, rocks, or other objects has been redirected to the Holocaust, an event whose grip on the American public imagination has itself become obsessive."[36] Critics complain that such projects trivialize the Holocaust, noting that people are not and should not be identified with objects, especially banal, bureaucratic ones, while supporters claim that such projects are transformative, teach tolerance, and build community. "The discomfort with memorial projects arises from an inability to reconcile the radical incongruity between a profane signifier (a button, a penny, or a paper clip) and a sacred signified (the victims of genocide). Whereas from the collector's standpoint, the relationship honors victims, to the outsider it can appear arbitrary, improper, and even blasphemous."[37] What is key, however, is that in all these cases it is the number six million that has itself become the iconic sign to be embodied through the act of collecting.

A key impetus for such collecting projects involves the difficulty of imagining—or even actually counting to—six million. That initial problem of comprehension becomes the catalyst for memorialization, as collectors such as the students in Whitwell attempt to grasp the meaning of six million while simultaneously working toward it (and, in Whitwell, then exceeding it). In this respect the significance of six million and of six as numerical-memorial icons increases because socially and culturally we believe numbers can express concepts clearly, scientifically, and succinctly. At the same time, the technical challenge of actually counting to six million objects limits our ability fully to comprehend the victimhood of the Holocaust in a concrete, rather than abstract, manner. That limiting function enhances the importance of the number, transforming it into a transcendent, quasi-mystical figure that nonetheless remains somewhat out of reach. As an iconic number it points to the enormous scale of the Holocaust's victims while highlighting, at the same time, the difficulty of directly and fully comprehending the number. Where Magilow finds the value of such projects is in the process of trying to attain that goal and that comprehension, a process he sees as social, public, and truly collective memorialization, centered on a mass of objects deemed significant because they are not actual relics, and made symbolic through interactive play and their numeric value. So long as these objects, such as the paper clips, serve as media of memorialization, they remain valuable, not trivial.

However, there is a potential irony in such collecting projects. Whether the goal of six million is achieved and collecting ceases or, as in the case in Whitwell, where the collection surpassed its original goal and continues to this day, the accumulated mass of material objects—an inventory of what is in stock—might be seen as recalling Nazi techniques. Though one cannot deny the performative, memorial value of an inventory such as Whitwell's, it is possible to see an echo in such collecting projects of the Nazi objectification and dehumanization of Jews: the plunder of their sacred ritual objects, the amassing of their living bodies in ghettos and camps and of their corpses in mass graves, and, especially, the collection and commodification of their material belongings and even bodily remnants, such as hair, immediately prior to and following their murder, without attention to numeric order and precision, and, often, without sufficient accounting of/for the items.

Thus, while the Whitwell inventory of paper clips builds an institutional Holocaust memory through its stock of everyday items, housing the collection in a restored European railway car of the type used in Nazi deportations of Jews concretizes and contains that memory. At the opening ceremony, visitors walked through the railcar memorial fitted with glass panels, so that they could see the paper clips inside, "a symbolic resting place for millions of victims who have no graves."[38] Here the abstract quality of the paper clip as everyday object not directly associated with Jewish victimhood (despite Whitwell students' beliefs to the contrary) is made to represent Jews after all, packed like so many objects into a railcar. Or rather, Jews and other victims: in the final memorial collection, the participants decided to display eleven million rather than six million paper clips in the railway car, with another eleven million housed in a nearby monument "honoring children of the Holocaust."[39] This attempt to make Holocaust memory more inclusive, however, problematizes the students' memorial, collection, and counting efforts and threatens to erase the iconic meaning of the collection itself, since the eleven million number is not representative of the Holocaust in the same way. As historian Deborah Lipstadt, in *The Eichmann Trial,* has reminded us, Simon Wiesenthal had created this alternative arithmetic reckoning of the Shoah's victims—eleven million, comprising six million Jews and five million others, a composite number that is too high to represent the total number of Nazi murders and too low to include all victims, direct and indirect, of the Nazi regime—in order to make the Holocaust more universal and inclusive while maintaining Jewish numerical primacy.[40] As the Whitwell case attests, the eleven million figure continues to have a life of its own, with its own ritual candle lighting and other representations, alongside and in some cases supplanting the six million figure.

This is not the only numerical-memorial challenge to the iconic power of the six million figure. As Geneviève Zubrzycki has noted, in Poland, the number six million more likely refers to the total number of Polish losses during World War II, which includes almost the entirety of the Jewish Polish population and a nearly equal number of non-Jewish Poles. "The number of Polish citizens who perished during World War II (six million) and the number of European Jews killed during that period (six million) appear to place Poles and Jews on an equal plane of losses and suffering—adding to the competitiveness of Poles with Jews over who holds the 'monopoly' on suffering, a competitiveness heightened by the significant place of martyrdom as a root paradigm in the histories and identities of both Poles and Jews."[41] Interestingly, as Zubrzycki's research indicates, the iconic Holocaust number six million carries with it a different meaning in Poland, complicating public perception of six million as a Jewish figure and as a figure referring only to Jews, but also accentuating its significance as an icon and symbolic point of reference. In this case the competition over the meaning of the number should be understood as an aspect of the number's importance. These challenges to the iconic meaning of six million are perhaps the topic of a future study.

At present, the number six million dominates the reckoning and public recognition of Jewish loss during the Holocaust—a powerful numeric icon that has come to represent the Holocaust itself. A recent rendering of this iconic figure in print further accentuates its significance in the post-Holocaust landscape: the book, *And Every Single One Was Someone*, which, as discussed in the "Introduction," repeats the word "Jew" six million times. "It is meant as a kind of coffee-table monument of memory," wrote Jodi Rudoren in the *New York Times*, acknowledging the publication as more concept and conversation piece than literary achievement, intended more for institutional purchase and display than for individual consumption.[42] The "author" of the volume, Phil Chernofsky, first thought of the book's "shtick" in the late 1970s, when he taught at the Yeshiva of Central Queens and charged his students to write the word "Jew" on blank sheets of paper as many times as possible in half an hour; the total came to only 40,000. The publisher's goal is to print six million copies of the book. Rudoren compares it to Yad Vashem's ongoing effort to collect and record the identity of every single Jewish victim of the Holocaust in its Names Recovery Project (addressed ethnographically by Carol Kidron in chapter 2 of this volume): in June 2013 Yad Vashem publicized 4.2 million names in an oversized "Book of Names" unveiled in the renovated Block 27 exhibition at the Auschwitz-Birkenau State Museum; to date, it has recorded 4.5 million names in its Central Database of Shoah Victims'

Names.[43] These are interesting, very different projects. Chernofsky's book begins with the precision and certainty of the six million but then renders that number as a mind-numbing, anonymous mass of "Jews," thereby reducing the multiplicity of individual victims to one unnamed Jew, repeated six million times. In contrast, Yad Vashem's version is another collecting project, whose ultimate goal might strike many as forever out of reach, but that nonetheless can inspire participation and action; in Yad Vashem's "Book of Names" everyone is unique, individual, not anonymous. But despite their differences, both endeavors arise from the iconic significance of the number six million. In the continuing symbolization of the Holocaust, this figure, and the other numbers I have associated with it, have social afterlives; all of them provide Jews and non-Jews with numerical icons that assist in conceptualizing the Shoah and serve as mechanisms by which the future of its memory may be secured.

Notes

Thank you to workshop conveners and editors Michal Kravel-Tovi and Deborah Dash Moore for their helpful comments on earlier drafts of this chapter and for the fruitful discussions I had with the other workshop participants, especially my co-panelists Carol Kidron and Yael Zerubavel and respondent Geneviève Zubrzycki.

1. Virgil Cândea, "Icons," in *Encyclopedia of Religion*, ed. Lindsay Jones, 2nd ed. (Detroit: Macmillan Reference USA, 2005), 7:4352–4354, *Gale Virtual Reference Library*, April 30, 2014.

2. Dominik Bartmanski and Jeffrey C. Alexander, "Introduction: Materiality and Meaning in Social Life: Toward an Iconic Turn in Cultural Sociology," in *Iconic Power: Materiality and Meaning in Social Life*, ed. Jeffrey C. Alexander, Dominik Bartmanski, and Bernhard Giesen (New York: Palgrave Macmillan, 2012), 1–2.

3. Nikolas Rose, *Numbers, Powers of Freedom: Reframing Political Thought* (Cambridge: Cambridge University Press, 1999), 198.

4. Ibid., 208.

5. Translation quoted by Major William F. Walsh in *Trial of the Major War Criminals before the International Military Tribunal, Nuremberg, 14 November 1945–1 October 1946* (Nuremberg, Germany: International Military Tribunal, 1947), 3:570, December 14, 1945, http://www .loc.gov/rr/frd/Military_Law/pdf/NT_Vol-III.pdf, hereafter cited as *IMT* followed by volume, page number, and URL. The text of Höttl's affidavit, document 2738-PS/exhibit USA-296, is available at *IMT*, 31:85–87, http://www.loc.gov/rr/frd/Military_Law/pdf/NT_Vol-XXXI.pdf. One might think that the number, emerging from an August 1944 conversation, that is, before the Holocaust was over, would be a low estimate. It is important to note, however, that by this point the vast majority of the murders of the Holocaust had been committed. That does not imply we should discount the ongoing killing, especially the death marches, nor ignore the fact that the Nazis still placed a high priority on the Jewish genocide, but only that it is not, as we will see below, a remarkably inaccurate number.

6. *IMT*, 3:569, http://www.loc.gov/rr/frd/Military_Law/pdf/NT_Vol-III.pdf. The number is corroborated by U.S. attorney general Tom C. Clark in a letter to the Yiddish Scientific Institute dated December 10, 1945, which stated that "six million Jews were slaughtered by the Germans and their satellites" (cited in Max Weinreich, *Hitler's Professors: The Part of Scholarship*

in Germany's Crimes against the Jewish People, 2nd ed. [New Haven, CT: Yale University Press, 1999], 5).

7. "Himmler sei mit dem Bericht nicht zufrieden gewesen, da nach seiner Meinung die Zahl der getoeteten Juden grösser als 6 Millionen sein muesse. Himmler hatte erklaert, dass er einen Mann von seinem statistischen Amt zu Eichmann schicken werde, damit dieser auf Grund des Materials von Eichmann einen neuen Bericht verfasse, wo die genaue Zahl ausgearbeitet werden sollte." *IMT,* 31:86, http://www.loc.gov/rr/frd/Military_Law/pdf/NT_Vol-XXXI.pdf.

8. See *IMT,* 19:405, http://www.loc.gov/rr/frd/Military_Law/pdf/NT_Vol-XIX.pdf.

9. The Nuremberg trials were not the first time the number was mentioned; it appeared in scattered newspaper accounts, including the *New York Times* on January 8, 1945, which sources the number in an address by Jacob Lestchinsky to the Yiddish Scientific Institute the previous day.

10. Peter Black, e-mail message to author, February 24, 2012. The USHMM estimates were pieced together from a range of sources, including Raul Hilberg, *The Destruction of the European Jews,* 3rd ed. (New Haven, CT: Yale University Press, 2003), app. A, 1301–1321; Wolfgang Benz, ed., *Dimension des Völkermords: Die Zahl der jüdischen Opfer des Nationalsozialismus* (Munich: Oldenbourg, 1991); and Martin Gilbert, *The Routledge Atlas of the Holocaust,* 3rd ed. (New York: Routledge, 2002).

11. Compare Raul Hilberg, *The Destruction of the European Jews,* rev. and definitive ed. (New York: Holmes and Meier, 1985), 3:1219–1220, with the 3rd ed., 3:1320–1321.

12. See Donald L. Niewyk and Francis R. Nicosia, *The Columbia Guide to the Holocaust* (New York: Columbia University Press, 2000), 45.

13. Cited in Raul Hilberg, "The Statistic," in *Unanswered Questions: Nazi Germany and the Genocide of the Jews,* ed. François Furet (New York: Schocken, 1989), 155.

14. Furet, *Unanswered Questions,* viii.

15. Berel Lang, "Holocaust Memory and Revenge: The Presence of the Past," *Jewish Social Studies,* n.s., 2, no. 2 (1996): 5.

16. Ibid.

17. Tom Segev, *The Seventh Million,* trans. Haim Watzman (New York: Hill and Wang, 1993), 140.

18. Ibid.

19. Cited in Segev, *Seventh Million,* 142. See Numbers 31:2 in which Israel is told to attack the Midianites out of revenge for their previous aggression. See also Deuteronomy 32:35 in which God says "Vengeance is mine," suggesting that revenge is ultimately a divine, not human, matter.

20. Segev, *Seventh Million,* 151.

21. Ibid., 11.

22. Ibid., 432–434.

23. Ibid., 347. See also Segev's interesting footnote about other rhetorical uses of "six million" in ibid., 347–348.

24. See Primo Levi, *The Drowned and the Saved,* trans. Raymond Rosenthal (New York: Summit, 1988).

25. Daniel Mendelsohn, *The Lost: A Search for Six of Six Million* (New York: HarperCollins, 2006), 134.

26. See Yael Zerubavel's discussion of the definite article in chapter 3 of this volume.

27. Cited in Hasia R. Diner, *We Remember with Reverence and Love: American Jews and the Myth of Silence after the Holocaust, 1945–1962* (New York: New York University Press, 2009), 42.

28. Ibid., 43. Incidentally, the forest never reached its goal; see Segev, *Seventh Million,* 430n. On the issue of Israeli afforestation as Holocaust memorialization, see Oren Baruch Stier,

Committed to Memory: Cultural Mediations of the Holocaust (Amherst: University of Massachusetts, 2003), 179–181.

29. Diner, *We Remember,* 19. Interestingly, the stage directions for the "seder ritual" instruct those performing it to do so after the third cup of wine "just before the door is opened / for the symbolic entrance of the Prophet Elijah," making no mention of the traditional Haggadah text read at this point, "*Shfokh chamatcha*" (Pour out thy wrath), the recitation of a wish that God punish the nations of the world for their ignorance of the divine. For more on the relationship between the Holocaust and the Haggadah, see Liora Gubkin, *You Shall Tell Your Children: Holocaust Memory in American Passover Ritual* (New Brunswick, NJ: Rutgers University Press, 2007). For more on Maimonides's Thirteen Principles of Faith, see, for example, *Siddur Kol Yaakov / The Complete ArtScroll Siddur, Nusach Ashkenaz,* 3rd ed., ed. and trans. Rabbi Nosson Scherman, co-edited by Rabbi Meir Zlotowitz (New York: Mesorah, 1990), 178–181. "Ani Ma'amin" is also the title of a Hadag Nahash song, though only the refrain "ani ma'amin" shares anything with the classic statement of religious creed; the rest of the song is a litany of political criticism (see Hadag Nahash, "Ani Ma'amin," directed by Gal Muggia, http://vimeo.com/41743115; and Azzan Yadin-Israel, "A Measure of Beauty," *Jewish Review of Books* 3 [Fall 2010]: 44–45).

30. Diner, *We Remember,* 75.

31. Ibid., 70.

32. Ibid., 77.

33. Daniel H. Magilow, "Counting to Six Million: Collecting Projects and Holocaust Memorialization," *Jewish Social Studies,* n.s., 14, no. 1 (2007): 24.

34. See Zygmunt Bauman, *Modernity and the Holocaust* (Ithaca, NY: Cornell University Press, 2001).

35. See http://www.whitwellmiddleschool.org/?PageName=bc&n=69258.

36. Magilow, "Counting to Six Million," 26.

37. Ibid., 28.

38. Peter W. Schroeder and Dagmar Schroeder-Hildebrand, *Six Million Paper Clips: The Making of a Children's Holocaust Memorial* (Minneapolis: Kar-Ben, 2004), 55.

39. See http://www.whitwellmiddleschool.org/?PageName=bc&n=69258.

40. Deborah E. Lipstadt, *The Eichmann Trial* (New York: Nextbook/Schocken, 2011), 8–10.

41. Geneviève Zubrzycki, *The Crosses of Auschwitz: Nationalism and Religion in Post-Communist Poland* (Chicago: University of Chicago Press, 2006), 114–115.

42. Jodi Rudoren, "Holocaust Told in One Word, 6 Million Times," *New York Times,* January 26, 2014, 1.

43. Ibid., 12. For Yad Vashem's project, see http://www.yadvashem.org/yv/en/remembrance/names/, http://www.yadvashem.org/yv/en/pressroom/pressreleases/pr_details.asp?cid=795, and http://www.yadvashem.org/yv/en/remembrance/names/why_collect_names.asp.

2 Breathing Life into Iconic Numbers

Yad Vashem's Shoah Victims' Names Recovery Project and the Constitution of a Posthumous Census of Six Million Holocaust Dead

Carol A. Kidron

THE PRESENT ETHNOGRAPHIC STUDY examines the memory work constituted by the Yad Vashem's Shoah Victims' Names Recovery Project.[1] Since 1955, Yad Vashem has disseminated testimony pages amassing demographic data on the time and place of birth, profession, place, and form of death of Holocaust victims. Testimony pages have been stored in an archive and more recently in an online database that might potentially document all Jewish Holocaust victims. Recently, Yad Vashem has intensified efforts to recover "every person's name," calling upon the public not only to submit new testimony pages but to "fill up the database so that we may reach the six million mark." Aimed not only to compile a more complete commemorative list of names, the project hoped to salvage and represent the absenced and forgotten personal identities of victims.[2] Novel information technology facilitates sophisticated cross-referencing, corroboration, and validation of the names and identities in the database. Now at the four million mark and "counting," it could numerically approach, populate, and "corroborate" (and perhaps "vindicate") the iconic number of six million.

Yad Vashem also redesigned its previous exhibit, the Hall of Names, which displayed the testimonial pages. The original exhibit was no more than a marginal storage room located off the main linear path of the museum tourist route. It was transformed in 2004 into a monumental memorial exhibit displaying the archived testimony pages in a new fashion, blatantly representing the process of counting the six million and "completion" of the database.

Content analysis of the Names Recovery Project website and the Testimony Pages and ethnographic observations at Yad Vashem's Hall of Names exhibit raise numerous questions.[3] How does the project commemorate the Holocaust dead? Does, and if so, how does the institutional agenda of recovering "every

Page of Testimony   דף עד

*Pages of Testimony commemorate the Jews who were murdered during the Holocaust – Shoah. Please submit a
separate form for each victim, in block capitals.* **Fields outlined in bold are mandatory.**

Victim's photo Please write victim's name on back. Do not glue.	*The Martyrs' and Heroes' Remembrance Law 5713-1953 determines in section 2 that: "The
task of Yad Vashem is to gather into the homeland material regarding all those members of
the Jewish people who laid down their lives, who fought and rebelled against the Nazi enemy
and his collaborators, and to perpetuate their* **names** *and those of the communities,
organizations and institutions which were destroyed because they were Jewish".*

Victim's family name:	Maiden name:
Victim's first name **(or nickname):**	Previous / other family name:

Title:	**Gender: Male / Female**	Date of birth:	Approx. age at death:

Place of birth (town, region, country):	Citizenship:

First name of victim's father:	Family name of victim's father:

First name of victim's mother:	Maiden name of victim's mother:

Victim's family status and no. of children:	First name of victim's spouse:	Maiden name of victim's spouse:

Permanent residence **(town, region, country):**	Street:

Victim's profession:	Place of work:	Member of organization or movement:

Places and activities during the war – arrest / deportation / ghetto / camp / death march / hiding / escape /
resistance / combat (circle relevant):

Residence during the war (town, region, country):	Street:

**Circumstances of death: prison / deportation / ghetto / camp / mass murder / death march / hiding /
escape / resistance / combat or unknown - Shoah:**

Place of death (town, region, country):	Date of death:

*I, the undersigned, hereby declare that this testimony is correct to the best of my knowledge. I understand that this
Page of Testimony and all the information on it will be publicly accessible.*

Submitter's first name:	Family name:	Previous / maiden name:

Street, house no., Apt.:	City	State / Zip code:

Country:	I am a Shoah survivor : Yes / No	**My relationship to the victim** **(family / other):**

During the war I was in a camp / ghetto / forest / in hiding / had false papers / the resistance (circle relevant):

Date:	Place:	Signature:_____

2011-2012

ונתתי להם בביתי ובחומתי יד ושם... אשר לא יכרת" ישעיהו נ"ו ה'

"... And I shall give them in My house and within My walls a memorial and a name ... that shall not be cut off" Isaiah, 56:5

Testimony page. Courtesy Yad Vashem.

Hall of Names exhibit. Photo by the author.

person's name" and "reaching the mark" of all six million dead constitute novel commemorative practices? How does display of the very act of counting amassed Testimony Pages in the Names Recovery Database and the Hall of Names exhibit grapple with the commemorative challenge of Holocaust absence and incomprehensibility?

In keeping with the critical perspective of the politics of Holocaust memory,[4] the recovery project may be interpreted as the posthumous nationalization of the Holocaust dead mnemonically "put to work"[5] in the service of the Israeli state. However, macropolitical studies deconstructing the *what* and *why* of discourse and practice often do not account for the *how* (in our case) of commemorative discourse and practice in everyday life. Moreover, on their own, academic critical studies often fail to unpack the micropractices and processes that constitute novel cultural products that will in turn ultimately affect not only the microsite but also macro-sociopolitical realities.[6]

A semiotic analysis of part-whole (synecdochal) relations between the component parts of the project—namely, the recovered individual testimony pages or numbers of dead—and the whole—namely, the iconic six million—provides a bottom-up reading of the way Yad Vashem specifically revivifies the "virtual" presence of the previously absent dead. In contrast to a census of the living that open-endedly enumerates a population, the a priori six million mark constructs what might be termed "a census of the dead" that places the very act of counting and recovery of the absent yet potentially present dead parts of the whole on display. As newly recovered testimony pages, or "parts" of the absent "whole" or six million, are counted and fed into the Yad Vashem database and exhibit, they breathe life into the iconic number and materialize the "incomprehensible" experience of Holocaust victimhood. Ultimately, the re-empowered whole (number of ever-increasing testimony pages/victims) envelops and takes supremacy over the "shallow" personal lives of its individual parts, perpetually signifying the momentum of self-completion of the iconic number—six million. Thus, the project, as unique cultural product, creates an illusion of the emergent entirety of Holocaust presence and creatively grapples with the crisis of Holocaust representation by successfully representing the sublime devastation of Holocaust suffering thought otherwise to be "beyond representation."[7]

Beyond the Politics of Holocaust Memory

Commemorative projects aim to transform absence into presence.[8] The cultural feat of representation fabricates renewed presence so that participants may experience what has become absent. Representation of the absent past is morally valorized, as it honors lost individuals and communities and provides a strategically potent political and ideological model for the present. Recent scholarship, however, has focused not on semiotic processes of representation but on the politics of memory and the instrumentalization of the past for political gain. Benedict Anderson's frequently cited work on the nation as imagined community outlines a series of mechanisms through which the nation-state reshapes and reifies group identities constituting and sustaining national cohesion and allegiance.[9] According to Anderson, the museum, the census, and the map "work together to shape the way the State imagines its domain, the nature of human beings it rules, and the legitimacy of its ancestry."[10] Particularly relevant to the study at hand, the museum constitutes and displays an imagined ancestral history unifying heterogeneous populations, rallying them to the call of sociopolitical agendas made meaningful by the culturally constructed lessons of collective pasts.

Yet, while Anderson examined the political instrumentalization of an invented ancestral past, collective memory scholars such as Handelman, Huyssen, Nora, Schudson, White, and Zerubavel,[11] narrow their gaze to the way in which the dead are enlisted to sustain, reinvigorate, or rewrite national, ethnic, or communal grand narratives. Handelman explores the way memorial ceremonies ritually transform fallen soldiers into symbolic parts of the collective/state or whole, meaningfully standing for the whole. Commemoration of their sacrifice emerges as a key component of the nation's civil religion. Burial of Israeli Defense Forces (IDF) soldiers in the national cemetery enables the bodies of the fallen to reconstitute national roots in the Land of Israel after diasporic rupture. Traditional aesthetic and textual streamlining of tombstones ensures that, despite individual differences, all soldiers would be identically classified and documented along the same bureaucratic rubrics (name, date of birth and death, and army unit) devoid of idiosyncratic biographical references. Streamlining assures the construction of identical graves that together semiotically merge to create one potent signifier of the iconic soldier who sacrificially died to preserve the collective and the state. Only in this way may the individuals fallen together make up the part that can stand for the whole. Although this is most certainly the semiotics of many national military cemeteries, according to Handelman, the uniquely precarious nature of Jewish-Israeli ties to territory and the conflicted political context simultaneously necessitates perpetual enlistment of new sacrificial parts and policing of the displayed commemoration of individual difference in ways that would preserve the integrity of the whole.

Numerous scholars have examined the mnemonic processes and practices of the enlistment of the Holocaust dead in the service of Israel's civil religion.[12] Feldman's study of high school trips to Poland in particular explores the way the dead sustain national grand narratives and empower the nation-state as sole sanctuary for the Jewish people.

In the same vein, scholars have deconstructed commemorative practices at Yad Vashem. Bartov presents a post-Zionist reading of Yad Vashem's museology, claiming that the newly renovated exhibits further tighten the hegemonic grip of the state-run institution on Holocaust memory so that it may be put to work to sustain the teetering, morally suspect, xenophobic political vision of the state.[13] Yet these scholars do not consider the semiotic or sociopolitical potential of the practice of counting the Holocaust dead or what I have termed a census of the dead.

Extending Anderson's and Appadurai's conceptualization of the population census as one of many hegemonic bureaucratic practices facilitating the social construction of the imagined national community, demographic data pertaining to the dead amassed in Yad Vashem's testimonial pages, housed in their archives, and displayed in the Hall of Names can be understood as a hegemonically constructed and enlisted census of the dead.[14] Resonating with Handelman's analysis of the enlistment of Israeli fallen soldiers, the nationalization of the Holocaust dead permits the Israeli Holocaust memorial to enlist posthumously the Holocaust dead as revered citizens.[15] The enlistment, bureaucratic classification, and nationalization of the culturally diverse and often "unaffiliated" Holocaust dead in the national Holocaust memorial potentially reinforce the foundational grand narrative in Israel's civil religion, reinstate the state as sanctuary and redeemer of the Jewish people, and finally re-empower Yad Vashem as valorized guardian of the Holocaust past in its "completed entirety."

However, as sole interpretation, this top-down reading of the census of the dead as a means to nationalize and politically instrumentalize the six million obscures salient microsemiotic processes of commemoration.[16] Only a study of how the census "culturally works" on the ground to pull off the impossible feat of representing the individual absent dead, transforming them into semiotic parts that sustain the iconic whole can explain how the iconic number of six million dead retains its symbolic and political potency. This study, therefore, presents a semiotic analysis of the way institutionally recovered and evocatively displayed names and numbers, or census of the dead, presents the process of counting the dead and completing the historical record to revivify the presence of the absent iconic six million.

Content Analysis and Ethnographic Observation

The Names Recovery Project Website

Yad Vashem began the Names Recovery Project in 1954. In the first three decades of the project, survivors primarily filled out testimony pages. By the late 1980s Yad Vashem had only recovered approximately one million names, roughly 25 percent of which were accessed from other sources of documentation. According to the project website, from the mid-late 1990s and more urgently from 2004 on, Yad Vashem issued a *call via the mass media to individuals, families, and communities* "to fulfill [their] our moral duty to respect the victims last behest and remember them in this way and *to recover the names of the remaining 5 million victims.*" The project is depicted as having been "a race against time" to access and document information from those still alive who might testify to their deaths, "before those who remember them are no longer with us."

According to the website, the project also ambitiously aspires to "reconstruct the life stories of each individual Jew murdered in the Shoah" and preserve individual legacies of millions of Holocaust victims who would otherwise be lost in the oblivion of forgetting. As stated on the website, "since 1955, Yad Vashem has been fulfilling its mandate to preserve the memory of Holocaust victims by collecting names, the ultimate representation of a person's identity, as it is written: 'And to them will I give in my house and within my walls a memorial and a name (Yad Vashem), an everlasting name that shall not be cut off' (Isaiah 56:5)." The site goes on to explain that "the number six million is described as so large it is almost impossible to comprehend. It does not convey who they were, where they lived, information about their families, what their dreams were, how they died, or whether and how they were related to us." Presented also as a corrective of the Nazi bureaucratic dehumanization, which turned individual lives into numbers, the project claims to return the name, face, and even personal biographical story to the number as follows:

> Our aim is to present Jewish people as human beings with discernible identities, which the Germans planned to destroy in the name of their murderous racist ideology. From the dust and loss, we are committed to restoring the human faces of the victims and uncover families and communities as well as their culture that was annihilated during the Holocaust. The Nazis sought to dehumanize the Jews, turn them into numbers, murder them and systematically obliterate every memory of them. This not only changed the scale and

scope of the murder, but also called for a new kind of remembrance. (www .yad.vashem.org)

This text discursively frames the Names Recovery Project as motivated by two seemingly different yet semiotically complementary agendas. First, as search and salvage mission, the project aims to complete the archive by accessing the remaining two million names that would allow them "to reach the mark" of the commemorative list of six million victims. However, the site also clearly admits that even if completed the number is inherently "limited" as it is incomprehensible in all its magnitude. Echoing Zelizer's distinction between referentiality and symbolization,[17] the evocative power of the six million as symbol, which semiotically envelops its parts to iconically signify and stand for those parts, is now suspect of having failed to represent its constituent parts / reduce its parts.[18] In an attempt to both complete and reinvigorate the semiotic force of the six million, the site calls for the second agenda, namely the restoration of individual stories and "humanity" of the dead. Precisely the merging of both agendas—the bureaucratic mechanism of counting to recontain and restore an integrated whole and the restoration of individual biographies and faces—provides the necessary "breadth" (in numbers across the board) and "depth" (disclosing the lives behind the numbers) to salvage the whole of the six million as symbol and stable representation of Holocaust victimhood.

Although the text presents the project as a totally novel and path-breaking endeavor, it is culturally grounded in Jewish paradigms of memory. The website portrays the Names Recovery Project as a contemporary offshoot of traditional Jewish memory work, positioned auspiciously after two key foundational events: the revelation at Sinai and the recitation of the Exodus from bondage in Egypt on Passover. On a more micro and familial level, the site calls upon each Jewish individual and family to fulfill their personal obligation to redeem the identities of forgotten Holocaust victims just as one would recite Yizkor (liturgical memorial) prayers for personal loved ones. Interpreting the text, the contemporary Names Recovery Project is grafted upon and thereby legitimated and empowered by what Yerushalmi has described as deep cultural Jewish metacodes and practices of memory.[19]

The project agenda and the grafting of the mission within culturally embedded Jewish paradigms of memory is brought home most powerfully on the website in a promotional video clip by Rabbi Lau, previously chief rabbi of Israel. As Holocaust survivor and valorized spiritual leader, Rabbi Lau takes on the role of spokesman for Yad Vashem, legitimating its hegemonic control over the database of the dead. After explaining how and why the names project is consistent with Jewish dictates of memory, Rabbi Lau states:

It is not enough for all of you to give your grandchildren or children the names of the dead, it is not enough to put the names of the dead in the Zichor Books in survivor organizations or on memorial walls in your synagogues. You must fill out the testimony pages. But it is also not enough to fill out the pages—we must fill the database so we have all the 6 million. All of them must be preserved together in the central database here in the national museum. (www.yad.vashem.org)

The rabbi most univocally depicts the project agenda as the process of salvaging, submitting, and counting all the victims or parts toward creating a complete or full database, which would then fill the incomplete iconic number and symbol. He also clearly illuminates the transition from traditional Jewish and Jewish-Israeli commemoration, where names of the dead were privately or communally recollected and stored, to centralization of all Holocaust victims in a national database under the auspices of Yad Vashem.

The Testimony Page: Identifying and Classifying the Dead

The testimony page serves as the main bureaucratic media of the Names Recovery Project.[20] According to the website, testimony pages can be filled out by survivors or their descendants, as well as friends or acquaintances of victims. The pages are stored for perpetuity in the Central Database of the Names Recovery Project. Approximately 60 percent of the forms (approximately 2.5 million) are "displayed" in Yad Vashem's Hall of Names exhibit. The pages are standard A4 in length, made up of multiple rubrics, including full name (as well as a number of rubrics permitting the recording of multiple names in different languages—e.g., Yiddish, Hebrew [or other language of country of origin]), date and place of birth, place of residence before the war, profession, parents' and spouse's names, and place and circumstances of death. There is also an empty square for a photograph of the victim when available. On the bottom of the form, the submitter is requested to record their own details: name, place of residence, and relationship to the victim followed by a signature. Those submitting forms are described on the website as "witnesses testifying to the lives and biographical details of the victims." According-ing to the online tutorial, only a form containing information in a minimum of three descriptive rubrics (e.g., name, place of birth, name of parent of victim) may be submitted. If containing less than three rubrics, the page is considered empirically unsound and is not "counted."

The importance of submitting a form for every single victim and ultimately counting each and every one of the Holocaust dead is emphasized in numerous ways on the website. First, the category of "Holocaust victim" is liberally defined, permitting the inclusion of those previously excluded from victim lists. Expanding the Israeli Census Bureau's definition of Holocaust survivors,[21] the website pointedly reads, "in this instance the Holocaust victim is defined as a Jew who was murdered when his or her country of residence was ruled or occupied by the Nazis or by regimes that collaborated with the Nazis where Jews who died in the few months after the end of WWII because of exhaustion or sickness caused by traumatic Shoah experiences are also considered victims."

Second, the website highlights the importance of submission of a separate page for each victim, suggesting ways to bypass the problem of insufficient demographic information or duplication. The website states, "each Holocaust victim, children included, must be registered on a separate Page of Testimony. Even when the child's name is unknown, the 'witness' is called upon to submit a separate page by entering 'child' in the Family Status field and specifying parents names and gender."

To avoid duplication of testimony pages and inaccurate enumeration, potential witnesses are asked to search Yad Vashem's database of names prior to submission of their testimony pages. The website then recommends that a testimony page be submitted "as a token of personal commemoration" even when the victim's name already appears in the database. The representation of a potential duplicate page as token of personal commemoration discursively frames the submission process and resultant commemoration as a personal moral imperative that overrides concern over possible duplication and perhaps even accuracy of enumeration. However, possible duplication inevitably "creates" a bureaucratic dilemma. Although according to the website, Yad Vashem staff cross reference the pages submitted with data from other sources, it offers no information regarding removal of duplicate pages. In contrast to a census of the living, which builds its authority on scientific validity, the Yad Vashem census of the dead juggles competing agendas of bureaucratic accuracy and moral imperative of collective memory.

Beyond these instructions for submission, the website also outlines the agenda and symbolic significance of the submission of testimony pages:

> [Pages] serv[ing] as lasting memorials for Holocaust victims. Preserved as "symbolic tombstones" in the Hall of Names at Yad Vashem, Jerusalem, these Pages restore the personal identity and dignity to the victims of Nazis and their accomplices. Each Jew who perished during the Holocaust deserves a Page of Testimony.

Yad Vashem frames and represents the testimony pages evocatively as personal symbolic tombstones. Each page individually memorializes one Holocaust victim. The aggregation and envelopment of all the pages/tombstones undertakes the sacred act of bringing to final rest the unburied and unknown dead in the database and Hall of Names exhibit. In keeping with the text appearing on the wall at the entrance to the exhibit—"the testimony pages are tombstones of the victims and the newly classified dead have become posthumous citizens of the State"—the recovery and display of salvaged pages museologically constitutes an alternative national cemetery for posthumous citizens of the Jewish State.[22] A stark contrast emphasizes the sinister and dehumanizing Nazi bureaucratic process versus the redemptive process of Yad Vashem's census of the dead, as museological messenger of the Jewish state.

The Online Database of Names: Generating the Virtual Second Life of the Dead

According to the website, the Central Database of Shoah Victims' Names currently contains four million names, including approximately 2.5 million names from scanned testimony pages and the remainder from deportation lists and camp and ghetto records. Nearly all four million names have been digitized. The Central Database was made available to the public online on the Yad Vashem website in 2004.

Visitors surfing the database can search for, view, and print any and all digitized testimony pages. No password or payment is required. After searching for and viewing a page, the visitor may click on the "mini-biography" feature, receiving a screen containing what is termed the victim's "personal story." The very brief story is a digitally compiled paragraph amassing data from the fields in the testimony page and other documents in Yad Vashem's archives. Each mini-biography allows the visitor to click on links to access further historical information about the places the particular victim lived in and died in and, if relevant, major collective historical events in his or her biography. The website trumpets the mini-biography or "stories behind the names" feature as "a revolutionary milestone in Holocaust remembrance and learning," placing the individual story back into historical context.

The database not only enables visitors to find details with a few clicks of a button, and at times even photos of deceased relatives, friends, and/or acquaintances, but it also creates new connections between the living. Website visitors may discover names and places of residence of individuals who submitted pages, thereby discovering lost/unknown relatives or friends. If contacted, distant or long-lost relatives or friends might provide survivors and their descendants with further information pertaining to loved ones' Holocaust history. The website includes dramatic tales of reunions between survivors and surviving family members made possible by the database. In this way, the Holocaust dead are embedded within an ever-expanding network of a living community of memory. This genealogical heritage work is depicted as potentially strengthening Jewish identity worldwide.

Interpreting the Semiotic Potential of the Recovery Project Website and Testimony Page

In an attempt to deconstruct the Names Recovery Project's cited aims, means, and self-attributed achievements, one key theme threads through the website's multiple pages. Beyond the recovery of unaccounted for names/victims, with the help of the testimony page the project enlists diverse personal details that reconstruct what is repeatedly termed the personal biography / life story / face of the victim. Biographical reconstruction is subtly depicted as transforming the archived names and numbers in multiple ways. Reconstructed life stories aim to restore narrative "depth" to the previously "shallow," "flat," and faceless names/numbers rehumanizing the previously morally "stained" Nazi bureaucratic number. In response to potential Holocaust denial, narrative depth "fills out" the number, adding empirical weight so to speak to each number and by extension corroborating the total number of six million. Grappling with a crisis of representation, the reconstructed biography enables the surviving collective to identify with the individual "victims/numbers" and by extension, the incomprehensible number of six million. Every time a visitor to the digitized virtual cemetery on the website clicks on the resultant chain of links moving from a victim's name to the web page and finally to the story behind the sites of their suffering, they revivify the victim/number, working against the "flatness of the archive."[23]

These commemorative practices thus produce a hybrid mnemonic artifact that merges the more contemporary museological experiential and individual turn with elements of a more traditional function of the archive/census. On the one hand the experiential and individual component of the project preserves and digitally displays the underlying depth of each number—the individual story/face—or part of the whole. On the other hand, as traditional archive, the database collapses and flattens the individuality of each victim/number so as to bureaucratically and efficiently amass the totality of parts into the empirically sound whole.[24] Thus, complementing the "additive value" (5,999,000 plus one = 6,000,000) of the numbers/parts, where each number "functions" merely to add up to the whole, the depth of the story behind each number bolsters the monumental commemorative potential of the otherwise elusive whole.

Although publicly accessible archives potentially permit for discovery of genealogical information by relatives and historians and enable restoration of some degree of narrative depth to the lives of the dead, the grassroots enlistment of previously unconnected survivors, descendants, and even unrelated volunteers to access and submit biographical details enigmatically creates an entire network of formerly unrelated individuals now "related" to and responsible for (and thanks to their details on the form accountable for) the revivified presence of the dead. In a posthumous act of "procreation," the newly revivified deceased victims become the virtual catalyst spawning a new network of living relations/communities. Recalling the posthumous baptism of Latter-day Saints (Mormons),[25] where baptism of the dead by proxy by the living creates an ever-expanding Mormon family, this living network reverses the temporal order of familial procreation as the living perpetually revive the dead with new and amended biographical details.

However, there are numerous limits to this commemorative feat. A closer look at the testimony page and at the emergent personal story discloses an absence of actual narrative depth. The rubrics on the page cannot produce anything other than a meager list of demographic details. Even if the "witness" might have personal tales to tell, no field elicits individual lived experiences or distinctive traits. There is literally no room on the form or in the rubrics/categories of classification left for a story of any kind. As seen in the following hypothetical example, in great contrast to the video archives of survivor personal testimonies, the so-called personal story behind the number on the website is nothing more than a digitally generated string of data taken from the testimony form put together by grammatical connective tissue.[26] For example, the story might read: "Chaim Rosenberg was born on April 10th 1900 in Cluj Romania, he was the son of Natan Rosenberg. He married Tova Friedman and he was a tailor. He was incarcerated in the Ghetto of Cluj in 1944 and later sent to Auschwitz on April 15th 1944 where he was gassed to death on ____." The blank space indicates the absence of demographic data regarding the victim. As shallow as this narrative is, it is probably the most complete artifact possible on the database as the great majority of pages simply do not contain sufficient information to reconstruct even a brief life story. Most testimony pages provide far less biographical detail, implying that there are very few specific personal biographies or life stories actually recovered. The average "story" on the website is no more than two sentences long. In keeping with Hull's insights regarding the way the aesthetics and logic of formatting bureaucratic documents often override the process of representation and meaning making,[27] the database may be producing a simulacra of virtual rather than "real" individual narrative depth. If so, we might ask whether the individual counted parts or numbers may be too shallow to revivify the whole. Does the absence of depth imply that the six million may remain a floating or empty signifier?

The dilemma surrounding the inclusion of duplicate forms also raises difficult questions regarding the empirical validity of the total/whole number of counted victims. Since the inception of the archive, surviving relatives and friends have submitted duplicate forms for the same victims utilizing different family names and place names in different languages and spellings for the same person. Despite the reference on the website to the removal of duplicates, whether for the lack of facilities or due to ambiguous archival policy, according to Anders and Dubrovskis[28] many duplicate forms remain. Duplicate forms for the same individual have also yet to be integrated to guarantee that each number in the database represents and records the life of a real and not bureaucratically duplicated victim. Considering the Zionist Israeli and Jewish valorization of the act of witnessing and commemorating the martyred collective dead, if as stated on the website all forms are "personal commemorative tokens" of the living witness, how can duplicates be removed from the archive? If the very act of submission is culturally valorized, then the contribution of duplicate forms or even incomplete forms of the Holocaust dead to the public stock of Holocaust history/memory would have to be recorded for perpetuity in some (alternative) way. Paradoxically, however, as long as the Names Recovery Project aims to enlist and create a (newly connected) network of witnesses committed to the "partnership" of commemoration and continues to be dependent upon these witnesses to access the missing two million names/forms in order to reach their goal, they may not be able to preserve an empirically valid census. This would disempower the "semiotic potency" of the six million. This analysis suggests an inherent tension between two competing imperatives: that of the accuracy and viability of the individual numbers/parts versus that of completing the six million or whole. Yet as will be seen below, the design of the Hall of Names exhibit aesthetically bolsters the supremacy of the whole over the parts, and re-empowers the semiotic potential of the "whole number."

The Hall of Names Exhibit

In the original exhibit, similar to predigitized archival storage areas, old binders filled book shelves throughout the room set up without textual reference or museological design that would signify the agenda of reaching the goal of an a priori completed number of pages. At the head of the room a glass casing displayed a sample testimony page.

In great contrast, the newly transformed Hall of Names exhibit (http://www1.yadvashem.org/yv/en/museum/hall_of_names.asp), designed by Moshe Safdie and Dorit Harel, is positioned as the last exhibit in the linear pathway of main exhibits in Yad Vashem, located before the much-discussed terrace from which the visitor may experience what Young terms a "redemptive" view of the Judean Hills.[29] Visitors enter the exhibit on a ring-shaped platform between two cones in the center of the room. One cone ascends upward ten meters toward the ceiling. A skylight at the top of the cone sends beams of light throughout the cone. Inside this upward-extending cone are some 600 photographs of Holocaust victims, accompanied by fragments of testimony pages. The second cone extends downward into the ground and ends in a base filled with water. The "well" is carved out of the mountain's bedrock. The victims' faces are reflected in the water at the base of the lower cone. Visitors stand in the center of the room and move around a circular railing between the cones looking both up and down. The entire outer edge of the circular room is covered from floor to ceiling in black shelves, upon which are stacked closed and numbered black binders containing approximately 2.5 million testimony pages. At the far end of the hall is a glass screen onto which pages of testimony are projected. Next to the screen a doorway leads to a computer center where visitors may search the database with the assistance of the Hall of Names staff.

The exhibit may be read as enveloping the Holocaust dead as individual parts into the monumental whole of the Jewish nation-state. It thereby constitutes a totality of victim-citizens from masses of otherwise unaffiliated and culturally and ideologically diverse individuals. We could not have more blatant empirical evidence for this than the raison d'être on display on the wall of the entrance to the site that reads: "the testimony pages are tombstones of the dead who have become posthumous citizens of the State." Parallel to Handelman's[30] aesthetic uniformity of the masses of individual IDF graves in the military cemetery, the walls of the circular Hall of Names display rows and rows of identical black binders with identical white labels that envelop the individual testimonial pages hidden from view. These binders merge to create an impermeable black and white wall as the

Hall of Names exhibit: close-up of black binders. Photo by the author.

boundary demarcating the spaces between pages (and individual victims) and binders disappears. What emerges is the monumental and ominous totality of Holocaust victimhood. The iconicity of bureaucratic monumentality once again envelops the particular and the individual.[31]

Although Handelman and Hansen-Glucklich have claimed that the empty shelf space awaiting new binders and newly recovered pages may be said to signify the presence of absence and the inevitable failure of representation,[32] I would assert otherwise. In great contrast to the tomb of the unknown soldier that signifies the finality of anonymity and the failure of individual identification and commemoration, the evocative absence of binders at the end of many of the rows of binders literally leaves room and hope for the recovery of new pages/parts that are destined to fill up the empty shelves. Empty space thus can signify the processual generation of re-presence rather than absence. Yet how is this sense of generated re-presence constituted?

The visitor standing and walking in the narrow pathway around the circular monochromic exhibit viscerally experiences the sense of being enveloped in recursive movement. Densely packed identical black walls of binders appear to reach a momentum of circular motion, closing in on themselves and encapsulating the visitor.[33] In this way the Holocaust dead on display and the visitor come to share in the same hermetically sealed totality. The design thereby constitutes the experience of virtual totality in the making. I say "totality-in-the-making" as the hundreds of binders in virtual movement around a shelf appear to move into empty shelf space illusively "filling them up" until the visitor no longer "sees" a gap in the bookcases. Recalling Anderson's claim that "the fiction of the census is that everyone is in it,"[34] the processual momentum created by circular monochromic design and, of course, the act of counting toward the six million mark at Yad Vashem creates the illusion that the whole is virtually complete despite the absence of its parts. As Macdonald notes,[35] the enchantment of museums, particularly those taking on culturally sanctified representation, emulates the generative potential of religious ritual, which cosmologically recreates reality. In this way the census—or the act of counting on display—as commemorative artifact may be understood as a "verification ritual" ascertaining the presence and not the absence of a completed storehouse of sacred dead Holocaust citizens.[36] One might consider that Yad Vashem's ability to signify what remains essentially absent moves beyond the verification of presence into the realm of the virtually real[37] or what Kapferer terms a "dynamic reality."[38]

If we turn our attention to the microlevel of each "paper tombstone" or testimony page and its commemorative potential in the census on exhibit, here too individual identity is streamlined and "sacrificed" within standardized bureaucratic rubrics to create the whole. Despite the declared goal to breathe life into each and every individual biography, there is absolutely no room for individual biographical details that are not covered by the formulaic rubrics or personal comments regarding the submitter's ties to the victim. Although the "life" and death of the individual is most certainly commemorated for posterity on the form, and they most definitely "count" in the emerging totality of the census on display as it struggles to approach the six million mark, the individual life and its idiosyncratic details quickly "give way" as they are fed into the categorical rubrics of the census. With the exception of the genealogical tourist's one-time search for relatives, visiting researchers seek the compiled history produced not by the individual testimonial page but by the assembled information on multiple pages. They search, for example, for all those who perished in Auschwitz, or in the Warsaw ghetto, or who were born in Budapest and deported in 1944. In this way the information cannot possibly do more than supplement the historical record documenting and counting collective Jewish presence and ultimate death occurring in different ways and in different sites of suffering and charting chronological developments of Jewish communities in different European cities and towns. Whether utilizing contemporary information technology or traditional formats, testimony pages first and foremost contribute to and therefore authenticate the historical record with the individual victim merely facilitating corroboration and authentication of communal and collective history. In this way, the pages contribute to Holocaust history.

In contrast, even to the monothetic military cemetery, as objects on display in the exhibit, the testimony pages or "tombstones" are totally hidden from view within binders. They are inaccessible to the visitor, enveloped in the movement toward totality. Once pages are numbered, placed on display within identical binders on identical shelves, it might be claimed that the limited depth of the life story made available to the visitor on the website (as discussed above) when viewing a testimony page or digitally generating a life story is now totally lost. For the sake of comparison consider the museological choice at the new museum commemorating 9/11 at Ground Zero. Photos of all victims are displayed on glass consoles, and visitors may touch any picture to "pull up" and read a full file (appearing on the console) containing demographic details of the victim and a personal story about the victim written by surviving family members.

Although the tower of photos and testimony pages in the center or vortex of the room "opens" up and displays individual pages for visitor perusal and empathic identification with the parts of the whole—unlike the walls of the other exhibits at Yad Vashem, the wide tower design and the positioning of the pages far above the heads of visitors does not permit the visitor to read the individual details on the form nor to stand eye to eye (as they would watching a video clip of a survivor testimony) with the individual victim on the page. Again, the aesthetics of the display serves to distance the pages from the visitor as hundreds of documented individual pages and victims ascend in a circular motion up, around, and away into the vortex of the monumental tower. Thus the tower, too, displays the overpowering totality of the whole rather than reconstituting an actual re-presence of the individual dead. Despite the avowed agenda of returning the face to the numbers, in the exhibit, as in the database, the whole takes precedence over the re-presence of the individual lives of its parts.

Discussion

Interweaving Appadurai and Handelman's insights, Yad Vashem's project might be intriguingly considered a census of the dead on display, counting, stream-lining, and encompassing the Holocaust dead as individual parts into the monumental whole in the service of the Israeli nation-state.[39] The project bu-reaucratically classifies and thereby constructs citizens from masses of otherwise unaffiliated and/or conflicted individuals. Clearly, the text on the wall depicting testimony pages as "tombstones of posthumous citizens of the State" certainly supports this reading. However, I have proposed that an interpretation of the Names Recovery Project and the Hall of Names exhibit as solely the product of the politics of memory in the service of the nation-state overshadows insights to be gleaned from a grounded analysis of the semiotic mechanics of the com-memorative process while also eliding the novelty of this particular form of "na-tional enlistment" of the dead. Indeed, without a semiotic analysis we cannot possibly begin to answer fully the key questions of this study: How does the a priori mark of the six million constitute a unique commemorative process and a no less unique culturally grounded commemorative product? How has the "his-toric" archive been transformed by turning the archival collection of testimony pages into a census on display? Beyond the political imperatives, are there semi-otic imperatives to urgently fill and display the database and reach and perform the mark of six million?

A semiotic analysis of part-whole (synecdochal) relationships in the Names Recovery Project and at the Hall of Names exhibit has provided a multivocal and bottom-up reading of the way institutionally recovered and evocatively displayed names and numbers might reinvigorate and sustain the iconic whole of the six million. The six million or whole is reinvigorated as number and as sublime "in-comprehensible" experience of Holocaust victimhood out of the recovered and bureaucratically configured testimony pages or "parts." The discursive framing of the project agenda as a process of "completion" of the absent whole, which is the six million, transforms the commemorative function of each testimony page as number in the emergent census of the dead. The agenda also alters institu-tional criteria for the submission and enumeration of pages/numbers. Although the names and faces humanize the icon, it maintains its supremacy and intan-gible totality.

For the sake of comparison, in a census of the living processual counting of the population open-endedly constitutes the sum total of the populace by creating numbers so to speak that were previously absent. Duplication of individuals in the census or empirically incomplete evidence of the existence of a member of the population would not be valid nor would it be tolerated as serving any other purpose than enumeration. In great contrast, the pre-existence of the sum total of six million in the census of Holocaust dead implies that the testimony page or part merely materializes or corroborates the number or part of the whole that was already semiotically present. Without, however, the recovery of the testimony page as bureaucratic materialization of each and every number, the semiotic force of the whole six million would be depleted.

Institutional policies surrounding duplicates as "tokens of commemoration" and the submission of forms without a victim's name points to the critical function of every part in its role to resuscitate the whole. Yet it also points to the dual agenda of this particular census, as its moral mission aims not only to enumerate the absent dead but also to create an ever-growing network of related witnesses in Israel's Jewish community of memory. It may also point to the ethical supremacy of the agenda of completing the whole, at times even overriding the scientific criteria of the census.

The display of the act of counting the pages and "filling" the empty shelves in the Hall of Names exhibit publicly performs the museum's semiotic battle with Holocaust absence, the crisis of representation, and the depleted semiotic potency of the iconic number. On the one hand, the museological display of millions of testimony pages and hundreds of binders that are in the process of infinite multiplication toward completion aesthetically sets up an illusion that the spatial gaps on the empty shelves will soon be filled. The a priori number complemented by the exhibit design, therefore, together generate the sense that the pages will ultimately fully materialize the presence of the archive/census and potentially reach totality. In this way too the design of the exhibit further encapsulates and contains the parts and thereby the whole of the illusive past—constituting a "second life" to both the iconic number and Holocaust memory.

The novelty of the project and the exhibit also suggests that in all its "hegemonic" national monumentality Yad Vashem's Names Recovery Project in general and Hall of Names in particular are more than a strategic or bombastic monument to the distortion and instrumentalization of memory in the service of statecraft.[40] Although commemorative sites such as Ground Zero are now struggling to present a delicate balance between a more user-friendly display of the individual lives of victims and monumental commemoration of the totality of mass violence,[41] Yad Vashem's unique hybrid artifact marks a pioneering attempt to grapple aesthetically and digitally with tensions between the display of the individual and the collective. The archive/census also dialogues in new ways with the changing role of museology in partnership with old and new bedfellows. As old bedfellows, the project is still encumbered by the drawbacks of archival classification and the flatness of any census. However, thanks to their new bedfellows, enlisted internet-based interactive consumers form a posthumously generated and "genealogically" related community of memory resuscitating the traditional "dead memory" of the historical record.[42] The simulacra of digital technology's options for genealogical tourists on the web even appears to transform the "duty memory"[43] of subjugated citizens into a "living memory."[44] Nevertheless, the Hall of Names exhibit most certainly makes a museological choice to permit the whole to take supremacy over the parts. Once bolstered by the counted parts on display framed most blatantly to complete the a priori mark, the whole envelops the parts in the hope that its monumentality may virtually restore the absence of missing parts and thereby redeem the cultural and national icon of the six million.

This chapter suggests a number of meta-analytical implications for the study of enumerative processes in general and commemorative counting in particular. Although salient, top-down political analyses of hegemonic processes cannot sufficiently unpack the processes of national enumeration without analyses of semiotic practices on the ground. Precisely this kind of grounded analysis discloses the very subtle processes of movement and momentum,[45] direction and closure as numbers move to "complete themselves." The delicate balance (or at times conflicted relations) between the representation of individual numbers and their additive value calls for further semiotic studies of synecdochal part-whole relations. Finally, the double entendre of additive "value" implies research might continue to explore the inherent tension between positivist precepts at the heart of enumeration and moral agendas that frame efforts to sustain the symbolic potency of numbers that represent those who count.

Notes

1. Michael Lambek and Paul Antze, "Introduction: Forecasting Memory," in *Tense Past: Cultural Essays in Trauma and Memory,* ed. Paul Antze and Michael Lambek (New York: Routledge, 1996), xi–xxxviii.

2. I employ the term "absenced" rather than "absent" to imply that the dead are not merely "not present" but they have been actively made absent in mass destruction. In keeping with Handelman (Don Handelman, *Models and Mirrors—Towards an Anthropology of Public Events* [Cambridge: Cambridge University Press, 1990]), absence of presence must be turned into the presence of absence through complex forms of commemoration. Moreover, due to the limits of representation of the incomprehensible number of dead (see Saul Friedlander, *Probing the Limits of Representation* [Cambridge, MA: Harvard University Press, 1992]; and Michael Bernard-Donals and Richard Glejzer, *Between Witness and Testimony: The Holocaust and the Limits of Representation* [Albany: State University of New York Press, 2001]), the re-presentation of the dead "made absent" necessitates even more novel commemorative practices to be outlined below.

3. Ethnographic observations at Yad Vashem's Hall of Names exhibit and content analysis of the Names Recovery Project website and the testimony pages were undertaken. In keeping with Barbara Kirshenblatt-Gimblett's methodological approach, the spatial configuration and layout of museum exhibits and the public representation of archival information may be observed and interpreted as "agencies of display" where the public display of objects in particular configurations tell a meaning-laden narrative in context. Ethnographic observation of "what [the] museum means to show" in the exhibit and on the website, therefore, potentially provides access to the intent, logic, and meaning of the project. See Barbara Kirshenblatt-Gimblett, *Destination Culture: Tourism, Museums, Heritage* (Berkeley: University of California Press, 1998), 30. For a further outline of ethnographic methodologies in museums, see Bill Hillier and Kali Tzorati, "Space Syntax: The Language of Museum Space," in *A Companion to Museum Studies*, ed. Sharon Macdonald (Oxford: Wiley-Blackwell, 2011), 282–301.

4. Don Handelman, *Nationalism and the Israeli State: Bureaucratic Logic in Public Events* (Oxford: Berg, 2004); Omer Bartov, "Chambers of Horrors: Holocaust Museums in Israel and the United States," *Israel Studies* 2, no. 2 (1997): 66–87; and Irit Dekel, "Way of Looking: Observation and Transformation at the Holocaust Memorial, Berlin," *Memory Studies* 2, no. 1 (2009): 71–86.

5. Michael Schudson, "Dynamics of Distortion in Collective Memory," in *How Minds, Brains and Societies Reconstruct the Past*, ed. D. L. Schacter, J. T. Coyle, G. D. Fischbach, M. M. Mesulam, and L. E. Sullivan (Cambridge, MA: Harvard University Press, 1995), 346–364.

6. "Macro" realities refer to state-sponsored processes versus "micro," which refers to experiences of commemorative processes on the ground.

7. Saul Friedländer, "The Shoah between Memory and History," *Jewish Quarterly* 37, no. 1 (1990): 5–11.

8. Handelman, *Nationalism and the Israeli State*.

9. Benedict Anderson, *Imagined Communities: Reflections on the Origin and Spread of Nationalism* (London: Verso, 2006).

10. Ibid.

11. Handelman, *Models and Mirrors*, 202–233; Handelman, *Nationalism and the Israeli State*; Andreas Huyssen, *Twilight Memories: Marking Time in a Culture of Amnesia* (London: Routledge, 1995); Pierre Nora, "Between Memory and History: Les Lieux de Mémoire," *Representations* 26 (Spring 1989): 7–25; Schudson, "Dynamics of Distortion"; Geoffrey M. White, "National Subjects: September 11 and Pearl Harbor," *American Ethnologist* 31, no. 3 (2008): 293–310; and Yael Zerubavel, *Recovered Roots: Collective Memory and the Making of Israeli National Tradition* (Chicago: University of Chicago Press, 1995).

12. Saul Friedlander, "Memory of the Shoah in Israel," in *The Art of Memory: Holocaust Memorials in History*, ed. James Young (Munich: Prestel, 1994), 149–157; Charles S. Liebman and Eli'ezer Don-Yiḥya, *Civil Religion in Israel: Traditional Judaism and Political Culture in the Jewish State* (Berkeley: University of California Press, 1983); Maoz Azaryahu and Aharon Kellerman, "Symbolic Places of National History and Revival," *Transactions* 24, no. 1 (1999): 109–123; Jackie Feldman, *Above the Death Pits, Beneath the Flag: Youth Voyages to Holocaust Poland and Israeli National Identity* (New York: Berghahn, 2008); and Handelman, *Nationalism and the Israeli State*.

13. Bartov, "Chambers of Horrors"; see also Dekel, "Way of Looking," 71–86.

14. Anderson, *Imagined Communities*; and Arjun Appadurai, "Patriotism and Its Futures," *Public Culture* 5, no. 3 (1993): 411–429.

15. Handelman, *Nationalism and the Israeli State*.

16. Patrizia Violi, "Trauma Site Museums and Politics of Memory: Tuol Sleng, Villa Grimaldi and the Bologna Ustica Museum," *Theory, Culture and Society* 29, no. 1 (2012): 36–75.

17. Barbie Zelizer, *Remembering to Forget: Holocaust Memory through the Camera's Eye* (Chicago: University of Chicago Press, 1998).

18. Zelizer draws a distinction between referentiality and symbolization. Referentiality references and documents the particular historical details of events and individuals. In great contrast symbolization forgoes upon empirically accurate documentation of historical detail for the sake of the semiotic force of iconic representations that can stand for and semiotically contain multiple particular individuals and events.

19. Yosef Hayim Yerushalmi, *Zakhor: Jewish History and Jewish Memory* (Seattle: University of Washington Press, 1982).

20. See http://www1.yadvashem.org/yv/en/downloads/pdf/daf_ed_en.pdf.

21. "Those living under the Nazi Regime or any country under the direct influence of the Nazi Regime between the years 1933–1945." Dorit Berger, Census Bureau of Statistics, personal communication, July 28, 2001.

22. Tim Cole, "Nativization and Nationalization: A Comparative Landscape Study of Holocaust Museums in Israel, the US and the UK," *Journal of Israeli History* 23, no. 1 (2004): 130–145; Jennifer Hansen-Glucklich, "Evoking the Sacred: Visual Holocaust Narrative in National Holocaust Museums," *Journal of Modern Jewish Studies* 9, no. 2 (2010): 209–232; and Dekel, "Way of Looking."

23. Appadurai, "Patriotism and Its Futures."

24. Ibid., 413.

25. Jeffrey A. Trumbower, *Rescue for the Dead: The Posthumous Salvation of Non-Christians in Early Christianity* (Oxford: Oxford University Press, 2001).

26. Due to both copyright issues and ethical considerations, a hypothetical case has been presented that emulates biographies on the website.

27. Matthew S. Hull, "Documents and Bureaucracy," *Annual Review of Anthropology* 41 (2012): 251–267.

28. Edward Anders and Juris Dubrovskis, "Who Died in the Holocaust? Recovering Names from Official Records," *Holocaust and Genocide Studies* 17, no. 1 (2003): 114–138.

29. James Edward Young, *Writing and Rewriting the Holocaust: Narrative and the Consequences of Interpretation* (Bloomington: Indiana University Press, 1988).

30. Handelman, *Nationalism and the Israeli State.*

31. Hull, "Documents and Bureaucracy."

32. Handelman, *Nationalism and the Israeli State;* and Hansen-Glucklich, "Evoking the Sacred."

33. Carol A. Kidron, "Embracing the Lived Memory of Genocide: Holocaust Survivor and Descendant Renegade Memory Work at the House of Being," *American Ethnologist* 37, no. 3 (2010): 429–451.

34. Anderson, *Imagined Communities,* 170.

35. Sharon Macdonald, "Enchantment and Its Dilemmas: The Museum as a Ritual Site," in *Science, Magic and Religion: The Ritual Processes of Museum Magic,* ed. Mary Bouquet and Nuno Porto (Oxford: Berghahn, 2005), 209–227.

36. See Dunn in Greta Uehling, "The First Independent Ukrainian Census in the Crimea: Myths, Miscoding and Missed Opportunities," *Ethnic and Racial Studies* 27, no. 1 (2004): 149–170.

37. Michal Kravel-Tovi and Yoram Bilu, "The Work of the Present: Constructing Messianic Temporality in the Wake of Failed Prophecy among Chabad Hasidim," *American Ethnologist* 35, no. 1 (2008): 64–80.

38. Bruce Kapferer, "Ritual Dynamics and Virtual Practice: Beyond Representation and Meaning," *Social Analysis* 48, no. 2 (2004): 33–54.

39. Appadurai, "Patriotism and Its Futures"; and Handelman, *Nationalism and the Israeli State*.

40. Schudson, "Dynamics of Distortion."

41. Aaron Hess and Art Herbig, "Recalling the Ghosts of 9/11: Convergent Memorializing at the Opening of the National 9/11 Memorial," *International Journal of Communication* 7 (2013): 2207–2230.

42. Nora, "Between Memory and History."

43. Ibid.

44. Maurice Halbwachs, *The Collective Memory* (New York: Harper Colophon Books, 1980), 68–87.

45. Kidron, "Embracing the Lived Memory."

3 Putting Numbers into Space

Place Names, Collective Remembrance, and Forgetting in Israeli Culture

Yael Zerubavel

Nation-states cultivate collective remembrances around a wide range of temporal and spatial commemorative sites.[1] Temporal commemorative sites are primarily anchored in the calendar, which serves as a mnemonic framework for collective remembrances of specific events and figures that together contribute to the creation of an overall narrative about the nation's origins and historical development. Anniversaries, memorial days, and holidays are among temporal commemorative sites that underscore key points in the nation's collective memory.[2] Their anchoring within the calendar ensures that the performance of memory will recur annually, thus serving as a major venue for mnemonic socialization.[3] Spatial commemorative sites provide another venue among a range of locations such as cemeteries, memorial sites, monuments, and historical places around which various memorial practices may develop to underscore the significance of that past. The country's map, encoded with names that evoke the past, thus emerges as an alternative site for cultivating a national memory.

Clearly, the primary function of place names revolves around their role as geographical designators. The selection of a name that draws on a historical person or group of people, a mythological figure, or a specific event adds a mnemonic function, leading to its identification as a *commemorative toponym*.[4] Such toponyms interweave time and space, past and present, national and local memories as they add a spatial dimension to collective memory. The creation of commemorative toponyms is a familiar mnemonic practice that is found cross-culturally. This chapter addresses a more specific Israeli mnemonic practice that establishes commemorative toponyms based on *numerical commemoration*,[5] namely, a memorialization of the past that focuses on the number of people who died for the national cause in a particular event. I refer to the toponyms based on such numbers as *numerical commemorative toponyms*.

To further highlight the use of numbers in this mnemonic practice, the discussion includes a comparison to another type of numerical toponyms that memorializes historical events through a reference to their historical date. I refer to this type as *calendrical commemorative toponyms.* These toponyms too rely on numbers as a key component of their reference to the past, and similarly add a mnemonic meaning to their function as space designators. The analysis of both categories of commemorative toponyms thus brings into focus the symbolic value of numbers as a site of memory. The present discussion does not aim to offer a detailed historical study of the process of naming but rather to highlight symbolic patterns of numerical commemorative toponyms and offer a broad interpretive framework for their analysis as semiotic signs.

The most basic form of the numerical commemorative toponym consists of a reference to the generic category of the designated space followed by the definite article and a number. In its basic form, then, the numerical commemorative toponym employs the collective number of people who died as the only reference to a specific historical event. The wide range of types of space named through numerical commemoration is illustrated by such examples as <u>Hill</u> of the Five (*Ma'ale Ha'Hamisha*),[6] <u>Square</u> of the Three (*Kikar Ha'Shelosha*),[7] <u>City</u> of Eight (*Kiryat Shemona*),[8] and <u>Street</u> of the Four (*Rehov Ha'Arba'a*).[9] Numerical commemorative toponyms may also appear in extended forms: One pattern of an extended toponym includes the reference to the group's collective identity, as is the case in Street of the Two <u>Nurses</u> (*Rehov Shetei Ha'Ahayot*) or Street of the Twenty-Three <u>Seafarers</u> (*Rehov Kaf-Gimal Yordei Ha'Sira*).[10] Another pattern,

Street sign in Tel Aviv provides the Hebrew name of Street of the Four and its English and Arabic transliterations with no reference to its meaning. The sign also includes the individual names of the four but no reference to the historical event in which they died. Photo by the author.

more typical of settlement names, adds an abstract concept prior to the number, as is illustrated by *Mishmar Ha'Shelosha* (Sentinel of the Three) or *Netiv Ha'Asara* (Path of the Ten).[11]

A different, yet salient pattern of numerical commemorative toponyms in Israeli culture introduces the number through the mediation of Hebrew letters. This practice draws on the principles of *gematria*, which assign a numerical value for each letter of the Hebrew alphabet. Israeli toponyms based on numerical commemoration reveal a tendency to use actual numbers for groups that are smaller than ten and shift to letters in representing groups that exceed ten, though exceptions may be found.[12] Since numbers that are larger than ten require the combination of two or more letters, such toponyms assume the appearance of an acronym in which the quote sign (*gershayim*) is inserted between the letters. The written form of the toponym thus visually marks the function of the letters as number substitutes. With the exception of names in which the letter combination creates a recognized Hebrew word and the toponym is pronounced as that word, most toponyms are pronounced as the combined names of the Hebrew letters that represent the number. Thus, for example, Square of the Thirty-Nine is called *Kikar Ha'Lamed-Tet,* drawing on the names of the letters *lamed* (equals 30) and *tet* (equals 9) rather than the Hebrew word for the number 39.[13]

Jewish tradition assigns a sacred status to Hebrew letters, as demonstrated by their use in designating chapter numbers in the Hebrew Bible or days of the

The sign for Street of the Eleven in Herzliya represents the number 11 by the letter combination *ha'yod-alef* in Hebrew with its English transliteration. No reference is made to the individual identities or the historical event in which they were killed. Photo by Ilanit Palmon. Courtesy of the author.

month in the Jewish calendar. The introduction of the letters as number substitutes in the toponyms therefore actively contributes to the sanctity of these names. Indeed, the shift from numbers to letters signals code switching from a profane, everyday communication to an elevated Hebrew commemorative discourse. Thus, a newspaper headline reporting the death of "thirty-five fighters" who were on the way to the besieged settlement *Gush Etzion* in January 1948 cites their actual number; but the formal death announcement in the same issue refers to "the *lamed-hei* national heroes who died while rushing to the rescue of their besieged brethren," representing their numerical value in letters.[14] Similarly, a newspaper article published in Palestine in 1946 related the death of "the twenty-three seafarers" in 1941, but in discussing an initiative of memorialization efforts the text switches to the "*kaf-gimmel*" seafarers, representing the same number in letters.[15] The prominence of the letters in the commemoration of the thirty-five fighters is also visually articulated in the large monument to them near kibbutz *Netiv Ha'Lamed-Hei,* which features at its center the two letters that make up this number: *lamed* and *hei.*

Calendrical commemorative toponyms similarly draw on the Hebrew alphabet to represent numbers. One pattern of this mnemonic practice refers to the year according to the Jewish calendar and therefore follows the traditional custom of time reckoning by presenting the numerical value in letter combinations. The toponym based on a year is often, though not uniformly, pronounced as if a word. Another pattern of calendrical commemorative toponym introduces a date including the day and the month with no reference to the year. Indeed, each of these patterns represents a link to a different semiotic framework: while a toponym based on a specific year is clearly connected to the linear progression of historical time, a toponym based on the day and the month with no indication of the year shifts its reference to the annual cycle that represents commemorative time.

A toponym based on a year typically highlights its significance as a major historical "turning point."[16] Such toponyms are more prevalent among street names than place names and often appear in more than one locality. A typical example is *Rehov Tarpat* (1929 Street), which focuses on the year marked in Israeli collective memory as the first major outbreak of national hostilities between Jews and Arabs in Palestine.[17] Another prominent example is *Rehov Tashah* (1948 Street), which memorializes the birth of the state of Israel. A calendrical street name may also relate to a significant year for local rather than national memory. The most frequent pattern is the founding year for the specific settlement in which the toponym appears, as illustrated by *Rehov Tarna* (1891 Street) in Hedera, *Shederot Tarsat* (1909 Boulevard) in Tel Aviv, and *Rehov Tar'ad* (1914 Street) in Ramat Gan. A rare example of a settlement name that features a year is *Pa'amei Tashaz* (In the Footsteps of 1947), which commemorates 1947 as the year in which eleven new settlements were founded in the Negev desert.[18] Most calendrical toponyms relating to important events in Jewish history are based on the day and the month according to the Jewish calendar. Thus, for example, a street named *Hei Be'Iyar* (Fifth of the Hebrew Month Iyar) memorializes the date of the declaration of the state of Israel that is celebrated annually as Israel's Independence Day. Conversely, calendrical toponyms that commemorate historical dates of universal significance, such as May 1 Street (*Rehov Ehad Be'Mai*) and September 11 Square (*Kikar Ha'Ahad Asar Be'September*)[19] relate to the Gregorian calendar and represent the day of the month in numbers. This dual calendrical system and the alternative choice of numbers and letters reinforce the distinction between events that are seen as particularly significant for Jewish history and others pertaining to "general" history. This distinction also echoes secular Israelis' habitual reliance on the Gregorian calendar in everyday life, while reverting to the Jewish calendar for marking sacred time (i.e., Jewish holidays). An unusual case of a hybrid toponym that mixes the two dating systems is *Rehov Kaf-Tet Be'November,* which relates to the Gregorian month (November) but represents the day (29) in Hebrew letters (*kaf-tet*). This toponym follows a distinct mnemonic pattern for this specific date which marks the United Nations General Assembly's Resolution 181 to end the British Mandate for Palestine, supporting the partition of Palestine to a Jewish and an Arab state in 1947. Use of the Gregorian month thus underscores the perceived significance of this date as a critical

Street sign for November 29 Street in Hedera provides the date with its English transliteration and no historical reference. The name features the letter combination representing the number 29 as customary in Jewish dating and the month according to the Gregorian calendar. Photo by Ilanit Palmon. Courtesy of the author.

turning point in Western and Middle Eastern histories and serves as a reminder of global support of the establishment of Israel by the UN vote. At the same time, representation of the day of the month by letters follows Jewish custom of reckoning time and thereby foregrounds the significance of this date in Israeli and Jewish collective memories.

Collective numerical commemoration of those who died for the national cause emerged in the Zionist Hebrew culture in the aftermath of World War I. Kibbutz *Givat Ha'Shelosha* (Hill of the Three), founded in 1925, is the earliest case of a numerical commemorative toponym that I found.[20] A few years later, the rise in military clashes and casualties during the Arab Revolt of 1936–1939 and the establishment of numerous frontier settlements during those years opened more possibilities for adopting numerical commemorative toponyms. These new toponyms articulated the importance of the ethos of patriotic sacrifice and the ideological commitment to settling the land, and affirmed the symbolic link between place, sacrifice, and memory in the process of nation building.

The charged struggle for national independence in the late 1940s and post-independence Israel further enhanced numerical commemoration as Israeli national memory added new sites of memory related to the 1948–1949 war. Numerical commemorations of fallen Israelis included such settlement names as *Givat Ko'ah* (Hill of the Twenty-Eight), *Ein Ha'Shelosha* (Spring of the Three), *Mishmar Ha'Shiva* (Sentinel of the Seven), *Netiv Ha'Lamed-Hei* (Path of the Thirty-Five), and numerous streets and sites at the local level. Toponyms representing the number of dead were also extended to two cases of Jews from Palestine who were part of military operations during World War II and drowned in service: the "twenty-three seafarers" relates to Palmah members who drowned while on a mission to blow up an oil refinery in Lebanon in May 1941, and the "one hundred and forty" memorializes Jewish volunteers in the British army who drowned while on board the SS *Erinpura* on the way to Malta in 1943.[21]

In the following years, the practice of numerical commemorative toponyms was extended to other cases of collective deaths that occurred away from Israel but involved acts that targeted Jewish Israeli citizens. The settlement *Nir Hen* (Meadow of the Fifty-Eight), established in 1955, commemorates the passengers of an Israeli civilian plane shot down for entering Bulgaria's airspace that year.[22] The murder of the eleven Israeli athletes at the Munich Olympics in 1972 shocked the Israeli public and led to multiple numerical commemorations.[23] Another category of numerical commemorative toponyms relates to groups of Jews who died because of their real or presumed ties to Israel. Examples include *Yad Ha'Tish'a* (Memorial for the Nine) in Herzliya and *Rehov Ha'Tish'a* (Street of the Nine) in Haifa, both commemorating a group of Iraqi Jews sentenced to death for alleged spying for Israel in 1969,[24] and streets named The Forty-Three after a group of Moroccan Jews who drowned on their way to Israel in 1961.[25]

From the 1960s on, the numerical commemoration of casualties declined. The three most prominent commemorations added since then revolve around air force accidents with escalating numbers of casualties. The death of ten fliers in a plane crash in 1971 memorialized by the settlement *Netiv Ha'Asara* was followed by the death of fifty-four paratroopers in a helicopter crash in 1977 memorialized at the site named Hill of the Fifty-Four (*Givat Ha'Nun-Dalet*) and in a monument shaped in the form of the Hebrew letters that represent that numerical value.[26] In 1997, two helicopters collided in northern Israel and the accident resulted in seventy-three casualties. Numerical commemoration of the seventy-three casualties is featured at the memorial site where the accident occurred and Park of the Seventy-Three (*Gan Ha'Shiv'im U'Shelosha*) was established in their memory in Ness Ziona.[27] Other examples of numerical commemorative toponyms include Street of the Twenty-Two (*Rehov Ha'Kaf-Beit*) in Safed, memorializing schoolchildren who had been killed while on a trip in the Galilee in 1974 and the renaming of a railroad station Haifa Center of the Eight (*Haifa Merkaz Ha'Shemona*) after eight railroad workers who were killed during the Second War of Lebanon in 2006.[28]

Monument to the Fifty-Four in the Jordan Valley, shaped in the form of the letters *nun-dalet*, representing the number 54. Photo by Lee Rotbard. Courtesy of the author.

This chapter is based on the analysis of sixty historical events that received numerical commemorations (not counting multiple sites for the same event). Given the difficulty in identifying this mnemonic practice, the present study does not seek to represent all historical cases, but draw on the substantial data that this sample provides in order to analyze the emerging patterns of numerical commemoration. The sample demonstrates the existence of an active mnemonic tradition extending over eight decades, from the mid-1920s to 2011.[29] Most of those numerical commemorations address historical events that took place in Palestine before 1948 and later in the state of Israel. A few cases relate to events that occurred outside of the country but deemed connected to it directly or symbolically. The commemorative numbers encoded in toponyms that I identified range between 2 and 140: the highest figure encoded in a settlement name is fifty-eight (as it appears in *Nir Hen,* Meadow of the Fifty-Eight), while the highest number encoded in a street name is one hundred and forty referring to World War II. Most of the earlier toponyms focused on numbers on the low end of this spectrum, frequently ranging between groups of three to seven. Toponyms referring to the 1948–1949 war include higher numbers (the "Twenty-Eight," the "Thirty-Five," the "Seventy-Eight"),[30] yet are well below the earlier highest figure of 140.

The Social Meanings of Numerical Commemoration Toponyms

The idea of creating numerical commemorative toponyms inevitably calls for a discussion of the social implications of employing numbers and numerical values as sites of memory. First and foremost, this mnemonic practice represents the significance of collective and egalitarian memorialization. The prominent role of the number in this mnemonic framework thus articulates several premises: First, patriotic death evokes the society's moral obligation to remember the dead.[31] Second, the shared fate of death in a particular event is a sufficient basis for relating to the dead as a distinct social group. Third, the nature of patriotic sacrifice privileges the commemoration of the group over its constituent members, and individual members are addressed through their group membership.[32] And fourth, all those included in the group carry the same value and are equally represented within it. The privileging of a group over an individual identity through numerical commemoration may be traced back to the case of ancestral groups or martyrs, such as the "three fathers," the "four mothers," the "ten martyrs" (*aseret harugei malkhut*), and the case of the thirty-six righteous men (*lamed-vav tzaddikim*).[33] Similar extended numerical commemorations of ancestral groups or groups associated with national beginnings are found cross-culturally.[34]

An emphasis on a collectivist orientation underlying numerical commemorative toponyms displays a high *commemorative fit*[35] with a Western mnemonic culture that emerged in the aftermath of World War I. A growing concern over the memory of the dead, the emergence of collective memorials such as the Tomb of the Unknown Soldier and the Cenotaph, and the standardization of military graves articulated both the spirit of collectivism and the egalitarian ethos of national memorial practices at that period.[36] At the local level, Jewish society in Palestine was developing other mnemonic practices that subscribed to a collectivist-nationalist ethos and gave rise to national myths of heroism and sacrifice and new memorial sites and rituals.[37] Hebrew youth were socialized in schools and youth movements to place a high value on group solidarity, equality, and readiness for sacrifice,[38] and the collectivist ethos resonated powerfully in the ideology of Socialist Zionism, which led to the development of communal settlements such as the kibbutz and the moshav. It is therefore not surprising that these types of settlement also took a lead in adopting numerical commemorative toponyms. The collectivist orientation is evident also in other Hebrew commemorative toponyms, such as the Sons or the Defenders, which refer to the fallen as a group.[39]

Attachment to numerical commemoration as a mnemonic form articulating an egalitarian-collectivist ethos became most visible in cases where an earlier individualized memorialization appeared to privilege one person within the group over others who had lost their lives in the same event. A later establishment of a numerical commemorative toponym thus represented a corrective move to reintroduce the other members of the group into the Israeli mnemonic landscape. This was the case when kibbutz *Maoz Haim* and the museum *Beit Sturman* were named after Haim Sturman, one of three men who had been killed by a road mine in 1938.[40] In 1958, twenty years after the historical event and on the tenth anniversary of the state of Israel, a national ceremony marked the renaming of a national park previously known by its Arabic name, *Sakhne,* to the Hebrew name *Gan Ha'Shelosha* (Park of the Three), commemorating them as a group.[41] Another prominent example relates to the memorialization of those who died in Tel Hai in 1920. Although all eight casualties were included in official Israeli memory, the extensive commemoration of Yosef Trumpeldor, a former officer in the Czarist army and a known Zionist leader, turned him into a national hero with multiple toponyms and other sites of memory to his name. Thirty years after the event, a new development town was first named *Kiryat Yosef,* again singling him out, yet the name was quickly modified to *Kiryat Shemona,* City of Eight, to honor all those who died in Tel Hai.[42] Still another case revolved around a group of fourteen people who were killed in the Galilee in June 1946. One of them, Yechiam Weitz, was buried separately in Jerusalem and kibbutz *Yechiam* was named after him. Twenty years later, and following the discovery of the remains of the rest of the group, a collective monument at the site where the fourteen had been killed was named Monument for the Fourteen (*Yad Le'Yad*).[43] In all these cases, the later addition of a numerical commemorative toponym was designed to restore a *commemorative balance* by shifting the focus from one individual to the group as a whole.

The inclusive approach to the memorialization of patriotic death displayed by numerical toponyms reflects the reality of the national struggle during the prestate period and the 1948–1949 war that blurred the distinction between military and civilian casualties.[44] Although soldiers are typically associated with readiness to fight for the nation whereas civilians who die within the context of a war are often perceived as victims, the application of the same commemorative form to the dead blends sacrifice and victimhood within the framework of death for the country. The inclusion of soldiers who were killed in action along with soldiers who died in accidents and civilians who were killed by the enemy or terrorist acts demonstrates this trend. This blurred line is also articulated linguistically in Hebrew in which both "sacrifice" and "victim" are included within the semantic field of a single term, *korban*. Along the same lines, the Hebrew term *kedoshim* (holy ones), traditionally used in reference to Jewish martyrs, is used in reference to both soldiers and civilians who are victims of terrorist acts.[45]

The examination of the range of the numbers of dead that form the foundation for existing numerical commemorative toponyms is particularly instructive. The current range of 2 to 140 indicates avoidance of higher possible figures that represent total casualties suffered in a single large-scale battle or an entire war. Given that a toponym provides high visibility to such collective figures, the canonization of higher numbers through numerical commemoration might highlight the magnitude of losses that would make such a toponym too unsettling. It is quite possible that the outstanding number of 140 was canonized through numerical commemoration because it relates to World War II, and it was important to the Jewish society to underscore its participation in the war and its contribution to the Allies' cause. The more dominant reluctance to feature high numbers through numerical commemorative toponyms is best demonstrated in the avoidance of using the "Six Million" as a toponym, although this collective number representing Jews who perished in the Holocaust is widely used in other contexts, as discussed elsewhere in this volume. Instead, other generalized references to "the Holocaust martyrs" (*Kedoshei Ha'Shoah*) and specific Jewish communities have become commemorative street names.[46] The one exception of a numerical commemorative toponym relating to the Holocaust that I have found is Memorial to the Eight (*Yad Ha'Shemona*) near Jerusalem, which memorializes eight Jews who had been reported to the Gestapo by Finns and were subsequently killed. Yet this toponym was introduced to the Israeli mnemonic landscape by Protestant Finns, that is, outsiders to Israeli society, and it focuses on a relatively small number of Holocaust victims.[47]

In the earlier phase of its development, the trend of escalating numbers that appeared in numerical commemorative toponyms within the range of 2 to 140 was connected to the Israeli-Arab conflict, with some notable examples as mentioned above. Death in an armed conflict was relatively rare in the early decades of the twentieth century and deemed a sufficient basis for a collective remembrance. But, in time, the recurrence of small numbers of casualties made them increasingly less distinct and accounts for the tendency to shift toward relatively larger numbers and more discrete circumstances in the following decades. Thus, collective deaths incurred by terrorist activities spurred numerical commemorative toponyms in the 1970s, when such events were relatively rare, but when the First Intifada broke out and collective deaths in terrorist acts became more frequent, they did not produce additional numerical commemorative toponyms. The tendency to create numerical toponyms to mark collective deaths at sea or in the air appears to have a particularly strong commemorative fit with cases in which there are little or no remains of the dead given the abstract and collectivist framework of this mnemonic practice.

"Two Who Knows?" "Two I (Do Not) Know"

The same qualities of numbers that are conducive to their mnemonic function as articulating a collectivist and egalitarian approach to the dead also problematize their use and undermine their effectiveness as sites of memory in other respects. The following discussion on the vulnerability of Israeli numerical commemorative toponyms explores these issues and offers a comparison with the practice of calendrical commemorative toponyms that likewise introduces numbers into space. Perhaps the most obvious difficulty surrounding numerical commemorative toponyms stems from their most important feature: the reference to the dead as a group through reliance on their collective number. While the abstract character of numbers and the brevity of the toponym are compatible with its function as a space designator, these features obscure the individual identities and the specific historical event referenced by this remembrance. Thus, for example, when the sign of a street named *Rehov Ha'Arba'a* (Street of the Four) appears with no indication of the names of the memorialized dead, the numerical toponym represents the erasure of their individual memory even as it preserves their collective remembrance. Even where individual names of the dead are included on street signs (as in the first photograph in this chapter), the names alone do not provide the necessary information to learn about the historical circumstances of their deaths.

Clearly, during the prestate period in which this naming practice emerged, the small Jewish society of Palestine (with a population of 355,000 in 1936 and 630,000 in 1947) and its close social networks made public knowledge of the historical events and identities of the dead seem as a given. This assumption is evident in the linguistic structure of the minimal numerical commemorative form where the definite article is a critical component preceding the number (the four, the five). The inevitable erosion of public knowledge due to the passage of time that challenges all mnemonic traditions is nonetheless exacerbated by the elusive character of the numerical toponym. Faced with these anonymous signs, one struggles to find the answer to these questions: Who are "the four" or "the two" referred to on these signs? What did they do? How did they die?

Furthermore, the anonymous and abstract number at the center of this practice stands in a marked contrast to the importance that Jewish tradition assigns to names as a primary site of memory. Naming children after ancestors is a cherished Jewish practice, and conversely, the obliteration of one's name is presented in the Bible as a powerful curse that relegates one to oblivion. The idea of a number replacing an individual identity may be particularly disturbing in the post-Holocaust era given the Nazis' notorious practice of using numbers to identify their victims, embodied in the form of a tattoo on the arms of those interned in Auschwitz. The central motto of Yad Vashem, Israel's Holocaust Memorial Authority—"Every person has a name"—which draws on a title of a poem by Israeli poet Zelda, highlights the significance attached to names within this context. The project of recovering the names and biographies of Holocaust victims is thus seen as a major restorative act representing moral victory over the Nazis. In the post-Holocaust period, the continuing use of a mnemonic practice that obscures individual identities through the use of a number can easily become problematic.

The abstract and rational basis of numerical commemoration may also undermine the mnemonic function of the toponym by inhibiting an emotional response to patriotic sacrifice that other, more expressive forms of memorialization evoke. Use of letters as numbers substitutes may serve as a corrective strategy that diffuses the cold aura associated with numbers and brings the toponym closer to a "word." At the same time, the process of distancing of the number by letters and pronouncing the toponym as the names of those letters introduces a *mnemonic veil* that obscures the original mnemonic function of the toponym. The veiling becomes more acute when the letter combination happens to form an established Hebrew word and the toponym is pronounced as that word. Even though the written form of the toponym indicates that the letters appear as an acronym, this status is not apparent in speech and can be easily overlooked. The word that the letter combination forms, therefore, masks the numerical representation and challenges the assumption that members of the society would know that the letters stand for numbers. The following examples illustrate this point. A street name *Shderot Paz* (Boulevard of the Eighty-Seven) in Kiryat Gat memorializes soldiers of a religious unit who were killed in that area in the 1948 war. The two letters that make up their number, 87 (*pei-zayin*), also form the word *paz,* which means "gold." As a result, the street name is pronounced as Golden Boulevard, which obscures its origin in numerical commemoration. Similarly, the settlement *Nir Hen* (Meadow of the Fifty-Eight), which commemorates the passengers and crew of the El Al plane who were shot down in Bulgaria in 1955, creates the letter combination (*het-nun*), which also forms the word *hen* implying "grace." The settlement name is therefore pronounced as Graceful Meadow. In both cases, the established words formed by their respective numerical values produce a mnemonic veil, concealing the original commemorative function of these toponyms.

In some cases, however, the word that the letter combination forms may add a meaning that contributes to the commemorative framework. Thus, for example, the letter combination *kaf-het,* which represents the number twenty-eight, also makes up the word *ko'ah,* implying both power and strength. The numerical toponyms produced by this letter combination, *Givat Ko'ah* and *Metsudat Ko'ah* (Hill of the Twenty-Eight and Fortress of the Twenty-Eight, respectively), also mean Hill of Power and Fortress of Power. The association of the numerical commemorative toponyms with power and strength enhances the commemorative fit with Israeli national heroic culture even while overshadowing its numerical reference.[48] Another interesting example of a dual meaning of a letter combination based on numerical value is Memorial of the Fourteen. The letter combination that stands for fourteen, *yod-dalet,* also means both a "hand" and a "memorial." The commemorative toponym *Yad Le'Yad* (Memorial of the Fourteen) thus creates a pun in Hebrew that affirms and reinforces its mnemonic function.

A rare mnemonic form of numerical commemorative toponyms takes the concealment of its numerical base one step further by embedding the letters representing the number within a longer established word. In this case, the letter combination loses its status as a distinct component of the toponym. This is illustrated in the toponym *Menorah,*[49] in which the first and the last letters (*mem* and *hei*), which represent forty-five, are separated by other letters. The toponym was selected to memorialize forty-five men of a religious unit who had been killed in 1948 near Modiin, but the word *menorah* also introduces a connection to the history of the Maccabean revolt in the second century BCE and the tradition of Hanukkah in which a menorah is lit for eight days. The outcome is a multilayered commemorative toponym that reaffirms the symbolic connections between the Maccabean revolt and 1948 constructed by the Zionist master commemorative narrative.[50] At the same time, the double distancing of the numerical commemoration by the mediation of the letters and by their separation within a longer word makes the memory of the ancient revolt and the Hanukkah tradition more salient than the commemoration of the 1948 war. These choices may reflect the late origin of this commemorative act in the early 1980s, when religious Zionist values became more pronounced within mainstream Israeli culture.

Numerical commemorative toponyms are particularly vulnerable to the issue of the accuracy of the number that is at the core of this collective memorialization. Yet when new historical information or a different approach to counting questions an established collective number, such challenges may lead to the discrediting of a numerical commemorative toponym: if the name is preserved despite contestation, its historical validity becomes questionable; and if changed, the revision of the toponym is likely to present practical complications and might require further socialization to establish continuity with the earlier commemorative number. The lack of a good solution for such contestations can easily result in the formation of incompatible toponyms commemorating the same event. The coexistence of Street of the One Hundred and Thirty-Eight (in Haifa) and Street of the One Hundred and Forty (in Tel Aviv) alluding to Jewish soldiers on board of the SS *Erinpura* who drowned in 1943 demonstrates this difficulty.[51] Similarly, incompatible numerical commemorations of the group of Moroccan Jews who drowned on the way to Israel in 1961 are presented by streets named The Forty-Three (*Rehov Ha'Mem-Gimel*), while other official commemorations of this event refer to The Forty-Four (*Mem-Dalet*).[52] A more recent challenge to the long-established commemoration of the "twenty-three seafarers" calls for changing it to the "twenty-four seafarers" so as to include the British officer who lost his life in the same mission and whose death was disregarded in the earlier counting.[53]

This issue of accuracy becomes even more acute when the historicity of the memorialized event is questioned. This happened in numerical commemoration relating to a group of ninety-three female teachers and students of the religious school Bais Yaakov who committed suicide during World War II in order to avoid being captured by the Germans. The story about the ninety-three spread during the Holocaust and appeared credible because it follows a familiar plot structure of traditional narratives of Jewish martyrdom (*kiddush ha'shem*),[54] yet subsequent research by Jewish historians and Holocaust scholars concludes that this "event" has no historical foundation.[55] Nonetheless, several cities have maintained a toponym revolving around the ninety-three, revealing that numerical commemoration can easily blur distinctions between history and myth in ways that subvert the aura of scientific grounding, historicity and precision associated with numbers.[56]

Another major problem of this mnemonic practice arises when identical numerical commemorative toponyms established in different locales memorialize different historical events and identities. This occurs more frequently in the case of street names based on low numbers, such as Street of the Four (in Tel Aviv, Jerusalem, Acre, and Beit She'an) and Street of the Seven (in Netanya, Beit Shemesh, Kiryat Ata, Azor, and Safed). What appears as the same toponym in multiple localities actually draws on diverse local memories with different historical referents. Another sort of confusion stems from a toponym that features a letter combination that appears identical to another toponym with a different referent. Thus, for example, the letters *het-nun* that make up the numerical commemoration of the fifty-eight in *Nir Hen* (Graceful Meadow) also represent the initials of the poet *H*aim *N*ahman Bialik's first and middle names in the toponym *Shederot Hen* (Graceful Boulevard) in Tel Aviv. Given their identical appearance, and without a clear account of their respective meanings, it is impossible to know that *Nir <u>Hen</u>* and *Shederot <u>Hen</u>* represent different types of commemorative toponyms, the former based on numerical commemoration, and the latter encoding the name of a prominent figure.

While calendrical commemorative toponyms provide a more specific historical context than numerical commemorative toponyms, the limited scope of this information similarly calls for further contextualization to ensure their full interpretation as mnemonic forms. The effectiveness of calendrical toponyms therefore depends on the level of one's knowledge of history, the saliency of their historical referents within public memory, and the availability of further information related to the toponym. Street names that memorialize major Jewish national historical landmarks (such as the years 1929 or 1948, or key dates like the fifth of Iyar) may serve more effectively as sites of memory than street names that memorialize local turning points (such as the year of founding), which are likely to be less widely known.

In both cases of toponyms, their effectiveness rests upon one's recognition of these mnemonic forms even if one cannot decode the specific reference to

Street sign for Tarmav Street in the neighborhood *Kerem Ha'Teimanim* (the Yemenites' Vineyard) in Tel Aviv. The sign includes the reference to 1882 as the first year of the Yemenite Jewish immigration to the Land of Israel. Photo by the author.

the past. The mnemonic function of calendrical commemorative toponyms is further challenged by the marginalized significance of the Jewish calendar for secular Jewish Israelis who, unlike religious Jews, do not refer to it on a daily basis and therefore may have greater challenge decoding the historical referent of a Jewish year represented through letter combination. A recent article alluded to a television show in which Israeli youths answered the question, "when did the *Tarpat* events' take place," with the statement that they occurred in *Tashah*.[57] Their answer discloses not only ignorance about Israeli history but also the lack of understanding that *Tarpat* and *Tashah* stand for different years (1929 and 1948, respectively) which makes their answer absurd.

Like numerical commemorative toponyms based on collective numbers of the dead, calendrical commemorative toponyms face the dilemma of identical names that refer to different events. Thus, for example, the same street name *Rehov Tarpad* (1923/1924) that appears in Ramat Ha'Sharon and Bnei Brak memorializes their respective beginnings.[58] Similarly, *Rehov Tarmav* (1881/1882) in the Yemenite neighborhood in Tel Aviv marks the beginning of Yemenite Jews' immigration to Palestine in 1882, whereas the same street name in Rishon Le'Tsiyon memorializes the year it was founded. The potential confusion that such duplications create makes the addition of historical information on street signs critical, though awareness of this need varies greatly across townships.

On Remembrance and Forgetting

This chapter focused on numerical commemorative toponyms related to specific events involving death for the national cause and calendrical commemorative toponyms marking major historical events in Israeli national and local memories. Both types of toponyms introduce the past through numbers into Israeli national space, thereby transforming the landscape into a symbolic map of the past. Designed to memorialize and reinforce Israeli collective memory of the past, these toponyms participate in a broader mnemonic framework that cultivates memory of significant historical events.

Numerical commemorative toponyms represent an emphasis on collectivist and egalitarian ethos and the value of patriotic sacrifice, displaying a commemorative fit with the period in which they emerged and developed. The toponyms reinforce the collectivist orientation of Israeli national memory, highlighting the priority of group remembrance over that of individuals. The mnemonic value of this form lies in its ability to respond to the social expectation that official memory recognizes all those who lost their lives in the same event and gives each an equal weight. Yet like any mnemonic form, toponyms are inherently selective in their representation of the past. While they aim at reinforcing the collective remembrance of a specific past, they distance, marginalize, or suppress other aspects of the past. Thus, emphasis on collective remembrance masks and blurs memories of individuals who make up that group as well as the memory of individuals and marginalized groups that are excluded from that form of commemoration.

With the passage of time, memory of the individuals and the historical event to which the abstract and impersonal toponym alludes inevitably fades away. Similarly, the brief and detached reference to a historical date that the calendrical toponym memorializes presents an elusive form, further curtailed by the duality of the Jewish and Gregorian calendars as systems of dating in Israeli culture. In both cases, use of letters as part of the commemorative framework further complicates and undermines the mnemonic function of the toponym. Even though the spatial presence of the toponym conveys the promise of permanence, commemorative toponyms by themselves cannot guarantee immunity from the trajectory of collective forgetting. Without further historical information and additional commemorative practices that reinforce public knowledge of their historical referents, numerical and calendrical commemorative toponyms remain weak sites of memory. Given that their role as space designators is more salient, it can easily veil the reference to the past and thereby obscure their mnemonic function. Thus, the formal creation of a toponym by itself, without creating a further *commemorative density*[59] that would support it, runs the risk of becoming increasingly ineffective with the passage of time.

With the weakening of Israeli collectivist ethos, national heroic myths and symbols that had emerged during the prestate period declined. Growing attention to the representation of individuals who make up the collective is apparent in the inclusion of individual names on monuments and other forms of personalized memorialization within the framework of a collective memorial.[60] A tendency to blur the lines between heroic sacrifice in active duty, soldiers' death in accidents, and loss of life in terrorist acts has offered a more inclusive context for numerical commemoration that has kept this practice active. Numerical commemorative toponyms thus provide a venue for publicly memorializing collective deaths that may have otherwise been ignored given their specific circumstances.

Analysis of these particular mnemonic forms suggests, however, that the difficulties of decoding numerical and calendrical commemorative toponyms weaken their effectiveness as sites of memory. Their brief and abstract references to the past through numbers, whether relating to a group of the dead or a date, and the use of Hebrew letters as number substitutes, complicate the role of the toponym as a mnemonic form. Even when cultural recognition of these mnemonic patterns signals a symbolic shift to a commemorative framework, difficulties of interpreting the specific historical referents leave these forms inherently vulnerable to forgetting. The coexistence of similar toponyms with different referents and conversely, incompatible toponyms that relate to the same event in various localities, demonstrate two possible complications that undermine the mnemonic function of numerical and calendrical toponyms.

The selectivity of this mnemonic practice is also articulated in the delineation of the boundaries of the commemorated group. The case of the twenty-three seafarers illuminates how the social construction of group boundaries determines the commemorated number. The demand to modify the commemoration to the twenty-four seafarers focuses on the ethno-national criterion that was used to define the group and points out that the canonized lower figure erased the memory of the British officer who had died in that event. The issue of inclusion and exclusion also relates to the current Israeli policy of providing the transliteration of Hebrew toponyms in English and Arabic on road signs without references to their meaning or historical referents. Lack of knowledge of Hebrew leaves the meaning of such numerical and calendrical toponyms inaccessible to non-Hebrew speakers. Transliteration of the Hebrew names thus accommodates the function of the toponym as a space designator only, reserving their mnemonic function exclusively for Hebrew speakers as members of the Israeli national mnemonic community.

The Hebraization of Israeli national space raises broader issues than those explored in this chapter, yet the present discussion suggests the significance of the toponym as a political vehicle to promote remembrance and forgetting and to define the symbolic boundaries of the nation. While numerical and calendrical commemorative toponyms introduce Jewish memory of the past into the landscape, they also serve to obscure and suppress the Arab past. The reintroduction of maps and signs bearing erased Arabic toponyms in the greater Tel Aviv area is therefore performed as an act of protest by members of the organization *Zochrot* (We Remember, linguistically marked in the feminine form) to challenge this process of forgetting. The diverse meanings of commemorative toponyms thus reveal the dynamic process of commemoration and its political character and highlight the tensions between history and memory, national and local memories, and the interplay between remembering and forgetting.

Notes

I would like to thank Deborah Dash Moore and Michal Kravel-Tovi for inviting me to participate in the workshop that inspired my work on this topic. I am grateful for the feedback I received on an earlier version from them as well as Maoz Azaryahu, Michael Feige, Anat Helman, Tamar Elor, Tamar Katriel, Derek Penslar, and Eviatar Zerubavel and participants in the stimulating seminar on "Contested Memories and the Politics of Change" sponsored by the Allen and Joan Bildner Center for the Study of Jewish Life at Rutgers University during 2013–2014. Special thanks to Lee Rotbart for her devoted research assistance and to Ilanit Palmon for her help in photographing street signs.

1. Pierre Nora, *Les Lieux de mémoire,* vol. 1, *La République* (Paris: Gallimard, 1984), is his first volume in a series of studies on memory in France; see also Pierre Nora, "Between Memory and History: Les Lieux de Mémoire," *Representations* 26 (Spring 1989): 7–25.

2. See the discussion of calendrical and spatial commemorative sites in Yael Zerubavel, *Recovered Roots: Collective Memory and the Making of Israeli National Tradition* (Chicago: University of Chicago Press, 1995), 138–144; and Eviatar Zerubavel's comparative study of calendars as a site of national memory in "Calendars and History: A Comparative Study of the Social Organization of National Memory," in *States of Memory: Continuities, Conflicts, and Transformations in National Retrospection,* ed. Jeffrey K. Olick (Durham, NC: Duke University Press, 2003), 315–337.

3. See Eviatar Zerubavel, "Social Memories," in *Social Mindscapes: An Invitation to Cognitive Sociology* (Cambridge, MA: Harvard University Press, 1997), 87.

4. See Maoz Azaryahu, "The Power of Commemorative Street Names," *Environment and Planning D* 14, no. 3 (1996): 311–330; and Reuben Rose-Redwood, Derek Alderman, and Maoz Azaryahu, "Geographies of Toponymic Inscription: New Directions in Critical Place-Name Studies," *Progress in Human Geography* 34, no. 4 (2010): 453–470.

5. I introduced the concept *numerical commemoration* in Zerubavel, *Recovered Roots,* 45. For further discussion of this distinct Israeli tradition, see Yael Zerubavel, "'Numerical Commemoration' and the Challenges of Collective Remembrance in Israel," *History and Memory* 26, no. 1 (2014): 5–38.

6. The kibbutz *Ma'ale Ha'Hamisha* was named after five members of the founders' group who had been killed while working in a nearby settlement shortly before the kibbutz was founded. See "Ma'ale Ha'Hamisha," http://www.maale5.com//Default.aspx [in Hebrew].

7. Square of the Three in Tel Aviv is named after three members of the Jewish Haganah (Defense) underground who were killed in December 1947. A small monument at the square provides their names and the historical context of their deaths.

8. *Kiryat Shemona* was named after the eight people who were killed in Tel Hai in 1920 and memorialized annually on Tel Hai Day, the Eleventh of Adar. For a full discussion of the rise of Tel Hai as a national myth, see Zerubavel, *Recovered Roots,* 39–47, 84–95. See also "Kiryat Shemona," http://www.k-8.co.il/AboutUs/history/Pages/default.aspx [in Hebrew]. Note that the linguistic pattern of *Kiryat Shemona* follows the biblical name *Kiryat Arba* and, therefore, differs from the predominant pattern that includes the definite article prior to the number.

9. Street of the Four appears in numerous localities. Examples include Tel Aviv, in which the four memorialized were killed by an explosion at a local police station in February 1946 (*Davar,* February 24, 1946, 1 [in Hebrew]); in Acre, where four workers of the electric company were attacked and killed upon entering the town in March 1948 ("Street of the Four in Acre," *Eretz Zokheret Yoshveiha,* www.ezy.co.il/memoSite.asp?memorial_id=41 [in Hebrew]); in Beit She'an, where four people were killed by terrorists who entered the town in 1974 ("Street of the Four," http://www.ezy.co.il/memoSite.asp?memorial_id=113 [in Hebrew]).

10. Street of the Two Nurses memorializes two nurses who were killed by Arabs on the way to the hospital in Jaffa in 1936. Street of the Twenty-Three Seafarers refers to a group of Palmah members sent by the British by sea to blow up an oil refinery in Lebanon in May 1941. The boat and the men drowned at sea before they had a chance to carry out their mission. See the "Tel Aviv Street Guide," http://www.tel-aviv.gov.il/thecity/pages/streetsguide.aspx?tm [in Hebrew].

11. *Mishmar Ha'Shelosha,* a cooperative agricultural settlement (moshav), was named after three men who had been killed a month before it was founded in 1937. See "Mishmar Ha'Shelosha," *Labor Movement,* http://tnuathaavoda.info/places/home/places/1155802705.html. *Netiv Ha'Asara,* a moshav founded in Northern Sinai in 1973, was named after ten

soldiers who had died in a plane crash in 1971. The moshav was relocated to the Negev in 1982 when Israel returned Sinai to Egypt. See "Netiv Ha'Asara," http://www.netiv-10.co.il/12432 /%D7%94%D7%99%D7%A1%D7%98%D7%95%D7%A8%D7%99%D7%94 [in Hebrew]; see also Yehuda Ziv, *A Moment in Situ: Stories behind Place Names* [in Hebrew] (Jerusalem: Tsivonim, 2005), 22, 24.

12. In some instances of numbers larger than ten I found alternative numerical commemorations (by numbers or letters) of the same event in different locations. For example, the sixteen members of the Haganah who had been killed in 1948 in Atarot were memorialized in a street name based on the number (*Rehov Ha'Shisha Asar* in Jerusalem) and a street name with the letters that represent the same numerical value (*Rehov Ha'Tet-Zayin* in Tel Aviv). Similarly, streets named after the eleven Israeli athletes killed in the Munich Olympics are often based on a letter combination but in some cases are based on the number (see also note 23).

13. Square of the Thirty-Nine in Haifa is named after Jewish workers of the oil refinery who were killed by Arab workers in 1947. See "Kikar Ha'Lamed-Tet," "Haifa Street Guide," http://www.haifa-streets.co.il/Lists/List1/DispForm.aspx?ID=6140 [in Hebrew].

14. An article titled "Thirty-Five Haganah Members Were Killed by an Ambush" quotes the actual number, while an obituary refers to the letter combination that represents its value. Both were published on the same first page of *Ha'aretz*, January 18, 1948 [in Hebrew]. Similarly, *Ha'tsofe*, January 20, 1948 [in Hebrew], carried the news headline referring to the number ("Thirty-Five Fighters Sent as Reinforcement"), whereas a headline of an article about the funeral on the same date stated "Last Journey of the Lamed-Hei Heroes of Israel," employing the letter combination.

15. "Project [in Memory] of Hannah Szenes" [in Hebrew], *Davar*, April 21, 1946. Although the title focuses on the memorialization of another heroic figure, it first discusses the case of the twenty-three seafarers.

16. Zerubavel, *Recovered Roots*, 9–10.

17. See the title of a recent publication by Hillel Cohen, *1929: Year Zero of the Jewish-Arab Conflict* [in Hebrew] (Jerusalem: Keter, 2013) that critically examines the history and views of 1929 as a turning point in the Israeli-Palestinian conflict.

18. *Pa'amei Tashaz* (In the Footsteps of 1947), a moshav, was established in 1953 (Regional Council Merhavim, http://www.merchavim.org.il/cgi-webaxy/item?41 [in Hebrew]).

19. May First Street appears in Holon, Azor, and Ramla. September 11 Square is found in Or Yehuda; see "Kikar Be'Or Yehuda," *Eretz Zokheret Yoshveiha*, http://www.ezy.co.il /memoSite.asp?memorial_id=260 [in Hebrew].

20. Kibbutz *Givat Ha'Shelosha* was named after three men from Petah Tikva, whom the Ottoman authorities had charged with treason and who died in prison in Damascus in 1917. See http://www.ptarchive.co.il/he/ArchiveItem.aspx?t=1&p=1&iid=15 [in Hebrew]; and Ziv, *Moment in Situ*, 22.

21. On the twenty-three seafarers, see note 10. The 140 men belonged to the 462 Transport Company of the British army that was on its way from Alexandria to Malta when its ship was destroyed by the Germans. A state memorial was created for them in the national cemetery on Mount Herzl. See Maoz Azaryahu, *In Their Death They Commanded: The Architecture of Military Cemeteries in Israel, the Early Years* [in Hebrew] (Tel Aviv: Ministry of Defense Press, 2012), 57–69.

22. See Ziv, *Moment in Situ*, 26; and "Moshav Nir Hen," Rural Settlement website, http://www.homee.co.il/%D7%9F%D7%A0%D7%99%D7%A8-%D7%97/ [in Hebrew].

23. Street of the Eleven (*Rehov Ha'Yod-Alef*) in Herzliya, Street of the Eleven Athletes in Tirat Ha'Karmel, Haifa, Park of the Eleven in Bat Yam, Stadium of the Eleven in Ashdod, and Square of the Eleven (*Kikar Ha'Ahad-Asar*) in Bnei Brak are among multiple sites

memorializing the Israeli athletes killed at the Munich Olympics in 1972 by means of numerical commemoration.

24. See *If Eighty, It Is Not a Legend: Herzliya's 80th Anniversary* [in Hebrew] (Herzliya, Israel: Herzliya Municipality, 2004), 47; see also "Street of the Nine," "Haifa Street Guide," http://www.haifa-streets.co.il/Lists/List1/DispForm.aspx?ID=5895 [in Hebrew].

25. The destruction of the boat was reported in "Hope Was Lost" [in Hebrew], *Davar*, January 13, 1961. Streets named after the dead appear in multiple localities, including Jerusalem, Dimona, Bat Yam, and Safed.

26. See "Andartat Ha'Nun-Dalet," Jordan Valley Tourism, http://www.bikathayarden.co.il /index/%D7%90%D7%A0%D7%93%D7%98%D7%AA-%D7%94%D7%A0%D7%93 [in Hebrew].

27. For a detailed study of the memorialization of the seventy-three soldiers who were killed in this crash in 1997, see Michael Feige, "The Monument to the Helicopter Disaster and the Paradox of the Privatization of the Commemoration of Fallen Soldiers" [in Hebrew], *Iyunim Bitkumat Yisrael* 20 (2010): 122–143. For the park in Ness Ziona, see "Gan Ha'Shiv'im U'Shelosha," *Masa Aher*, http://www.masa.co.il/article/6450/%D7%92%D7%9F-%D7%94 -73-%D7%91%D7%A0%D7%A1-%D7%A6%D7%99%D7%95%D7%A0%D7%94/ [in Hebrew].

28. Ahiya Raved, "Haifa Central Station Named after Those Killed by the Katyusha Rocket" [in Hebrew], *Ynet*, July 9, 2007.

29. The process of locating these cases presented a challenge since there is no central database of street names to draw on and this naming pattern had not been identified or studied elsewhere. The sixty cases were therefore collected over time by using search engines, directories, publications on memory, memorials, and naming, as well as by word of mouth.

30. A fortress where twenty-eight soldiers were killed in 1948 was named *Metsudat Ko'ah* (see in Society for Preservations of Israel Heritage sites, http://www.shimur .org/%D7%A6%D7%A4%D7%95%D7%9F/articles/%D7%9E%D7%A6%D7%95%D7%93%D7 %AA%20%D7%9B%22%D7%97%20-%20%D7%A8%D6%B5%D7%A2%D7%95%D7%AA%20 %D7%AA%D7%97%D7%AA%20%D7%90%D7%A9 [in Hebrew]). A moshav commemorating the group was named *Givat Ko'ah*, that is, Hill of the Twenty-Eight (see "Givat Ko'ah," http:// www.givat-koah.co.il/ [in Hebrew]). Street of the Seventy-Eight (*Rehov Ayin-Het*) memorializes those who were killed in the attack on the caravan to Hadassah Hospital on Mount Scopus in Jerusalem in March 1948, many of whom were medical staff. See Ziv, *Moment in Situ*, 25–26.

31. Yael Zerubavel, "Patriotic Sacrifice and the Burden of Memory in Israeli Secular National Hebrew Culture," in *Memory and Violence in the Middle East and North Africa*, ed. Ussama Makdisi and Paul A. Silverstein (Bloomington: Indiana University Press, 2006), 77–100.

32. Georg Simmel, *The Sociology of Georg Simmel*, trans. and ed. Kurt H. Wolff (New York: Free Press, 1950), 107, 111.

33. See Joseph Dan, "The Narrative of the Ten Martyrs: Martyrology and Mysticism," in *History of Jewish Mysticism and Esotericism* [in Hebrew] (Jerusalem: Zalman Shazar Center / Historical Society of Israel, 2008), 2:744–776. The tale of the thirty-six righteous men (*lamedvav tzaddikim*) who live in every generation unknown to others differs from other numerical commemorations since it does not refer to a specific historical event but rather represents a revolving group throughout the ages. Yet here, too, group membership has priority over individual identity which is demonstrated in the Yiddish reference to each member as a "*lamedvavnik*" (i.e., one of the thirty-six). See Gershom Scholem, "The Thirty-Six Hidden Righteous Men in Jewish Tradition," in *Scholem's Studies of Hasidism* [in Hebrew], ed. David Assaf and Esther Liebes (Jerusalem: Magnes, 2008), 316–320.

34. Although I found cross-cultural examples of extended numerical commemoration of symbolic ancestors and martyrs in Jewish and Christian traditions and in several cases related to modern national memories, their use as toponyms appears limited and I have found no

example of a minimal numerical commemoration outside of Israel. For more detailed discussion of cross-cultural examples, see Zerubavel, "Numerical Commemoration," 7–10.

35. Zerubavel, *Recovered Roots*, 220.

36. George Mosse, *Fallen Soldiers: Reshaping the Memory of the World Wars* (New York: Oxford University Press, 1990), 34–50, 82–99; and Jay Winter, *Sites of Memory, Sites of Mourning: The Great War in European Cultural History* (Cambridge: Cambridge University Press, 1995), 78–116.

37. Jonathan Frankel, "The 'Yizkor' Book of 1911: A Note on National Myths in the Second Aliya," in *Religion, Ideology, and Nationalism in Europe and America: Essays Presented in Honor of Yehoshua Arieli* (Jerusalem: Historical Society of Israel / Zalman Shazar Center, 1986), 355–384. On key Israeli national myths of heroism and sacrifice, see Zerubavel, *Recovered Roots*.

38. Tamar Katriel, "*Gibush*: The Crystallization Metaphor in Israeli Cultural Semantics," in *Communal Webs: Communication, Culture, and Acculturation in Contemporary Israel* (Albany: State University of New York Press, 1991), 11–34; Oz Almog, *The Sabra: The Creation of the New Jew* (Berkeley: University of California Press, 2000), 226–254.

39. Maoz Azaryahu, *Namesakes: History and Politics of Street Naming in Israel* [in Hebrew] (Jerusalem: Carmel, 2012), 72–74, 141–142, 177–178.

40. Kibbutz *Maoz*, founded in 1937, was renamed *Maoz Haim* in 1938 drawing on Haim Sturman's first name. See "Kibbutz Maoz Haim," http://www.maoz.org.il/ [in Hebrew]. In 1941, the museum *Beit Sturman* (Sturman House) was established in his kibbutz, *Ein Harod*. See "Beit Sturman," http://www.beit-shturman.co.il/he/ [in Hebrew].

41. See Esther Zandberg, "Garden of Eden Made by Man" [in Hebrew], *Ha'aretz*, April 6, 2001.

42. See note 8.

43. See the discussion of parents' complaints about the individualized memorialization and the process that followed in Ilana Shamir, *Commemoration and Remembrance: Israel's Way of Shaping Its Mnemonic Landscape* [in Hebrew] (Tel Aviv: Am Oved, 1996), 37–39. See also "Mystery of the Burial of the Thirteen Solved Twenty Years Later" [in Hebrew], *Davar*, May 22, 1966; and "A Monument Was Unveiled to Those Who Died at the Bombing of the Akhziv Bridge" [in Hebrew], *Ma'ariv*, June 5, 1969.

44. The state extended the status of fallen soldiers to all casualties of the war from November 30, 1947, to March 1, 1949. See Maoz Azaryahu, *State Cults: Celebrating Independence and Commemorating the Fallen in Israel, 1948–1956* [in Hebrew] (Sde Boker, Israel: Ben-Gurion Research Center and Ben-Gurion University Press, 1995), 112.

45. On the shift from "sacrifice" to "victimhood" in Israeli culture, see Zerubavel, "Patriotic Sacrifice," 80–84. See also Galit Hasan-Rokem, "Martyr vs. Martyr—The Sacred Language of Violence," in *A Reader in the Anthropology of Religion*, ed. Michael Lambek (Malden, MA: Blackwell, 2008), 590–595.

46. Maoz Azaryahu indicates that the idea of naming a street The Six Million was raised in Tel Aviv in 1947 (*Namesakes*, 65); a similar proposal was recently raised in Nahariya (Jackie Houri, "Nahariya's Municipality Is Changing Street Names" [in Hebrew], *Ha'aretz*, October 26, 2010) but did not materialize.

47. On the history of *Yad Ha'Shemona*, see Gershon Nerel, "Yad Ha'Shemona: A Unique Moshav of Finns and Israelis in the Judean Hills" [in Hebrew], *Ariel* 168 (December 2004): 100–111.

48. The fortress, which had been called in Arabic *Nebi Yusha*, was renamed *Metsudat Ko'ah* after the twenty-eight dead soldiers (see note 30). To eliminate confusion with the moshav *Givat Ko'ah*, the name of the fortress was changed to the Yesha Fortress (*Metsudat Yesha*). In

2004 the site resumed its earlier numerical commemorative toponym *Metsudat Ko'ah* (Fortress of the Twenty-Eight). See Ziv, *Moment in Situ*, 25.

49. *Menorah* is the only case I found of a numerical commemoration incorporated into a larger word. A similar strategy was employed in another commemorative toponym, kibbutz *Dorot* (Generations) in 1941, where the name was constructed as an acronym memorializing three members of the Hoz family who had been killed in a car accident in 1940 through their first name initials (*Dov* Hoz, his wife *Rivka*, and daughter *Tirtza*). See Ziv, *Moment in Situ*, 28–29.

50. See Alter Welner, *Armed in Front of the Camp: The Story of a Religious Unit* [in Hebrew] (Tel Aviv: Defense Ministry Press, 1984), 263–264. On controversies that arose in the naming process, see Shamir, *Commemoration and Remembrance*, 67. Modiin was the place from which the Hasmonean family originated, and menorah is the ritual lamp at the ancient temple in Jerusalem which was lit to mark the rebels' victory in liberating Jerusalem and the temple and the miracle of oil that lasted eight days. On the symbolic connection between antiquity and modern Zionist revival advanced by Zionist memory, see Zerubavel, *Recovered Roots*, 22–33.

51. The figure of 140 is mentioned in a 1946 article "In Memory of the 140" [in Hebrew], *Davar*, April 30, 1946, 6, yet the "Haifa Street Guide" explains that *Simtat Kof-Lamed-Het*, also known by its acronym *Simtat Kalah* (Alley of the One Hundred and Thirty-Eight), memorializes the 138 Palestinian Jewish volunteers to the British army who died at sea when their ship was bombarded, and makes no reference to the updated figure of 140 ("Simtat Kof-Lamed-Het," "Haifa Street Guide," http://www.haifa-streets.co.il/Lists/List1/DispForm.aspx?ID=5448 [in Hebrew]). The "Tel Aviv Street Guide" mentions both the earlier counting of 138 dead and the updated number, which is the basis of the current name *Rehov Kof-Mem*, also known by its acronym *Rehov Kam* (Street of the One Hundred and Forty). See "Rehov Kof-Mem," "Tel Aviv Street Guide," http://www.tel-aviv.gov.il/thecity/pages/streetsguide.aspx?tm [in Hebrew].

52. Streets commemorating the forty-three Moroccan Jews exist in Jerusalem, Bat-Yam, and Ma'alot, yet the official number of the dead noted on the official monument in Mount Herzl and used in the annual memorial ceremonies dedicated to their memory refers to the "forty-four" (*Mem-Dalet*). The latter also appears on a special medal issued in their memory; see "The Boat Egoz," Israel Medal and Coin Corp., http://www.israelmint.com/?section=449&product=2520&lineItem=419 [in Hebrew].

53. See the report by Dr. Moses Ami-Oz and Neri Erelli, "The Twenty-Four Seafarers," Ministry of Defense, 2011, http://dl.dropbox.com/u/75665001/%D7%AA%D7%A7%D7%A6%D7%99%D7%A8%20%D7%93%D7%95%D7%97%20%D7%94%D7%9B%D7%92.pdf [in Hebrew]. See also Roi Chikie Arad, "The Man Who Was on the Boat with the Twenty-Three Seafarers" [in Hebrew], *Ha'aretz*, February 21, 2013.

54. On the issue of the credibility of invented tradition that follows traditional patterns, see Yael Zerubavel, "The Historical, the Legendary, and the Incredible: Invented Tradition and Collective Memory in Israel," in *Commemorations: The Politics of National Identity*, ed. John R. Gillis (Princeton, NJ: Princeton University Press, 1994), 105–123.

55. On the case of the ninety-three Bais Yaakov women, see Judith Tydor Baumel and Jacob J. Schacter, "The Ninety-Three Bais Yaakov Girls of Cracow: History or Typology?," in *Reverence, Righteousness, and Rahamanut: Essays in Memory of Rabbi Dr. Leo Jung*, ed. Jacob J. Schacter (New York: Jason Aronson, 1992), 93–130. See also Ruti Kadosh, "The Heroines Who Did Not Exist" [in Hebrew], *Ma'ariv*, April 21 2009.

56. Cities with streets commemorating the ninety-three teachers and students include Tel Aviv, Haifa, Petah Tikvah, Netanya, and Rishon LeTsyion. Bnei Brak, a city known for its large ultra-Orthodox population, established the Park of the Ninety-Three.

57. See Moshe Skal, "The Events That Transformed the Relationship between Arabs and Jews" [in Hebrew], review of *Tarpat,* by Hillel Cohen, *Ha'aretz Sefarim,* December 27, 2013, 8–9.

58. The same toponym, *Rehov Tarpad* (1923/1924), represents the founding of Ramat Ha'Sharon in 1923 ("Historical Landmarks," Ramat Ha'Sharonhttp://ramat-hasharon.muni .il/%D7%90%D7%91%D7%A0%D7%99-%D7%93%D7%A8%D7%9A-%D7%91%D7%94%D7%99 %D7%A1%D7%98%D7%95%D7%A8%D7%99%D7%94/ [in Hebrew]) and the founding of Bnei Brak in 1924 ("Bnei Brak," http://www.bnei-brak.muni.il/Pages/default.aspx [in Hebrew]).

59. See Zerubavel, *Recovered Roots,* 8–9.

60. On the decline of national heroic myths and symbols and the growing emphasis on individuals in Israeli mnemonic culture, see Zerubavel, "Patriotic Sacrifice." For changing trends in commemorative toponyms and the preference for names associated with nature and landscape, see Amit Pinchevski and Efraim Torgovnik, "Signifying Passages: The Signs of Change in Israeli Street Names," *Media, Culture and Society* 24, no. 3 (2002): 375, 378; and Azaryahu, *Namesakes,* 224–231.

PART II

COUNTING THE LIVING:
PUTTING THE "JEWISH" IN SOCIAL SCIENCE

4 Jewish "Crime" by the Numbers, or Putting the "Social" in Jewish Social Science

Mitchell B. Hart

Jews, Race, and Criminality

In 1911, Rudolf Wassermann, who headed up the Munich branch of the Bureau for Jewish Statistics, published an article in the bureau's official journal titled "Is the Criminality of the Jews a Racial Criminality?"[1] Wassermann practiced law professionally and had received a doctorate from the University of Erlangen for a dissertation on the history of criminal statistics. He was certainly not the only Jewish statistician or social scientist who took an avid interest in the subject of Jews and crime, but he was, as far as I am aware, the only one who could lay claim to being a genuine criminologist.[2] Thus, he brought a particularly deep knowledge of criminology and statistics to the subject of Jews and crime, or Jewish criminality.

Wassermann began his article by noting that the subject of the criminality of the Jews had stirred up a great deal of debate over the past few decades, and that "Not one year passes that does not bring forth another new work!" on the topic. "Most of the opinions," he continued, "revolve around the question whether the criminality of the Jews is predominantly due to occupation or race."[3] In other words, should we explain the criminal behavior of Jews as a product of social forces or heredity?

Wassermann noted that the journal in which his own piece was appearing had already dealt with this topic numerous times. And indeed, the journal *Zeitschrift für Demographie und Statistik der Juden* (Journal of demography and statistics of the Jews), which started in 1905, had published a good deal on the subject of Jews and criminality: brief pieces that related official government statistics, summations of scholarly and popular scientific articles that appeared in other journals or newspapers, and original articles produced by Jewish scholars associated with the Jewish statistical movement. While statistical studies by Jews had begun appearing already in the 1880s, an organized movement of what came to be called Jewish statistics formed in the first years of the twentieth century. The Bureau for Jewish Statistics (which published the *Zeitschrift für Demographie und Statistik der Juden*) was founded in Berlin in 1904 and constituted the institutional center of a European-wide network of bureaus committed to the collection and analysis by Jewish scholars of statistical material related to Jewry.[4]

By no means, however, was this the only forum in which the statistics generated about Jews and crime were disseminated and discussed. The subject of Jews and crime, in fact, was an important category in the broader Jewish social scientific enterprise and a common theme in Jewish and general newspapers and journals.[5] And the question of causality lay at the heart of the Jewish social scientific enterprise, including the engagement with criminality. To what extent, social science asked, could biology or environment, broadly and variously defined, account for the purported Jewish traits or behaviors that statistics appeared to reveal?

The idea of "taking stock" seems particularly apt as a way of capturing the project under analysis here. In the first place, Jewish social scientists took race, and the Jewish race, seriously as a historical reality. The "Jewish stock" could be either pure or mixed, worthy of preserving or in need of reform and regeneration; it could be a source of pride or a source of shame. Jewish thinkers interested in the racial question worked with all these notions at one time or another. Taking stock, then, meant taking race seriously and working with it as an analytical category and social-historical reality. Yet it also can be seen to have had a moral component. The social scientific analyses under discussion here evaluated the relationship between Jews and crime and took stock of the degree to which the purported Jewish nature or character could be held responsible for the overrepresentation of Jews in some types of criminal activity. Jewish social scientists did not deny that Jews were involved in crime. They accepted the statistics that appeared to demonstrate that Jews engaged in certain sorts of crimes in greater numbers than their Christian compatriots. The issue they grappled with was one of causality.

Debates over Jews and crime, and the central role of statistics in narratives produced about the subject, offer one of the clearest illustrations of the ways in which the category of "the social" functioned in Jewish social scientific or statistical discourse. Jewish social thinkers did not, as far as I am aware, spend a great amount of time theorizing over the nature and definition of the social as a category. While the social remained rather vague and ill-defined as a sphere of study within Jewish statistics, the social emerges—at least in retrospect—as a clearer, more coherent notion when it is deployed as an explanation for statistical averages and rates and in ongoing debates over purported Jewish physical, mental, and moral traits. Ultimately, through debates over causality a very clear and distinct notion of the social is articulated in Jewish social scientific texts.

More particularly, as the title of Wassermann's article demonstrates, the social within Jewish social scientific texts emerges as a direct response to the racial. This debate was assuredly not limited to discussions of Jews and crime but framed and infused much of the social scientific work produced about the Jews during this period. For instance, analyses of the relationship between Jews and capitalism focused not only on quantitative data about Jews' involvement in certain forms of trade and industry but on the question of why Jews seemed to be overrepresented in some areas of economic activity and underrepresented in others. If the statistical data revealed that Jews were overrepresented in occupations such as businessman, stockbroker, and trader, did this mean that Jews were racially predisposed to capitalism, or could this overrepresentation better be explained with reference to severe legal limitations European governments and the church placed on Jewish economic activities for centuries? Were Jewish bodies, brains, and behavior a product or manifestation of some inherent and unchanging Jewish essence or of forces—historical and contemporary—external to the Jew and, thus, amenable to change?[6]

Representation and Overrepresentation of Jews and Crime

This idea of statistical overrepresentation was critical to the social scientific debates about Jews over the past two centuries or more, including Jews and crime. The notion of overrepresentation was not worked out with reference to the Jews, though crime statistics did play a central role. The notion of overrepresentation depended on the idea of "the average man" (*l'homme moyen*). These concepts, in turn, were instrumental in the development of the categories normal and abnormal or pathological, categories that carried with them clear moral judgments that became central to social scientific narratives produced about Jews (though by no means solely about Jews). Criminality, of course, lent itself particularly well to the production of such narratives. All groups within a particular society or class of society could claim its share of criminals. As we shall see, Jews were said to be statistically overrepresented—that is, departed from the average or norm— in particular realms of criminal activity, and this overrepresentation had to be explained.

In the 1820s the Belgian statistician Adolphe Quetelet formulated the influential idea of the average man. Through the accumulation and analysis of massive amounts of data related to births, deaths, marriages, and other phenomena, Quetelet claimed that one could discover the fundamental laws of society. According to Allan Sekula, "Quetelet argued that large aggregates of social data revealed a regularity of occurrence that could only be taken as evidence of determinate social laws." This regularity had political and moral as well as epistemological implications: "The greater the number of individuals observed, the more do individual peculiarities, whether physical or moral, become effaced, and leave in a prominent point of view the general facts, by virtue of which society exists and is preserved."[7] Quetelet believed that crime statistics, or "moral statistics," revealed most clearly both the "general facts" by which society exists and, at the same time, the forces that threatened to undermine society.

For our purposes, what is most significant is that this insight into social regularities through statistical data led Quetelet, following Gauss, to construct a bell curve of the average man that served to define what was normal and pathological or deviant for both individuals and societies. In the words of Sekula, "In an extraordinary metaphoric conflation of individual difference with mathematical error, Quetelet defined the central portion of the curve, that large number of measurements clustered around the mean, as a zone of normality. Divergent measurements tended toward darker regions of monstrosity and biosocial pathology. Thus conceived, the 'average man' constituted an ideal, not only of social health, but of social stability and beauty."[8] For Quetelet, as Piers Beirne has written,

> the average man was one who regularly chose the mean course between the extremes of deficiency and excess. The virtues of the average man thus comprised "rational and temperate habits, more regulated passions . . . foresight, as manifested by investment in savings' banks, assurance societies and the different institutions which encourage foresight." Against the average man, who did not commit crimes, Quetelet frequently juxtaposed the criminality of vagabonds, vagrants, primitives, gypsies, the "inferior classes," certain races with "inferior moral stock," and "persons of low moral character."[9]

"Divergent measurements," or overrepresentation, thus carried a clear moral judgment. These categories of normal and pathological, whether explicitly articulated or not, came to frame almost all discussions and debates about the modern Jewish condition. It does, however, bear pointing out that Jews were hardly the major focus of most European statisticians' and social scientists' research into the nature and causes of crime; this honor fell mainly to the poor and working classes, to women, immigrants—indeed, to what the French historian Louis Chevalier famously referred to as "the laboring and dangerous classes."[10] Debates over Jewish normalcy and pathology occurred as part of a more general deliberation among social scientists, policy makers, and others about the physical and moral status of nation-states and their populations.

Statistics offered, so it was widely believed, a clear means by which normality or pathology could be represented.[11] In the case of the Jews, were they statistically overrepresented in certain categories of criminality or in other realms that constituted the categories of social scientific investigation such as university attendance or banking and high finance? Did Jews suffer disproportionately from certain diseases such as tuberculosis, diabetes, or certain types of cancer? On the other hand, did they enjoy a relative immunity to some diseases? What might explain this condition of overrepresentation, and when this condition was deemed pathological—as it so often was—how might the Jews be returned to normalcy? These questions impelled and shaped the entire Jewish social scientific enterprise. Through such inquires the concept of the social emerged.

Overall, Jewish social scientists were interested in what the numbers had to say about Jewish collective abnormality or pathology. Yet, as we'll see, Jewish social scientists might be said to have at the same time normalized "Jewish criminality" insofar as the narratives they constructed around comparative statistics explained this criminality as the product of forces external to Jews themselves, that is, not as a result of more fundamental biological or psychological Jewish traits but as an almost natural result of particular social conditions. The normalization of "Jewish crime" was, therefore, an effect rather than a cause of the social scientific discourse generated about Jews and crime. Indeed, insisting on the normal or normative nature of crime per se, and Jewish crime in particular, would not have been an effective explicit strategy, given that a prime impetus for Jewish scientific engagement with Jewish crime was a desire to counteract a growing anti-Semitic discourse on the subject that also relied heavily on statistics.

Anti-Semites, including opponents of Jewish emancipation and integration, had used numbers related to Jews and crime at least since the late eighteenth century for political and polemical purposes. To take the best known example, in 1782 Johann David Michaelis rejected Christian Wilhelm von Dohm's plea on behalf of Jewish civic emancipation and made the purported statistical overrepresentation of Jewish involvement in criminal activities central to his argument. According to Michaelis,

> We can see, principally from reports of investigations of thieves, that the Jews are more harmful than at least we Germans are. Almost half of those belonging to gangs of thieves, at least those of whose existence is known to us, are Jews, while the Jews are scarcely 1/25th of the total population of Germany. If this 1/25th part supplies the same number of riff-raff as the whole German people, or even more, then one must conclude that at least in respect to thievery, which I consider to be the lowest of the vices, the Jews are twenty-five times as harmful or more than the other inhabitants of Germany.[12]

Michaelis's insistence that Jews were thieves and robbers was hardly new. As Otto Ulbricht and other historians of early modern central Europe have shown, by the early eighteenth century the image of the Jew as thief or crook pervaded German Christian discourse. As Ulbricht has written, "writers no longer distinguished between *Gauner* and *Spitzbuben* (crooks and scoundrels) and Jews."[13] It's not clear, however, just where Michaelis got his numbers, since he refers only to

Diebes-Inquisitions-Acten, or "reports of investigations of thieves," as a source. Historians of German criminal statistics agree that the first, and highly unsatisfactory, attempt at an organized collection of statistics about crime dates from the first decade of the nineteenth century. Not until the 1830s did anything resembling reliable data appear in government publications.[14] Nonetheless, it is notable that already in the late eighteenth century, however questionable, numbers had become part of the discourse and debate over Jews, criminality, and emancipation and integration.

Michaelis's essay elicited a sharp response from the Jewish philosopher Moses Mendelssohn. Mendelssohn's reply contained within it the fundamental features of the argument that so many Jewish social scientists would make a century and more later, and so it is worth quoting at length:

"Ritter Michaelis does not seem to know any other vices besides fraud and roguery," wrote Mendelssohn. "I think, however, that where the wickedness of a people is to be evaluated one should not entirely overlook murderers, robbers, traitors, arsonists, adulterers, whores, killers of infants, etc. But even if one were to judge a people's wickedness only by the quantity of thieves and receivers of stolen goods among them," he acknowledged, "this number should not be viewed in terms of that people's proportion of the entire population. The comparison should rather be made between traders and peddlers among the Jews on the one hand, and among other peoples on the other. I am sure that such a comparison would yield very different proportions." Flipping the perspective and numbers, Mendelssohn observed, "The same statistics, I do not hesitate to maintain, will also show that there are twenty-five times as many thieves and receivers of stolen goods among German peddlers as among Jewish. This is aside from the fact that the Jew is forced to take up such a calling, while the others could have become field marshals or ministers. They freely choose their profession, be it a trader, peddler, seller of mousetraps, performer of shadow plays or vendor of curios."

Mendelssohn went on to explain what might motivate Jews to turn to thievery to secure funds. The political system that Michaelis defended, was, in fact, to blame.

> It is true that quite a number of Jewish peddlers deal in stolen goods; but few of them are outright thieves, and those, mostly, are people without refuge or sanctuary anywhere on earth. As soon as they have made some fortune they acquire a patent of protection from their territorial prince and change their profession. This is public knowledge; when I was younger I personally met a number of [Jewish] men who were esteemed in their native country after they had elsewhere made enough dubious money to purchase a patent of protection. This injustice is directly created by that fine policy which denies the poor Jews protection and residence, but receives with open arms those very same Jews as soon as they have "thieved their way to wealth." Although he is

inspired by Scripture, Herr Ritter Michaelis seems to have a bias against poverty. Among the Jews, however, I have found comparatively more virtue in the quarters of the poor than in the houses of the wealthy.[15]

Mendelssohn does not question the value or use of numbers in a debate over criminality, only that the numbers need to be understood correctly. He faults Michaelis for focusing only on certain relatively minor crimes such as theft and roguery, while ignoring such crimes as murder, rape, and assault that are arguably far more serious. And he explains the cause of Jewish crime with reference to variations in occupational patterns and levels of wealth and poverty, that is, as a social phenomenon.

Statistics, Race, Religion, and Crime

This type of social explanation for Jewish crime remained a constant among Jewish (and many non-Jewish) social scientists over the following one hundred and fifty years, even if, as we shall see, these same social scientists could also allow at times for a more complicated explanation that relied on some combination of the racial and the social. Yet, a number of crucial elements that in the 1780s only appear in nascent form developed much more fully over the following century. While numbers certainly did play some role in discussions about Jews and crime, and Jews and society more generally, the centrality of statistics to criminology, and thus to scientific narratives about Jews and crime, only coheres in the last quarter of the nineteenth century in Germany. Individual German states were already collecting statistics on crime in the early decades of the nineteenth century,[16] but it was really only after German unification in 1871, and the publication of comprehensive annual statistics through the Reich Statistical Office beginning in the early 1880s, that official numbers assumed prominence in German and German Jewish narratives about Jews and crime.

While scholars disagree about just when criminology emerged as a truly independent, scientific discipline, statistics had come indisputably by the last quarter of the nineteenth century to be understood as an essential tool for criminologists. Moreover, by the late nineteenth century, scientific discourse on race that had only just begun to take shape in the 1780s had, as is well known, become central to much, though not all, of the social scientific debate. This included debate about Jews. Questions of race and environment, biology and culture constituted central categories of that debate, and statistics featured prominently. By the 1880s, then, race, crime, and statistics had become components in a scholarly and popular public debate over the nature of Jews and their relationship to the larger surrounding society and state.

Earlier works that dealt with Jews and crime certainly contained numbers; but statistical tables and statistical thinking did not drive them, unlike works that began to appear in the last quarter of the nineteenth century. For example, in a work on "Jewish thieves and scoundrels" from 1820, we find hundreds of individual names and case histories, but not one statistical table.[17] The Prussian authority on crime A. F. Thiele's oft-cited book, *Die jüdischen Gauner in Deutschland: ihre Taktik, ihre Eigentümlichkeiten, und ihre Sprache* (The Jewish crook in Germany: Tactics, traits, and language), includes at the outset tentative figures about Jewish thieves in Germany. Yet these numbers do not constitute the main material for making sense of Jewish criminality in Germany. Rather, Thiele builds his narrative from hundreds of individual stories, from police records, transcripts of evidence, and court cases. Furthermore, the moral character of individuals, rather than social or biological conditions, constitutes the main explanatory frame for understanding crime. In Thiele's own words, "Only the biography characterizes the Gauner."[18] Thiele's work comes to more than 700 pages, and there is not one statistical table in it.

We can get a sense of the shift that occurred in the 1880s by comparing Thiele with the anonymous publication *Der Juden Antheil am Verbrechen* (The Jewish participation in crime),[19] which relies heavily on Thiele (at times lifting and reproducing sentences without attribution), but begins with an assertion about "just how important and invaluable confessional statistics [statistics organized according to religious affiliation] are for a judgment on the essence of Jewry."[20]

By the 1880s and 1890s, criminal statistics had become a discernible, even essential component of scientific and popular narratives about Jews, the state, and society. On one side, opponents of Jewish emancipation and integration used criminal statistics to make their case for the racial difference of Jew and German, and thus the impossibility of civic and social assimilation. Wilhelm Giese began his 1892 work, *Die Juden und die deutsche Kriminalstatistik* (The Jews and German criminal statistics), by telling readers that while pondering the Jewish Question, he realized that the oft-pronounced differences between the German and Jewish *Volkscharacter* must also be reflected in the realm of criminality. This seemed so self-evident that he then asked himself whether there existed enough statistical material to make a comparison between Jewish and German criminality. "I found in the German criminal statistics much more than I had expected; indeed, the difference in the racial character [of the two groups] appeared before my eyes after only a most superficial examination."[21]

The official criminal statistics of the German Reich counted convictions and divided these according to religion; there were four main categories: Protestant, Catholic, all other Christians, and Jews.[22] Giese, though, as he informs us, combines the first three into one category, "*Deutsche* (German)," so that he is left with only two categories: Germans and Jews. He then uses these to create his statistical tables. In the taxonomy of the official Reich statistical studies, Jews constitute a religious group, alongside Catholics and Protestants. For Giese, as for so many others, Jews are a distinct national and racial entity. They are not, as the emancipationist and integrationist advocates had been insisting since the last half of the eighteenth century, different from their Christian German neighbors only because of their faith. They were different in their very beings; they were a separate and distinct *Volk,* manifested in their bodies and behavior.[23] Thus, different rates of crime reveal a deeper, essential difference in the German and Jewish soul or spirit.[24]

Jewish advocates also insisted on the centrality of official state statistics to an understanding of the truth about Jews and criminality, though they disagreed with anti-Semites about the nature of that truth. For instance, in his 1885 work on Jewish crime, the Mainz Jewish lawyer Ludwig Fuld asserted that the problem or question of Jewish criminality must be and will be addressed through crime statistics—in this case, the official Prussian statistics of 1881. Only these could counter the large numbers of tendentious numbers (*Tendenzstatistik*) that have appeared over the past few years. The latter statistics stemmed from what Fuld called a "revitalization" of the question of the relationship between crime and religion: Does "the religion of a people (*eines Volkes*) influence its criminality"? This revitalization came in turn, he argued, from an increasingly "wild race hatred."[25] *Tendentious numbers* must be countered by truth (*Wahrheit*). It is the "duty and right of Science" to respond to the "hackneyed anti-Semitic fable of Jewish criminality," a fable that unfortunately even prominent German philosophers accept and propagate.[26] Exact research demands not metaphysics, but numbers, "not a deductive but an inductive approach."[27] Anti-Semites, working from a deductive approach, began with their own "metaphysical" understanding of the nature of the Jew and then sought the numbers that would allow them to construct a "scientific" argument to support this a priori belief. An inductive approach, according to Fuld, would begin with the numbers and allow those to determine one's theory or truth. Fuld does not question the value of numbers per se or the categories used to construct the narratives that give meaning to those numbers; he assumes that numbers reveal something significant about group identity and social realities. But in the end, numbers must drive the theory.

In this case, numbers must help provide an answer to the question about the nexus of religion and crime, specifically about the influence of the former on the latter. According to Fuld, the numbers revealed that in terms of crime rates, those of sectarians fell below Jews, Jews fell below Catholics, and Catholics below Protestants. This fact yields "the general rule that the adherents of a religion that is not the majority within a country, that in other words is not in a ruling position, far more seldom find themselves in trouble with the law and before a criminal judge than do believers in the majority religion. . . ."[28] Since the anxiety and fear that came with being a minority was so much greater, so too were the social controls exerted by each religious community of such minorities. Fuld called this "a social law." And his explanation for Jewish crime, which he granted exists, was indeed a social one, albeit not rooted in notions of class or economic differences, as were the majority of analyses by Jewish statisticians that appeared in the last years of the nineteenth century.

Fuld offered a social explanation for rates of Jewish crime, motivated in large part by his desire to repudiate a racial discourse about Jews that relied increasingly on statistics. Thus, it shared a number of fundamental components of the dominant narrative about Jews and crime emerging in the 1890s. It was, however, perhaps less convincing than one based on occupational or class differences. By the time Fuld was writing, an argument that sought to explain contemporary Jewish behavior with reference to some overarching centralized Jewish religious control—what Fuld called the social law of Jewish anxiety over its minority status and the consequent exertion of powerful controls by the Jewish religious establishment—seemed to slight or ignore a fundamental process of modern German Jewish life: the breakdown of communal religious authority and control, though not, of course, the disappearance of minority consciousness.

Economies of Jewish Crime

Discourse about Jews and crime that focused on economic or occupational differences could account for statistical evidence in a more subtle and convincing manner, while also taking note of dramatic transformations in German Jewish life over the past century, transformations that included not only civic and political emancipation but also social, economic, and cultural integration into the German middle classes. Just as important, perhaps, this sort of argument made a strong case for the *normalization* of Jews, and it did so by demonstrating through official statistics that Jews committed crimes not as Jews—or more precisely not because of their Jewishness—but as *bourgeois Germans.*[29]

Such an argument, rooted in social-economic rather than racial or religious forces, had the potential, irrespective of the intentions of those who made the case, for normalizing and Germanizing Jews as members of contemporary society. For example, in 1896, four years after Wilhelm Giese's anti-Jewish work appeared, the Committee for the Defense Against Anti-Semitism, known as the Abwehr, published the first volume of its projected series on aspects of Jewish life in Germany.[30] The committee had been founded in 1890 by German Christians ashamed of the growth and strength of an organized, politicized anti-Semitism in their country. In the words of a writer for a Jewish newspaper, the committee had "taken up the task of analyzing and explaining the conditions of the Jews in Germany, with regard to the various realms and relations of civic and public life. And insofar as this is possible, they aim to do this using official [statistical] data (*amtlichen Materials*)."[31] Many Christians and Jews, the anonymous author continued, remain unaware of facts related to important issues and questions, such as the participation of Jews in military service, or in artisanal and industrial work, and this lack of factual knowledge makes the defense against anti-Semitic attacks impossible.

Tellingly, the first volume of the series dealt with the criminality of the Jews in Germany. In the introduction to the volume the editors write that one of the chief claims of the anti-Semites is that Jews have a particular affinity for crime, and that this poses a great threat to the well-being of the countries in which they live. This claim is made so often that it is taken as truth, regarded as a fact. At the same time, numerous studies, clothed in the pretense of science, seek to demonstrate this claim. In contrast, the editors explain that their volume on Jews and criminality will, "without bias or prejudice, offer up the objective truth through raw numbers (*nackten Zahlen*) to those interested. These numbers offer, on the basis of all extant official material, the actual facts."[32] The use of the phrase "raw numbers" is revealing. Akin to Fuld, the authors of the Abwehr study believe in the value of numbers generated by the German state about Jews. But these numbers must be organized and interpreted correctly, and this is, of course, what the opponents of Jews cannot or will not do. One must begin with the raw numbers and not an already arrived at theory; an inductive, and not deductive, approach must be taken.

The statistical tables, which cover the years 1882–1892, demonstrate "with enormous clarity the extraordinary difference between the criminality of the Jews and the criminality of non-Jews. There is an entire realm of crimes and misdemeanors in which the Jews are only minimally represented, and others in which they are heavily implicated." Having pointed out the variability and distinctiveness of Jewish and non-Jewish criminality, the authors then pose a crucial question: "Now, is this phenomenon to be explained by race, which remains [as a subject] unsettled, or by religion?" Then they add a second, political query: "It also needs to be asked, is the particular criminal proclivity of the Jews a greater danger to the State than the proclivity of the non-Jews?"[33] The study notes that the percentages related to crimes such as murder, manslaughter, larceny, and other serious offenses are far lower for Jews than for non-Jews and suggests that this balances out those realms in which the numbers for Jews are higher.

What crimes, then, did Jews commit at higher rates than Christians? These were of two major kinds: crimes against the state or religion, mainly related to such things as Sunday or Sabbath laws, or laws related to public order; and white-collar crimes. At this juncture the particular social argument about crime, and indeed about almost all purported Jewish differences, can be seen most clearly.

The Abwehr study stressed the need to situate crimes in their particular economic and social contexts, in the opportunity provided by certain occupations (such as banker or stockbroker rather than factory worker or farmer), and by social position. Thus, it is imperative, they argued, that comparisons of crimi-nality between Jews and non-Jews *not* be a comparison of the rates from within one geographic region or German state (e.g., Prussia, Bavaria, etc.). That is, when looking to criminal statistics to reveal something about why Jews commit the crimes they do, it makes no sense to compare Jewish rates of crime to the en-tire population of an individual region or state. This would necessarily distort the true meaning of the numbers. It is the occupational or economic, rather than the geographic or regional, that is determinative. One ought to compare the criminal ratios of particular social and economic sectors of the population, so that Jews are compared not to the entire non-Jewish population but only to those non-Jews of the same profession or occupation.

The authors of the study use the state of Saxony, where there was, they say, no Jewish community to speak of, as an example. This makes it possible to examine the criminal statistics for this region and draw conclusions from them, without any sort of claim of there being a negative Jewish influence. They write that of the thirty-five categories in which the statistics for Jews prove unfavorable, there are at least eighteen in which the numbers for Christians in Saxony are just as un-favorable. For instance, counterfeiting: throughout the Reich, the Jews commit this offense at rates above the average; so, too, do Christians in Saxony. Readers are then offered a long list, over half a page, of offenses to which Christians in Saxony participate at disproportionate rates. These are economic or white-collar crimes, all of them characterized as crimes to which individuals of the upper social and economic strata would be prone. Christians in Saxony also engage to a high degree in pimping, public lewdness, distribution of pornography, and other moral offenses. By the late nineteenth century these sorts of crimes involving il-licit sexual practices had become widely associated with Jews.

Anti-Semitic propaganda, of course, made much of Jewish involvement in the white slave trade, as both pimps and prostitutes. Even the organized Jewish communities throughout Europe and North America recognized this involve-ment as a problem and vowed to remedy it. However, racial anti-Semitism saw such activities as proof not of a historically contingent set of conditions (i.e., the poverty and vulnerability of Jewish girls and women immigrating to the West from eastern Europe) but of a more general Jewish degeneracy and insisted that Jewish immorality and disease (literal and figurative) were threatening to poison the pure German or Aryan body (both individual and social).[34] An argument such as that proffered by the Abwehr, in which a region of Germany all but free of a Jewish presence can be shown to suffer from the same rates of sexual crimes and pathologies, demonstrates the fallacy of the anti-Semitic position. Surely something other than an insidious Jewish influence must account for Christian Saxon sexual perversion, as well as the other sorts of crime patterns revealed by the numbers.

The industrialized kingdom of Saxony shows evidence of high rates of crimes that much of the rest of Germany does not. That is, Saxony deviates in its crime rates from Germany as a whole. Saxony, in this regard, is proximate to Jews in terms of types of crimes committed in high numbers. But it would be absurd, the study insists, to assert some sort of kinship or connection between the two groups. The explanation lies, rather, in two social phenomena: "that the inhabitants of the Kingdom of Saxony, like the Jews, involve themselves to a higher degree in financial endeavors broadly defined, and that they are urban dwellers."[35] It goes on, "If one bears both of these facts in mind, then one finds the key to the particular types of crime engaged in by Jews: financial crimes and misdemeanors."[36]

These are not, the authors emphasize, what the anti-Semites label Jewish crimes; they are not explicable by racial or religious traits but by the particular nature of Jewish activities in the city. Christians, when found in similar social and economic conditions, commit the same sorts of crimes—as the Christians in Saxony demonstrate.[37] Finally, the occupational statistics show that Jews are involved in trade to a much greater degree than are Christians in the Reich as a whole, and so it should not be surprising that their numbers when it comes to crimes involving finance are relatively higher.[38]

This sort of social, rather than racial, argument made by the Abwehr study was adopted by numerous later Jewish statisticians and social scientists. For instance, in the first issue of the *Zeitschrift für Demographie und Statistik der Juden,* Arthur Ruppin made the argument in his analysis of "the criminality of Christians and Jews in Germany, 1899–1902."[39] Ruppin, who was the director of the Bureau for Jewish Statistics in Berlin and the editor of its journal, noted that the statistics revealed that Christians and Jews commit different types of crime at different rates. Christians commit far more physical and violent crimes, while Jews commit more "abstract" crimes—occupation-based crimes, crimes against moral codes, and against public order. Ruppin then explains these differences: (1) Jews enjoy, on average, a higher standard of living, and this accounts for the infrequency of crimes against property, like robbery; (2) Jews are, on average, more highly educated than non-Jews, and this accounts for lower levels of crimes described as "brutal," involving force; and (3) differences in occupational structure and in urban/rural concentration. Jews are most likely to be involved in crimes involving trade and big business and in the free professions (e.g., crimes that violate the laws against work on Sundays or libel). Interestingly, Ruppin here appears to violate the methodological rule set forth by the Abwehr study discussed above. He does not limit his comparison of Jewish and Christian crime to particular occupational or economic sectors but rather compares "Jews" and "Christians" without further differentiation. Thus, we cannot know from Ruppin whether urban Christian bankers who attended university were more or less physically violent than their Jewish counterparts.

In any case, Ruppin, like most other Jewish social scientists, made a fundamentally social argument about Jews and crime, and they understood this argument in large part as a response to the racial determinism espoused by opponents of Jews.[40] However, Jewish social scientists by no means rejected race as a valid or viable explanation for individual and collective traits or as a force in society or history. At the end of his article on Jewish and Christian crime in Germany, Ruppin held out the possibility that biology might have something to do with explaining differences in types of crimes committed by these two ostensible religious groups.[41]

Recall that Rudolf Wassermann posed the question: Is the criminality of the Jews to be conceived as a racial criminality or as the product of social conditions? The question was not merely rhetorical, and his answer illustrates the complicated, even confused, relationship of the social and the racial in much of this literature. "I am able," he concluded, "to summarize my views on the form and the causes of criminality among the Jews in the following way:

1. The criminality of the Jews expresses essentially the type of criminality associated with the general strata of the population to which the Jews belong socially.
2. Therefore, in all probability, it [criminality] is influenced by social class. A series of other considerations supports this.
3. It is by no means self-evident, however, that other factors—that is, one's racial make-up—are not involved in contributing to the criminal impulses of individuals; and there is also no denying that in the case of the Jews—and to whom does this not apply?—social conditions in part have to be traced back to racial characteristics."[42]

In the end Wassermann seemed to embrace and endorse a social rather than a racial explanation for criminality, both Jewish and Christian.

The Jewish Trust in Numbers

Wassermann's unreflexive use of the categories Jews and Christians to organize his thoughts on criminality is illuminating. In its appropriation and reproduction of these categories, Wassermann's article—and he was hardly alone in this—already came equipped, as it were, with an explanatory framework. That is, the statistical table has already produced a "problem" to be addressed and solved just by organizing crimes and criminals along the lines of Jewish and Christian. This is not to say that Jews did not commit crimes, just as Christians did. However, when the statistical tables organize the numbers around the categories of Jewish and Christian, they make Jewishness a factor a priori and, therefore, demand an explanation along these lines. What was at issue was not whether Jewishness or

Judaism had anything to do with explaining why Jews commit crimes; that was a presupposition or intellectual given that came built in, so to speak, to the existing social scientific discourse. The issue was the etiology of Jewish criminality. Hence, Wassermann's question was asked in one form or another by dozens of criminologists and social scientists: Is Jewish criminality a racial or social criminality?

Neither Wassermann nor other Jewish social scientists questioned the validity of the categories themselves. They did not query the very notion of a "Jewish criminal" or "Jewish crimes," or the incommensurabilities involved in these categories, the use of ostensibly religious identities, Christian and Jew, to solve a question about purported racial traits and differences. At most, as in the case of the German Jewish lawyer Maximilian Paul-Schiff, one encounters a sarcastic repudiation of the idea that criminal statistics yield any useful information. But this was a methodological point, rather than a nosological or epistemological one.[43]

In general, Jewish statisticians and social scientists believed in the numbers produced about Jews, believed in the categories used to create the statistical tables and charts, and even often believed in the content of the narratives that told of Jewish degeneration, perversion, and decline. This belief or trust in the numbers and narratives did not mean merely acceptance, though, of course, it meant that. Rather, it was part—and a central part—of their faith in social science to reveal the truth about the condition of Jews in the modern world, for better or worse. Indeed, Jewish social scientists insisted that only social science, with statistics at the center, could do this (in contrast to the disciplines of history or theology). Jewish social scientists did not, and could not, repudiate the value of statistics per se, only the interpretations and meanings others often gave them.

Nor did Jewish social thinkers reject or repudiate the idea of a Jewish race or racial arguments per se. Jews accepted the comparative statistics produced and disseminated by anthropologists, physicians, national economists, and sociologists about Jewish difference in almost every realm of life. What they, for the most part, rejected was the racial hierarchy often found in what we would call normative narratives and the belief in a strong bio-racial causality. Jewish social scientists at this time did not, moreover, reject racism; throughout their writings one finds an insistence that Jews belonged to the white race, which European and North American Jewish social scientists also assumed was the ideal. Rather, the accusation by European and North American authorities that the Jews were below Anglo-Saxons or Aryans, and that there was an intrinsic tension or contradiction in the ontological categories white and Jew had to be countered, not that Jews were a race per se.

In fact, at times a notion of Jewish superiority, deemed genetic or racial, emerged in Jewish analyses, including the discussions of Jews and crime. Briefly, it was argued that in the first place, the fact that Jews committed white-collar crimes, rather than the physically brutal crimes of rape and murder, demonstrated a moral superiority, a refinement of spirit, over the Christian or Gentile community. Second, the crimes Jews committed demonstrated their intellectual superiority: crimes related to finance, to the stock market and banks, fraud and embezzlement, these crimes required intelligence and cunning; Gentiles committed physical crimes, Jews committed crimes of the mind. In the end, the proclivity on the part of Jews to certain types of crime was not itself a racial trait; rather, it was a secondary characteristic of the primary trait of superior intelligence, and this was a racial or genetic trait.[44] Thus, the categories racial and social, so often seen as opposed or incompatible, were not mutually exclusive in this discourse. Jews could be and were defined as a race, or as an ethno-nation, whose purported collective traits were nonetheless due to historical and social forces.

What was "the social," then, in Jewish social scientific texts? It was not, to be sure, a clearly theorized concept, nor was it a tangible space or realm that existed apart from the economy or polity. Nor can it be equated with "the environment"—which included geography and climate as causal factors—nor with culture. Rather, for social scientists, the social was a set of forces that had been produced by the particular historical and contemporary position inhabited by Jewry. As an explanatory frame, it took its place somewhere between the idea of individual moral character and bio-racial determinism. As the literature on Jews and crime illustrates, a more particular notion of the social was constructed through and around numbers as a means by which Jewish scholars and others could intervene in the larger debate over race and environment, biology and culture. The social was context, of course, but also cause.

Notes

I would like to thank Deborah Dash Moore and Michal Kravel-Tovi for organizing and hosting the conference at the University of Michigan on Jews and numbers, and for inviting me to participate. I also wish to thank them for their astute and critical reading and editing of this essay, which improved it immensely.

1. Rudolf Wassermann, "Ist die Kriminalität der Juden Rassenkriminalität?," *Zeitschrift für Demographie und Statistik der Juden* 7, no. 3 (1911): 36–39. The English translation can be found in Mitchell B. Hart, ed., *Jews and Race: Writings on Identity and Difference, 1880–1940* (Lebanon, NH: Brandeis University Press, 2011), 145–149.

2. By "Jewish statistician" or "Jewish social scientist," I mean self-identified Jews who made the Jewish past and present the primary object of their scholarly inquiry. There certainly were Jews, such as Gustav Aschaffenburg in Germany or Cesare Lombroso in Italy, who were leading authorities on criminology, but the Jews were not the focus of their interests.

3. For instance, the essay by the eminent German criminologist Franz von Liszt, *Das Problem der Kriminalität der Juden* (Giessen, Germany: Alfred Töpelmann, 1907), and the article by the head of the bureau of legal statistics in Amsterdam, J. R. B. de Roos, "Über die

Kriminalität der Juden," *Monatsschrift für Kriminalpsychologie* 6 (1909): 10. The latter figures prominently in Wassermann's article.

4. On the history of the Jewish statistical movement, see Mitchell B. Hart, *Social Science and the Politics of Modern Jewish Identity* (Stanford, CA: Stanford University Press, 2000).

5. Much of the statistical material used by Jewish social scientists derived from official government studies, either at the local or national level; Jewish social scientists also relied heavily on numbers that appeared in the works of researchers who included Jews in their studies but were not focused exclusively on them. On the attraction of Jews and crime as a subject for popular discourse, see Daniel M. Vyleta, *Crime, Jews and News: Vienna 1895–1914* (New York: Berghahn, 2007); and Michael Berkowitz, "Unmasking Counterhistory: An Introductory Exploration of Criminality and the Jewish Question," in *Criminals and Their Scientists,* ed. Peter Becker and Richard F. Wetzel (Cambridge: Cambridge University Press, 2006), 61–84.

6. On the European discourse about Jews and the economy, see Derek J. Penslar, *Shylock's Children: Economics and Jewish Identity in Modern Europe* (Berkeley: University of California Press, 2001).

7. Allan Sekula, "The Body and the Archive," *October* 39 (Winter 1986): 19–20. In addition, see Piers Beirne, *Inventing Criminology: Essays on the Rise of "Homo Criminalis"* (Albany: State University of New York Press, 1993), chap. 3.

8. Sekula, "The Body and the Archive," 22.

9. Beirne, *Inventing Criminology,* 89.

10. Louis Chevalier, *Labouring Classes and Dangerous Classes in Paris in the First Half of the Nineteenth Century* (London: Routledge, 1973). See also Ann-Louise Shapiro, *Breaking the Codes: Female Criminality in Fin-de-Siècle Paris* (Stanford, CA: Stanford University Press, 1996). The term "les classes dangereuses" dates back to 1840, coined by H. A. Frégier. See Clive Emsley, *Crime and Society in England: 1750–1900,* 2nd ed. (London: Longman, 1996), 36.

11. This does not mean that everyone agreed that statistics was the only or even the best means of understanding and representing crime and its effects. For a fascinating discussion of the continuing attraction and importance of individual case studies of crime in Germany, see Peter Fritzsche, "Talk of the Town: The Murder of Lucie Berlin and the Production of Local Knowledge," in *Criminals and Their Scientists,* ed. Peter Becker and Richard F. Wetzel (Cambridge: Cambridge University Press, 2006), 377–398.

12. Johann David Michaelis, "Arguments against Dohm (1782)," in *The Jew in the Modern World: A Documentary History,* ed. Paul Mendes-Flohr and Jehuda Reinharz (Oxford: Oxford University Press, 1995), 42. On Michaelis and the Jews, see Jonathan Hess, "Johann David Michaelis and the Colonial Imaginary: Orientalism and the Emergence of Racial Antisemitism in Eighteenth-Century Germany," *Jewish Social Studies,* n.s., 6, no. 2 (2000): 56–101; Jonathan Hess, *Germans, Jews, and the Claims of Modernity* (New Haven, CT: Yale University Press, 2002), chap. 2; and Michael Berkowitz, *The Crime of My Very Existence: Nazism and the Myth of Jewish Criminality* (Berkeley: University of California Press, 2007), 69. On Michaelis more generally, see Michael C. Legaspi, *The Death of Scripture and the Rise of Biblical Studies* (Oxford: Oxford University Press, 2010).

13. Otto Ulbricht, "Criminality and Punishment of the Jews in the Early Modern Period," in *In and Out of the Ghetto: Jewish-Gentile Relations in Late Medieval and Early Modern Germany,* ed. R. Po-Chia Hsia and Hartmut Lehmann (Cambridge: Cambridge University Press, 1995), 49.

14. See Helmut Graff, *Die deutsche Kriminalstatistik: Geschichte und Gegenwart* (Stuttgart: Ferdinand Enke, 1975), 28–30. Ulbricht ("Criminality and Punishment," 51) also makes the point that reliable statistics date only from the early nineteenth century.

15. Moses Mendelssohn, "Remarks Concerning Michaelis' Response to Dohm (1783)," in *The Jew in the Modern World: A Documentary History*, ed. Paul Mendes-Flohr and Jehuda Reinharz (Oxford: Oxford University Press, 1995), 48. On this exchange in another context, see Michael Berkowitz, "A Hidden Theme of Jewish Self-Love? Eric Hobsbawm, Karl Marx, and Cesare Lombroso on 'Jewish Criminality,'" in *The Cesare Lombroso Handbook*, ed. Paul Knepper and Per Jørgen Ystehede (London: Routledge, 2012), 256–258.

16. Herbert Reinke, "Die 'Liason' Strafrechts mit der Statistik," *Zeitschrift für neuere Rechtsgeschichte* 12, no. 1 (1990): 169–179.

17. Carl Philipp Theodor Schwenken, *Notizen über die berüchtigsten jüdischen Gauner und Spitzbuben* (Marburg u. Cassel: Johann Christian Krieger, 1820).

18. Quoted in Peter Becker, "Criminological Language and Prose from the Late Eighteenth to the Early Twentieth Century," in *Crime and Culture: An Historical Perspective*, ed. Amy Gilman Srebnick and René Lévy (London: Ashgate, 2005), 32.

19. The full title is *Der Juden Antheil am Verbrechen, auf Grund der amtlichen Statistik über die Thätigkeit Schwurgerichte, in vergleichender Darstellung mit den christlichen Confessionen* (Berlin, 1881). On these mid-nineteenth-century works on Jews and crime, see Berkowitz, *Crime of My Very Existence*, chap. 1.

20. Anonymous, *Der Juden Antheil*, 6.

21. Wilhelm Giese, *Die Juden und die deutsche Kriminalstatistik* (Leipzig, 1892), 1.

22. Ibid., 3.

23. The German word *Volk* cannot be adequately translated into English. The German term resonates far more deeply, carrying with it notions of mythical, national, and racial identity that the English "folk" fails to convey.

24. Giese, *Die Juden*, 7.

25. Ludwig Fuld, *Das jüdische Verbrechertum: Eine Studie über den Zusammenhang zwischen Religion und Kriminalität* (Leipzig: Theodor Huth, 1885), v.

26. Ibid., vi.

27. Ibid., 3–4.

28. Ibid., 6.

29. This sort of argument about criminality, class, and integration was made by Todd Endelman about English Jewry in his seminal work, *The Jews of Georgian England, 1714–1830*, 2nd ed. (Ann Arbor: University of Michigan Press, 1999).

30. Verein zur Abwehr des Antisemitismus, *Die Kriminalität der Juden in Deutschland*, vol. 1 (Berlin: Mitteilungen des Vereins zur Abwehr des Antisemitismus, 1896).

31. Anonymous, "Die Kriminalität der Juden in Deutschland," *Im Deutschen Reich* 2, no. 1 (1896): 21. See also Daniel Vyleta, "Jewish Crimes and Misdemeanors: In Search of Jewish Criminality (Germany and Austria, 1890–1914)," *European History Quarterly* 35, no. 2 (2005): 299–325.

32. Anonymous, "Die Kriminalität," 21–22.

33. Ibid., 24–25.

34. See Jay Geller, "From Mohels to *Mein Kampf*: Syphilis and the Construction of Jewish Identification," in *The Other Jewish Question: Identifying the Jew and Making Sense of Modernity* (New York: Fordham University Press, 2011), 88–131; Sander Gilman, *The Jew's Body* (London: Routledge, 1991); and Edward Bristow, *Prostitution and Prejudice: The Jewish Fight against White Slavery, 1870–1939* (Oxford: Oxford University Press, 1982).

35. Anonymous, "Die Kriminalität," 27–28.

36. Ibid., 28.

37. Ibid.

38. Ibid.

39. Arthur Ruppin, "Die Kriminalität der Christen und Juden in Deutschland 1899–1902," *Zeitschrift für Demographie und Statistik der Juden* 1, no. 1 (1905): 6–9.

40. For further examples, see Bruno Blau, *Die Kriminalität der Juden* (Berlin, 1906); the relevant sections in Arthur Ruppin, *Die Juden der Gegenwart* (Berlin, 1904, rev. 1911); and Maurice Fishberg, *The Jews: A Study of Race and Environment* (New York: Walter Scott, 1911). For a discussion of these and other studies that situates these arguments within intra-Jewish political debates of the time, see Hart, *Social Science*.

41. Ruppin, "Die Kriminalität der Christen und Juden," 9.

42. Wassermann, "Rassenkriminalität," 149.

43. See Maximilian Paul-Schiff, "Zur Statistik der Kriminalität der Juden," *Zeitschrift für Demographie und Statistik der Juden* 5, no. 5 (1909): 70–75.

44. For one example of the argument about Jews, crime, and intelligence, see Arthur Ruppin, "Die sozialen Verhältnisse der Juden in Preussen und Deutschland," *Jahrbücher für Nationalökonomie und Statistik* 23 (1902): 781–784. On the more general argument about Jews and intelligence, see Sander Gilman, *Smart Jews: The Construction of the Image of Jewish Superior Intelligence* (Lincoln: University of Nebraska Press, 1997).

5   Counting People

The Co-production of Ethnicity and Jewish Majority in Israel-Palestine

Anat Leibler

> We beg them [the king, his family, and his chief minister] to join with us in checking the abuses being perpetrated by tyrants against that class of citizens . . . and we call on the king to mete out justice, and we express our most sincere desire for but one king, one law, one weight, and one measure.
>
> Quoted in Witold Kula, *Measures and Men*

TWO POLITICAL PECULIARITIES distinguish Israel from many democratic states. First, it rests on a duality of being both a liberal democratic state under the rule of law and the homeland of one exclusive ethnic group that rules militarily over another ethnic group. Other states with separate ethnic groups have managed to reconcile this contradiction by creating separate polities and territories for the group segregated from the political system, but Israel has never systematically implemented such a system. Leaving the ethnic conflict unresolved fosters a coexistence of several civic incorporation regimes in one society or an *ethnocracy,* a regime motivated to maintain Jewish supremacy.[1] Second, Israel is a state whose geographic borders with Arab neighboring countries are unsettled and continuously contested. In fact, some scholars see in Israel's ongoing tendency to expand its borders a "spatial nationalism" and a constitutive element of the country's identity.[2] These two peculiarities are rooted in the early years of the Jewish-Palestinian conflict.

Since its founding in 1948, the state of Israel has developed policies to encourage Jewish reproduction, especially among Mizrahi Jews, based on concerns that Israel confronted a demographic imbalance in which the birthrate of its Palestinian population had increased while its Jewish population demonstrated a decrease in reproductive rates. These demographic trends were conceptualized as a threat to the national plan of establishing a Jewish state with a Jewish majority.[3]

Indeed, demographic enumeration and the question of the numerical ratio between Jews and Arabs were part of the political agenda of Mandatory Palestine in the early years of the twentieth century due to the presence of two national ethnic groups. Palestinian Arabs, the majority ethnic group in the country, posed an obstacle to Zionist ambitions to settle the country and dominate it. Establishing numerical superiority was of utmost importance and manifested in struggles over the numerical representation of each group through demographic enumeration, which was pursued in order to prove the economic capacity of the state to absorb massive immigration. Zionist leaders, headed by David Ben-Gurion, addressed this problem by promoting ongoing Jewish immigration that sought to tip the demographic balance between the two groups. Other leaders of the Yishuv challenged this ideology, arguing that the national conflict should be resolved by accepting the demographic composition of Palestine as given and avoiding intensive attempts to change it. This type of view was held by Chaim Weizmann, the president of the Zionist Confederation, who proposed an alternative approach of a binational state in Palestine. These two views represented two different emphases in the process of state building: the Ben-Gurion camp saw increasing the size of the Jewish *population* in Palestine as most important, while the Weizmann camp focused on the *territory* of Palestine as the state for both groups. Weizmann lost this battle and Ben-Gurion's approach became the ideological foundation of the policy of "population exchange" in the 1948 war.

One of Ben-Gurion's allies was Roberto Bachi, an Italian demographer who worked in Zionist institutions. As a social reformist and a distinguished scientist, his demographic studies and social plans were widely accepted by Yishuv leaders, especially his "political demography" approach. Bachi presented it as a comprehensive theory of demography as well as a methodology from which he drew a new understanding of political action through population management. His involvement in the Yishuv's political agenda occurred in two major interconnected areas: first, his advocacy of prenatal policies, which was connected to a nation-building strategy of achieving numerical dominance of the Jewish population in areas to be incorporated in the Jewish state, and, second, the development of ethnic distinctions within the Jewish population in order to track differential fertility and changing cultural features. Within his approach, at its first stage until the mid-1940s, Bachi used statistical practices of grouping and characterizing the "Mizrahi type" in order to locate the most fertile Jewish group in Palestine. Then, toward the late 1940s, in response to the One-Million Plan to bring mass Jewish immigration from Arab countries, Bachi shifted his focus from a concern about the quantity of Jews in Palestine to their quality. He transformed his agenda from increasing the numerical ratio of Palestinian Jews and Palestinian Arabs to conducting social research on characteristics of Mizrahim and suggesting social policies to control the shape of Israeli society in anticipation of mass Jewish immigration from Arab countries.[4] With his political demography approach, he provided a new understanding of the use of statistics to the local community by defining the problem of numerical imbalance in a fresh way: he raised the question of Jewish reproduction through the prism of probabilities and statistical research, which regrouped Jews in Palestine according to an intersection between reproduction rates and socioeconomic characteristics. Bachi was a credible scientist, a social reformist, and a Zionist technocrat—a unique figure who would later become head of Israel's Central Bureau of Statistics at the founding of the state in 1948. This, in addition to his connections with Yishuv leaders, made his demographic practices an "obligatory passage point" and helped establish Ben-Gurion's stance toward the national conflict.[5] Bachi's work was not instrumental or technical. His view of the demographic future of the country was intrinsically connected with a perceived threat to the homogeneity and quality of Jewish society and formulated the basis of a systematic paradigm of eugenics.[6]

I have argued that the consolidation of the Mizrahi type as part of state infrastructural categories of ethnicity took place in the prestate period, a decade before the arrival of mass immigration of Jews from Arab countries to Israel. Without Bachi's reworking of the popular category "Mizrahi" into a scientifically systematized category, this binary social epistemology could not be as strong and legitimate as it actually was.[7] In this chapter I consider population enumeration and demography as a political technology, which was deployed in efforts to triumph in the national conflict with Palestinian Arabs, as well as a plan of social engineering for a better preparedness toward an expected mass immigration.[8] As I show in the next section, the Israeli case resembles other countries in their nation-building processes: "demography" and "territory" were two different objects of official statistics in Europe during the nineteenth and early twentieth centuries. However, the emphasis on demography as a main national concern in Israel worked in a unique way: while enumerating "the population" as equal social or economic units is a performative action that deploys and employs a liberal view of society, Bachi's work helped to establish and systematize a deep ethnic split between two Jewish ethnic groups.

Analytical Perspective: Demography versus Territory

Mark Twain wrote in his autobiography: "Figures often beguile me, particularly when I have the arranging of them myself; in which case the remark attributed to Disraeli would often apply with justice and force: There are three kinds of lies: lies, damned lies, and statistics."[9] This famous line, which ascribes to statistics the status of lie, expresses a common distrust of statistical numbers as a credible form of representation, especially when they are produced by commercial companies, interest groups, political parties, not to mention governments. Official statistics are skeptically seen as shaped by partisan interests of different sectors and political groups. Therefore, they are far from being naïve and neutral. This general suspicion of "statistics" does not comprehend their power to categorize or grasp the depth of their implications. If numbers are powerful and lure us, then how deep is the influence of the infrastructure of classifications within which numbers are ordered? We neither "trust" nor "distrust" categories since we fail to see their fabrication as resulting from different kinds of processes. Once categories appear in official sites of states and their agencies, they usually become invisible. Yet, as social studies of statistics have shown, they are salient and constitutive.[10] As such, they become the apparatus within which numbers are stored. Assuming categories are the "host" of numbers, one can trace the trail of constructing official numbers in relation to their main object, which they aim to describe and represent. When we look at national statistics of states-in-the-making prior to their institutionalization and standardization, we can identify the main object of statistics as formulated by experts and statistical pioneers. Through this analytical prism we gain insights into the country's main object of concern.

The history of statistics describes its roots in dual traditions and practices. The first tradition is German, which emphasizes the political strength of the state or "matters of the state." The second one is British, which developed around population and its regularities.[11] The meaning of the German word *Statistik*, first used by Gottfried Achenwall in 1749, concerned the science of states. Its descriptive form included no reference to numbers; it was organized around four objects that expressed the idea of the power of the state: territory, population, products (economy), and administrative functions.[12] The British tradition of statistics evolved from below, a liberal spirit of reformists focused on describing the population.[13] This duality reflects two leading themes in the deployment of statistics and the object it represents—"state" or "society." Statistics as a scientific form of representation, its practices, and its knowledge, were co-constructed in historical processes of nation-state building.[14] Each country performed a different mode of representation. In some countries statistics described the state—territory, army, economic capacity and administration—while in others it depicted the population and its habits in such domains as hygiene, mortality, morbidity, crimes, and economic welfare.

The main object of state statistics as formulated by technocrats and statistical pioneers either focused on population or territory as constituting objects of the development of official statistics. Countries with conflicts between different ethnic groups intensified demographic practices. Others with high levels of regionalism based on geographical distinctiveness claimed a territory as a single national space in order to make it a "One and Indivisible Republic" on their way to becoming a sovereign political entity, as happened in post-Revolution France and Italy during the Risorgimento.[15] Both countries created a modern mapping of territory as an act of appropriation by the new elite that strengthened the centralized government.[16]

This chapter opens with a famous quotation of a petition from Brittany by people who connected civil rights with uniformity of measures: "We beg them [the king, his family, and his chief minister] to join with us in checking the abuses being perpetrated by tyrants against that class of citizens . . . and we call on the king to mete out justice, and we express our most sincere desire for but one king, one law, one weight, and one measure."[17] The unification of all measures, including people, and their standardization through projects of registrations, enumerations, surveys, and censuses of states in their making created a "standard grid" that can be recorded and monitored by the centralized state but also granted citizenship rights to their residents.[18] Historically, the cacophony of measurements, institutions, laws, and taxation was an obstacle in the way of France becoming one nation.[19] Unlike the French case in which the unification project promoted the concept of *national citizenship* as a single national and legible society, demographic practices in the Israeli case helped to establish a society with different levels of incorporation regimes.

Jewish Demographic Supremacy over a Binational Resolution

The pursuit of Jewish demography was perceived as crucial to the existence of the Jewish people as well as to Zionist goals.[20] Arthur Ruppin, a well-known Zionist leader, developed this field at the beginning of the twentieth century, first in Germany and then in Palestine.[21] His sudden death in 1943 stopped his sociodemographic study of the Jewish nation.[22] Prestate demography exerted significant political significance in determining boundaries of the Jewish population in Palestine through repetitive counting of all Jews in the Yishuv.[23] While Jewish demography was practiced regardless of any geographical borders, Zionist organizations during the period of the Yishuv provided evidence for the economic, cultural, and numerical superiority of Palestinian Jews over Palestinian Arabs. They used numbers to introduce the size of the Jewish community in Palestine to the western world as a justification for the establishment of a national home.[24] A controversy concerning the number of Jewish immigrants stimulated the British Mandate to scrutinize population movements and put special efforts into developing statistics for determining the *economic* capacity of the country.[25] In fact, however, through its colonies, Great Britain made a significant contribution to the development of vital statistics and other demographic features of the population.[26] In Palestine, the British Mandate conducted two censuses. The first, in 1922, right after its occupation of the Middle East, was part of the standard routine of British institutions to better facilitate their governance. The second census was conducted after the 1929 riots between Palestinian Arabs and Palestinian Jews and was carried out in order to determine the exact ethnic composition of the country and the size of the two national groups.[27]

Zionist organizations used surveys of different kinds to estimate the number of their members. For example, the Histadrut counted workers in order to define the working classes as well as to regulate the flow of workers from city to city.[28] The Histadrut (umbrella labor union) also reported strikes in detail as a means of indicating its power over employers and to increase its political influence and involvement in the Jewish community in Palestine. This activity also carried symbolic importance. Numbers reflected power and organizational governance.[29] In addition, Zionists often portrayed the size of the Jewish population in Palestine as a moral indication of the strength of the "nation." Many Zionist local leaders expressed awareness of Jewish numerical inferiority. For example, in their introduction to the 1918 census, conducted by the *Zionist Federation,* the editors were almost apologetic for Jewish numerical inferiority in Palestine: "thousands of Jews migrated to other countries; suffered from illness and died of hunger; these numbers therefore, represent merely remains of refugees."[30] Other leaders, such as Yitzhak Ben-Zvi, admitted the inescapable fact of Palestinian Arab demographic majority in Palestine and looked for ways to change this balance through political actions.

In 1936 an Arab revolt broke out in Palestine, followed by a long strike of Palestinian Arab laborers that lasted until 1939.[31] These years, considered to be a formative period for the birth of the Palestinian national movement, shaped the national conflict.[32] The Zionist leadership's commitment to consider demographic balance a pivotal aspect of the conflict, as well as their aim to dominate the country by solidifying a Jewish majority, intensified this struggle. An alternative option favored a binational solution that would freeze the ethnic ratio of Palestinian Jews and Palestinian Arabs of the Yishuv. This new version of a binational approach reflected the ideology of Brith Shalom. Formed in 1925, Brith Shalom articulated its ideology in reaction to the Arab revolt in 1929. Its supporters included major Jewish intellectuals such as Judah Magnes, Martin Buber, and Gershom Scholem, who opposed Ben-Gurion's supremacist approach. Although it faded by 1933, a second attempt to propose a binational solution reemerged at the beginning of the 1940s. Chaim Weizmann, whose views were clearly heard in the World Zionist Organization, communicated the need to limit Jewish immigration and strive toward recognition of the two nations' rightful claims to the land in order not to provoke additional battles.[33] But the pro-demographic superiority camp won the intra-Yishuv political conflict. And, eventually, belief in the necessity of Jewish demographic supremacy over the land became the ideological foundation for a policy of "population exchanges" in the 1948 war. Weizmann was marginalized from any political circles of power and dismissed from his presidency of the World Zionist Organization in 1946, while Ben-Gurion, with his demographic approach, became the first prime minister of the state.

Though Jewish demography, the enumeration of Jews in Palestine and around the world, was already an established practice at the beginning of the twentieth century, more professional statistical accounts in Israel started with the work of Roberto Bachi at the beginning of 1940s. The next section describes the efforts that Bachi and some of the Yishuv leaders creatively developed to increase Jewish reproduction as a means of nation building.

"A Failure to Fulfill a Minimum Quota of Children"

During the 1940s Bachi ran a campaign for making Jewish reproduction a visible and publicly discussed theme in Zionism's political agenda. Bachi thought that the existence of the Jewish nation depended upon high birthrates, but he also acknowledged the fact that this idea had not yet solidified in the Zionist leaders' thinking. He set himself the goal of alerting the Yishuv on this subject and making it part of Zionist ideology by working on two levels: bringing to public awareness the idea that the nation's endurance should be the concern of every Jewish resident in the country, while developing social policies that would strengthen the size of the local Jewish community. To promote this goal, he wrote in one of his pamphlets, sent to leaders in the Yishuv, that the Zionist organizations should be engaged in social welfare policies aimed at increasing Jewish reproduction.[34] He employed the term "political demography" to emphasize the existential implications, on top of the political ones, of what he saw in a demographic prognosis of decreased Jewish reproduction.[35] As early as 1942 he had warned politicians and the public of a potential disaster and argued that the actual existence of the nation was conditional upon the size of the Jewish community in the country:

> If a fundamental change will not take place in the demographic process, the existence of our nation in Palestine is in a great danger. Indeed, the Land of Israel absorbed immigration in the past and is going to absorb mass immigration in the future, but the critical point of the revival of our nation in this Land should be through natural reproduction (i.e., "internal immigration") ... if we want the valuable [Zionist] projects, which were created with great efforts in the last 60 years to remain in faithful hands, we should protect the future of our Yishuv by sufficient reproductive rates.[36]

Only an increase in the reproductive capacity of the Yishuv could strengthen the nation in pursuing its goals, argued Bachi. Reproduction was not a private matter; human conduct was a political task that should be managed by Zionist ideology:

Some think that the fertility rates is a private matter and if the individual has no interest in carrying the burden of a family there is no need to change the situation [the individual's position] with moral propaganda. . . . I think differently. Indeed, I do not believe that a sudden revolution in fertility rates can happen only as a result of propaganda, but it seems that in a country that was built mainly on the foundation of the pioneering efforts of those who sacrificed themselves for the rebirth of the nation in its land, we must not be skeptical and think that society has no ability to influence the individual.[37]

Moreover, Bachi asserted, objections against the intervention of "society" in matters such as reproduction, which belong exclusively to the private sphere, resembled those heard one hundred years ago against state regulations concerning employer-employee relations or when society began to intervene in family life for the sake of public hygiene. "Yes, society has the option and the right to intervene in the question of reproduction to prevent the anarchic deed of the individual, which will likely destroy the construction of our country that was built with tremendous efforts," he wrote.[38] Bachi perceived his demand for more children as an ideological imperative rather than something to be forced by the state. Yet, Bachi also suggested policies aimed at institutionalizing this imperative through legislation and regulations of prestate Zionist institutions, which were accepted by the Jewish public. After 1948, demographic reproduction would become a political mission via daycare, tax credits, and child support.

Ben-Gurion may be the most well-known spokesperson for constructing the female body as a national womb, but Bachi was the one who informed Ben-Gurion by giving him data on this issue. In 1943, Ben-Gurion was surprised to find out that low birthrates were located at the very heart of the Zionist movement—in the kibbutzim.[39] During a discussion about a severe shortage of labor in the kibbutzim held at a meeting of his political party, he gave a speech in which he cited the "experts" who supplied him with data about Jewish birthrates and claimed very enthusiastically and with his well-known charisma, the following collectivist argument:

We need to demand from the female and male members [of the kibbutzim] that they fulfill a minimum quota of children. I do not suggest legalizing it in the Histadrut [umbrella labor union] constitution. The most important, significant, and difficult things we have been doing, and that we are still doing, are not written in any article of a constitution, but with our moral and ideological consciousness we demand of ourselves to do them. . . . Every couple needs to know and feel that if they fail to fulfill this norm, they have not done their duty to themselves, to society, to the nation, to the movement and to the new life we would like to create here.[40]

Ben-Gurion's speech referred not to reproduction in the entire nation; it only referenced the kibbutzim, a closed and homogeneous political group whose members originated mainly from central and Eastern Europe. In those years the population of the kibbutzim formed the local elite: groups of Zionist pioneers who arrived from Eastern Europe at the beginning of the twentieth century. These ideologically committed men and women founded collective agricultural settlements to fulfill the Zionist enterprise of "building the Land and being built up in the Land." The next part of his speech emphasizes this distinction:

> We cannot always obtain assistance from other mothers. We will not act in the same way as the voracious capitalist that hires for himself the stomach of a beggar to digest the delights he greedily and continuously eats. We will not hire or "draft" other mothers to nurture their children in anguish so that we can use them to root out potatoes from our gardens.[41]

In his speech, Ben-Gurion was referring to Bachi's study of patterns of marriage and reproduction among different groups in the Yishuv.[42] There Bachi acknowledged differences in birthrates between Mizrahim and Ashkenazim. Bachi, not Ben-Gurion, used an ethnic dichotomy. Ben-Gurion had a different view of the human composition of the Yishuv. He considered the population of the kibbutzim as his own group, which did not need to be ethnically categorized under the dichotomous category of Ashkenazim (Jews with ethnic origins in western European countries as distinguished from Mizrahim with ethnic origins in North African and Middle Eastern countries). For him, they were male and female comrades, literally "members" of the "group," or the *kvutza,* the original name for kibbutz. Mizrahi mothers were "other" mothers who had a higher quantitative potential of delivering children, but they were members of neither the Zionist movement nor the Zionist settlements; therefore, their children would not be the desirable future generation. "We plan to live here more than one or two decades," asserted Ben-Gurion. "We are not refugees; we have no intention to go back after the war [World War II] to Germany or to 'emancipated' Poland, not even to Soviet Russia . . . [therefore], we require youth of our own, children of the guys and girls of our groups. . . ."[43] Clearly, the "we" refers to no other than the pioneers who emigrated from eastern and central Europe. Yemenite or Kurdish Jews, for example, were not part of this "we."

In 1944, Bachi met with Ben-Gurion to provide an account of the decline in the Jewish birthrates of the Yishuv and the diaspora, as well as the birthrate among Arabs in Palestine. Ben-Gurion seemed to be interested, though not fully aware of the problem,[44] and promised to take care of the issue and bring it to the executive body of the Jewish Agency.[45] Following this meeting, Bachi wrote a report, *The Demographic Development of Jews and Arabs in the Land of Israel,* and sent it to Ben-Gurion with copies to the most important Zionist leaders of the Yishuv: Eliezer Kaplan, Moshe Shertok, Dr. Avraham Katznelson,[46] and Chaim Weizmann.[47] Despite Ben-Gurion's enthusiasm when speaking about the subject in a closed political meeting, in 1944 he felt no urgency to extend this message to the entire Yishuv.[48] Ben-Gurion refused to participate in a conference intended to encourage reproduction because he did not want to be directly associated with this subject or to be addressed by people's requests for privileges. He also had doubts as to his ability "to do something for the sake of the important matter that is so close to your [Bachi's] heart."[49]

Hence, the idea and initiative for politicizing reproduction and making it part of official policy was not Ben-Gurion's at all. Most of the pro-natal campaign was managed in cooperation with the Committee for Encouraging Internal Reproduction, whose members came from local Zionist organizations. With the support of this committee, Bachi delivered lectures all over the country and wrote articles, mainly in the popular media. He titled the campaign "Against the Only-Child Family." Bachi attended numerous meetings of different committees, some with top leaders of the Yishuv,[50] conferred with delegations, and addressed the issue in meetings of communal settlements. He ran the campaign as a show to entertain the public: Bachi initiated public trials in the three major cities of Jerusalem, Tel Aviv, and Haifa. Conducted with the participation of the national committee, these trials aimed to provoke public opinion about the decreased reproduction rates.[51] At the center of the trial stood a mother of an only child, accused of four crimes: (1) having an abortion due to economic considerations, (2) endangering the existence of the future of the Jewish nation in general, (3) putting the existence of the Yishuv at risk, and (4) damaging her only child by making him lonely. An impresario managed these trials, which were widely reported in the Hebrew daily newspapers of the time. Expert witnesses such as pediatricians, an economist, a rabbi, a housing clerk, and a teacher gave their testimony, in addition to parents who were put on trial.

The first witness, who offered a very long expert testimony, was none other than Bachi. His testimony filled eight pages in which he raised two major arguments. First, he stressed the need to encourage "internal immigration," his term for reproduction, and not *Aliyah* (external immigration by Jews), based on his assumption that the source of future immigration would be from Asia and Africa, hence putting in question its quality.[52] Second, the demographic imbalance between Arabs and Jews in Palestine became an urgent problem since not only did "our neighbours" have higher rates of reproduction, but they had lower mortality rates in those few years. This strengthened the demographic threat of the Arab population on the Zionist state.

Bachi offered a conceptual framework for thinking about alternative solutions to the "demographic problem." He translated general political concern about the "demographic balance" into a scientific object of investigation by characterizing the ethnic and national groups in Palestine according to their different stages of social development, forming a theory of modernization, and laying down the foundation for predictions about infant births and mortality. The Palestinian Arabs, according to his analysis, were in a stage where they suffered less from infant mortality but, at the same time, their birthrates did not drop as had happened with European groups in the nineteenth century. "Prevailing primitive ways of life, associated in many cases with a strong desire for children," he wrote, "bring fertility to a very high level."[53] This was his explanation for the imbalance. Increased rates of fertility, for instance, were not only higher than European populations during the nineteenth century, argued Bachi, but also higher than those of other Muslim populations. Thus, he predicted that the Palestinian Muslim population would reach a million and a half by 1960.

Bachi also mapped the geographical areas in which demographic growth exceeded the average. At the time of writing these predictions, in 1946, the Jewish population was 600,000,[54] one-third of the total population in Palestine. The natural tendency of the two groups, Palestinians Arabs and Jews, worked against the development of the Yishuv becoming an independent Jewish state. His numerical predictions expressed political pessimism:

> According to the current demographic situation, 1,000 Jews entering the age of fertility will have 1,065.5 children; those will eventually reach the age of fertility, too. At the same time, 1,000 Muslims will give birth to 2,287 children with reproductive capability. In other words, the fertility of Jews is sufficient only to cover Jewish mortality, while the fertility of Muslims in Palestine multiplies their number by 2.3 in the short period of one generation.[55]

Bachi perceived the demographic balance as a competition between the two nations, which would be resolved either by Jewish mass immigration or by lowering the Arabs' reproductive capacity. He thought that success depended on the question of what the Zionist leadership would be willing to do in order to change this balance in favor of Jews.[56] In his view, talking about increasing Jewish reproductive rates was not sufficient; change also required the institutionalization of practices to be conducted by agencies of the yet-to-be-born state. In 1948, several years after he started his campaign against the only-child family and just before the Declaration of Independence in May, Bachi articulated his vision regarding the state's role in encouraging reproduction. It illuminates his actions in hindsight since the beginning of the 1940s. "In order to establish a reproduction regime," he observed, "we need to place the care for increased reproduction and multiple-child families as a cornerstone of Zionist policy. This is the enduring function of the state as well as of our central and local organizations."[57]

In 1944 Bachi recruited the national committee, the formal government of the Yishuv, to endorse reproduction.[58] By the end of that year, he submitted to the committee a general plan with suggestions for political demography.[59] A year later the committee published a summary of its activities in which it claimed that

Bachi was the one who continuously drew Ben-Gurion's attention to the subject. Later, the committee announced its social program, titled "The Politics of Endorsing Internal Immigration," whose objective was to invigorate the Yishuv through more reproduction. It was based on three of Bachi's publications and on several memoranda he wrote during his work with the committee on policies that should be taken up by the Zionist organization.[60] The program included several steps.

First, Bachi suggested establishing a trust fund to help large families and increasing workers' salaries with the birth of every new child. The mechanism for allocating money was interesting: it would not be given directly through the workplace to each new parent, but, instead, a special institution would tax workers, regardless of their marital status, as well as employers, and collect this money as insurance for the time the worker would become a parent. In addition, Zionist organizations would add their own money to strengthen this resource. When a worker expanded his family, he would be eligible for financial child support.[61] This proposal was legalized after 1948, and while it suffers from constant threat of budget cuts, it remains one of Israel's social welfare institutions. Bachi's second suggestion involved helping large families in various ways: by giving the father of such a family preference in employment and obtaining loans; reducing payments for social, educational, and health services; and canceling tuition for elementary school for families with three or more children. These families would be eligible for public housing and financial support to pay their mortgage. Employers would have to create a half-time job for women who were mothers of several children. Also, hospitals would send new mothers to special postnatal convalescent homes for a week or two. The committee's plan also included a budget. This comprehensive social program would later constitute the basis for the new state's social welfare policy.

Bachi's work toward a pro-natal plan also characterized the different groups in the Yishuv with different patterns of reproduction. This work led him to create a more systematized classification of these groups.

A Partition Plan for Solving Numerical Inferiority

During his first years in Palestine, Bachi saw Mizrahi families as a possible solution to his political ambition to increase the ratio of Jews to Arabs. His prenatal campaign aimed at making the political leaders as well as the Ashkenazi public aware of the need to raise birthrates in general. In the postwar years, when the Yishuv leadership had to withdraw a plan of bringing one million immigrants from Europe and replace it with immigrants from Muslim countries,[62] Bachi shifted his focus from calculating birth probabilities to making recommendations for "managing" the Mizrahi population. He feared that high rates of reproduction by Mizrahim would change the "face" of the country and its Jewish society. In scientific language Bachi warned of a cultural threat through demography.

Explanations of the increased fertility of Mizrahim resulting from a younger marriage age and a shorter interval between each child, failed as an explanation when reproduction rates were compared to European Jewish women whose husbands are white-collar or academic professionals. The methodological rule of *ceteris paribus,* all other things being equal, did not apply when the two groups are so different. As in the nineteenth century, the apparent equality of statistical categories—which has replaced the old social statuses, such as class, family, and religion, with objective and scientific categorization—simultaneously permitted the measurement of deviant groups that behaved differently from the "average man" or the "statistical man." Such individuals were measured as equal but then regrouped and redefined scientifically as a "social problem."[63] The practice of regrouping signified the rise of the "social question" as Mitchell Hart has shown in chapter 4 of this volume.[64]

Clearly, conceptions of a politics of demography were interwoven with envisioning the future state. Adding to Bachi's intensive involvement in committees, meetings, public trials, lectures, radio broadcasts, and other public performances in the matter of Jewish internal immigration, his writings about the political consequences of the balance between the two national groups support the argument that he viewed the demographic profile of Jews as intrinsically related to the national conflict and therefore, as an inseparable part of the process of nation building and state formation:

> The numerical balance between Jews and non-Jews is influenced not only by the size of future immigration, but to a very considerable extent, by the reproductive capacity of the Arab and Jewish populations. For the time being, there is a very big difference between the size of the Arab and Jewish family and the "true" rate of natural increase of the two populations. A wise and firm Jewish demographic policy may prevent this difference from becoming larger in the future and may even reduce it. . . . It would, however, be blindness on the part of the Zionist movement, not to see the consequences of the fact that, within the same political framework there are at present two populations—the larger group, which has an increased natural rate of reproduction, and exceeded the smaller group [with low rates of reproduction].[65]

In a section labeled "Political Conclusions," Bachi analyzed the state of reproduction rates among Jews and Arabs. It is written as instructions for state building based on scientific predictions that portray the nature of the state in the future. It also discusses at length the issue of what would solve the problem of demographic balance.[66] Bachi suggested a comprehensive plan as a solution to the numerical ratio between Palestinian Arabs and Jews in the territory of Palestine. Although some of his suggestions had already been articulated by other leaders of the Yishuv, unique in Bachi's plan was its basis on geostatistical calculations reflected coherently and clearly in public discussions.[67] Bachi did not only echo these options but also helped to put them on the public agenda.

The first option was to establish a binational legal entity, a confederation that would give both peoples the same rights, regardless of being from the minority or majority group. Given the fact that Jews were more advanced from an economic, social, and cultural point of view, added Bachi, it would prevent them from developing a "minority complex" as a result of their numerical inferiority. This option suggests refraining from the struggle for Jewish supremacy through external immigration. The second suggestion was even more extreme in terms of options that were conceived as legitimate in those days: a democratic Palestinian state of Jews and Arabs. The state would become Jewish when Jews reached the majority. Bachi disapproved of this second option and thought that the free play of birthrates would not work in the interest of Jews. The future Jewish state, he asserted, would need at least one million external immigrants to obtain a Jewish majority, though even this would be by a narrow margin and probably for a short time only.

The third suggestion to make a Jewish majority in Palestine a certain and grounded fact was to partition the country. Bachi's plan included far-reaching steps toward that goal. Since the aim of Zionism would be to create a Jewish state, with a substantial Jewish majority, and since solutions based on a binational state were not acceptable, a partition plan would be the most reasonable way to resolve the political problem. It could be realistic only under three conditions:

> (i) that it *takes out* from the future Jewish State a substantial part of the Arab population; (ii) that the present process of attracting the surplus of the Arab population from the internal hills to the coastal plain (Jewish State) is *interrupted,* and that the surplus of the Arab population in the internal hills is encouraged to settle in other regions; (iii) that a "reserve" of land for the future development of the Jewish population is kept as far as possible in regions where the Arab population is not dense (e.g. the Negev [the southern desert of Palestine] or part of the Jordan Valley, etc.). (Emphasis added)[68]

The last part of Bachi's program is a political plan of ethnic cleansing, a purification of part of the country of Palestinian Arabs. Although Bachi's main concern in this document is proliferation of the Palestinian population, the areas Bachi suggested as potential territory for settling future Jewish immigrants (especially from Muslim countries) also included sections that geographically bordered the northern and the southern parts of the country. Almost a decade after this document was written, newly arrived Mizrahim were settled in these underdeveloped areas or in cities abandoned by Palestinian Arabs who were ex-pelled from or fled the country—cities such as Lod and Ramleh. This settlement policy created the political, social, and economic periphery of the country.

Additional evidence for the claim that this program was not only to be ap-plied to Palestinians but also to future immigration of Mizrahim comes from the fact that this supremacist solution was conditioned by a fourth recommendation: Bachi urged paying attention to the "oriental" communities of the Yishuv since their numerical ratio was about to increase. But this attention, he urged, "should follow organic principles. It should not choose the way of philanthropy or so-cial assistance, but that of social reconstruction, in order to eliminate the vicious circle of chronic poverty renewing itself generation after generation."[69]

Political demography, therefore, was not only a technology of governing so-ciety; it was a very basic science for planning the new state and establishing offi-cial social policy toward the population. Only a few years later, after 1948, Zionist leaders explicitly translated political demography into the notion of seeing the Mizrahi woman as the "national womb." Bachi's conception of political demog-raphy was directly associated in public with concerns about the demographic numerical ratio between Jewish members of the Yishuv and Palestinian Arabs living in Palestine, yet the Against the Only-Child campaign showed that the context was wider and included birthrates among different groups within the local Jewish community. This national concern about indigenous Palestinian Ar-abs increased in 1948 and facilitated such practices toward Palestinians as their exclusion from citizenship through the first census. Thus, political demography had dealt with the two inseparable themes of encouraging internal immigration of Jews as part of nation building and keeping Palestinian Arabs a minority as part of state formation.

Moving from Quantity to Quality

While ethnic classifications were widely used by bureaus of statistics after World War II, and Bachi understood that the science of populations can contribute to the "national enterprise" through identifying reproductive regularities, it was considered unacceptable to sort the Jewish population in Palestine according to inner ethnic divisions during the prestate years. Grouping and classifying Jews according to their ethnic origins was perceived as emphasizing inner ethnic divi-sions of Jews in Mandatory Palestine. It was "viewed as a product of the long term dispersal of the Jewish people in the Diaspora."[70] According to a central impera-tive in Zionist ideology, "Return to the Homeland" involves creation of the "New Jew," the "Sabra," liberated from the culture and psychology of exile. Overcom-ing the old habits of one's country of origin was the Israeli Jews' source of le-gitimate identity.[71] Therefore, naming and characterizing "ethnicity" accentuated differences rather than cohesion and solidarity. Schools inculcated this ideology of ignoring ethnic differences among Jews.

In 1944 in a memorandum addressed to Ben-Gurion, Shertok, Katznelson, and Weizmann, the political leadership at the time, Bachi reiterated his awareness of the need to comply with this ideological imperative. At the same time, he challenged it by suggesting the necessity for coexistence between Zionist ideology and demographic observation about the natural character of Mizrahim:

> The theoretically beautiful position that we are all Jews and do not acknowledge the existence of ethnic groups, a recognition that led us to manage our own social, economic and educational affairs according to unified standards for all the ethnic groups, means, in many cases, neglecting the *real* needs of these ethnic groups, or pushing the Mizrahim into directions that do not fit their *natural* character. (Emphasis added)[72]

Categorizing ethnicity was not a simple task of looking for regularities among coherent social groups that seemed to be a "law of nature." There existed no stable, clear demographic object to observe and measure. Bachi dealt with a phenomenon whose definition and coherence were yet to be constructed, as he reported in hindsight: "the irregularity and changing structure of the population; the heterogeneity of the social structure of the Jewish population which renders of little value the use of 'general average' for the entire Yishuv; the lack of any complete census of population after 1931, and the consequent necessity of using estimates of population which become more and more unreliable with the elapse of time . . . ,"[73] all made the scientific and systematic research of the Jewish population necessary.[74]

Tensions between Zionist ideology and the diversity of the emerging new society was resolved through a particular objective category of ethnicity limited by time: "place of birth." This is a temporal category since place of birth applies only to the first generation of Israeli Jews, and father's place of birth applies only for the second generation; by the third generation this category was supposed to disappear.[75] Place of birth reconciled discrepancies between official Zionist ideology, which moved toward rejecting classification of ethnicity, and a desire to study differences between Jewish groups. Moreover, place of birth not only solved the contradiction between Zionism and constructing ethnicity, it also served as a category that replaced "race" for Mizrahim, who were visible Jewish minorities in Palestine.

Bachi did his first demographic research in Palestine on the birthrates of women from Haifa and Jerusalem, based on 40,000 cases of infant mortality and live births collected in the 1938 British census.[76] In his analysis he found that the ratio between the two cities was almost double (1:1.77), which he interpreted as caused by the fact that most women in Haifa were born in Europe, while Jerusalem was populated by the old Sephardic Jewish Yishuv. A few years later, Bachi divided this data set into three independent variables of mother's birthplace, father's occupation, and residence. With these variables Bachi demonstrated that the number of births correlated with the country of origin (divided into two major groups of Asia-Africa and Europe-America), place of residence, and occupational status. This early work reveals Bachi's innovative conceptualization of geostatistics, as well as his sociological view regarding the correlation between occupational status and country of origin. In a lecture he delivered to gynecologists in 1944 he explained the logic behind the ethnic classification and argued that when making comparisons to the "average family," the population of Hebrew women in Eretz Israel was divided into three major types: Asian, European, and local Israeli woman. This was due to the exceptional variability among Jewish women in Mandatory Palestine, whose birthrates could not be measured and studied as a coherent group.

As noted at the beginning of the chapter, the categories Ashkenazim and Mizrahim or Sephardim derived in part from long-established religious and cultural traditions, including language (Yiddish versus Ladino or Judeo-Arabic). But Bachi gave these categories a wider meaning that referred to social, cultural, and economic aspects of people's lives. He used additional indicators to determine distinctiveness of these two groups beyond language, religion, and cultural traditions; he added biological traits, geographical location, education, and hygiene.[77]

Bachi strove to describe a coherent statistical object. In this task, revealing the natural number of births would enable the statistician to account for the biological distinctiveness of Mizrahim. Assuming controls for social and cultural interventions, the natural number of birthrates would be displayed. In other words, if fertility among Jews of European descent was "natural," according to Bachi, a woman could deliver as many as five or six children. But statistics showed that reality was very far from this prediction; the average fertility of a European Jewish woman was 1.7 children.[78]

Bachi's demographic accounts also examined the correlation between hygiene and sanitary conditions and infant mortality among Mizrahim.[79] He based his analysis on identifying the demographic stage of Mizrahim as similar to the stage of the European nations at the beginning of the Industrial Revolution during the transition to an urban economy. Bachi then applied this teleological reasoning to each group he was studying: Muslims, Jews in the diaspora, Mizrahim, Ashkenazim, and Sephardim. Generally speaking, claimed Bachi, the first stage occurs in the eighteenth century when scientific progress as well as the advancement of medicine and hygiene still had no significant effect on sanitary conditions among the population, with no decrease in the level of morbidity. The next stage occurs in the nineteenth century, when scientific advancement and the reorganization of hygiene and medicine caused a great decline in infant and child mortality. While in the third stage fertility started to fall for reasons that were not entirely clear, in the fourth stage morbidity almost stops and fertility drops considerably to a point where natural reproduction rates become negative, meaning, in every new generation, fewer children are born. How did this apply to the groups in Israel-Palestine?

The argument about the need to trace demographic trends related to the actual existence of the Jewish nation in its own homeland: "It is our desire and in our capability to create a social structure that will contain the capacity for self-preservation," Bachi contended.[80] The presence of Jewish groups and their reproductive rates, he maintained, create the capacity to build a state. His idea that the Jewish Yishuv in Palestine has the "capability to create a social structure"[81] is interesting, since Bachi viewed the social structure as emerging from state policy, whereas sociologists usually think of social *structure* as a given, out of which the state arises. This causality is not imaginary. It was, in fact, a main component of Zionist ideology. But, at the same time, it added a component that treated demography not only as a technology of knowing but also as a technology of making a new society. Moreover, concern about the ability to create a social structure for the new state was neither abstract nor focused on levels of Jewish reproduction. Mainly, Bachi worried about the quality of future generations conditioned by which group would contribute more to the demographic growth of the Jewish community in Palestine. In this contest, he contrasted Mizrahim with Ashkenazim:

> In spite of the rapid movement of the Mizrahim's amalgamation into the European groups, we cannot ignore the fact that the Mizrahi community still greatly contributes to the reproduction of the entire Yishuv. This contribution facilitates the declining of the general [demographic] deficit; but, on the other hand, it can also cause a significant change in the *quality* of our community's composition. (Emphasis added)[82]

Bachi presented "society" as a problem due to its problematic groups; his solution was to make all aspects of society legible through statistics, by offering a technology to know these groups. In a lecture on the "demographic problem" a year before the establishment of the state, Bachi delivered a provocative analysis, based on eugenics, to an audience of health workers:

> A few years ago, in a time when the Jewish birth rates of our community were low, I calculated what the demographic consequences would be of the natural reproduction of two extreme groups of Mizrahim and Ashkenazim. For example, if we compare Austrian and Yemenite women, we would get the following: 100 Austrian mothers will have 60 daughters . . . and 100 Yemenite mothers will give birth to 300 daughters who will take their place in the next

generation. We could calculate what the consequences would be of their natural reproduction in the generation of their granddaughters: 100 Yemenite women will have 900 granddaughters, while the Austrians will have only 33. These are, of course, extreme groups.[83]

Clearly, this analysis represents a eugenic attitude common in those days, and it accompanied the Zionist ideology of other leaders and social scientists. Bachi's scientific numerical predictions, which had never before been so systematically presented in Palestine by any professional, provided an instrumental framework to understand the complexity of the demographic problem between Jews and Palestinian Arabs as it intersected with a threat to the homogeneity and quality of Jewish society. This case resonates in similarity to the dispute between Yule and Pearson at the turn of the nineteenth century in which Pearson's statistical techniques were technical means for solving a problem conceived only in relation to a political project of elite social reform and eugenics. Pearson's statistical approach was perceived as a "prediction or problem solution which partially define the situated instrumental knowledge-constituting interests of the scientists."[84] More specifically:

> Eugenic problems and concerns were, in turn, significant foci of scientific activity, and central to the biometrical enterprise, because they were sustained by general social interests. Eugenics was at this time an important ideological strand in a body of thought closely associated with the rising professional middle class.[85]

Bachi's lecture raises another critical concern: the process of dichotomizing two groups, negating one by the other, making one a dark reflection of the other. By opposing one group to the other as two extreme examples of Mizrahim and Ashkenazim, Bachi created a dichotomy to represent the "great divide" between two "pure" and opposite types of social groups of Israeli-Jewish society. Moreover, by using probability, he anticipated future demographic tendencies, which would have an impact on the quality of society and, therefore, require social intervention. Later in the article Bachi discusses the differences between the two ethnic groups in a more comprehensive way, constructing Mizrahim as the major object of statistical inquiry, as well as of other disciplines.

Here is an example how his statistical logic operates: "While Ashkenazim have one bed per person on average, the Kurds and Sephardim have one bed for 2.5 persons on average." He continues in this vein: "Ashkenazim have on average one window per person, while the Persians and Kurds have one window per four persons," before concluding, "Sephardim have a 54% level of good hygiene, while Ashkenazim have 98%."[86] The same goes with the possession of a bathtub, water, and electricity, indices on which Mizrahi households were measured in comparison with Ashkenazim. Here we can see how quantification objectified the Mizrahi as a statistical category. They are no longer described with adjectives but have become a measurable object. However, the Ashkenazim were not really measured. Instead they signified the relationship between the normal and the deviant. "It is clear," concluded Bachi based on these examples, "that if we want to have any idea of the sociological profile of our community in the next few years, we have to have a special interest in the social problems of the Oriental Ethnic Group [*edot hamizrakh*], of Mizrahim."[87]

Discussing the proliferation of Mizrahim could have been reasonable if their ratio in the population was high. However, the ratio of Mizrahim in the population before 1948 was actually very small: between 1919 and 1948 they comprised only 10 percent of the total Jewish immigration. Not until after the establishment of the state did their percentage grow. From 1948 to 1951, the first three years of the new state, they increased to 50 percent of Jewish immigrants, and in the years 1952 to 1954 the ratio soared to 76 percent of total Jewish immigrants.[88] Why, then, did Bachi bother with such calculations and predictions in the prestate years?

With the development of statistics and corresponding numerical representation of "society," statistical practices signified the distinction between traditional and modern society and replaced the old social order with a new one by giving people new and equal positions in the social configuration.[89] The last point refers to the identification of statistics with values such as democracy and equality, that is, that statistical counting transforms human beings into homogeneous units with a common denominator. Each unit (individual) is equal to others and, hence, cannot have privileges over others. By signifying the individual with numbers, he or she becomes unmarked and has the same social importance as others from different classes.[90] This is an apparent equality. The replacement of the old social statuses, such as class, family, and religion, with objective and scientific categorization, simultaneously permitted the measurement of deviant groups that behave differently from the "average man" or the "statistical man." Those individuals ostensibly identified as equal were subsequently regrouped and redefined scientifically as a "social problem."[91] Thus, the modern method of classification has become a legitimate method of labeling.[92] In the Israeli case, however, statistics was not only means of counting and identifying; it was also a means of establishing inequality.

Roberto Bachi—A Social Reformist

At first, the enormous efforts Bachi invested in making demography an urgent issue on the national agenda had no impact. Naturally, the pressing need for rescuing refugees from the clutches of the Nazis to bring them to the haven of Eretz Israel-Palestine exerted a more dramatic appeal than dry graphs showing the need for healthy Palestinian Jewish immigrants (internal immigration of Jews who live in Palestine).[93] Toward 1944, however, his efforts succeeded and his proactive approach was recognized as pioneering by Zionist leaders. Delivering Jewish children became a well-addressed theme in the newspapers, theaters, and public discussions: "Babies. Everyone is having babies. . . . We've stopped taking anything into account. We don't dare. The Va'ad Leumi edict—it's in the air."[94]

Was this a one-time work of an enthusiastic scientist? Bachi's demographic enterprise during the prestate years would influence the epistemology of Israeli society for many generations to come. In January 1948 he was nominated to establish the Israeli Central Bureau of Statistics, a state institution that he led until 1972. As chief statistician, Bachi embedded his dichotomist view of the Jewish ethnic grouping—Asia/Africa versus America/Europe origins—in state infrastructure of statistical classifications. Moreover, Bachi was not a "lone actor." He worked through a diverse network of politicians of different levels of seniority as well as medical doctors and nurses who were all enrolled in the only-child family project, people interested in birthrates and population management practices. On the national level, he provided numerical data to Ben-Gurion on a regular basis and presented his calculus in numerous public activities and political and professional committees. His work at Hadassah Hospital, assessing probabilities and correlating variables, related to reformist practices of studying and diagnosing certain populations and intervening in their hygiene habits. His classifications traveled well beyond Hadassah's projects, which were subsequently assembled into his network.

Bachi's statistical work offered a comprehensive epistemological tool to identify an essential ethnic group by intersecting ethnicity with the "national demographic problem." His acts of persuasion with main leaders of the Yishuv involved translating national concerns through scientific practices. Bachi's success related to his ability to provide a new way of understanding the *present* in terms of the *future*. His numerical predictions on the nature of the development of the population made statistics and demography a necessary technology, indispensable for public policy and social planning. Demography in those prestate years offered a technology for imagining an unknown future when one million immigrants of Mizrahim stood at the country's doorstep, threatening to change its profile.

Lastly, most readers would see the divide between Jewish and Arab Palestinians as construed by demographic statistics as obviously relevant to the political narrative of state building, whereas my dissection of Jews into subgroups complicates that simplistic divide. The Zionist enterprise was articulated through demographic practices of population management, but these demographic practices also helped to shape Zionist ideology into one of internal colonialism. Zionism was not only a project of "white settlers" who colonized the country and its indigenous Arab population; it also colonized its own population of Mizrahi Jews. Political demography mobilized not only in relation to the national competitors, but it also aimed at describing Jewish society. Practices such as constructing demographic regularities of weak populations, all developed during the nineteenth century, brought "society" into being, that is, brought to the public's awareness the existence of an entity that is larger than the small communities where people lived.[95] The different practices in which Bachi was engaged during the prestate period portrayed society with the intention of making social reforms possible. His work in the Hadassah Medical Organization's Bureau of Medical Statistics nurtured reformist projects with personnel that included nurses, epidemiologists, and social workers.

For Bachi, as well as for nineteenth-century reformers, only the depiction of society and its groups could reveal statistical regularities and open the way for social reforms, social intervention, and social engineering. The same aspect of the development of statistics during the nineteenth century and in Israel in the prestate period was also used to measure deviant groups by documenting rates of suicides, crimes, poor education, poverty, and disease. While the duality of the new technology of social intervention helped to improve human conditions, it expressed a paternalistic point of view. The conditions under which a "social law" was formulated could be changed by the intervention of the benevolent class, even as it marked the distance between observers and observed.[96]

Notes

I would like to thank the editors of this volume, Michal Kravel-Tovi and Deborah Dash Moore, for their invitation to present my work in an insightful workshop on Jewish numbers at the Frankel Center for Judaic Studies, University of Michigan, and for their valuable comments on this chapter. My thanks are also to two anonymous readers for their useful reviews. Part of the empirical data presented in this chapter was already published in the journal *Social Studies of Science* (2014): 271–292.

1. On civic incorporation regimes, see Gershon Shafir and Yoav Peled, *Being Israeli: The Dynamics of Multiple Citizenship* (Cambridge: Cambridge University Press, 2002). On ethnocracy and spatial nationalism, see Yoav Peled, "Ethnic Democracy and the Legal Construction of Citizenship: Arab Citizens of the Jewish State," *American Political Science Review* 86, no. 2 (1992): 432–443; and Oren Yiftachel, "'Ethnocracy': The Politics of Judaizing Israel/Palestine," *Constellations* 6, no. 2 (1999): 364–390.

2. For spatial nationalism, see Adriana Kemp, "Labour Migration and Racialisation: Labour Market Mechanisms and Labour Migration Control Policies in Israel," *Social Identities* 10, no. 2 (2004): 267–292; and Ariella Azoulay and Adi Ophir, *The One-State Condition: Occupation and Democracy in Israel/Palestine* (Stanford, CA: Stanford University Press, 2012).

3. Calvin Goldscheider, "Demographic Transformations in Israel: Emerging Themes in Comparative Context," in *Population and Social Change in Israel,* ed. Calvin Goldscheider (Boulder, CO: Westview, 1992), 1–36; Shoham Melamed, "Motherhood, Fertility, and the

Construction of the 'Demographic Threat' in the Marital Age Law," *Theory and Criticism* 25 (2004): 69–96; Jacqueline Portugese, *Fertility Policy in Israel: The Politics of Religion, Gender, and Nation* (Westport, CT: Praeger, 1998); and Nira Yuval-Davis, *Woman-Nation-State* (Basingstoke, UK: Macmillan, 1989).

4. Though this chapter is not about the etymology of ethnic wordings, a clarification is required: the popular category Sephardim, or Edot Hamizrah, was commonly used by social agents and scientists as well as the general public since the days of the "Big Aliyah" to Israel in 1950. It referred to immigrants whose origin was Arab countries. Then, during the 1970s and especially with the rise of the local social movement "Black Panthers," the term was slowly transformed to "Mizrahim" to signify a unification of many small ethnic groups into one collective with a shared destiny. At the same time, and with a slight difference, the popular coupled categories Sephardi versus Ashkenazi, signify a long-established religious and cultural heritage, including language and prayer melody that reaches farther back than the recent ethnic history of the Israeli society.

5. The term "obligatory passage point" (OPP) was coined by Michel Callon to describe the process of constructing a network around a controversy. By framing a problem and identifying the relevant actors, the role of a given primary actor becomes indispensable. The OPP is a point of negotiation positioned around a primary actor through which other actors must pass. For more on OPP and actor network theory, see Michel Callon, "Elements of a Sociology of Translation: Domestication of the Scallops and the Fishermen of St. Brieuc Bay," in *Power, Action and Belief: A New Sociology of Knowledge?*, ed. John Law (London: Routledge, 1986), 196–233; Bruno Latour, *Science in Action: How to Follow Engineers and Scientists through Society* (Cambridge, MA: Harvard University Press, 1987); and Michel Callon and Bruno Latour, "Unscrewing the Big Leviathan: How Actors Macrostructure Reality and How Sociologists Help Them to Do So," in *Advances in Social Theory and Methodology: Toward an Integration of Micro- and Macro-Sociologies*, ed. Karin Knorr-Cetina and Aaron Cicourel (London: Routledge and Kegan Paul, 1981).

6. Anat Leibler, "Disciplining Ethnicity: Social Sorting Intersects with Political Demography in Israel's Pre-state Period," *Social Studies of Science* 44, no. 2 (2014): 271–292.

7. Ibid.

8. Anat Leibler, "Statisticians' Ambition: Governmentality, Modernity and National Legibility," *Israel Studies* 9, no. 2 (2004): 121–149.

9. Mark Twain, *Chapters from My Autobiography* (Project Gutenberg, 2006): 471, http://www.gutenberg.org.

10. On the constitutive power of categories and a review of the social literature on the subject, see Geoffrey C. Bowker and Susan Leigh Star, *Sorting Things Out: Classification and Its Consequences* (Cambridge, MA: MIT Press, 2000); and Stefan Timmermans and Steven Epstein, "A World of Standards but Not a Standard World: Toward a Sociology of Standards and Standardization," *Annual Review of Sociology* 36 (2010): 69–89.

11. Paul F. Lazarsfeld, "Notes on the History of Quantification in Sociology—Trends, Sources and Problems," *Isis* 52, no. 2 (1961): 277–333; Theodore M. Porter, *The Rise of Statistical Thinking, 1820–1900* (Princeton, NJ: Princeton University Press, 1986); and Anthony Oberschall, *Empirical Social Research in Germany 1848–1914* (Paris: Mouton, 1965).

12. Silvana Patriarca, *Numbers and Nationhood: Writing Statistics in Nineteenth-Century Italy* (Cambridge: Cambridge University Press, 1996), 66–67.

13. Population in this tradition was subordinated to the need and goals of state administration. John Sinclair, who adopted the German term in the eighteenth century, wanted to distinguish himself from the German origin by emphasizing inhabitants of a country rather than a

state: "to ascertain the 'quantum of happiness' enjoyed by the inhabitants of a country and the means of its future improvement." Quoted in Porter, *Rise of Statistical Thinking*, 25–27. On the British tradition of statistics, see Ian Hacking, *The Taming of Chance* (Cambridge: Cambridge University Press, 1990), 118–119; and Alain Desrosières, "How to Make Things Which Hold Together: Social Science, Statistics and the State," in *Discourses on Society: The Shaping of the Social Sciences,* ed. Peter Wagner, Bjorn Wittrock, and Richard Whitley (Dordrecht: Kluwer, 1991), 195–218.

14. See, for example, Alain Desrosières, *The Politics of Large Numbers: A History of Statistical Reasoning* (Cambridge, MA: Harvard University Press, 2002); Ian Hacking, "Prussian Numbers 1860–1882," in *The Probabilistic Revolution: Ideas in History,* ed. Lorenz Krüger, Lorraine J. Daston, and Michael Heidelberger (Cambridge, MA: MIT Press, 1987), 1:377–393; Hacking, *Taming of Chance*; Porter, *Rise of Statistical Thinking*; Theodore M. Porter, "Lawless Society: Social Science and the Reinterpretation of Statistics in Germany, 1850–1880," in *The Probabilistic Revolution: Ideas in History,* ed. Lorenz Krüger, Lorraine J. Daston, and Michael Heidelberger (Cambridge, MA: MIT Press, 1987), 1:351–376; and Libby Schweber, "Styles of Statistical Reasoning: The French Liberal Tradition Reconsidered," in *The Age of Numbers: Statistical Systems and National Traditions* [in French], ed. Jean-Pierre Beaud and Jean-Guy Prévost (Sainte-Foy: Presses de l'Université du Québec, 2000), 299–324.

15. Marie-Noëlle Bourguet, "Décrire, Compter, Calculer: The Debate over Statistics during the Napoleonic Period," in *The Probabilistic Revolution: Ideas in History,* ed. Lorenz Krüger, Lorraine J. Daston, and Michael Heidelberger (Cambridge, MA: MIT Press, 1987), 305–316; and Desrosières, *Politics of Large Numbers*, 25.

16. Patriarca, *Numbers and Nationhood*, 124–125. Italy during the mid-nineteenth century period of Risorgimento is an interesting case of a transition from descriptive statistics focused on the density of the residents in each Italian state to numerical statistics as a means of unifying the nation into one administrated territory. Italian statisticians replaced non-numerical descriptive statistics with numbers and rearranged Italian territory into administrative regions represented by abstract numbers. The new regions did not always overlap with existing political units (Patriarca, *Numbers and Nationhood*, 141–144). As a consequence, the revision of Italian territory into one uniform space deprived of any physical-historical characterization began to inform discourses on society and practices of representation. The employment of numbers contributed to bring about a "dot-like world, an individualistic, neo-liberal image of society" (Patriarca, *Numbers and Nationhood*, 140).

17. Quoted in Witold Kula, *Measures and Men* (Princeton, NJ: Princeton University Press, 1986), 203–204.

18. James Scott, *Seeing like a State: How Certain Schemes to Improve the Human Condition Have Failed* (New Haven, CT: Yale University Press, 1998), 1–2.

19. Scott, *Seeing like a State*, 32.

20. Raphael Falk, *Zionism and the Biology of Jews* (Tel Aviv: Resling, 2006); and Mitchell B. Hart, *Social Science and the Politics of Modern Jewish Identity* (Stanford, CA: Stanford University Press, 2000).

21. For a thorough account of Ruppin's intellectual trajectory from Germany to Palestine, see Derek J. Penslar, *Zionism and Technocracy: The Engineering of Jewish Settlement in Palestine, 1870–1918* (Bloomington: Indiana University Press, 1991), 80–110; Falk, *Zionism and the Biology of Jews*; Etan Bloom, "The 'Administrative Knight'—Arthur Ruppin and the Rise of Zionist Statistics," in *Demographie—Demokratie—Geschichte: Deutschland und Israel,* ed. Josef Brunner (Göttingen, Germany: Wallstein, 2007); and Mitchell B. Hart, "Jews, Race, and Capitalism in the German-Jewish Context," *Jewish History* 19, no. 1 (2005): 49–63.

22. Bloom, "Administrative Knight."

23. Roberto Bachi, January 1948, RG 41/107/18, Israel State Archive (henceforth ISA).

24. David Ben-Gurion, *Medinat Yisrael Hamechudeshet* [The Israeli state renewed] (Tel Aviv: Am Oved, 1969), 57.

25. Yaakov Reuveni, *Mimshal Hamandat Be'eretz Yisrael, 1929–1948: Nituach History-Medini* [The mandatory government in the Land of Israel, 1929–1948] (Ramat Gan, Israel: Bar-Ilan University Press, 1993), 205–206.

26. Hacking, *Taming of Chance*, 116–117; and Gyan Prakash, *Another Reason: Science and the Imagination of Modern India* (Princeton, NJ: Princeton University Press, 1999).

27. Benjamin Eliav, *Hayeshuv Biyemey Habait Haleumi* [The Yishuv in the days of the national home] (Jerusalem: Keter, 1976), 48; and Shmuel Dotan, *Hama'avak Al Eretz Yisrael* [The struggle over the Land of Israel] (Tel Aviv: Misrad Habitahon, 1981), 99.

28. David De-Vris, "Tnuat Hapoalim Beheifa Bashanim 1919–29: Mechkar Bahistoria Shel Poalim Ironiyim Be'eretz Yisrael Hamandatorit" [Labor movement in Haifa in the years 1919–29: A historical study of urban workers in the Land of Israel during the British Mandate] (Ph.D. diss., Tel Aviv University, 1992).

29. Ben-Gurion, *Medinat Yisrael Hamechudeshet*, 57.

30. Hamisrad Haeretz Yisraeli, Shel Hahistadrut Hatzionit, Sfirat Yehuday Eretz Yisrael [World Zionist Organization, Palestine Zionist Office, Enumerating Jews in Palestine], 1918.

31. Tamar Hermann, "The Bi-national Idea in Israel/Palestine: Past and Present," *Nations and Nationalism* 11, no. 3 (2005): 381–401.

32. Shafir and Peled, *Being Israeli*.

33. Gershon Shafir, "Capitalist Binationalism in Mandatory Palestine," *International Journal of Middle East Studies* 43, no. 4 (2011): 611–633. For more on the binationalist approach, see Hermann, "Bi-national Idea in Israel/Palestine"; and Shafir and Peled, *Being Israeli*.

34. Roberto Bachi, n.d., File 466, Israeli National Science Archives in the Ben-Gurion Archives (henceforth SA, BGA).

35. Bachi, n.d., File 370, SA, BGA.

36. Bachi, 1942, File 694, SA, BGA.

37. Ibid.

38. Bachi, 1942, File 86, SA, BGA.

39. Kibbutz in the plural.

40. Bachi, 1943, File 68, SA, BGA.

41. Ibid. See also *Ha'aretz*, March 28, 1943.

42. Bachi, 1944, File 49, SA, BGA.

43. Bachi, 1943, File 68, SA, BGA. See also *Ha'aretz*, March 28, 1943.

44. Ben-Gurion was constantly concerned about the demographic ratio between Palestinian Jews and Palestinian Arabs in Palestine, but he was not aware of the internal immigration trends.

45. Bachi, 1944, File 84, SA, BGA.

46. Avraham Katznelson was a physician, member of the national committee from 1931 to 1948, and director of the health department of the Zionist Executive. David Tidhar, *Encyclopedia of the Founders and Builders of Israel* (2012), 2794.

47. Ibid.

48. Bachi, 1944, File 83, SA, BGA.

49. Bachi, 1944, File 79, SA, BGA.

50. Ibid.

51. Ibid.

52. For a discussion of the One Million Plan, see Dvora Hacohen, "Mass Immigration and the Israeli Political System," *Journal of Israeli History* 8, no. 1 (1987): 99–113.

53. Bachi, 1946, File 370, SA, BGA; confidential document.

54. Ibid.

55. Bachi, n.d., File 73, SA, BGA.

56. Bachi, 1946, File 370, SA, BGA.

57. Bachi, May 1948, File 466, SA, BGA; emphasis added.

58. Although the committee's status in the Yishuv was weaker than the Jewish Agency's position, it functioned as the official regulatory body of the Yishuv, which took care of education, health, welfare, and religious affairs. Bachi, 1944, File 79, SA, BGA.

59. Bachi, 1944, File 73, SA, BGA.

60. Bachi, 1946, File 466, SA, BGA; n.d., File 370, SA, BGA.

61. Bachi, n.d., File 466, SA, BGA.

62. Hacohen, "Mass Immigration."

63. Hacking, *Taming of Chance*, 118–119.

64. Paul Rabinow, *French Modern: Norms and Forms of the Social Environment* (Cambridge, MA: MIT Press, 1989), 169.

65. Bachi, n.d., File 466, SA, BGA.

66. Ibid.

67. Bachi's use of geostatistics was based on the method of representation of the population with its demographic characteristics on a geographical map in order to gain a better grasp of the national and ethnic distribution of different groups over the country.

68. Bachi, n.d., File 466, SA, BGA.

69. Ibid.

70. Calvin Goldscheider, *Israel's Changing Society: Population, Ethnicity, and Development* (Boulder, CO: Westview, 2002).

71. A more relevant source of identity was the type of settlement to which people belonged, since it indicated one's style of living as well as political affiliation. Ibid.

72. Bachi, 1944, File 83, SA, BGA.

73. Bachi, 1946, File 370, SA, BGA.

74. Ibid.

75. Goldscheider, *Israel's Changing Society*. See also Calvin Goldscheider, "Ethnic Categorizations in Censuses: Comparative Observations from Israel, Canada, and the United States," in *Census and Identity: The Politics of Race, Ethnicity, and Language in National Censuses*, ed. David I. Kertzer and Dominique Arel (Cambridge: Cambridge University Press, 2002), 71–91.

76. Roberto Bachi, *Yehudey Yerushalayim* [Jews of Jerusalem] (Jerusalem: Jewish Agency, 1941).

77. Bachi, 1944, File 49, p. 233, SA, BGA.

78. Ibid., 235.

79. Bachi, 1942, File 86, SA, BGA.

80. Ibid.

81. Ibid.

82. Ibid.

83. Bachi, 1947, RG 94/3558/8, p. 1, ISA.

84. Barry Barnes and Donald Mackenzie, "On the Role of Interests in Scientific Change," in *On the Margins of Science: The Social Construction of Rejected Knowledge*, ed. Roy Wallis, Sociological Review Monograph 27 (Keele, UK: University of Keele, 1979), 49–66.

85. Ibid., 61.

86. Bachi, 1947, RG 94/3558/8, p. 4, ISA. Although Bachi usually conflated Mizrahim (Asian-African origin) and Sephardim (Italian, Bulgarian, and Palestinian Jews), in this lecture he unified them into one category of Sephardim.

87. Bachi, 1947, RG 94/3558/8, p. 5, ISA.

88. Central Bureau of Statistics, Special Publication no. 36, *Registration of Population, Settlements, and Regions* (Jerusalem: CBS Publications, 1955).

89. Desrosières, *Politics of Large Numbers,* 31–32; Karl H. Metz, "Paupers and Numbers: The Statistical Argument for Social Reform in Britain during the Period of Industrialization," in *The Probabilistic Revolution: Ideas in the Sciences,* ed. Lorenz Krüger, Gerd Gigerenzer, and Mary S. Morgan (Cambridge, MA: MIT Press, 1987), 2:337–350; and Porter, "Lawless Society," 351–376.

90. Porter, *Rise of Statistical Thinking,* 25; Stephen Stigler, "The Measurement of Uncertainty in Nineteenth-Century Social Science," in *The Probabilistic Revolution: Ideas in History,* ed. Lorenz Krüger, Lorraine J. Daston, and Michael Heidelberger (Cambridge, MA: MIT Press, 1987), 1:287–293.

91. Hacking, *Taming of Chance,* 118–119.

92. Desrosières, "How to Make Things," 195–218.

93. From a letter that Dorothy Bar-Adon, a Zionist activist in the American Women's Zionist Association, known as Hadassah, describing Bachi's enterprise. Bachi, 1944, File 606, SA, BGA.

94. Bachi, 1944, File 68, ISA, BGA. The national committee was central to the political life of the Yishuv and functioned as the official representative of the national institutions, the nation, and the collective in every encounter with the British Mandate.

95. Peter Wagner, "'An Entirely New Object of Consciousness, of Volition, of Thought': The Coming into Being and (Almost) Passing Away of 'Society' as a Scientific Object," in *Biographies of Scientific Objects,* ed. Lorraine Daston (Chicago: University of Chicago Press, 2000).

96. Hacking, *Taming of Chance.*

6 Wet Numbers

The Language of Continuity Crisis and the Work of Care among the Organized American Jewish Community

Michal Kravel-Tovi

> We know more than ever about ourselves. Coupled with continuing efforts to extend and enrich such knowledge, this augurs well for the future of American Jewry.
>
> Sidney Goldstein, "Beyond the 1990 National Jewish Population Survey"

"WE KNOW," Sidney Goldstein, a professor of sociology at Brown University, assures his audience: we know ourselves. In his Marshall Sklare honorary address—an annual celebratory ritual of Jewish social scientific knowledge—Professor Goldstein publicly performs the sense of security that the American Jewish community places in social science. He uses the unmarked first-person plural "we" to refer to a wide range of leaders in the organized American Jewish world who care deeply about their community's future. The confidence Goldstein possesses in the potential of social science stems especially from the value of quantitative knowledge—the value of numbers. Indeed, much depends on the reality of numbers for Goldstein and his colleagues: the social scientists, public intellectuals, professionals, and lay leaders of the organized American Jewish community who have come to inhabit—and ultimately quantify—the Jewish communal sphere in the United States over the last three decades. They have filled it with rates, weights, and figures and adorned it with charts, tables, and graphs. In and through their discourse about numbers, the leaders of the American Jewish community have fashioned American Jewry as a numerically imagined community. When these communal leaders "speak of Jews"—to paraphrase Lila Corwin Berman's work—they speak of numbers.[1]

This chapter focuses on the intimate link between social-scientific discourses entailed in the production of numerical, sociodemographic knowledge of the

American Jewish community and an affective economy that shapes the distribution of that knowledge in that communal sphere. I will argue that the "statistical system" of American Jews has flourished by occupying a space of discursive tension—where seemingly incongruent features of numbers and emotions converge.[2] In particular, I will illustrate how Jewish sociodemographic statistics in the context of what came to be called during the 1990s the "continuity crisis" has been framed by both a rigorous scientific discourse of enumeration and an emotional language about the prospects of American Jewry. Each with its own cultural authority, the dauntingly dry language of numerically based social science and the poignant language of sentiment converge within the field of American Jewish statistics to mutually constitute and synergistically generate a powerful discourse about the population of this community. In what follows, I call this discourse "wet numbers"—a term that bears both metaphorically and analytically on the discursive dynamics under discussion.

The notion that statistics is a "dry" modality of knowledge is common. It indicates a colloquial association of numbers with inherent rigorousness, but also "dullness," of scientific data. As opposed to words that lend themselves easily to poetic playfulness, numbers are dry. They represent what is "out there" in an objective, straightforward, and factual manner, in a form well suited to tables and graphs. Because numbers provide hard data, their dryness is their strength; but it is also their point of weakness. The following quote conveys well this double-edged association of quantitative data with dryness: "You complain that your report would be dry. The drier the better. Statistics should be the driest of all reading."[3] In a similar vein, statistics can sometimes be described as "cold" (e.g., as in "cold data")[4] or "thin" (as in "thin description"),[5] terms that transmit a sense of frustration with the remoteness and even reductionism that are perceived to characterize quantitative data.

If the power of numbers to accurately represent reality is linked with metaphors of dryness and coldness, what do we make of numbers that are framed within affect-laden discourses? Perhaps it makes sense to think of such numbers in terms of their "heat," as if dry kindling sparks fires of emotionality. Indeed, in many contexts of enumeration, including the case under discussion here, statistics often create "heated debates" about the categories employed or about the resultant numbers and their interpretation. Certainly, the release of the 1990 National Jewish Population Survey (NJPS)—the statistical study that is the focus of my discussion of the continuity crisis—generated "heated" methodological debates related to the rate of intermarriage. Likewise, the release of the 2000–2001 NJPS a decade later animated "heated" public and scholarly arguments related to the estimated size of the American Jewish population.

But in framing my discussion in terms of wet, rather than hot, numbers, I wish to call attention to another discursive aspect of the continuity crisis. In particular, the concept of "wet numbers" enables us to think metaphorically about American Jewry as a biopolitical system—that is, as a community that has turned its social body into an object of both scientific knowledge and political intervention. The idea of wetness points to the affective work invested by the leaders of the American Jewish community in the production and distribution of population statistics. Building on this metaphor of wetness, I would say that wet numbers foreground an understanding of how the numerical sociodemographic discourses about the American Jewish population are soaked in "blood, sweat, and tears." By indexing body fluids, wetness highlights an embodied connotation of political intervention in the social body: the diluted blood of the social body, as well as the sweat and tears of those Jewish leaders who work hard, under bleak sociocultural conditions, to advance knowledge of a population about which they care deeply.

This chapter stands empirically and theoretically at this intersection of power/knowledge. By bringing the Foucauldian notion of biopolitics to bear on the study of American Jewry, I highlight the ways in which rigorous engagement of the organized Jewish community with sociodemographic knowledge of American Jews has reinforced the "Jewish population" as an object of knowledge and intervention. Put differently, biopolitics enables us to understand the strong institutional reliance on numerical, sociodemographic data as a means of transforming the loosely defined, multifaceted, and often obscure notion of "Jewish community" into a firmly knowable, measurable "Jewish population." When Professor Goldstein confidently proclaims, "we know more than ever about ourselves," he refers to this form of political knowledge.[6]

A productive starting point for studying such biopolitics might involve listening to how sociodemographic statistics are framed and narrated in communal domains. After all, the community claims to know itself to a great extent through population statistics; and, as we learn from Foucault, it is through discourse that different regimes of truth (e.g., about the population and its "facts") are established and negotiated. Without undermining the importance of unpacking concrete methodological, and often politicized, processes of statistics making (e.g., the decisions made about what questions to include in a survey, how to define a Jew, and the means through which to collect and make sense of results), I seek to emphasize here discursive processes that constitute the generation and circulation of statistical data. Given the intimate link between biopolitics and statistics, this chapter explores how producers, consumers and mediators of sociodemographic statistics on American Jewry talk and write about this quantified form of "social knowledge and its making."[7] Such a point of entry into a biopolitical field helps to decipher the webs of meaning that are spun and communicated among social scientists, public intellectuals, policy makers, and the public in communal conversations that unfold around statistics. In arguing for this point of entry,

I refer not only to the strategic choice to speak the language of numbers in the first place, a debated strategy in itself;[8] in addition, I seek to foreground modes of speaking through which statistics are delivered and the kind of communal values assigned to them. As the community both establishes and negotiates statistics as a central discursive domain through which it speaks to itself about itself, what types of rhetoric, tone, and metaphor partake in that domain's creation? On what moral, political, and institutional sources of authority do Jewish scholars, scientists, and communal leaders draw when they speak about Jewish statistics?

I ground my efforts to address these questions in an ethnographic and sociohistorical study that includes various communal sites and textual materials in which NJPS sociodemographic statistics regarding the American Jewish population have been generated, circulated, and discussed during the 1990s and early 2000s. In particular, this study draws on fieldwork conducted in both academic and professional settings, on interviews (primarily with Jewish social scientists and senior managers working within the Jewish organizational world), and a range of textual materials (mainly press releases, newspapers, and popular journal articles featured in the Jewish press).

Before turning to the 1990s' continuity crisis, I want to describe briefly the broader historical context in which American Jews have come to engage with population numbers.

The American Jewish Statistical System

The engagement of American Jews with counting themselves rests upon the fact that Jews (like other religious groups in the United States) cannot be surveyed in the national decennial census—a prohibition associated with church-state constitutional restrictions.[9] Therefore, and in contrast to a number of other diasporic Jewish communities,[10] American Jews have developed their own statistical system.[11] This system should be contextualized in both American and Jewish traditions of impassioned counting.

The faith that Americans place in numbers, writes Ian Hacking, is fundamental. Tracing this faith to its established roots in the Constitution (article 1, section 2), he concludes, half-jokingly, that "you could say that the second most important feature of the American dream was that people should be counted."[12] Similarly, Paul Starr describes statistics as a core component of the American cultural diet: "Every day, from the morning paper to the evening news, Americans are served a steady diet of statistics."[13] In her historical account of numeracy in the United States, Patricia Cline Cohen substantiates these strongly worded descriptions by demonstrating how statistics became, between the seventeenth and nineteenth centuries, both normalized as a discourse and enthusiastically embraced as a mode of knowledge.[14] In another study referring to more contemporary American domains of numerical expertise, historian Sarah Igo describes how, throughout the twentieth century, polls and surveys have been intimately interwoven into the cultural fabric of the American mass public.[15] The effects of surveying Americans have been multifaceted and far-reaching. Within the history of the aggregation and saturation of America's public spheres with "facts," lies the story, Igo argues, of intertwined developments of American public culture and American social sciences.[16]

Preoccupation with numerical inquiry among Jews within the American context should also be understood in relationship to a more general, global Jewish concern with demography. As Diana Tobin, president of a West Coast Jewish think tank, argues: "Counting Jews globally is an important lens through which we should be seeing the world."[17] Jewish demography has become central to the political life of both Israel and the Jewish diaspora. In the first case, demography has been considered essential to buttress the paramount Zionist value placed on security and defense, a sacred discourse of the nation-state.[18] In the second case, for Jews living outside of Israel, demography both articulates and frames a politics of diasporic identity. Although local sensibilities inevitably shape global Jewish engagements with statistics, these demographic entanglements with matters of Jewish collective life maintain a common discourse and agenda. International Jewish gatherings (such as the World Jewish Congress and the Conference on World Jewish Population) often bring together demographic studies within a comparative discussion.[19] These internationally linked projects of social-scientific inquiry into Jewish demography have shared a relatively common perspective—one undergirded by narratives of decline. Across contexts, research engagements with Jewish demography tend to breed grave discourses of crisis and urgency, underlining a felt need for practical intervention.[20] No doubt, the American Jewish statistical system rests within this broader ideological and institutional formation. In fact, this interpretative framework of crisis has emerged as a hallmark of the American Jewish social-scientific voice.

In 1880, almost three hundred years after the first Jew set foot on Roanoke Island, and more than two hundred years after twenty-three Jewish settlers arrived in New Amsterdam, the first nationwide statistical survey on American Jews took place. Conducted and compiled jointly by the Board of Delegates of American Israelites and the Union of American Hebrew Congregations, Statistics of the Jews of the United States represents the first systematic effort to produce a quantified portrait of American Jews.[21] Over the decades that followed, statistical forms of knowledge made further inroads into the American Jewish communal sphere, primarily through studies featured in the *American Jewish Year Book*. The American Jewish Committee (AJC), one of the leading Jewish organizations of the twentieth century, played a singular role in this process; it not only shared responsibility for this yearly publication but also partook in the establishment and funding of the institutional infrastructure for social-scientific research. In 1914 the AJC founded the Bureau of Jewish Statistics and Research, which would later become the Bureau of Jewish Social Research.[22] The rich data generated by the bureau and its successors, together with essays published (from the 1930s onward) in the scholarly journal *Jewish Social Studies,* positioned discourse on Jewish demography as one of the prime categories of interest for both communal activists and social scientists.[23] In fact, these forums for Jewish statistical research formed crucial parts of an emerging intellectual trend that would fully come to fruition within the organized Jewish community during the post–World War II period. Those trends would eventually constitute what Berman describes as the social-scientific turn.

Berman's concept of "a social-scientific turn" might help explain both the reemergence since 1970 of national surveys and the growing investment of Jewish communal agencies in local statistical projects.[24] This expansion in Jewish social-scientific production has been remarkable in its scope. It has included three national population surveys (in 1970, 1990, and 2000–2001) and approximately 140 local community studies conducted since the 1980s.[25] Local communal studies have often been celebrated as a productive means of self-evaluation, producing policy-relevant data in a context that is, practically speaking, considered to matter the most. "Local studies turn out to be [more] important because planning is done at the local level," explains Ira Sheskin, an advocate and researcher of community studies; "being able to quantify things, even if you 'know' them, is so important for planning," argues Jennifer Rosenberg, the New York UJA-Federation's research director, with regard to the formidable 2011 New York City survey.[26] As widely embraced as this form of communal research has become, it has also sparked a fair amount of criticism. Widely variable in method, and considered by many social scientists to be lacking in rigor, communal studies served as the backdrop for the 1970, 1990, and 2000–2001 national population surveys. In each of these surveys, the Jewish Federation aimed to mobilize the instruments and authority of social science in order to capture the national community in its entirety, rather than its scattered localities.[27]

These centralized statistical projects gained institutional footing through the establishment in 1986 of what later came to be called the Mandell Berman North American Jewish Data Bank (which serves as a repository of social-scientific studies of North American Jewry) and the founding in 1996 of the Berman Jewish Policy Archive (a central electronic library for matters of Jewish communal policy). Despite these community projects of centralization, the American Jewish statistical system has remained a rather fragmented and decentralized field. Without a clear coordinating institutional center, the social-scientific study of American Jewry occurs across a broad range of locations and through heterogeneous (and sometimes competing) frameworks. Some projects and researchers are based in general research universities and some in religious Jewish universities; some researchers hold positions in departments and centers of Jewish studies,[28] while others are located in a range of extra-academic and professional sites such as think-tank institutions and research departments housed within Jewish organizations.[29] In various ways, the statistical projects in all of these research contexts are made possible as a result of close links between Jewish social scientists and the organized Jewish world. It is within this political economy, in which funding and science making circulate, that the 1990 NJPS was crafted.

Crisis Numbers and the National Jewish Population Survey

In the wake of the 1991 publication of the NJPS *Highlights Report,* numerical forms of knowledge came to permeate the American Jewish communal sphere at an unprecedented level.[30] Statistical data—featured in a range of venues of Jewish and general media, communal sermons, organizational statements, and academic publications—have grown so pervasive that several Jewish journals have since devoted special issues to the engagement of Jews with counting themselves.[31] This deep-seated communal preoccupation with numbers precipitated the suggestion by Bernard Reisman, a Jewish communal studies professor at Brandeis, that "perhaps one should undertake a sociological study of the response to the survey."[32]

The 1990 NJPS provided a synoptic and detailed profile of American Jewry, formulating a wide array of sociodemographic parameters: age, sex, household structure, marriage, fertility, geography, philanthropy, education, labor, social stratification, and Jewish identity. As extensive as the survey was, its public reception seemed to focus on a single number: 52 percent. This number referred to the percentage of Jews who intermarried between 1985 and 1990. In fact, the survey suggested that there was much to celebrate about Jewish life, with regard, for example, to levels of education, professional achievement, and wealth. However, a clear tone of alarm and pessimism overshadowed such positive trends due to the reception of the data.

That the intermarriage rate of 52 percent became iconic of the survey as a whole and provoked such a grave sense of collective crisis in the communal imagination should come as no surprise. As Mitchell Hart demonstrates, already in early twentieth-century Europe, Jewish social scientists drew attention to intermarriage, treating it as a social pathology that, both quantitatively and qualitatively, afflicted the Jewish community.[33] The perceived danger of intermarriage to Jewish survival positioned this social phenomenon as "of particular interest and significance for Jewish social scientists"[34]—one that bore on weighty issues of Jewish demography and assimilation.

In a separate though not unrelated context, Lila Corwin Berman describes how Jewish social researchers in twentieth-century America have sought to understand the American Jewish experience by applying sociological tools to study intermarriage.[35] By attempting to discover social patterns of endogamy and drawing a connection between intermarriage and assimilation, this scholarship has constituted intermarriage as a sociological problem and prescribed in-group marriage as its scientifically validated solution.[36] Along these lines, the 1990 NJPS intermarriage rate of 52 percent engendered an unprecedented communal panic that soon came to be ubiquitously referred to as the continuity crisis. Controversy over matters of scientific accuracy aside, this number took on a life of its own: it informed public statements and debates, it gave birth to numerous policy commissions, and it fostered both local and national initiatives regarding Jewish identity and continuity.[37]

Clearly, narratives of Jewish decline are not new; nor are they unique to the communal dynamics responding to the 1990 NJPS and, to a lesser extent, to the 2000–2001 NJPS. A preoccupation with the concept of survival, and with quantification of this existential anxiety, forms an enduring, though not uncontested, feature of Jewish communal discourse. The "ever-dying people," as Simon Ravidowicz's oft-cited article argues, have consistently understood themselves as the "last Jews," or the "last survivors"; they have often similarly felt "as if they were standing at the grave of their people, its history and language."[38] This "crisis mentality"[39] was thus not invented with the 1990 NJPS. Rather, this study, as Jonathan Woocher, a senior federation professional, described to me, "gave it [the crisis mentality] a number." A decade later, the 2000–2001 NJPS introduced another number that would soon become infamously associated with the public discussion about demographic decline: the estimated number of 5.2 million Jews, a reported decline from 5.5 million Jews over a ten-year period. In the words of Michael Steinhart, a mega-philanthropist of American Jewry: "the news should have set off a code orange for Jewish organizations . . . all would agree that the Jews in America . . . are demographically endangered . . . the NJPS, after all, revealed palpable evidence of a crisis."[40]

"Numbers," as the saying goes, "speak for themselves," which means that they are assumed self-evidently to encapsulate and convey instantly recognizable and incontestable messages. The following quote, taken from internal correspondence between a prominent social scientist involved in the 2000–2001 NJPS and federation professionals articulates this notion with clarity.[41] As he writes: "numbers have certain connotations attached to them. The gap between 48% and 52% is more significant than that between 42% and 48% . . . yes, I can count . . . but thresholds matter." The message is clear: even if numbers do speak for themselves for politically attuned ears, they must still be spoken. It is through the ways in which they are spoken, and the discursive formats in which they are embedded, that numbers convey their meanings.

The overarching meaning of a continuity crisis represents a clear case in point. By and large, this framework invokes a historically loaded association of Jewish vulnerability. Most notably, when American Jews are depicted as an "endangered species," descriptions of Jewish demographic decline reinforce themes of "loss" and "catastrophe" so characteristic of post-Holocaust consciousness. For example, intermarriage is often portrayed metaphorically as "a silent Holocaust." In a similar vein, population decrease is often dramatically represented in light of the moral burden laid upon generations of Jews to replenish Jewish numbers after Auschwitz. Like Jewish statistics in early twentieth-century Europe,[42] both academic and communal discourses on matters of Jewish population are informed by medical perceptions of sickness and degeneracy, thereby heightening the sense of crisis by placing it within a morally loaded biological discourse of life and death. Within this framework, intermarriage becomes a "syndrome" or a "symptom," and any disengagement with the organized Jewish community is "contagious, approaching epidemic proportions."[43] This medical language metaphorically associates the ills of the social body with the physical body, a compelling connection with respect to its biopolitical framework.

The continuity crisis, as a rhetorical construct, has not only mobilized such emotionally laden medical language but also foregrounded emotionality itself by relying on a pessimistic language of affect. To paraphrase Ochs's idea (chapter 8 in this volume) about how numerical discourses are implicated in a "hyperbole of optimism," one could say that the continuity crisis was significantly augmented by a "hyperbole of pessimism." To be sure, practices of counting and numerical representations do bring to the fore volatile social issues—sometimes deemed existential—related to group membership, communal boundaries, and political power. Decisions about how to count Jews, for example, imply the loaded question of who is a Jew and highlight sensitivities about minority experience within a non-Jewish sociopolitical order. However, the emotional discourse of the continuity crisis is far from being an inherent tenet of numerical knowledge or an inevitable consequence of emotionally arousing issues; it is, rather, a language actively mobilized to frame and inflame passion.

Unsurprisingly, somber associations mark the forms of affect that frame the continuity crisis. Expressions of depression, anxiety, and concern recur throughout the description and interpretation of the data. These emotions are voiced not only by professionals and educated observers but also by social scientists and other scholars who position themselves as concerned members of the community. This is clearly reflected, for example, in Professor Bernard Reisman's depiction of the mood in two forums dedicated in the early 1990s to the published results of the NJPS:

In both cases, I and most of the other participants, initially emerged depressed and confused . . . the first day was not so much the demographers' findings but the depressive affect and concomitant sense of helplessness among the participants. And then I reasoned if we, who were mainly academics, were so demoralized and immobilized, would it not be likely that the professional and lay leaders would have even a more severe reaction?[44]

The debate between scholars and other advocates of decline, versus those who endorse a narrative of transformation about American Jewry, has indeed come to be framed in emotional terms as a debate between pessimists and optimists or between those who are in a panic and those who are euphoric. Sidney Goldstein reflects:

The tone of the debate has gone well beyond neutral and objective academic and scientific discussion, to embrace such value distinctions as "pessimists" and "optimists" . . . unfortunately, an increasingly emotional tenor has come to affect the debate on Jewish population and, to say the least, this has contributed little to the quality of the debate.[45]

On the other end of the spectrum, and almost twenty years later, we can find Professor Steven M. Cohen who construes bleak emotional language as both a logical response to the concerning population-related effects among American Jews and a rhetorical achievement.[46] And yet, during a panel on demographic narratives held in the course of the 2011 Association for Jewish Studies conference, he seems to be unsure about how to mobilize this rhetoric: "I'm still wishing, or my dream is, can we rhetorically express anxiety, dread, *harada* [anxiety in Hebrew] about intermarriage without pushing away all those intermarried?"[47] The potential benefits and risks of the emotional language of crisis appear in Jack Wertheimer's answer to my question about his own emotional style of public address. A prominent historian of American Jewry, who collaborates extensively with social scientists and Jewish professional leaders, he replied:

I am shocked at the passivity and the seeming lack of concern when what I see is something that is worthy of concern, and so this emotional language is designed to grab people by the throat and get their attention . . . but I'm also an engaged scholar. [He explains:] I have children and I worry about what kind of Jewish community my grandchildren will live in . . . but I feel that I need to limit the amount of crankiness because otherwise people are just going to tune me out completely.[48]

Professor Wertheimer's statement exemplifies another critical point: the conflation of personal and communal voices, and the "personalization" of social-scientific data. Grounded in a sacred Jewish institution—that is, the family—this kind of discourse animates experiences and sentiments that lie beyond and beneath the faceless and often alienating effect of "sheer numbers."

Statistics, as a culturally authorized way of "seeing" the community in the aggregate, become also an important lens through which individuals learn about their scientifically represented selves and "see" their situated family dynamics. Take, for example, Dr. Rabbi Hayim Herring's memories of the days directly following the release of the 1990 NJPS in the conservative congregation he then led in Minnesota: "There's a lot of emotion that is so intrinsic to the NJPS story because we are not talking solely about numbers, but about people's lives. At that point, everybody suddenly knew somebody who is either intermarried or has an intermarried family member . . . rabbis," and he included himself, "do not just speak data to make a point, our job is to move people emotionally, to change ways of thinking, and numbers may become beneficial in that way."[49] This statement reveals that the emotional language of crisis is not the fabrication of a media hungry for dramatic headlines. Rather, it is located in an intricate web of actors and public speakers—from social scientists and national leaders to congregational rabbis—that report numbers and make emotion-laden arguments.

To better understand these discursive frameworks that govern how numbers are layered with affect, I will turn now to the idea (and ideal) of the "engaged Jewish social scientist." This idea helped Wertheimer explain his affective tone of public address. This notion also plays a formative role in allowing and augmenting the affective discourses among social scientists. In particular, I argue that within the close intersection of Jewish social science and the organized Jewish community, the work of Jewish social scientists is construed in terms of care and commitment to the American Jewish community. These terms underwrite the political and moral legitimacy which allows Jewish scholars of American Jewry to speak passionately and dramatically, rather than in a detached manner, about scientifically based population numbers. The operation of the model of "engaged scholarship" uncovers an intimate link between counting American Jewry and caring for it.

The Engaged Jewish Social Scientist

While the American Jewish statistical system has taken many forms across its multiple incarnations and locations, it ultimately rests upon an underlying feature: an intimate and symbiotic relationship between the Jewish institutional world, composed of an intricate network of institutions of communal government and collective operation, and social science as a rule-governed social system of epistemic norms, standards, and authorities. This relationship rests not only on the political economy of scholarly production, meaning the actual process through which funding and research circulate between those who produce data and those who use or commission it, but also on ideas and ideals regarding the role of scholars and social-scientific scholarship in American Jewish communal life. This set of ideas and ideals is captured in the phrase of engaged scholar.

Because this chapter focuses on the discursive practices of wet numbers rather than on the practices of Jewish social science making, I cannot fully explore here the various terms of engagement that underwrite the model of the engaged scholar. Nor can I situate these terms in relation to other scholarly fields in which public engagement and political activism have been formative in how academics position themselves (e.g., feminist or black scholars). These matters deserve their own separate exposition. Yet, I want to point out some general features that characterize this model especially as they shed light on the dynamic of wet numbers.

Following Hart's work on Jewish social science and Berman's exploration of the Jewish social-scientific turn, I also came to think of the mutually constituting concepts of "engaged scholar" and "Jewish social scientist." In particular, I came to think of the social scientists who took part in the continuity crisis as Jewish social scientists.[50] After all, most if not all of the scholars I met identified themselves as Jewish. What Sam Heilman once wrote about the sociological scholarship of Jews still holds today: "Jews have been more interested in studying Jews than has anyone else."[51] Moreover, the scholars I met during my fieldwork often brought their Jewishness to the forefront when presenting their work. For example, in their writings in the Jewish press (such as in *Sh'ma* or *The Forward*)—in contrast to how they write in general academic venues—social scientists tend to use what Sarah Benor describes as Jewish English,[52] sprinkling their arguments with Jewish and Israeli expressions in Hebrew or Yiddish. During a two-day Brandeis University conference on the sociodemography of American Jewry held in October 2011, it wasn't uncommon for scholars to embellish their presentations with biblical verses (in either Hebrew or English), thereby performing their Jewish competencies and credentials. An Israeli colleague of mine, in a tellingly cynical response to this pattern, whispered to me on one of these occasions: "Do you think they compete to see 'who is more Jewish'?"

Interestingly, when, at the beginning of my interviews with social scientists, I invited them to share with me their intellectual and personal narratives that constitute their scholarly trajectories, the designation "Jewish social scientist" on my part went unnoticed and was sometimes even incorporated into their narrative. Only once, in an exceptional incident that proves the rule, did my definition provoke a response: "I'm not a Jewish social scientist!" Professor Calvin Goldscheider protested before providing his narrative, "I'm a social scientist of the Jews. There's a big difference."

The possible difference between a Jewish social scientist and a social scientist of the Jews clearly foregrounds the relationship between my own positionality and that of the social scientists I have studied. The fact that the term "Jewish social scientist" can be seemingly applied to them (Jewish social scientists who have by and large chosen to work *for* and in collaboration with Jewish organizations and centers of power) and myself (a Jewish social scientist who has chosen to work *on* Jewish organizations in an attempt to unpack the mechanisms of their power) demonstrates the inclusive breadth of the term. Goldscheider's comment in particular reveals the double-edged nature and endemic tension captured in the notion of the Jewish social scientist. Does the adjective "Jewish" qualify the scholar's background and identity or his research focus?[53] If it refers to both, what kinds of professional discourses are permitted within this coalescence of commitments and positions?

The model of the engaged scholar, which is often invoked and idealized in the context of the American Jewish statistical system, only deepens this ambiguity: with what, exactly, is the engaged scholar engaged? Is it with his scholarship or with something else, outside of and prior to it? Is the Jewish social scientist engaged with Jewish scholarship, Jewish life, or the connection between them? Do I—a scholar engaged with what matters to me and disturbs me as an Israeli Jew (e.g., the central role of anxious demographic discourses in public Israeli life) fall within the contours of the category of the engaged scholar or am I excluded from it? As these questions demonstrate, ambiguity and instability are endemic to the model of engaged scholarship, an aspect of Jewish social science in North America that both enables and complicates the field. Precisely the lack of precision encapsulated in this model fuels the American Jewish statistical system and defines the permissible wet nature of the voice that animates that data.

Within a variety of academic and communal forums, the persona of the Jewish scholar described by journalists, scholars, and communal leaders is of an individual who "cares" deeply. What he cares about is often defined through an open, indefinite set of tropes, such as "the Jewish people," "Jewish life," or "the Jewish future." These vague, often interchangeable, objects of care reference the Jewish community writ large or the American Jewish community in particular. In this framework, Jewish social-scientific scholarship—in the here and now—is constituted as a "service," a token of commitment. Steven M. Cohen, in his Marshall Sklare Award lecture in 2012, articulated the interconnections he envisions between Jewish service and scholarship: "our ever-growing conversation among several generations of scholars committed to studying, serving, and sustaining the Jewish People."[54] And in the appreciative words of Barry Kosmin, a senior demographer, for his late colleague, sociologist Egon Mayer, Jewish "care" marks Mayer's career and life story. Although the trajectory of Mayer's life is obviously distinct, Kosmin expands the notion of care to characterize the whole scholarly community. He writes:

> We return to what I believe inspired all of Egon's lifework: his concern for the Jewish people and its future. Jewish social science is not an uncontested field of study. The passions arising from differences in ideology, theology, and

discipline run deeply in our community of scholars. People care, believe and argue at a decibel level that is above that in most areas of the academy.[55]

Whether or not Kosmin is right in his relational diagnosis, he captures in this description the prescriptive, normative feature of care. In an address that can be understood as another example of the romanticized status of care for the Jewish community in social-scientific scholarship, Frederick M. Lawrence, president of Brandeis University, greeted over lunch the participants of the sociodemography of American Jewry conference (October 2011), which I attended. While praising the accomplishments of the Steinhardt Social Research Institute, Professor Lawrence preached to his audience about the centrality of care as the essential Jewish ethic of social-scientific labor:

> There are some people out there who work only with their heads but here, at Brandeis, we work with both our heads and our hearts. If there is something we care about deeply we should have the people do a good job . . . let's continue to work on the things that are important to our heads. God knows that they are also important to our hearts.

Professor Lawrence's message echoes the sentiments of Professor Goldstein, nearly two decades earlier, that Jewish scholarship ideally "comes from both the head and heart." Both professional and communal Jewish engagements are harmoniously integrated in Goldstein's descriptions of the field, representing what might be understood as a caring expertise. Referencing both a Jewish data bank and advisory committee, he noted, that they "have, I believe, been most fortunate in enlisting the assistance of a strong array of social scientists who are dedicated both to the highest standards of research and to the maintenance of a strong Jewish community." Given the growing scarcity he identifies in the availability of adept personnel, Goldstein goes further to recommend that

> early and high priority [should] be given to training in research methods of more social scientists who can be counted on to devote all or part of their career to work *in and for* the Jewish community . . . such an expansion of our personnel resources should be done [among other methods] by appeals to the Jewish conscience of qualified students.[56]

To be sure, the ways in which intellectual vigor should be utilized for Jewish causes, and the politics of those causes, are hardly points of agreement. Jewish social scientists obviously vary in the degree and nature of their subjective investment in Jewish communal life, and differ in how they understand and negotiate the repercussions of that investment for science making. Some take upon themselves the social role of the public intellectual, while others confine themselves to more academically and institutionally bounded domains. Whereas one scholar is fascinated by methodological innovations, a second publicly articulates his passionate commitment to *yidishkeyt* as what "keeps him in the business." Despite these differences, and even occasional discord, an ideology of Jewish communal care permeates the overlapping spaces of scholarship making and community building. The purpose of gathering knowledge itself becomes a modality of community building. Through the lens of Jewish biopolitics, the logic of Jewish social science envisions data as a tool for population service, planning, and intervention. It is thus not unusual to find such justifications for statistical projects in the genre of Jewish social-scientific writing. As Professor Goldstein, director of the academic advisory committee for the 1990 NJPS, unequivocally writes: "to have Judaism, we have to have Jews, and the right kind in the right kinds of places."[57]

Blood, Sweat, and Tears: The Wet Language of Population Crisis

Statistics, as Theodore Porter teaches us, is a language or a strategy of communication imbued with an aura of objectivity and uniformity.[58] The language of numbers carries with it an array of cultural assumptions about truth, precision, and representation; it also implicates a range of historically situated understandings of objectivity. Indeed, the 1990 NJPS statistics appeared on the American Jewish scene packaged in the language of hard science and dry methodology. Employed strategically, this dry language claimed institutional authority and garnered public trust. It was implicated in the "boundary work" that established the social researchers involved with the 1990 NJPS as a reliable professional community, impervious to political pressures and united in adherence to rule-governed standards.[59] In so doing, this language created conditions for staging the expertise of both the Council of Jewish Federations (the institutional patron of the NJPS study) and the academics involved.[60] In anticipation of any potential critique, the 1990 NJPS was, from the outset, presented to the public as a rigorously scientific survey.[61]

The dryness of biopolitics, however, can be misleading. As Ian Hacking writes: "biopolitics is, of course, less fun to study than the anatamo-political. The numerical manipulations of the body politic are and always were dusty, replete with dried-up old books."[62] This dryness is misleading because, as Porter argues in the context of administration, this very "grayness helps to maintain [statistics'] authority."[63] But this kind of misleading grayness, or dryness, is only one source of authority for the publicly distributed biopolitical language of American Jewish statistics; the other is the economy of affect that enfolds the language of dry science.

Historically, the realm of emotion, as opposed to that of science, has been marginalized as a modality of knowledge in western cultures. Emotions have been adversely associated with the embodied, the irrational, the intuitive, and, therefore, the feminine.[64] However, as a modality of speech, emotions have achieved hegemony in popular domains of public rhetoric. Frank Furedi argues that a culture of emotionalism has fostered a climate in which a display of feelings has acquired a formidable cultural status, informing how individuals are expected to speak about and conduct themselves in public.[65] Lay people, celebrities, politicians, and even academics draw on emotionalism when they speak publically. Richard Posner writes in regard to public intellectuals: "the emotionality of the public intellectual . . . stands in particularly striking contrast to the official image of the academic."[66]

Following Don Handelman's work on the synergetic relationship between bureaucratic logic and national sentiments, a relationship that helps him explain the power of the modern machinery of the nation-state,[67] I argue for a synergetic relationship between the dry language of numbers and the wet language of emotions in the biopolitical apparatus of American Jewry. The synergy, literally the "working together," of the numerical social data and the emotional qualities attached to that data helps to explain the pervasive presence and nature of social-scientific knowledge in the American Jewish communal sphere. Each discourse enhances the cultural grip of the other. Because numerical depictions of reality represent "social facts" and are considered to be the very means of truth making, numbers may "rationalize" and legitimate the emotions that they arouse. As Sherry Israel, a Brandeis professor who participated in the advisory committee of the 2000–2001 NJPS is quoted as saying, "if you design a study that's methodologically sound, you get what's out there. The community and its facts will speak for themselves."[68] When supported by numbers, emotions appear seemingly well-grounded in reality. Simultaneously, because emotionality pervades everyday life in profound ways, it lends meaning to an abstract reality captured by numbers, as if indicating what "really counts" about that reality. Secured in their position as "knowers"—as those who speak in the language of science and truth—and anchored in their political, moral authority as engaged scholars, these actors allow themselves to be immersed in the seductive power of emotional language without being "contaminated" by its supposed inferiority as a mode of knowledge.

Obviously, the synergetic relationship between statistics and emotions has its own limits and vulnerabilities—particularly with regard to the degrees of suspicion often leveled at both constructs. Because the production of numbers is at best complicated and often inaccessible to a large public or, at worst, subject to manipulation, statistics is often highly susceptible to critique and skepticism; moreover, as both Sheila Jasanoff and Sarah Igo show, historically, the popular reception of the "cult of experts" in twentieth-century America has been ambivalent.[69] Though sometimes treated with expressions of admiration and confidence, experts often endure distrust and even ridicule. Indeed, a great degree of public skepticism has sometimes greeted the emotional tone attached to numerical discourses of the continuity crisis. In particular, emotional overtones of referring to Jews as an endangered species and calls for a prompt and effective response have been dismissed as a mere "panic"[70] or portrayed as a traditional, conservative reaction on the part of a leadership that thrives on crisis heroism.[71] Alternatively, the emotional tone of crisis is sometimes taken as a calculated tactic of communication in the service of fund raising.[72] Others reject the crisis-laden notion of "Jewish continuity" altogether, choosing instead to celebrate notions such as "Jewish engagement" and "Jewish revival." Indeed, the heyday of Jewish continuity as an institutional catchphrase appears to have passed. This affective discourse seems to have its own disaffecting implications—alienating and numbing listeners.

Both the strengths and limitations of this synergy teach us about the fairly restricted modes of biopolitical operation available to American Jewish leaders in the nonstate voluntary-based American context in which they operate. Without fetishizing the state as an omnipotent actor, this study points to the particular and perhaps greater array of challenges that the nonstate context presents to those who strive to count, produce, and act upon the population. When Israel, as the Jewish nation-state, aims to reproduce its Jewish population, a wide array of legal frameworks, policy procedures, and bureaucratic institutions buttress its efforts. It attempts, as a matter of course, to import and reproduce Jews through a state-run conversion apparatus, and both immigration (*aliyah;* ascendance) and fertility policies. The state also possesses at its disposal various means of both direct and indirect mechanisms of governmentality (e.g., throughout the state-run education and army systems) that are more complicated for operation in a voluntary-based context such as that of the American Jewish community.

By contrast, when the organized American Jewish community strives to manage its Jewish population, it is handicapped by both the fragmented nature of its institutions, and, most significantly, by the voluntary-based and liberal-oriented forms of belonging that constitute that community. True, the organized American Jewish community is the biggest and most institutionally developed among Jewish diasporic communities. It relies on impressive established networks of funding, agencies, and organizations that serve as instrumentalities through which the polity can actually act to intervene in the social body. Perhaps "Birthright Israel" represents the most notable example of the impressive operational governmental capabilities of the community at the time of, and in fact as a response to, the continuity crisis.[73]

And yet, this working infrastructure is far more limited than a state in the range of interventionist options available. For example, despite continuing concerns over the Jewish family, the liberal-oriented organized community has never embraced fertility and other family-related policies. Furthermore, because matters of personal investment, engagement, and agency exist in the gap between

Jewish bodies and Jewish souls—between a measurable, but possibly empty, Jewishness and a meaningful one—Jewish voluntarism further complicates the loaded engagement with Jewish demography. It confuses the question of who is a Jew by casting doubts even on the value of counting Jews in the first place.

For a community in which, as some argue, every Jew can be deemed "a Jew by choice"—a community in which even the willingness to fill out a forty-five-minute NJPS questionnaire is understood as an indication of voluntary Jewish commitment—Jewish leaders must ultimately appeal to the realm of heightened emotional speech to motivate voluntary participation. In a tacit acknowledgment that numbers cannot, in themselves, be heard—that they do not, in fact, speak for themselves—or, alternatively, that they unintentionally normalize acculturation, these leaders speak not only in the name of science and its "facts" but also in the language of affect. The affective economy distributed through their reporting of numbers demonstrates how biopolitical logic in such a voluntary communal context depends upon language and its ability to influence personal decisions made by Jews. After all, the accumulated effect of individual life choices (from the question of whom to marry to whether to raise Jewish children and encourage Jewish habits) reflects back on the size ("quantity") and composition ("quality") of the social body. In this sense, the discourse of wet numbers assumes a potentially greater significance as a rhetorical tool for what Nikolas Rose calls "technologies of the soul": technologies aimed at the production of certain subjectivities.[74]

The concept of wet numbers enables us to think metaphorically about the affective, wet nature of such voluntary communities or less strongly equipped biopolitical systems. American Jewish leaders face a delicate task. These leaders speak the language of wet numbers—a language that attempts not just to count Jewish bodies but also to take account of, and indeed to touch, Jewish souls. Because their work inevitably draws on post-Holocaust schemes of Jewish biopolitics, reproduction of the population depends upon the constant production of a sense of collective crisis. As opposed to other situations framed in terms of collective crises that bear directly on the lives of individuals (e.g., natural disaster, war, or economic recession), the continuity debate does not necessarily imply a crisis for individual Jews in America. They simply may not care. The affective economy of wet numbers that shapes the ideological and institutional apparatus of continuity operates to replenish the care and responsiveness of the community in relationship to what might otherwise simply be taken as dry statistics. Working against the grain of indifference and apathy, Jewish leaders and researchers strive to prescribe care: care about Judaism, the Jewish people, and crises that potentially endanger Jewish survival. So essential is care to Jewish social science that, ironically enough, some of the social scientists who have played such important roles in establishing numerical regimes of knowledge have themselves come to distrust those very regimes; they worry that the numbers they count are not sufficiently "full" with care. As Professors Saxe and Kadushin put it: "the community needs Jews who count more than it needs to count Jews."[75] As this quote illustrates, even if the "population" is a prime object of study and intervention, it is eventually the "community" that must be targeted—and redeemed.

Given the intimate relationships between statistically based social sciences and policies of population intervention, this chapter invites future research examining discourses of biopolitical communal policies. Investigating the public communication (or, alternatively, the public silence) about fertility and conversion policy, or the politics of out-reach and in-reach, for example, all stand to teach us about "the limits and the forms of the sayable"[76] in the relationship between a community or a polity and its subjects. After all, just like numbers, biopolitical policies do not speak for themselves.

Notes

I would like to thank Deborah Dash Moore, Riv-Ellen Prell, Shaul Kelner, and Lila Corwin Berman for insightful and productive feedback on earlier drafts of this chapter. I am profoundly grateful to Josh Friedman for carefully editing and thinking with me about this chapter. Deborah Dash Moore embraced and encouraged this research project from its earliest stages, and I am indebted to her for her constant support and inspiration as well to the Mandell L. Berman Foundation for enabling my fellowship at the Frankel Center for Judaic Studies at the University of Michigan.

1. Lila Corwin Berman, *Speaking of Jews: Rabbis, Intellectuals, and the Creation of an American Public Identity* (Berkeley: University of California Press, 2009).

2. See Paul Starr, "The Sociology of Official Statistics," in *The Politics of Numbers,* ed. William Alonso and Paul Starr (New York: Russell Sage Foundation, 1987), 7–57.

3. The quote is taken from the letter of a nineteenth-century British officer to Florence Nightingale, cited by the historian Theodore M. Porter in his *Rise of Statistical Thinking, 1820–1900* (Princeton, NJ: Princeton University Press, 1986), 34.

4. Julia Paley, "Making Democracy Count: Opinion Polls and Market Surveys in the Chilean Political Transition," *Cultural Anthropology* 16, no. 2 (2001): 137.

5. See chapter 7 of this volume.

6. For more on the Foucauldian understanding of biopolitics, see Thomas Lemke, *Biopolitics: An Advanced Introduction* (New York: New York University Press, 2010); Michel Foucault, "Governmentality," in *The Anthropology of the State: A Reader,* ed. Aradhana Sharma and Akhil Gupta (Malden, MA: Blackwell, 2006), 131–143; and Michel Foucault, *History of Sexuality* (New York: Pantheon, 1978).

7. Charles Camic, Neil Gross, and Michèle Lamont, "Introduction: The Study of Social Knowledge Making," in *Social Knowledge in the Making,* ed. Charles Camic, Neil Gross, and Michèle Lamont (Chicago: University of Chicago Press, 2011), 1–40.

8. A small number of scholarly works have unpacked the strategic choice of minority groups to mobilize the language of statistics. See Paley, "Making Democracy Count"; and Jacqueline Urla, "Cultural Politics in an Age of Statistics: Numbers, Nations, and the Making of Basque Identity," *American Ethnologist* 20, no. 4 (1993): 818–843.

9. The only serious attempt by the American Bureau of the Census to include a question about religion (in the context of the Current Population Survey [CPS] in 1957) proved a failure. As Kevin Schultz recounts regarding the debates surrounding this attempt, the failure is attributable to the fervent opposition of Jewish organizations. See Kevin Schultz, "Religion as Identity in Postwar America: The Story of the Last Serious Attempt to Put a Question on Religion in the U.S. Census," *Journal of American History* 93, no. 2 (2006), 359–384.

10. It should be noted that some Jewish communities (e.g., in Canada and Australia) work with data extracted from national censuses, while other communities, such as in the United States, work with their own, self-produced data.

11. Paul Ritterband, Barry Kosmin, and Jeffrey Scheckner, "Counting Jewish Populations: Methods and Problems," *American Jewish Year Book* (1988): 204–221.

12. Ian Hacking, "Biopower and the Avalanche of Printed Numbers," *Humanities in Society* 5, no. 3–4 (1982): 290.

13. Starr, "Sociology of Official Statistics," 1.

14. Patricia Cline Cohen, *A Calculating People: The Spread of Numeracy in Early America* (New York: Routledge, 1999).

15. Sarah Igo, *The Averaged American: Surveys, Citizens, and the Making of a Mass Public* (Cambridge, MA: Harvard University Press, 2007).

16. Berman, *Speaking of Jews.*

17. Diana Tobin, in *Sh'ma* 41, no. 673 (2010): 5.

18. Anat Leibler and Daniel Breslau, "The Uncounted: Citizenship and Exclusion in the Israeli Census of 1948," *Ethnic and Racial Studies* 28, no. 5 (2005): 880–902; and Justyna Stypinska, "Jewish Majority and Arab Minority in Israel's Demographic Struggle," *Polish Sociological Review* 1, no. 157 (2007): 105–120.

19. Sergio Della Pergola, *World Jewry beyond 2000: The Demographic Prospects* (Oxford: Oxford Centre for Hebrew and Jewish Studies, 1999).

20. See Edward Norden, "Counting the Jews," *Commentary* 92, no. 4 (1991): 36–43; and Robert Wistrich, "Do the Jews Have a Future?," *Commentary* 98, no. 1 (1994): 23–26.

21. Jacob Rader Marcus, *To Count a People: American Jewish Population Data 1585–1984* (Washington, DC: University Press of America, 1990).

22. Naomi W. Cohen, *Not Free to Desist: The American Jewish Committee, 1906–1966* (Philadelphia: Jewish Publication Society, 1972).

23. For example, see Uriah Zvi Engelman, "Jewish Statistics in the U.S. Census of Religious Bodies (1850–1936)," *Jewish Social Studies* 9, no. 2 (1947): 127–174; and A. J. Jaffe, "The Use of Death Records to Determine Jewish Population Characteristics," *Jewish Social Studies* 1, no. 2 (1939): 143–168.

24. Ira Sheskin, "Local Jewish Population Studies: Still Necessary after All These Years," *Contemporary Jewry* 15, no. 1 (1994): 26–38; and Ira Sheskin, "Comparisons between Local Jewish Community Studies and the 2000–01 National Jewish Population Survey," *Contemporary Jewry* 25, no. 1 (2005): 158–192.

25. Information delivered by Professor Ira Sheskin during the Brandeis Socio-Demographic Conference (October 2011).

26. Sue Fishkoff, "With Flurry of New Local Studies, Jewish Communities Seeing Trends and Making Changes," *JTA*, July 10, 2011, http://www.jta.org/2011/07/10/life-religion/with-flurry-of-new-local-studies-jewish-communities-seeing-trends-and-making-changes.

27. Sidney Goldstein, "A National Jewish Population Study: Why and How," in *A Handle on the Future: The Potential of the 1990 National Jewish Population Study,* ed. Barry A. Kosmin (1988), 1–9, http://www.jewishdatabank.org/studies/details.cfm?StudyID=626.

28. Currently, the most prominent centers of Jewish statistical research are the Cohen Center and the Steinhardt Social Research Institute, both at Brandeis University.

29. Such professional sites include the Jewish Agency for Israel, the American Jewish Committee, the Institute for Jewish and Community Research, and the Jewish People Policy Institute.

30. Barry Kosmin et al., *Highlights of the CJF 1990 National Jewish Population Survey* (New York: Council of Jewish Federations, 1991).

31. See *Contact: The Journal of Jewish Life Network / Steinhardt Foundation* 5, no. 3 (Spring 2003) and 8, no. 4 (Summer 2006); and *Sh'ma* 41, no. 673 (2010).

32. Bernard Reisman, "Reflections on the 1990 National Jewish Population Survey," *Contemporary Jewry* 14, no. 1 (1993): 166.

33. Mitchell B. Hart, *Social Science and the Politics of Modern Jewish Identity* (Stanford, CA: Stanford University Press, 2000).

34. Ibid., 75.

35. Berman, *Speaking of Jews.*

36. The connection between intermarriage and assimilation is not unique to American Jews. It is widely accepted theoretically and supported empirically in relation to other religious groups. See, for example, Milton M. Gordon, *Assimilation in American Life: The Role of Race, Religion and National Origins* (Oxford: Oxford University Press, 1964).

37. The long list of popular publications includes Alan Dershowitz, *The Vanishing American Jew: In Search of Jewish Identity for the Next Century* (New York: Touchstone, 1997); J. J. Goldberg, "America's Vanishing Jews," *Jerusalem Report,* November 5, 1992; Anthony Gordon and Richard Horowitz, "Will Your Grandchildren Be Jews?," *Jewish Spectator* (Fall 1996): 36–38; Egon Mayer, *A Demographic Revolution in American Jewry,* vol. 1, *David W. Belin Lecture in American Jewish Affairs* (Ann Arbor: Frankel Center for Judaic Studies, University of Michigan, 1992); Jonathan Sarna, "The Secret of Jewish Continuity," *Commentary* 98, no. 4 (1994): 55–58; Jack Wertheimer, "Family Values and the Jews," *Commentary* 97, no. 1 (1994): 30–34; and Jack Wertheimer, Charles Liebman, and Steven Cohen, "How to Save American Jews," *Commentary* 101, no. 1 (1996): 47–51. For a policy-oriented study of the implementation of the 1990 NJPS, see Hayim Herring, "How the 1990 National Jewish Population Survey Was Used by Federation Professionals for Jewish Continuity Purposes," *Journal of Jewish Communal Service* 76, no. 3 (2000): 216–227.

38. See Simon Ravidowicz, *Israel: The Ever-Dying People and Other Essays* (Madison, NJ: Fairleigh Dickinson University Press, 1986), 217.

39. Berman, *Speaking of Jews,* 144.

40. Michael Steinhardt, "On the Question of Crisis," *Contact: The Journal of Jewish Life Network* 5, no. 3 (2003): 9.

41. As opposed to my use of public sources (such as research and popular articles), or interviews, with regard to Jewish Federations of North America (JFNA) archival material, I decided, in agreement with JFNA professionals, to conceal the identities of those involved in the 2000–2001 NJPS.

42. Hart, *Social Science,* 76–80.

43. Elihu Bergman, "The American Jewish Population Erosion," *Midstream* 23 (October 1977): 9–19. For other examples, see Edward Shapiro, *A Time for Healing: American Jewry since World War II* (Baltimore: Johns Hopkins University Press, 1992).

44. Reisman, "Reflections," 351.

45. Sidney Goldstein, "What of the Future? The New National Jewish Population Study for American Jewry," in *Proceedings of the Rabbinical Assembly,* ed. Rabbi Jules Harlow (New York: Rabbinical Assembly, 1992), 3.

46. Steven M. Cohen, "The Demise of the 'Good Jew': Marshall Sklare Award Lecture," *Contemporary Jewry* 32, no. 1 (2012): 85–93.

47. Ibid.

48. Interview, October 2011.

49. Interview, January 2012.

50. See Berman, *Speaking of Jews;* and Hart, *Social Science.*

51. Samuel Heilman, "The Sociology of American Jewry: The Last Ten Years," *Annual Review of Sociology* 8 (1982): 155.

52. Sarah Benor, "Do American Jews Speak a 'Jewish Language'? A Model of Jewish Linguistic Distinctiveness," *Jewish Quarterly Review* 99, no. 2 (2009): 230–269.

53. My usage of gendered pronouns here reflects the gender bias within the field of Jewish social science in which men are more highly represented than women.

54. Cohen, "Demise of the 'Good Jew,'" 92.

55. Barry Kosmin, "An Appreciation of the Contribution of Egon Mayer to Jewish Population, Community, and Family Studies," *Contemporary Jewry* 26, no. 1 (2006): 168.

56. Sidney Goldstein, "Beyond the 1990 National Jewish Population Survey: A Research Agenda," *Contemporary Jewry* 14, no. 1 (1993): 159–160.

57. Goldstein, "What of the Future?," 4.

58. Theodore M. Porter, *Trust in Numbers: The Pursuit of Objectivity in Science and Public Life* (Princeton, NJ: Princeton University Press, 1995).

59. For more on boundary work, see Sheila Jasanoff, *The Fifth Branch: Science Advisers as Policymakers* (Cambridge, MA: Harvard University Press, 1990), 14.

60. For the staging of science, see Stephen Hilgartner, *Science on Stage: Expert Advice as Public Drama* (Stanford, CA: Stanford University Press, 2000).

61. In a dramatically different set of circumstances, one deserving of its own separate discussion, the 2000–2001 NJPS precipitated a vicious public debate in which both opponents and supporters of the survey mobilized a dauntingly technical language of statistics. Filled, as it was, with the procedural details about statistical sampling, screening, and stratification methods, it seemed as if the dryness of the discourse of and about American Jewry was the survey's most definitive feature. For examples of such dry discourse, see Leonard Saxe and Charles Kadushin, "The Arithmetic of U.S. Jewry," *Jerusalem Post,* November 17, 2003, 135; Uriel Heilman, "NJPS 2000–01: A Lost Cause?," *Jerusalem Post,* December 17, 2003; and J. J. Goldberg, "A Jewish Recount," *New York Times,* September 17, 2003, 27.

62. Hacking, "Biopower," 279.

63. Porter, *Trust in Numbers,* 51.

64. See Allison Jaggar, "Love and Knowledge: Emotion in Feminist Epistemology," in *Gender/Body/Knowledge: Feminist Reconstructions of Being and Knowing,* ed. Allison Jaggar and Susan Bordo (New Brunswick, NJ: Rutgers University Press, 1989), 145–171; and Catherine Lutz, "Emotion, Thought, and Estrangement: Emotion as a Cultural Category," *Cultural Anthropology* 1, no. 3 (1986): 287–309.

65. Frank Furedi, *Therapy Culture: Cultivating Vulnerability in an Uncertain Age* (London: Routledge, 2004).

66. Richard Posner, *Public Intellectuals: A Study of Decline* (Cambridge, MA: Harvard University Press, 2001), 127.

67. Don Handelman, *Nationalism and the Israeli State: Bureaucratic Logic in Public Events* (Oxford: Berg, 2004).

68. Heilman, "NJPS 2000–01."

69. See Jasanoff, *Fifth Branch;* and Sarah Igo, "Subjects of Persuasion: Survey Research as a Solicitous Science, or, The Public Relations of the Polls," in *Social Knowledge in the Making,* ed.

Charles Camic, Neil Gross, and Michèle Lamont (Chicago: University of Chicago Press, 2011), 285–306.

70. Calvin Goldscheider, "Are American Jews Vanishing Again?," *Contexts* 2, no. 1 (2003): 18–24; Calvin Goldscheider, *Studying the Jewish Future* (Seattle: University of Washington Press, 2004); and Bethamie Horowitz, "Stop Worrying: Details Follow," *The Forward,* December 22, 2006.

71. MacDonald Moore, "The Neodox: Prophets of Spreadsheet Tribalism" (unpublished manuscript).

72. Goldberg, "Jewish Recount."

73. Shaul Kelner, *Tours That Bind: Diaspora, Pilgrimage, and Israeli Birthright Tourism* (New York: New York University Press, 2010).

74. Nikolas Rose, *Numbers, Powers of Freedom: Reframing Political Thought* (Cambridge: Cambridge University Press, 1999), 197–232.

75. Saxe and Kadushin, "Arithmetic of U.S. Jewry."

76. Michel Foucault, "Politics and the Study of Discourse," in *The Foucault Effect: Studies in Governmentality,* ed. Graham Burchell, Colin Gordon, and Peter Miller (Chicago: University of Chicago Press, 1991), 59.

PART III

COUNTING OBJECTS:
MATERIAL SUBJECTS AND THE SOCIAL LIVES
OF ENUMERATED THINGS

7 "Let's Start with the Big Ones"

Numbers, Thin Description, and the Magic of Yiddish at the Yiddish Book Center

Joshua B. Friedman

To ENTER the gorgeous, multimillion-dollar facility of the Yiddish Book Center, located on the bucolic campus of Hampshire College in Amherst, Massachusetts, visitors open a heavy set of wood doors and walk through an entryway upon which can be read a slightly altered version of the famous quote by Yiddish linguist Max Weinreich: "Yiddish is magic—it will outwit history."[1] Passing through another set of doors, they are welcomed by a docent, usually an older retiree, or a work-study student from one of the area's colleges within the region's five-college consortium.[2] After perhaps a bit of small talk, they are shown to a small room with a flat-screen television embedded into one wall. The room's other walls, each painted in deep, matted shades of blues and reds, display museum panels that briefly summarize the center's work of language and culture rescue—its now famous efforts to salvage the world's Yiddish books, and its more recent attempts to record oral histories, promote the translation of Yiddish literature, and organize Yiddish language and Jewish cultural education programs, especially for younger generations of students. Surrounded by these panels are three rows of comfortable, upholstered wood benches, the kind that a religious institution in a different context might have used as pews.

After the visitors get situated, the docent starts a short documentary video titled *Bridge of Books* that tells the Book Center's story—the efforts of its charismatic founder, Aaron Lansky, to rescue the world's Yiddish books before assimilated Jews, unable to grasp their value, or aging Yiddish institutions, unable to survive as their membership bases eroded, could throw them away. "Books were our portable homeland," Lansky passionately explains. "Books define our national identity. We call ourselves, '*am hasefer*': the people of the book," he continues as images of the Book Center's building, Yiddish print blocks, and pictures of old Yiddish books flash across the screen.[3]

The film addresses visitors as if they are hearing this story for the first time. But for many of them, the narrative of the Book Center is already a familiar one.

Approaching the Yiddish Book Center, Amherst, Massachusetts. Photo by the author.

In 2004, Aaron Lansky published a memoir about his mission of Yiddish rescue. *Outwitting History: The Amazing Adventures of a Man Who Rescued a Million Yiddish Books* won a National Jewish Book Award and dramatically increased the institution's popular exposure and that of Yiddish more generally.[4] Followed by a speaking tour that took Lansky to synagogues, Jewish community centers and cultural institutions, the release of *Outwitting History* was also accompanied by the public launch of the organization's eponymous "25th Anniversary Campaign."[5] By the summer of 2006, the center was already planning construction of a new building wing, completed in 2009, that provided new classrooms and offices, a performance hall, and a state of the art, climate-controlled book storage facility.[6]

As revealed by his memoir's subtitle, Lansky's best-selling narrative starts with numbers. From the vantage point of its readers, a decision actually to visit the institution represents an opportunity to see an abstract, numerical representation of Yiddish books take on material form. A range of desires and expectations are embedded in that transformation—from the number to the book object; as reflected in Lansky's discourse about the intimate connection between Jews and their books, the experience of witnessing the center's collection is laden with emotion and with passionate historical as well as future indices. The association of Yiddish with the Holocaust, the emotional discourse of "millions" in Jewish life, and the much analyzed desire of American Jews to salvage fragments of the Eastern European Jewish past are all potentially latent in the act of visiting the center's collection. Add to this the fact that, over the course of the center's history, a number of these visitors would have sent their own books or, as more recently is the case, their parents' and grandparents' books to the center, and we can begin to have a sense of the different ways that these particular numbers have become involved—intimately—in the social life of Yiddish.

Numbers and Economies of Affection

These connections, between numbers and affective realms of intimacy and desire, offer an alternative take on the social significance of numbers within institutional contexts. Dominated by a focus on "dry" disciplines such as demography and statistics, critical scholarship on numbers has emphasized ideological opposition between numerical ways of knowing and realms of emotion and sentiment. As Shaylih Muehlmann notes in her own critical examination of numerical authority within the practices of nongovernmental organizations (NGOs) in northern Mexico's Colorado River delta, the association of numbers with dispassion has been constitutive of their power throughout the history of western modernity: "The idea that numbers are universal, objective, and neutral mathematical truths that cannot differ cross-culturally," Muehlmann writes, "is a defining feature of our age."[7] In the analysis of a variety of social projects associated with "modernity," including, for example, population management, the commodification of natural and symbolic resources, state-led development projects, and language revitalization (to name only a few), the authority of numbers is closely linked by scholars with connotations of dispassion, objectivity, and neutrality.[8] Numerical knowledge has played an especially powerful role in the politics of language endangerment. Jane Hill, for example, has identified enumeration as one of the central organizing themes of the rhetoric of endangerment that surrounds projects of linguistic maintenance and revitalization. This is evident, for example, in discourses of professional linguists and heritage institutions such as UNESCO, which continuously call "for more accurate enumeration of languages and their speakers in order to plan more precisely for action. . . ."[9] Similarly, Jacqueline Urla's account of the use of statistics in the Basque language revival movement highlights how the perceived objectivity of numerical knowledge is constitutive of the powerful role statistics play in the production of both ethnolinguistic identity and its attendant cultural politics.[10]

But if much of this scholarship has connected the power of numbers to connotations of objectivity and empirical precision, it has less rigorously analyzed the affective dimensions of an equally prevalent and ideologically informed quality of numbers—specifically, the "thinness" with which numbers describe their objects. I draw on the notion of "thin description" here in contrast to Clifford Geertz's famous discussion of ethnography as "thick description."[11] Where thick description aims to distinguish fine-grained differences between semiotic phenomena by embedding them in a historical and social analysis, numbers operate by abstracting and eliding those contextual differences so that elements may be enumerated. On the one hand, then, their thinness is part of why numbers appear to transcend any particular context or perspective and are thus treated as objective and universally valid mediums of description. But, on the other hand, that very thinness also makes numbers powerful indices of a range of affective dispositions that are "deeper" or more "thickly layered" than numbers themselves—a sense of mission, a call to action, a feeling of belonging.[12] In the Book Center's numbers of Yiddish books, for example, numbers hold out *something else.* First and foremost, a collected book; but beyond that, a bond with ancestors or the possibility that Yiddish, in written form, will be passed down to future generations.

The investigation of numerical thinness in particular should be seen as part of a broader concern among scholars with how thinness (sometimes real, sometimes imagined) seems increasingly to structure the experience of public culture within a mass-mediated world. As Theodore Porter observes about the relationship between thinness and thickness in the social sciences: "[t]hinness is, if not the natural state of things, an appealing modern project."[13] For ethnographers, such projects can be especially vexing. As much as contemporary anthropologists are rightfully critical about the reifications of "authentic" otherness that can structure claims about the thinness of modern life, they have generally been committed to the project of thick description. These commitments are often clearest in ethnographies of public and mass-mediated culture, which are frequently critiqued because, as Walter Armbrust notes, "they tend to be 'thin.'"[14] Figuring out how to approach thinness ethnographically can thus be its own methodological, analytical, and even ethical challenge. John Jackson's recent book *Thin Description,* for example, draws on ethnographic work with the African Hebrew Israelites of Jerusalem (AHIJ) to highlight how claims about the thickness of ethnographic description can underwrite a sense of definitiveness to anthropological research in ways that foreclose other accounts. As the people and communities anthropologists study are increasingly adept at representing themselves to global publics across a range of media forms, so too should the authority anthropologists often attribute to thickness be critically reconsidered.[15]

Against the backdrop of these scholarly debates, an especially valuable contribution of this volume is its contributors' attentiveness to the political, historical, and epistemological entanglements between thinness and thickness within the Jewish cultures of enumeration they analyze. As Michal Kravel-Tovi describes in chapter 6 of this volume, the power of demographic statistics, generally assumed to be prized for their "dry" scientific precision, lies also with their "wetness"—that is, whether they will be affectively moving enough to precipitate individual and collective action. Both Oren Stier (chapter 1) and Carol Kidron (chapter 2) evidence a concern with what I call thickness at the heart of numbers in postwar Jewish cultures of Holocaust memorialization. In Kidron's work, the possibility that the figure of six million may reduce the lives of Holocaust victims to an empty—in fact, thin—numerical signifier underwrites her analysis of Yad Vashem's efforts to recover aspects of the personal identities of victims. In Stier's analysis, that same number derives its power precisely in its capacity to transcend any particular act of enumeration. As an iconic embodiment of the Holocaust, Stier argues, six million functions to distill and summarize, thus not only enumerating the dead, but also explaining, justifying, and even avenging. In their analyses then, these authors bring out the contested and mutually constitutive relationships between numerical thin- and thickness, thus critically interrogating the social and historical conditions that sustain an authoritative, a moving, or otherwise satisfactory numerical description.

The focus in this chapter on the close relationship between thick and thin within the culture of enumeration at the Yiddish Book Center further grounds and concomitantly builds upon this analytical trajectory. Since the Book Center's founding in 1980, the organization has cultivated a national, primarily American Jewish public of members, volunteers, students, and, of course, financial donors. Portions of that public have donated their own parents' and grandparents' Yiddish books; some have named the Book Center as a benefactor in their wills; still others are invested in the center's mission to train new generations of young students to read, write, and speak Yiddish. The center's Yiddish public is thus made up of people possessing an array of expectations about what a center for Yiddish books is and what its responsibilities should be to the text artifacts it has collected. Against this backdrop, the thin numerical description of Yiddish books helps facilitate a broad range of affectively laden possibilities and desires that so many have invested in the center's collection. This is what I refer to as "the magic" of Yiddish at the Book Center. Producing that magic, as I will show, has become an implicit, ongoing practice at the institution. After all, not everyone who visits the Book Center always sees, or is willing to see, the cultural values or future possibilities of so many numbers of Yiddish books. Some people just see large numbers of objects. Others come seeking particular values (e.g., their actual grandparent's books) that may be hard to identify among so many text artifacts. Thin description at these moments can appear *too* thin. As such, if Yiddish books are to be imaginatively saturated with the full range of values so many have invested in them, both the center and its public must collaboratively partake in the interactional work of making thin description meaningful.

The ethnography of these practices within this American Jewish cultural institution offers an alternative ethnographic setting from the bureaucratic and biopolitical contexts in which numerical cultures are usually analyzed. Like other nonprofits that employ enumeration in their public discourse, for example, as a way of summarizing institutional accomplishments, there is little concern at the center with whether its numbers of collected books are scientifically validated or highly precise; and yet, it is specifically in their capacity to mediate affectively laden transactions with Yiddish that underwrite these numbers' power. In a pattern germane to the U.S. nonprofit sector more generally, which has come increasingly to depend on private donors, philanthropists, and foundations, the Yiddish Book Center banks, both literally and figuratively, on its ability to generate an emotional identification with the institution and its grand mission. At the center in particular, though, the centrality of affective attachment is especially salient. The decline of the North American population of secular, native Yiddish speakers has meant that the contemporary patrons of Yiddish institutions and cultural projects outside the ultra-Orthodox world are increasingly composed of people whose primary means of engaging with Yiddish are affective as opposed to communicative or literary in nature. As Jeffrey Shandler has observed about the Yiddish Book Center, the scale of the center's collection in comparison to its possible readers means that most people who confront the Book Center's Yiddish books do so affectively; that is, "with the nose as much as the eye."[16]

An ethnographic focus on thin, numerical description at the Book Center thus provides a new perspective with which to consider American Jewish engagements with Yiddish. In this case study, numbers help reframe and augment what Shandler has referred to as "postvernacular" Yiddish language and culture.[17] Postvernacularity in Shandler's analysis designates a range of practices and projects—from performance, to the collection of Yiddish material culture, to face-to-face conversation among Yiddish students—in which what is most significant is less what is being communicated in Yiddish than the "the symbolic value invested in the language apart from the semantic value of any given utterance in it. . . ."[18] But whereas postvernacular engagements with Yiddish have been addressed to questions of cultural and linguistic survival in general (i.e., how to reconceptualize the "life" of language, the relationship between language and culture, and so forth), the ethnographic focus here is on the affective dimensions of numbers and their place within institutional practice. This focus illuminates how numbers help structure the relationship between the Book Center's affective Yiddish economy and the political economy of U.S. ethno-religious cultural production in which the nonprofit cultural institution is embedded.

Based on eight months of research at the Yiddish Book Center in 2010 and 2011, as part of a twenty-month ethnographic research project on the contemporary American Jewish engagement with Yiddish in the United States, this chapter draws on participant observation and both formal and informal interviews with volunteer Book Center collectors, or "zamlers," as well as visitors, volunteers, and staff. It also uses textual analysis of Yiddish Book Center media, and formal analysis of the physical space of the center's headquarters. Clearly, the goal here is not to provide an exhaustive analysis of numbers within the Book Center's history and contemporary context. Nor should thin description be understood as the only or even primary project of the institution; the center has pursued, and continues to pursue, a variety of educational, translation, and cultural projects to educate its public about Yiddish language, history, and culture. But alongside these projects, the center has not been able to do without its numbers of collected books. Those numbers remain critical to the passions of the center's public.

The Yiddish Book Center: Making Yiddish Books "Count"

The Yiddish Book Center (originally the National Yiddish Book Exchange and previously the National Yiddish Book Center) was founded in 1980 by then twenty-three-year-old, New Bedford, Massachusetts native, Aaron Lansky. After majoring in modern Jewish history and studying Yiddish as an undergraduate at Hampshire College, Lansky began a graduate program in Eastern European Jewish studies at McGill University in Montreal. There he formulated the idea to "save the world's Yiddish books." According to his own account, now the official account of the institution, Lansky's notion responded to the limited number of Yiddish texts available to students and the danger of their disposal with the aging of the majority of native, non-ultra-Orthodox Yiddish speakers. To address the problem, he started posting fliers and advertising in newspapers that he was looking to collect Yiddish books from their elderly Jewish owners.

Lansky's story departs from the wonder of numbers. In promotional literature, tours of the Book Center's Amherst facility, and especially in his memoir *Outwitting History*, it is the sheer mass of book objects—"a million Yiddish books"—that transformed what was originally intended as a two-year leave of absence from graduate school into what is now his fourth decade of leadership within what is arguably the most well-known Yiddish institution in the United States. As he describes in his memoir, in 1980 when he "decided to save the world's Yiddish books . . . scholars believed 70,000 volumes remained"; however, "today," he explains, "my colleagues and I have collected more than one and one-half *million*"[19] (emphasis in the original).

In his memoir, as well as Book Center media more generally, the reader follows young Lansky as he travels to abandoned basements and attics, the homes of elderly Yiddish speakers and aging Yiddish institutions to salvage Yiddish books before they are thrown away. Traveling by moving van, Lansky encounters elderly Jews from the Old World who entrust him with their prized possessions. In that world, forgotten by most assimilated American Jews and their institutions, the printed Yiddish word possesses unparalleled value. "He says," Lansky recalls of an elderly book donor in *Bridge of Books*, "'this book here my wife and I we bought in 1927 we went without lunch for a week, we should be able to afford it!'"[20]

Two typical scenes of collection dominate his account, both of which high-light the close relationship between older Jews and their books: the intimate contexts of exchange between owners of Yiddish books and Lansky's young group of friends and last-minute salvage efforts of books from dumpsters, attics, or basements scattered across a 1980s urban and primarily North American landscape. "The encounters," with the older generation, Lansky explains, "were almost always emotional: People cried and poured out their hearts, often with a candor that surprised us all."[21] When books were not literally "handed down" from older generations, they are described as "rescued." In such narratives, Yiddish books are themselves invested with the qualities of human subjectivity. "*Di bikher zenen geven lebedike nefoshes,*" Lansky quotes of one book donor who had "recovered [several Yiddish books] at the last minute from the *meysim shtibl,* the room where corpses are prepared for burial at the local Jewish cemetery."[22]

This portrayal of the close, intimate relationship between Yiddish books and their owners articulates a productive ambiguity—one that is reconciled by the project of thin description. On one level, the mission of the center is to rescue Yiddish books as a way to transmit their content—the "Yiddish" contained within each object. But the emotionally potent image of artifactual, paper books, metaphorically endowed with the tears of their owners and invested with human capacities, histories, and potentials simultaneously suggests that the material book-artifact itself is the thing of highest value. In the first instance, the artifact is valuable ultimately because it is a sign. It signals that what lies inside this material thing is something of valuable Yiddish content, waiting, as it were, to be "articulated" by a new reader. In the second, the book's very materiality makes it valuable—literally, *worthy* of salvage.

The center's institutional rhetoric shifts between different meanings of "the book." "They had so much to tell us," Lansky says at one point in *Bridge of Books,* implicitly suggesting what might be recoverable through the Book Center's mission.[23] But who "they" are and where and what the thing is about which they had so much to tell is left undefined. Do valuable stories belong to the books' donors or their authors? Was a book within the center's collection valuable because it was *actually* held and read by the Yiddish-speaking ancestors or perhaps a book donor's actual parents or grandparents? Or was it valuable as a catalyst for new readers? Perhaps books embodied another quality altogether? Such questions are generally left open in the institution's rhetoric; within the conceptual space of that openness, the visitor is allowed, even invited, to fill in answers.

For most of the first two decades of the institution's existence, prior to the emergence of affordable book digitization technologies, there was little need to make any differentiation at all between these different senses of the book. Each Yiddish object salvaged was both a material link to the past and the material impetus for Yiddish to be studied and read in the future (hence the title of the documentary *Bridge of Books*). For a donor, collector, or volunteer sorting books at the center, helping to organize artifactual Yiddish books simultaneously imbued them with possible, readable futures. Even if the Book Center's staff and volunteers could not read the content of a given book, to run a hand over its cover, to recognize the passing of time in its smell, to marvel at handwritten notes in its margins, or struggle to make out its author's name, were all implicitly linked to the possibility that someone else, an anonymous other, might actually *read* from the very object imbued with the ancestors' tears.

Of course, for an ethno-religious community that had, as Jonathan Woocher argued, elevated "survival" to sacred proportions, it's easy to see why American Jews could become so invested in the materiality of paper Yiddish books.[24] The book offered a chance to salvage—even if only in a fragmented form—a language, literature, and culture that most American Jews have been unable (and often also unwilling) to maintain in their own, everyday lives. *Book* salvage opened up *Yiddish* salvage not only for those who could read Yiddish but also those who could count the language's books. "Is there a treasure in your attic?" asks an early Book Center flyer intended for distribution in synagogues, Jewish community centers, and other locations where potential owners of Yiddish books might be found. "Yiddish Books Are a Cultural Treasure of the Jewish People . . . Yiddish studies are on the rise, and students and scholars need books."[25] That each volume collected is "a treasure" linked the volunteer book collector, young student, or financial donor not just to the Book Center but also to both the transhistorical collective of "the Jewish people" and the growing public of "students and scholars" who "need books."

Understandably then, actual interactions of donation and collection became especially powerful, affectively loaded experiences. To be sure, the rate of book collection has slowed since the center first began its mission; thus, the practice of book rescue no longer plays a definitive, central role in the center's work that it once did. Collection does, however, continue. "Yes, we still collect Yiddish books," a museum panel in the video room described above reminds visitors. "We receive boxes, we deploy zamlers (volunteer collectors), and we're always ready to race off at a moment's notice whenever Yiddish books are in danger." As the vision of devoted volunteers rushing to collect books "in danger" suggests, the work of collecting artifactual Yiddish books represents an especially illustrative ethnographic window through which to observe how Yiddish books become invested with a broad range of possible values connected simultaneously to their content and their materiality.

Pointing to one set of these possible values is the designation of the center's book collectors as "zamlers." The concept of the zamler is most associated in Jewish history and collective memory with the pre- and immediate postwar collection missions of what is today the YIVO Institute for Jewish Research.

Self-consciously committed to Yiddish as the national language of the Jewish people, YIVO was established in 1925 in then Wilno, Poland (for Jews "Vilna" and today officially Vilnius, Lithuania), as the Yidisher Visnshaftlekher Institut (Jewish Scientific Institute). Serving as the national, social scientific center for the study of Jewish life, YIVO was a central institution within the Jewish diaspora nationalist movement in Eastern Europe. Its networks of zamlers were critical to its work, collecting materials and information (customs, rituals, material culture, etc.), generally from shtetl Jews whose culture YIVO's social scientists worried was disappearing.[26] Through the application of the title zamler to the Book Center's volunteers, the institution thus rhetorically embeds its own collection practices within a transnational history of Eastern European Jewish cultural salvage.

During the collection trips of the Book Center's zamlers, the personal, embodied participation of donors and collectors adds layers of individual investment into Yiddish books in ways that, through personal experience, affectively "thicken" and make tangible the grand, ethno-national narratives of Jewish loss, salvage, and continuity such as those encoded in the figure of the zamler. In interviews I conducted with nine zamlers as well as on four book collection trips with zamlers, I saw how personal, often familial experiences are imaginatively invested in book objects. Nearly every zamler I interviewed, for example, noted that their trips to collect Yiddish books generally accompany end-of-life periods for owners or the family of owners. This fact accords with (and sometimes echoes) Lansky's own accounts of book salvage throughout the history of the center—in which scenes of collection often transpire as individuals and families prepare themselves for their own death or that of a loved one.

The zamlers I interviewed talked often about readying themselves for the kinds of intimate connections between people and books described in the center's narrative. This does not mean that zamlers always, or even normally, encounter book donors with intimate, personal connections to Yiddish books. The majority of donors today, as both zamlers and the Book Center have noted, are often the children or even grandchildren of the actual owners of Yiddish books, and thus they tend to be at more of a remove from the intimate social relations the institution has attributed to the things it collects. But zamlers do encounter owners with the kinds of emotional attachments Lansky describes in his narrative. As one book donor told me, after donating the books of her father, who had been a Yiddish writer, "It [donating her family's books] feels like a parallel process to taking care of my mother" (who had kept her husband's books until her death), akin to the work of clearing out the house, arranging the burial, and tending to the other processes that accompany death and dying. For some zamlers, the possibility of confronting mourners is a reason to make collection trips as swift and professional as possible. One zamler, for example, playfully imagines himself as a "superhero" swooping in quickly and efficiently—prepared with boxes and tape—to safeguard precious Yiddish books, assuring his donors that their books will be well taken care of. Others explicitly see "zamlering" as an opportunity for them to perform care for the elderly by caring for their material Yiddish things.[27] "Sarah," who was trained in gerontology, describes her personal, two-decade investment in zamlering as an extension of her work with families confronting end-of-life issues. "I can't express enough my role as a caretaker for these donations, as a kind of safe transport," she would tell me, reflecting on the difficulty families can experience as they determine how to part with the belongings of their loved ones.[28]

Not all donors or zamlers are this passionate about Yiddish books or their owners. Another zamler, an active volunteer in his community, described his work on behalf of the center as similar "to any other volunteer job" that he does. But when such zamlers go to collect books, they cannot assume that the donor feels similarly detached—especially in light of the possibility that donors have recently lost loved ones. The same principle applies to the donors—even those with little attachment to their books may encounter Book Center volunteers as passionately invested in Yiddish book collection as the center itself. Generally meeting far away from Amherst, neither party knows the precise value of what they are collecting (in terms of the rarity of a particular volume, its provenance, literary value or future uses) for the institution and the world of imagined others who need books. In other words, with the underlying possibility in mind that books might indeed be personally connected to someone else, the investment of Yiddish books with value does not depend on an active, intense investment on behalf of each individual. Indeed, such an investment can unfold even out of an uncertainty about what to do with these objects now that a parent or grandparent no longer needs them or has died. As one donor explained, as Sarah and I arrived at her suburban home to receive a small collection of vintage Yiddish records, she wasn't entirely sure the records belonged to her mother. She had discovered them among her mother's things in the attic, while moving her into hospice. But her family had owned a Jewish retirement home, so perhaps when it had closed, the records had somehow ended up in a box of her mother's items. Yet, as the donor went on to explain, the records *could* have belonged to her mother, or *might* be valuable in some way to someone else.

With the value of books, the motivation for donation, or the possible futures of donations left so open in these interactions, the narrative and rhetoric of the Book Center itself necessarily endows meaning. Indeed, zamlers are familiar with the center's history and mission and have generally read *Outwitting History*. Sarah, for example, got involved collecting books after attending a program at the Book Center. She even met the charismatic Aaron Lansky in person. Thus, when zamlers come to a house, they come equipped not only with boxes and tape but also with the narratives and implicit meanings of what Yiddish books meant to the ancestors. Those narratives provide relatively stable meanings and roles that zamlers and donors are able to identify with and enact, thus providing context for what might otherwise be a meeting devoid of it.

These social relations, and the narratives they help sustain, are organized less by the actual backgrounds and life stories of individuals who are party to these exchanges than they are by the collectible object of the artifactual Yiddish book itself. That every Yiddish book, regardless of title, provenance, literary value, or otherwise, is deemed "a treasure" allows for a relatively anonymous public of zamlers and donors to engage in the iterative, and potentially affectively charged, work of collection. In interviews, this iterative nature stood out and produced and reproduced the identity of Yiddish books as treasures. "I've been doing this for twenty years," Sarah told me, "and there have been so many other life changes that I've gone through, but collecting books has been something that's stayed the same."[29] Or, as Walter, another volunteer zamler, told me after a collection trip to the home of a recent widow who had decided to donate her husband's books, "I always make sure that every donor knows their books are important." He does this, he explained, regardless of the titles or the condition of what they are actually donating.

With each one understood as a treasure, it is the trust zamlers and donors are able to place in the collected book's value that has allowed people like Sarah, who do not speak, read, or write in Yiddish, to participate in the work of Yiddish salvage. In her narrative, like those of other second-generation and baby-boomer Jews, Yiddish was a "secret language" that parents and grandparents spoke, "so that the children shouldn't understand." Of course, not all of the individual zamlers who participate in these practices resemble Sarah; some zamlers and book donors I interviewed were "native listeners"; others are native speakers but cannot read Yiddish. According to the center, the first wave of zamlers in the 1980s, like book donors, were generally native Yiddish speakers. But regardless of an individual's Yiddish proficiency, the inherent value attributed to each Yiddish book is what has allowed this broad public to engage in the particular salvage work of the Book Center.

Able to "count on" the value of each Yiddish book, counting itself can become an emotionally laden act of Yiddish rescue. By adding them incrementally to the overall, numerically defined collection, zamlers participate in the work of "saving Yiddish." Thus Alex, another zamler, in an expression of his "appreciation and love for the Yiddish language," literally keeps a count of the number of Yiddish text artifacts he collects on behalf of the center: "I'm now approaching the milestone of reaching—of having zamlered—" he corrects himself, "1,000 books and 1,000 pounds of books. I'm probably in the 800 some odd pounds of books, and roughly eight some-odd-hundred books and magazines as well as a few sheets of music and some newsletters and things like that."

Counting and even weighing for Alex is hardly emotionless in its routine nature; rather, by keeping personal, numerical accounts of the books he collects, he literally measures his contribution to the center's salvage project and by extension the larger Jewish project of cultural and linguistic rescue. Not all zamlers keep such accounts; but neither is he the only one I met who does so. What his accounts reveal is how the objects' quality of enumerability enables all the zamlers discussed here to invest themselves and others in the center's work. Like Walter, who makes sure his donors know that each book is valuable, or Sarah, who invests herself in the work of caring for elderly Jews and their families by caring for Yiddish books, zamlers can invest themselves in the Book Center, the Jewish people, and the Yiddish language itself precisely because Yiddish books are interchangeable.

As so many enumerable treasures, each one valuable regardless of its material condition, content, or provenance, we can thus also see the multiplicity of values, hopes, and expectations that Yiddish books index for these donors and zamlers. At the moment of collection, it is not always clear—even to donors and zamlers themselves—whether a book is valued because of its materiality or its content; rather books are valued as personally treasured material objects, as sacred artifacts of the Jewish people, and also as carriers of potentially irreplaceable Yiddish content. The capacity of these artifacts to be invested with such an array of values emerges out of the social and material conditions of the collection process itself: the lack of familiarity that marks the encounter between zamlers and donors reinforces the perduring ambiguity about the precise reasons that an object is being donated, and the explicit expectations about what will be preserved in the process. Indeed, a "Yiddish book" need not even be an actual "book" at all—but any item containing any amount of printed Yiddish writing that is materially durable enough to collect.[30] Like the center's rhetoric in which the exact meaning of the Yiddish book remains open for interpretation, so too in these collection missions must zamlers, and at times even donors, leave open the precise reasons that Yiddish books are valuable. In the conceptual space of that openness, Yiddish books can become saturated with any number of different desires, possibilities, and expectations.

Thin Description and the End(s) of the Book

In spite of this multiplicity, though, the very conditions of collection and the ultimate goals of the institution have in fact constrained what the center is actually able to fully preserve in and through the preservation of Yiddish books. Despite, for example, the emotional investment of a zamler such as Sarah, who grounds her care for book donors in the care she performs for their Yiddish things, the center has not been able, nor has it usually sought, to preserve evidence of the historical connections between Yiddish books and their actual, previous contexts of use and ownership. They have not generally, for example, kept records of who donated which book or kept, as an archive might, collections from particular donors intact.

To be sure, there are understandable reasons for this lack of attention to the histories of actual, artifactual books. From the outset of the collection mission, in light of the aging of the population of native Yiddish speakers, the center immediately prioritized the goal of quickly collecting as many Yiddish books as possible—conditions that, with a largely volunteer staff, lent themselves poorly to preserving the actual histories of the books collected. On the one hand, as in cases where books have been salvaged as opposed to donated, taken from the back-stocks of institutions or simply mailed to the center without ceremony, there exist no intimate connections of ownership to track. But more significantly, lack of attention to such connections reflected simply a matter of institutional priority. Lansky rightly recognized that each moment lost was a moment in which someone might mistake a potentially priceless Yiddish object, an irreplaceable piece of Yiddish literature or history, for an old, worthless book.

Ultimately then, if the form of the Yiddish book was valuable at the Book Center, it was not only because elderly Jews had an ethno-religious predisposition toward bounded, paper book objects; it was because the form of the book functioned as a sign. It testified, *for the Center and its collecting public,* to the universal value of the Yiddish content "inside." Published originally for reading publics of native Yiddish speakers, the printed, mass-produced nature of the book seemed to witness to the universal value of its content. Such qualities can be assumed to have played a critical role in both the emotional and broader political economy of salvage at the center; specifically, it would have enabled the center's largely volunteer staff quickly to save large numbers of potentially priceless, irreplaceable Yiddish things without expending too many resources on the work of determining whether or not the content beneath the surface of the cover was of any value. Those questions about content could be answered by briefly looking over the objects themselves, as they were loaded or unloaded, one by one, into and out of boxes.

Nowhere in the history of the Book Center is the prioritization of the content over the material qualities of Yiddish books clearer than in the institution's initial efforts to digitize its collection of individual titles. In 1997, after years of collecting vintage books and sending collections of duplicates to university and national libraries, the center drew on funds raised from the Steven Spielberg Righteous Persons Foundation and other private donors to establish the Steven Spielberg Digital Yiddish Library. Initial funding aimed to cover the cost of digitizing around 12,000 of the center's roughly 15,000 unique titles. However, because the Yiddish Book Center began digitization when the technology was generally more expensive and less advanced, the company to which the center outsourced its work, the Pitney Bowes Management Services Company, had to split each volume down its spine in order to feed the individual pages through the scanner. (The center only digitized books for which it had copies and has since adopted digitization methods that do not require book disarticulation at all.) As former Book Center vice president Nancy Sherman explained in a *USA Today* article about the initial scanning project: "We had to destroy the books in order to save them forever. . . ." "We've realized," she continued, "that our mission wasn't just about collecting books. It's about preserving them."[31]

Understandably in light of the above ethnographic account of zamlers, efforts by the Book Center to preserve Yiddish by recirculating and even dematerializing artifactual Yiddish books has not quelled a desire among the institution's public for the Yiddish original. Frequently, at the Book Center, while conducting ethnography, or striking up conversations with visitors about what they valued about the institution, I would end up hearing Lansky's narratives of book collection expressed back to me. "Nobody wanted this stuff," one older Book Center donor and Yiddish enthusiast explained, incredulous that American Jews couldn't recognize the value of Yiddish books. "Aaron went down in the rain, to dumpsters, to save them! Can you believe it?!" "My favorite part," explained another woman, "was the 'designated eater,'" referring to the rotating individual among Lansky's young friends, assigned to eat the large portions of food that Lansky recalls being fed in the kitchens of immigrant-generation Jews during his collection trips. Another interviewee describes having been at the "famous incident" in which Aaron and his friends picked books out of a New York City dumpster that, as this interviewee reflected, "Aaron uses in every fundraising letter."

This last interviewee is right. These stories are, in fact, famous. Stories of book rescue have become, for many American Jews, part and parcel of the story of Yiddish; they are shared scripts that the Book Center's public—most of whom are non-Yiddish speaking or reading American Jews—tell themselves and each other about the language. Thus, even as the center ultimately decided to "destroy the books in order to save them forever," for many individuals who ritualize, tell, and retell the story of the center, the magic of Yiddish—its ability to outwit history—still cleaves to the paper book and its material contingencies: the adventure story of young, passionate Jews who travel by moving van to postindustrial urban areas to salvage the Yiddish past at the last minute; the physical work of boxing, moving, and storing Yiddish books; the kitchens of elderly Jews; the ancestors' tears absorbed into acid-yellow, paper pages.

At the center, I often met people in search of both the actual books the center had salvaged and the deeper values the books were assumed to index through their materiality—evidence of a book's past, its intimate histories, or the possibility that one's donated book would be read in the future. But, particularly in light of the center's material practices of book collection and processing, I soon learned that a desire for these "deeper" phenomena could only be met through thin description—the treatment of Yiddish books as *so many* interchangeable objects. The following, drawn from my field notes, characterizes just how critical thin description is to accommodating these desires:

"You know I've never been here before," a middle-aged visitor tells Mark, a young Book Center staff member. Mark is preparing to lead a tour for the visitors. It's springtime, and also Hampshire College's admitted-students day, so the center is starting to receive more visitors after a long, slow winter. "We're up here for a wedding, but my father has been a member for a long time. He donated 4,000 books here you know." Mark and I raise our eyebrows, impressed. Only a few months ago, we had helped move roughly 1,200 books from the house of a Yiddish writer in the Bronx. We thus had a sense of what is involved in that kind of transport. "Hold on," he said, reaching into a pocket for his cell phone, "that's actually him. Hello? Hi, Dad, hmmm, OK."

The visitor looks over to Mark. "He wants to know how his books are doing." Mark looks back at the visitor, searching for the right thing to say. "He says he wants to talk to someone who can check on them," the visitor continues, handing the phone to Mark before either of us can give an answer. I search the visitor's face for some sign of irony: a wink, a wry smile, a nod of understanding about the unreasonableness of his father's request. Nothing.

"Hello?" asks Mark into the cell phone. The family and I watch. "Hello?" he asks again, "are you there?" He turns back to the visitor apologetically, "I think the signal got cut off," he explains, handing the phone back. Mark steps back, relieved, to start the tour.

At drinks later in a local Amherst bar, I asked Mark about the incident: "That was terrifying," he said, laughing into his beer at the prospect of embarrassment on his part and potential disappointment on the part of the guest, at having to inform him that his family's actual books were unaccounted for. "It must have been an act of God," he continued with an ironic laugh, "that the call was dropped."

Mark hyperbolically describes his potential for discomfort as "terrifying"; but, leading such tours, he generally has little to fear. Most of the time, in fact, tours like these meet praise and astonishment at what the institution has accomplished. If this particular exchange threatened to break down into disappointment or argument, it is because Mark is rarely asked to give such a *thick* account of the histories of particular Yiddish books—the exact places from which they came, where they might be found in the center, where they might have been distributed, and who may or may not be reading them. That visitor, unlike others, had not yet learned to see, within the thousands of Yiddish books before him, the belongings of his own father.

As I spent more time at the Book Center, walking with visitors as they wandered between shelves of collected Yiddish books, I saw how other individuals, unlike Mark's visitor, were more comfortable with, and even embracing of, a valuation of Yiddish books according to their identities as interchangeable objects. These visitors were comfortable with the collection's "thin description." As they searched through the rows of industrial metal shelving units that line the center's main floor, they often searched out the signs of previous affective connection (like those described in Book Center media): hand-written inscriptions, dedications, book plates, and ephemera tucked into the pages of the Yiddish books. The pleasure of discovery, as I learned through interviews with Book Center staff, eventually motivated a decision to leave pieces of ephemera in books for visitors or buyers to discover. Of particular value are experiences of personal "connection": a found book stamped with the seal from a visitor's hometown public library, a copy of a title one remembers from his father's or grandfather's shelf, a book published in the same Eastern European city from which one's relatives escaped. In these ways, precisely because any book can potentially enclose a personal, emotionally valuable sign of connection, each book can potentially be "one's own."

Similar relationships adhere in the dedication of shelves. Over the course of the center's history interested visitors have been able to dedicate individual shelves, often in the name of parents or grandparents. As Morgan, a staff member, explained to me, the possibility of seeing one's dedicated shelf has often motivated people to visit the center, and possibly contribute further to the institution. "Of course," she jokingly remarked, "everything but the light switches here have a name on them!" But experiences at shelves in particular, she went on to explain, can be "very emotional for people." What books fill up a dedicated shelf does not generally matter in these affectively loaded rituals of visitation. With books able to function as substitutes for other books, the potential of a single book to index a rich, emotionally laden history of use is distributed to each element, each "unit," on a shelf. As one tearful, middle-aged visitor nostalgically expressed at the sight of her shelf: "This is as close as I'm going to get to my grandmother's shtetl."

These rituals of visitation clearly convey the degree to which the production of emotional connection depends upon the thin description of Yiddish books—the willingness to treat them as so many interchangeable objects. As one couple from New York explained to me as they conducted genealogical research on the Book Center's lone public computer, positioned amid stacks of artifactual Yiddish books: "Sure, we could have done this from home, but for us it's a kind of pilgrimage. My father," continued the older gentleman of the couple, "came over from Ukraine, and donated his Yiddish books here, *so I like to think that they are around me while we're here*" (emphasis added).

Shelves of Yiddish books on display at the center. Photo by the author.

This gentleman's comments capture perfectly the attitude toward books that Mark's visitor missed while roaming through the stacks. One must "like to think" that one's own, particular books can be found among so many interchangeable objects. As his words reveal, the visitor knows full well that the books in the stacks are likely not his father's actual books. The material objects in front of him, rather, are materialization of numerical scale—of the numbers of Yiddish books that the center has collected—into which he must be willing to perceive his father's actual contribution. That is his role within the production of the Book Center's magic.

For a nonprofit organization that depends on the volunteerism of a large number of individuals, facilitating that magic is a critical part of institutional labor. The desire by a visitor or volunteer to participate in the institution's activities or to be inspired by them—however small—is always potentially bound up in the larger political economy of cultural production. Donation of a parent's book today can lead tomorrow to membership. As Morgan was well aware, a decision to become a member, dedicate a shelf, or participate in a program can eventually lead to a larger financial donation down the line. Cultivating and transforming what might begin as a single, emotional experience at the center into more extensive, emergent chains of exchange forms the lifeblood of cultural organizations such as the Yiddish Book Center.

It is not surprising then that, alongside the center's other projects of education and translation, the institution also implicitly encourages these forms of apprehension and appreciation of books for their thin, numerical identities. Not far from where I met the woman confronting her grandmother's shtetl, visitors can read an information panel explaining that the books on display are just a small fraction of larger numbers, "less than five percent," according to the panel, of volumes salvaged by the center since 1980. "Several hundred thousand more," the panel continues, "have already been integrated into the permanent collections of 500 major university and research libraries around the world." Elsewhere, a visitor can learn that "[i]n the early 1980s, approximately 80% of our books came directly from the homes of older, Yiddish-speaking Jews. Today such donations account for less than 5% of the books we collect; the rest now come from the suburbs, from American-born children and grandchildren." Those books that are not among the 5 percent on the main floor, or those in university or research libraries, are divided between two cold-storage facilities: the Lief D. Rosenblatt Library, which is an on-site facility open to the center's visitors, and a rented, off-site cold-storage facility located within driving distance of the center and inaccessible to visitors. Because the storage company arranges to pick up the books—stored in stacked cardboard boxes and loaded onto wooden pallets—most staff have never visited the facility.

Throughout the history of the center's work, books have naturally traveled among these different sites. This has the effect of playing havoc with various attempts to categorize the collection in particular ways—outside, that is, of its identity as an assemblage of interchangeable objects. Thus, even the most minimal of classificatory systems can be upset by the interchangeability of books. For example, the books displayed on the center's main floor and in the Rosenblatt Library, are organized alphabetically according to author's last name. With some exceptions, there are no sections for books on particular topics or even more general divisions such as fiction and nonfiction. Instead, when I was conducting fieldwork in 2010 and 2011, and at the time of writing this chapter, a series of large, elegantly printed block Hebrew letters adorned shelves on the first floor, to mark which authors' names could be found on those rows of shelves. However, as books are reorganized, sold, or donated, the actual books on any given shelf and even the shelving units themselves have to be reorganized and relocated. In the summer of 2010, for example, when the center decided to set up an exhibit space on the main floor, the Yiddish books and the shelves on which they rested had to be cleared away. This also required, of course, reorganizing the books and shelves that remained. Such efforts at rearranging the physical space of the institution have made it so that the Hebrew letters marking shelves could no longer be depended upon to correspond to the books that are actually found there.

This pattern holds true with various other meta-cultural designations of value on display at the center. For example, during the summer of 2011, the center installed a series of informational panels and small exhibits throughout its first-floor stacks. These panels, named the Unquiet Pages exhibit, were placed alongside and between the shelves of collected, artifactual Yiddish books. Each panel discussed some element of Yiddish literature, history, or culture. One panel, for example, covered Soviet Yiddish, another focused on women poets and writers,

A pallet of boxed Yiddish books on the center's loading dock, headed for the off-site cold-storage facility. Photo by the author.

and so forth. But like those who see their own family's books while visiting shelves they have donated, individuals must imagine the books by women writers, from the former Soviet Union, or otherwise, into the collection. The books actually on display adjacent to or underneath these panels did not correspond to these categories.

Even numerical descriptions themselves, expressing the proportion of books that can be found (or imagined to be found) in different areas of the center's holdings, "strain" to describe the objects to which they refer. Because, as one panel explains, "there's no way to know" how many more books the center will collect, it follows that it is in fact impossible to confirm whether the 5 percent of books on the main floor are *actually* 5 percent of the total collection. In a similar vein, the actual number of books collected tends to vary across the literature and rhetoric of the center; at certain moments, the numbers of books collected are set at "1.5 million," at others "over a million," and still others "countless."

Paralleling a lack of correspondence between books and their alphabetical markers, or books and the meta-cultural categories described in the Unquiet Pages exhibit, the accuracy of these reported numbers is hardly at issue. Under or "behind" these meta-cultural distinctions, the majority of Yiddish books at the center circulate among different locations of storage. To be sure, the center's lone librarian knows where to find most titles among those available on site (particularly those most frequently requested); and the center has maintained a limited number of special collections (such as its David and Sylvia Steiner Yizkor Book Collection). However, the more general movement of books through the center's facilities mirrors the way in which most visitors will approach Yiddish books—first and foremost according to their identity as materializations of the center's numbers.

In this sense, the difficulty of ensuring that a given category corresponds to paper book objects can be understood as an artifact of institutional accommodation to the variety of values that people imagine into Yiddish books. That artifact reflects not the absence of a system of categorization but rather an informal manner of valuation that exists in tension with and alongside other efforts by the institution to impose meaningful order. Thus, on tours of the center that I attended in 2011, guides routinely promoted an openness about how books should be categorized, handled, and valued by refusing to reduce the center to any particular kind of book-related institution. "So what is this place?" tour guides would routinely ask. "It's not a library, or a museum, or an archive, or a school . . . but it has components of all of these." The Book Center does not limit itself to modes of engagement with books that would typify these other institutions; it understands that some visitors will expect a museum, others an archive, and still others a school. By not organizing books strictly according to the norms of any of these institutions, the center has best been able to encompass the range of values and expectations that its public maintains; it achieves that end by the collection's thin description in which its collected artifacts are apprehended as "Yiddish books"— one million, over a million, or "countless" in number.

The Magic of Yiddish and the Future of Depth at the Book Center

> This month we'd like to tell you about a number of new projects in the works, a number of exciting programs, and an inspiring set of numbers. Let's start with the big ones: as you probably know, we've collected well **over a million Yiddish books** in the 30 years since Aaron Lansky began this effort. What's more, we posted our first Yiddish books online in 2009, and so far they've been **downloaded a quarter million times!** Right now, we're collaborating with the Jewish Public Library of Montreal to digitize **1,000 hours of audio books** and **1,500 reel-to-reel recordings** of interviews with major Yiddish writers, and we're in the process of scanning another **4,500 Yiddish books.** More than **900 people** have signed up for our popular online language-learning series, a *shmek yidish*, at least **77** have enrolled in our Jewish Metropolis online course which begins next week, and we'll soon welcome nearly **80 scholars** for a working conference on Translating Yiddish Literature.[32] (Bold in the original)

As I have sought to ethnographically illustrate in this chapter, when people visit the center's Yiddish books, they come looking for forms of value that are "deep" or "thick" in nature. Some seek out the depth of an emotional connection to ancestors; others desire a materialization of the memory of an actual parent or grandparent; still others value an act of witnessing a Jewish language in the process of revival. Given the highly voluntary nature of participation with the Book Center, there is a clear incentive for the institution to encourage and honor the broad range of expectations and values that people might invest in the organization's collection. At the same time, though, not all engagements with Yiddish books are always understood by the center's public as of equal value or equally likely to emerge from so many numbers of collected Yiddish originals. Understandably then, even visitors who themselves engage nostalgically or emotionally with Yiddish books still often expect the center to facilitate deeper encounters with Yiddish—encounters able to move beyond the thin surface of the book-as-number toward acquisition of its actual content.

Against this backdrop of assumption and desire, the production of value— the magic of Yiddish at the Book Center—can often be a matter of "playing the numbers." Walking through the center with one middle-aged man, carrying a single copy of his recently deceased father's Yiddish book, I could sense his discomfort about the numbers of books that surrounded him. "There are so many copies," he exclaimed, as his eyes ran over the shelves before him, taking account of the probability that his father's book would have a readable future amid the crush of volumes. When, at the end of his visit, I asked if he wanted to donate his book, he balked, seeming to reconsider the odds that his father's book would be read: "Maybe I'll just hold onto it," he replied.

Especially after the center digitized its titles, the odds of a donated, artifactual Yiddish book being read can appear even more unfavorable than in the center's earlier years. In this context, the institution has sought, in a sense, to balance its semiotic accounts—to produce possibilities of literacy and education on other fronts and through alternative mediums. In 2011, for example, Aaron Lansky published a series of mission statements in the institution's *Pakn Treger* (*Book Peddler*) magazine, declaring a shift in mission and detailing a broader expansion of the institution's priorities to encompass cultural education, language learning, and translation.[33] To be sure, this is hardly the first time the center has sought to emphasize that education in and about Yiddish is its ultimate goal.[34] But since 2010, the center has been especially decisive and unequivocal about its new direction. "Saving a million Yiddish books was just the beginning," the center's mission reads on its website. "Our priority now is to advance knowledge of the content and literary and cultural progeny of the books we've saved." To carry out this mission, the center has deepened the academic component of its current programs (like its summer language and culture program for college students), rolled out new culture and education programs for high school students and 20-somethings, and created initiatives to support translation. As the above e-mail update suggests, one should "start with the big ones"; but today, the center

"New numbers" at the center. A sign near the lone computer on the main floor, located amid stacks of paper books, describes the Yiddish Book Center's online collection. Photo by the author.

seeks to invest its public in new numbers as well—numbers of downloads, of audio material being digitized, and of eager participants traveling to Amherst to attend conferences.

For an institution that has captured the imagination of its public by iteratively and collaboratively producing a broad range of valuable possibilities through the thin description of emotionally saturated Yiddish books, these developments raise important challenges to how Jewish culture is produced at the Yiddish Book Center. On the one hand, with the ability to create endless digital copies, the kinds of values that Yiddish originals index can seem increasingly circumscribed: the beloved originals become collectible objects for emotional, sentimental, and nostalgic identification while possibilities of being read in the future seem increasingly remote. But, on the other hand, downloads and education programs do not offer the possibilities of rescue, witnessing and display, mourning and emotional investment that so many have linked to the organization's collected, artifactual Yiddish books. The effects of these shifts on the affective economy of the Book Center remain, at this point, in process: how (and indeed, whether) the center and its public will maintain the affective power of its Yiddish originals, or whether it will successfully and sustainably produce emotional investments in its new initiatives remain open questions at the Yiddish Book Center.

During my own period of ethnographic research at the center, these shifts in affective economy appeared in the difficulty that Book Center staff sometimes had explaining to visitors why it keeps so many copies that seem increasingly unlikely to be read. This was brought home to me one afternoon as I, together with a Book Center staff member, accompanied a Jewish day school teacher and his middle school students on a tour. As his students roamed through the center's Lief D. Rosenblatt cold-storage facility, looking over the copies of alphabetized Yiddish books, taking them off and putting them back on shelves, and trying to sound out their titles, their teacher skeptically engaged the staff member.

"To a certain extent, I'm not sure I see the point," the schoolteacher told us, as his students excitedly wandered through the climate-controlled room. "Now that the books have been digitized, why do you need so many extra copies? And they are growing old and decaying anyway. I just don't see the reason for keeping so many extra books."

"Well," the Book Center employee contested, "you simply don't know what people will want in the future."

"Do you think they should be thrown away?" I asked. "What about the cultural associations of Jews with books?"

"Well, but then the only reason to keep them is because we want to avoid something. And we do throw books away, we throw holy books away, we bury them. If you think about it," he went on, "packing lots of books into cold storage is a lot like burial."

If this visitor sees only "so many copies," I would argue, it is because he divests himself of his role within the collaborative relationships that create the "magic of Yiddish" at the Book Center. The center employee, who reminds him that "you simply don't know what people will want in the future," does not so much provide him with an answer than encourage him to endow the objects in front of him with readable and hence valuable futures. The lack of recognition on his part of this potential "now that the books have been digitized" is especially striking in light of the awe, fascination, and wonder of his own middle-school-aged students in the face of so many Jewish things. Even with this spectacle before them, their teacher sees only so many numbers of Yiddish books without a sense of potential that they might be valuable to others—*even the very students he's brought to see the center's collection.* Overwhelmed by the numbers of books, and thus what he perceives as an impossibility of their future readability, he is unable or unwilling collaboratively to invest them, along with the Book Center's staff member and myself, with their potential value. He does not care about numbers.

As a representative of the institution, though, the staff member—like the zamlers and other volunteers described in this chapter—do care; and arguably, they *must* care. For a nonprofit such as the Yiddish Book Center, which relies on volunteer giving among a national, nonlocal base of members and private donors, cultivating a broad range of desires, values, and expectations, and channeling them into a financial investment in the institution represents an important component of its labor. Thus, even if this schoolteacher doesn't "see the point" of collecting, storing, and displaying so many Yiddish books, the center must also think about others—like donors, zamlers, visitors, and even the teacher's own students—who may indeed continue iteratively to invest themselves in the center's collection of artifactual Yiddish originals, and whose investment might be converted into an institutional resource.

Ethnographic analysis of the interplay between the thinness and thickness of numbers at the Yiddish Book Center foregrounds the benefits, for the social analysis of numbers, of thinking beyond the kinds of bureaucratic and biopolitical contexts in which scholars analyze (usually social scientific) numerical cultures. The culture of numbers analyzed here, within an American Jewish nonprofit organization, constitutes a rich, interactive field of socio-institutional discourse and practice. In the thinness of the center's large numbers of Yiddish books lies an array of possibilities, the articulation of which depends upon ongoing collaborations among the volunteers, staff, and donors who animate the affective practices and political economy of the Yiddish Book Center. Across these practices, the power of numerical description is hardly grounded in the dominant associations of numbers with objectivity and accuracy; they are not at all purified from the affective, emotional realms of social life as is so often understood in both public and academic discourses. Indeed, in the ethnography offered here, the precision of numerical knowledge within the center's book practices is almost entirely beside the point. Accuracy, for example, in the numbers of books within the center's holdings matters far less than the imaginative possibilities that so many Yiddish books—when apprehended and valued according to their identities as interchangeable elements—can hold out for the center and its public.

In this sense, numbers of Yiddish books at the center are powerful, to return to the Weinreich quote with which I began this chapter, when they create *magic:* when they point to an array of desires, values, and expectations that are invested in the objects numbers so thinly describe. The nature of those expectations and desires are multiple and sometimes contradictory; at times, a desire for Yiddish to be read in the future can conflict with a concomitant yearning among the center's public to preserve the history of the collected Yiddish artifacts themselves. Thin description, as a collaborative practice, has allowed the center and its public to bridge and encompass these values and expectations; it is thus part and parcel of how the center has worked to bridge the generations and thus, it hopes, to "outwit history."

Notes

1. The quote is usually relayed as "Yiddish has magic, it will outwit history."
2. The Five College Consortium consists of Hampshire College, Amherst College, University of Massachusetts (Amherst), Mount Holyoke, and Smith College.
3. *Bridge of Books,* directed by Sam Ball (2001), from the Yiddish Book Center website, 13:36, http://www.yiddishbookcenter.org/our-story.
4. Aaron Lansky, *Outwitting History: The Amazing Adventures of a Man Who Rescued a Million Yiddish Books* (Chapel Hill, NC: Algonquin, 2004).
5. *Outwitting History* was published in October of 2004. In a December 2004 letter to members, Lansky writes: "Last month, I announced 'Outwitting History,' a historic $25 million campaign in honor of our 25th anniversary." Aaron Lansky, Untitled Letter to Members, December 13, 2004 (Mailings, Yiddish Book Center, Amherst, MA), p. 2.
6. Aaron Lansky, Untitled Letter to Members, August 7, 2006 (Mailings, Yiddish Book Center, Amherst, MA), p. 2. The plan for the building was first discussed in membership letters as a climate-controlled library; over time, it became more ambitious in scope.
7. Shaylih Muehlmann, "Rhizomes and Other Uncountables," *American Ethnologist* 39, no. 2 (2012): 340; see also Jacqueline Urla, "Cultural Politics in an Age of Statistics: Numbers, Nations, and the Making of Basque Identity," *American Ethnologist* 20, no. 4 (1993): 818–843.
8. On numbers and numerical disciplines in relationship to governmentality and population management, see Ian Hacking, "Biopower and the Avalanche of Printed Numbers," *Humanities in Society* 5, no. 3–4 (1982): 279–295; Michel Foucault, "Governmentality," in *The Foucault Effect: Studies in Governmentality,* ed. Graham Burchell, Colin Gordon, and Peter Miller (Chicago: University of Chicago Press, 1991), 87–104; Gilles Deleuze and Félix Guattari, *A Thousand Plateaus: Capitalism and Schizophrenia* (Minneapolis: University of Minnesota Press, 1991); and Jonathan Xavier Inda, *Targeting Immigrants: Government, Technology, and Ethics* (Malden, MA: Blackwell, 2006); and on commodification, see Muehlmann,

"Rhizomes," 339–352. On development, see, for example, Akhil Gupta, *Red Tape: Bureaucracy, Structural Violence, and Poverty in India* (Durham, NC: Duke University Press, 2012). On language maintenance and revival, see, for example, Lise M. Dobrin, Peter K. Austin, and David Nathan, "Dying to Be Counted: The Commodification of Endangered Languages in Documentary Linguistics," in *Proceedings of the Conference on Language Documentation and Linguistic Theory*, ed. Peter K. Austin, Oliver Bond, and David Nathan (London: SOAS, 2007), 59–68; Jane H. Hill, "'Expert Rhetorics' in Advocacy for Endangered Languages: Who Is Listening, and What Do They Hear?," *Journal of Linguistic Anthropology* 12, no. 2 (2002): 119–133; and Urla, "Cultural Politics." The articles cited analyzing the centrality of numerical discourse to rhetorics of endangerment are particularly relevant for the argument being developed here; they bring out the connotations of scientific objectivity that give numbers their power, while also pointing to the passions and anxieties these discourses are intended to inspire.

9. Hill, "Expert Rhetorics," 127–128.

10. Urla, "Cultural Politics."

11. Clifford Geertz, "Thick Description: Toward an Interpretive Theory of Culture," in *The Interpretation of Cultures: Selected Essays* (New York: Basic Books, 1973), 3–30.

12. For a related discussion of missions pursued at the intersection of numerical knowledge and book practice (in this author's case, the publication and circulation of large numbers of bibles), see Matthew Engelke, "Number and the Imagination of Global Christianity; or, Mediation and Immediacy in the Work of Alain Badiou," *South Atlantic Quarterly* 109, no. 4 (2010): 811–829.

13. Theodore M. Porter, "Thin Description: Surface and Depth in Science and Science Studies," *Osiris* 27, no. 1 (2012): 209–226.

14. Walter Armbrust, "Egyptian Cinema On Stage and Off," in *Off Stage / On Display: Intimacy and Ethnography in the Age of Public Culture*, ed. Andrew Shryock (Stanford, CA: Stanford University Press, 2004), 73. The quality of thinness is central as well to Andrew Shryock's observations, in the same volume, based on his analysis of the representational practices of ACCESS, an Arab American advocacy organization in Dearborn, Michigan: "The undeniable 'thinness' . . . ," of the organization's informational material, "is found in diverse media of multicultural display, and it is best understood, to use Andreas Glaeser's term, as a 'reduction' that facilitates representation. Thus, in museum exhibits, what the 'visitor' can know about Arab American immigration history, work, politics, religion or family life must be garnered from less than three hundred words of explanatory text per topic, plus photo captions." Andrew Shryock, "In the Double Remoteness of Arab Detroit: Reflections on Ethnography, Culture Work, and the Intimate Disciplines of Americanization," in *Off Stage / On Display: Intimacy and Ethnography in the Age of Public Culture*, ed. Andrew Shryock (Stanford, CA: Stanford University Press, 2004), 303.

15. John L. Jackson, *Thin Description: Ethnography and the African Hebrew Israelites of Jerusalem* (Cambridge, MA: Harvard University Press, 2013).

16. Jeffrey Shandler, *Adventures in Yiddishland: Postvernacular Language and Culture* (Berkeley: University of California Press, 2006), 176.

17. Shandler's valuable work on the contemporary engagement with Yiddish among American Jews in particular requires a more developed discussion than I can take up within the confines of this chapter, given my particular attention here to numbers in Jewish life. In the dissertation on which this chapter is based, I draw from ethnographic research on the engagement of American Jews with Yiddish to more fully develop, reconsider, and reanalyze the concept of postvernacularity. For a discussion of postvernacularity's influence on contemporary Yiddish scholarship, see Lara Rabinovitch, Shiri Goren, and Hannah S. Pressman, eds., *Choosing Yiddish: New Frontiers of Language and Culture* (Detroit: Wayne State University Press, 2013).

18. Shandler, *Adventures,* 4.

19. Lansky, *Outwitting History,* ix.

20. Ball, *Bridge of Books.*

21. Lansky, *Outwitting History,* x.

22. "The books were living souls." Lansky, *Outwitting History,* 55.

23. Ball, *Bridge of Books.*

24. Jonathan S. Woocher, *Sacred Survival: The Civil Religion of American Jews* (Bloomington: Indiana University Press, 1986).

25. "Is There a Treasure in Your Attic?," Flyer, n.d., National Yiddish Book Center.

26. For an excellent history of YIVO, including its relationship with zamlers, see Cecile Kuznitz, *YIVO and the Making of Modern Jewish Culture: Scholarship for the Yiddish Nation* (Cambridge: Cambridge University Press, 2014). For a recent discussion focusing specifically on YIVO's zamlers, see Sarah Ellen Zarrow, "'Holy Sacred Collection Work': The Relationship between YIVO and Its Zamlers," in *Going to the People: Jews and the Ethnographic Impulse,* ed. Jeffrey Veidlinger (Bloomington: Indiana University Press, forthcoming).

27. The term "zamler" comes from the Yiddish verb *zamlen* (to collect). By attaching the suffix "ing" to "zamler" (or, at other times, to the Yiddish verb's base *zamel*), Book Center volunteers modify the Yiddish according to English rules of morphology. In that capacity, "zamlering" seems to iconize in its very linguistic form the ideology embodied in the practice itself—that collecting books on behalf of the center can be performed regardless of a participant's level of Yiddish proficiency. To the extent that it was frequently the language of "zamlering" and "zamlered" that the volunteers I interviewed used, I follow these linguistic practices in describing their experience.

28. When quoting from interviews, I have used pseudonyms.

29. To clarify, Sarah is speaking about the nature of individual collection visits; all zamlers have noted that collection has become increasingly infrequent over time.

30. The relationship between the materiality of Yiddish writing and the practice of collection and text processing at the Book Center is a subject for a separate study. With regard to the claim here that durability and printedness underwrite what gets collected and processed at the center, this is not an official policy as much as, I would suggest, an artifact of the socio-material conditions of collection that are briefly discussed in this chapter (particularly, the important role of the center's volunteer public in those efforts). Thus, for example, texts in multiple languages, as long as Yiddish is among them, have been included in what gets collected, kept, and digitized by the institution. Tellingly, handwritten Yiddish text artifacts (letters, postcards, etc.) have not been systematically collected or redistributed in the manner of books. If thought to be of possible value, one staff member explained, such materials are sent to archives, or stored in boxes for possible future museum displays or projects. Nor have newspapers been systematically saved or inventoried; as one employee involved in the early collection trips of the Book Center described it, newspapers "would just fall apart" through the very process of collection itself.

31. Associated Press, "Pages of 12,000 Yiddish Books Digitally Preserved," *USA Today,* May 6, 2002, http://usatoday30.usatoday.com/tech/news/2002/05/06/digital-yiddish.htm. The number of books initially digitized also tends to vary in Book Center discourse; elsewhere the Book Center discusses 11,000 titles initially digitized.

32. Randy Silnutzer, "October update from the Yiddish Book Center," October 12, 2011, message sent from updates@bikher.org.

33. Aaron Lansky, "Flip Side," *Book Peddler* (Summer 2011): 20–25; and Aaron Lansky, "Road Map," *Book Peddler* (Fall 2011): 16–23.

34. It is difficult to put an exact date on when this transition took place, or even if it was a transition at all. Indeed, as early as 1985, one can read Aaron Lansky reminding readers in the institution's *Pakn Treger* magazine that "saving Yiddish books" is only a "first step"—"Our real work," Lansky goes on to explain, in a section extracted from the text and printed in large bold letters, is "building a bridge between the generations, saving a culture from extinction and revitalizing our own lives as Jews." Aaron Lansky, "Just between Us," *Book Peddler* (Winter 1985): 2–5.

8 "130 Kilograms of Matza, 3,000 Hard-Boiled Eggs, 100 Kilograms of Haroset and 2,000 Balls of Gefilte Fish"

Hyperbolic Reckoning on Passover

Vanessa L. Ochs

EXTRAVAGANTLY LARGE NUMBERS, such as the very ones referenced in the gargantuan larder of my title, are frequently marshaled around the time of the Passover holiday in print and online. They call to mind the large numbers within the Haggadah (Passover's liturgical text), the many available versions of the Haggadah and the high attendance at the seder (Passover's festival meal). They are consciously and creatively invoked in articles, reviews, advertisements, and public relations materials with the apparent expectation that they will elicit in readers optimistic visions of the flourishing of Jewish tradition, visions persuasive enough to counter or at least balance the persistently offered anxious or bleak appraisals of the present and future. I call this discursive practice hyperbolic reckoning and will examine three specific examples of how such cognitive schemes appear in American contexts and how they strive to cultivate optimistic readings on aspects of contemporary Jewish life. Acknowledged claims would elicit a positive affect or, at the very least, reduce anxiety. The first example concerns hyperbolic claims about the quantity of Haggadot in print. The second considers hyperbolic claims about the huge worldwide seders of Chabad, which include overwhelming obstacles to be surmounted and also require enormous quantities of food to be amassed and distributed. The third reflects upon hyperbolic claims about the number of American Jews attending seders.[1]

Before exploring the particular examples of hyperbolic reckoning in question and the visions of optimism they inspire, let me define the terms I am using. Claudia Claridge describes hyperbole as a literary trope:

> In a nutshell, a hyperbolic expression carries magnified, intensified content that exceeds the (credible) limits of fact in a given context. Put more precisely: at the basis of the definition lies the contrast between the hyperbolic expression and an assumed "literal" expression, which would represent the content and context more factually or faithfully. It is this contrast that triggers a transferred interpretation.[2]

Thus, as a strategic form of communication, hyperbole creates emphasis, focusing attention, making and arguing its point all at once. An intentional exaggeration, clearly not to be mistaken for empirical evidence or realistic representation, hyperbole must be easily and readily recognized as such by both producer and audience. In the context of epic literature, hyperbole is used as a form of praise that describes an individual's extraordinary characteristics or the depth of one's love or hate. Hyperbole is used as well to set the scene and expectations for a tall tale.[3] As a conscious artful conceit, hyperbole is invoked with the expectation that it will elicit specific emotional responses (such as pride, wonder, or recognition) from an audience that will receive the hyperbole in the proper and intended spirit; that is to say, the audience will be able to distinguish between hyperbolic assertion and a lie.[4]

As Joshua Ritter writes, hyperbole "pushes the bounds of logic whereby logical thought forms are opened up to radical perspectival expressions that evoke emotions, enthusiasm, and experiences."[5] For hyperbole to be effective, it cannot exist outside a conventionally understood and acknowledged narrative framework. When hyperbole relies upon numbers, they are generally presented as matters of common knowledge or as facts that need no corroboration. To ask: "How could you measure so high?" or "Where did you get your figures from?" is to accuse a hyperbolic strategy of having crossed a line, masquerading as truth, or being an outright lie or miscalculation; this would result in its failure to persuade.

These descriptions of hyperbole in secular discourse accurately characterize how it is generally deployed for emphasis in rabbinic literature in both *midrash,* traditional exegesis of biblical texts, and within *aggadah,* the nonlegal sections distributed throughout the Talmud. Rabbi Eugene Borowitz maintains that hyperbole, called *guzma,* is "the distinctive aggadic trope." In the service of making their points persuasively and even entertainingly, the rabbis, Borowitz claims, "regularly speak of the most fundamental religious truths in terms that are variously playful, purposely shocking, wildly imaginative and . . . extravagantly exaggerated. They and their community must have shared a rich context of acceptable communication. . . ."[6] Its usage is so commonplace and pervasive that Rabbi Ami, to make his point about hyperbole while being hyperbolic, stated in the Babylonian Talmud (Tamid 29a), "The Torah used hyperbole, the prophets used hyperbole and the sages used Hyperbole."

We turn now to the optimism evoked by forms of hyperbolic reckoning of Passover. Looking both backward and forward in time, it can be an affirmation of spiritual confidence that the God who redeemed the Hebrew slaves and brought them into the Land of Israel continues in the present to save, protect, guard, and guide. It can also be an attitude of confidence that Jewish transmission will take place and be sustained into the future through various sociocultural mechanisms such as families, schools, synagogues, cultural institutions, grassroots efforts, and products such as books, music, theater, and films. This latter form of optimism counters discourses of pessimism, which suggest that Jewish well-being (if measured by numbers of Jews) is under threat.[7] While not the only source of discourses of pessimism, the publication of surveys of Jewish demography and reflections upon them, as discussed by Michal Kravel-Tovi in chapter 6 of this volume, are one of the most repeatedly delivered persuasive and pessimistic forms of communication among Jews in America, in the Jewish media, and from synagogue pulpits.

My thinking about discourses of optimism that reference large numbers presented hyperbolically, and my positing that they are established on Passover as an alternative to discourses of pessimism, draws upon the ethnography of Juliana Ochs, who has analyzed how discourses of fear have been entextualized in contemporary Israeli culture. Her work shows how the particular fear of terror caused by suicide bombings at cafes and on busses experienced by Israeli Jews during the Second Intifada became attached to collective memories of anxiety, violence, destruction, and vulnerability linked to the Holocaust.[8] I derive my definition of a discourse of pessimism about Judaism in the American context from David L. Altheide's definition of a discourse of fear as "pervasive communication, symbolic awareness and expectation that danger and risk are a central feature of the effective environment or the physical and symbolic environment as people define and experience it in everyday life."[9] Thus, a discourse of pessimism in America describes and thus reifies the state of Judaism (markedly, as a religion and not as a culture) as being precarious, emphasizing reasons for worry, even despair, and leading often to calls for immediate action (in particular, making donations to various projects or institutions that propose to address "the problem"). Usually, such discourse inspires hand wringing over what is termed the "continuity crisis" that Kravel-Tovi has examined in chapter 6, if not by Jewish demographers themselves, who may be subjectively invested, then by Jewish professionals in synagogues, schools, and philanthropies who anxiously strategize how their programs might address the desperate situation that the numbers are said to affirm. This passage from an article in *Ha'aretz* by Rabbi Elianna Yolkut reflects upon how such anxieties are typically described in America. Note how numbers are used to prove and bolster the cause for concern; note, too, how demographic dips are readily intertwined with genocide as both memory and an imaginary:

> The Jewish community is obsessed with statistics, and continuously talks of the relationship between numbers and "Jewish continuity." Demographics is our primary source of worry. This is not shocking, nor surprising, given our painful history and our tiny numbers. We have faced genocide and mass exile over and over again throughout our history, which has been plagued with external and internal threats—often so devastating and painful that they are beyond imagination. As a result, we struggle with questions of demographics and of statistics, and worry about the amorphous term, "Jewish continuity."[10]

A widely disseminated discourse of fear emerged from responses to the 2013 Pew Research Survey, *A Portrait of Jewish Americans*, which included, in its summary, such observations as: "two thirds of Jews with no religion with minor children in the home say they are (*this was printed in bold, as if to underscore the threat visually and trigger pessimistic response*) **not raising their children as Jewish in any way.** . . ."[11] The report itself notes:

> The consequences of intermarriage were delivered with gravity, making claims about intermarriage and the raising of Jewish children as if they were uni-causal and self-evident: "Married Jews of no religion are much more likely than married Jews by religion to have non-Jewish spouses. Jews who have non-Jewish spouses are much less likely than those married to fellow Jews to be raising children as Jewish by religion and much more likely to be raising children as partially Jewish, Jewish but not by religion, or not Jewish at all. Furthermore, Jews who are the offspring of intermarriages appear, themselves, to be more likely to intermarry than Jews with two Jewish parents."[12]

While the survey, its methodologies, findings, and summary can be read in multiple ways, responses often express emotional distress; individuals contacted by the *New York Times* described the "very stark," report as having a "devastating" impact. Thus, when the survey reports figures indicating that among American Jews there is a growing rate of intermarriage, a high rate of divorce, and a low birth rate, these numbers are then interpreted to indicate a bleak diagnosis of the present state of affairs and a worse prognosis for the future. If membership in Jewish religious denominations has decreased, the figures are described as having "fallen precipitously"; congregations that are "downsizing" are said to be "losing members at an alarming rate."[13] This state of alarm inferred from the Pew Research Survey was captured by Jack Wertheimer of the Jewish Theological Seminary in New York when he likened American Jewry to an individual with a serious illness: "It's a very grim portrait of the health of the American Jewish population in terms of their Jewish identification."[14]

The Celebration of Large Numbers

Turning now to specific discourses deploying Passover's large numbers, I suggest that in the context of the holiday, a focus on large numbers in itself attracts attention and runs counter to expectation, for on Passover, small numbers take center stage. They are repeatedly highlighted in the Haggadah's liturgy and songs and in the ceremonial use and consumption of ritual foods at the seder. "During the Seder . . ." a Passover advertisement for Haggadot claims, "we find many numeric motifs: four cups, four sons, four questions . . . three matzahs . . . and, of course, 'who knows one?'"[15] One God; two dippings; three matzos; four cups, questions, and sons; ten plagues: in the context of the Passover seder, such cozily familiar small numbers as these provide clarity, precision, and manageability. Small numbers do the work of keeping the ritual orderly and telling the Exodus story, providing starting points, and serving as mnemonic devices for both traditional rabbinic interpretations and spontaneous parental homiletics.[16] Even children with adequate Jewish training, the ones who already know the answers to the "Mah Nishtana," the four questions about unusual aspects of the seder that the Haggadah ordains that they ask, may confidently already be able to parse the small numbers themselves by making textual references and repeating the lessons of their teachers. They may be able to state, for instance, that drinking four cups of wine at the seder symbolizes not just the celebration of freedom but also four different and discrete ways that scripture describes God's liberation of the Hebrew slaves in Egypt: (1) I shall take you out. (2) I shall rescue you. (3) I shall redeem you. (4) I shall bring you to the land.[17]

Thirteen is the upper limit of the seder's small numbers. It references God's attributes (as articulated in Exodus 34:6–7) and appears in the seder's penultimate popular cumulative song, the counting game, "Echad Mi Yodea?" (Who Knows One?). It takes but thirteen verses to account for everything in the Jewish universe, including God in heaven and earth, Jewish law, the patriarchs and matriarchs, the volumes of the sacred library, time itself, the facts of life, and tribal origins. Granted, when sung in one popular and exuberant folk melody, the singular God morphs into an unintended pantheon in each concluding refrain: *Echad Eloheinu, Eloheinu, Eloheinu, Eloheinu, Eloheinu* (One is our God, Our God, Our God, Our God, Our God).[18] Do the math: five Gods per refrain times thirteen verses equals sixty-five. But there is no untoward hint of polytheism intended in what could appear to be an exuberant stocktaking. Rather, the song affirms that the one God of the Passover narrative endures, not just in the remembered narrative of the ancient Israelites who knew exile and were once redeemed, but also for Jews alive now, those who continue wait with patience and trust for redemption.

But Passover does indeed also reference a few large numbers, ones found in the text of the Haggadah. They and the moods they invoke provide strong precedent for contemporary hyperbolic reckoning linked to optimism. The most familiar of the large numbers relate to those attributed to Rabbis Jose, Elezar, and Akiva who are imagined to be conversing. The rabbis refer to proof-texts in scripture to make ever more emphatic bids to describe the enormity of God's protective strength as demonstrated by the extent of God's wrath toward the Israelites' enemies. They outdo each other by multiplying the ten plagues God inflicted upon the Egyptians on land and sea. Says Rabbi Jose: "Ten in Egypt and fifty at the Sea." "No!" says Rabbi Elezar, multiplying by four: "Forty in Egypt, two hundred at the Sea." "No!" says Rabbi Akiva, multiplying by five: "Fifty in Egypt and two hundred and fifty at the Sea." The rabbis are neither hallucinating nor fibbing; they make their points emphatically according to their community's accepted hermeneutical hyperbolic practice.

These rabbis' large numbers certainly highlight the significance of the ten plagues, which, at the seder meal, are further emphasized ceremonially with the physical act of dipping ten drops of wine from one's cup. Along with other edible pedagogic aids available for family seders (the hidden matzo, called the *afikoman,* is for children, the most anticipated of these symbolic foods), the rabbis use of hyperbole demonstrates how retelling the familiar Exodus story can be enlivened, and be made fresh and compelling, even when repeated year after year. The gleefully exaggerated numbers provide a precedent for adults, who are ideally inspired to find new ways to reinsert themselves into the Exodus story, through the act of their own refreshed and inventive retellings, treating it as a personal memoir so that they may affirm: "It is because of what the Lord did for me when I went forth from Egypt" (Exodus 13:8). But rabbinic use of hyperbole goes a step further. It establishes a hopeful spiritual mood: it gives testimony to the boundlessness of their faith in a God of history who has expressed fidelity and love through the performance of miracles and could do so again. Ideally this, too, would set a precedent for the adults who embrace and affirm this worldview.

I offer a final instance in the Haggadah in which large numbers are proffered. It is a different optimistic image of Jewish flourishing, one that is not faith centered, but rather people centered. This number, so large that it is "uncountable," appears at the conclusion of the seder in the liturgy of the *Nirtzah* section, the last of the evening's ritual steps:

> Concluded is the Passover Seder,
> According to its law and custom.
> As we have lived to celebrate it
> So may we live to celebrate it again.
> Pure one, who dwells in his habitation
> Redress the countless congregation.
> Speedily lead the offshoots of the stock,
> Redeemed, to Zion in joyous song.[19]

The Israelites are referenced as the nation so numerous that they are *mi manah*, a countless congregation. This alludes to the priest Balaam's unintended felicitous oracle, emerging miraculously and against character from his mouth: "Who can count the dust of Jacob, Number the dust cloud of Israel?"[20] This passage in the Haggadah is followed by the wish, "Next year in Jerusalem!" This is a consoling vision of hope, not only appropriate but necessary for a people exiled by the destruction of their Temple. Imagine: Jewish people beyond number, all freely observing the complex traditions of the Passover holiday with precision and a full heart. Those who do so are rewarded with the redemptive promise of the most they could possibly ask for: the return of the Passover pilgrimage and sacrifice in a rebuilt Temple or, perhaps more plausible and hopeful to some, an eschatological vision of a heavenly Jerusalem.[21]

Practices of contemporary hyperbolic reasoning patterned after the various precedents in the Haggadah appear in the weeks preceding Passover when Jewish life goes into a most frenzied mode. This is a time given to feverish, anxious, and painstaking household cleaning for the sake of ridding homes of any traces of leavened foods.[22] New commodities are purchased, such as permitted holiday foods, housewares, clothing, and new editions of the Haggadah. Foods are cooked in advance of the seder for arriving family members and many guests; out-of-towners must be lodged. For merchants with a Jewish clientele, these weeks are the time for advertising, stocking up seasonal goods, displaying them, and selling them before they become irrelevant (few relish a Passover cake made from ground-up matzo once real flour is once again permitted; few purchase a Haggadah after the seders are held). For Jewish organizations, the weeks before Passover signal a calendric occasion to get in touch with current and future donors by sending out holiday-themed direct-mail solicitations. Some letters arrive accompanied by free Haggadot or, more typically of late, new liturgies or supplementary rituals with the organization's imprimatur to give added depth and meaning to one's seder. Others arrive with small jars of prepared haroset or kits including a feather, candle, and wooden spoon to use in the ceremonial home inspection for remaining crumbs of bread. Charitable Jews are expected to make donations this time of year, in particular to fulfill the obligation of providing for the Passover needs of the poor, *maot chittin*, literally the wheat fund, a practice to give the poor matzo and Passover foods or the money to buy them. It is a festive time in which the spiritual and material—emphatically, energetically, and tangibly—commingle in daily life, even in commercial exchanges. There is commotion, but it is generally so filled with happy anticipation (and the knowledge that the preparatory work will cease once the holiday arrives) that it is an optimistic tumult.

Instances of hyperbolic reckoning appear mostly in Jewish newspapers, magazines, and online platforms. Author-cooks such as Joan Nathan describe extravagantly delicious and unbelievably impressive Passover recipes; book reviews highlight noteworthy new Haggadah publications.[23] In Jewish and secular contexts, when hyperbolic reckoning is used, it explicitly or implicitly references either narratives that come from the Exodus story, passages from the Haggadah, or seder rituals (and possibly all of the above). It is always assumed that readers will find the allusions so familiar from their past attendance at seders that they rarely require explanation. They have become entextualized, that is, as described by Michael Silverstein and Greg Urban, they are "seen as building blocks or atoms of shared culture."[24] Private conversations among Jews about Passover often frame hyperbole as performative language, that is to say, as speech acts performed in a social context, designed to transmit cultural memories and values.[25] Language, in such instances, is ritualized: the act of speech brings attitudes and states of being into existence.[26] Seasoned producers and recipients of these instances of hyperbolic Passover discourse, complicit in the exchange, all know from experience that the Passover cleaning that takes day and night actually does comes to an end; that the boxes of Passover dishes pulled out of storage that weigh tons are heavy; and that the family with a million guests coming for the seders is having company. There is no reason to correct these statements. Use of hyperbole in these instances elicits not only mutual praise and sympathy; it also affirms and strengthens a sense of investiture in articulating communal values and memories.

So Many Haggadot!

This first example of hyperbolic reckoning concerns the number of Haggadot that are created, published, and distributed to consumers. An online advertisement on a publisher's blog makes an extraordinary claim about the number of copies that have been printed of a particular Haggadah. The blog of Mesorah Publications, familiarly referred to as ArtScroll and known for its "handsomely designed, accessible and uncompromisingly Orthodox print commodities," poses a most curious question in its headline, "Who Knows Two Million?" The question immediately evokes the familiar seder song "Who Knows One?" whose verses ask questions with obvious answers well known to seder-goers; in this case, the number one represents God.[27] But in this advertisement for ArtScroll's different Haggadot for adults and children available for the 2011 season, the large figure of two million initially evokes nothing at all in addition, given that the number, on Passover or at any other time of the year, has no particular Jewish resonance.[28] In fact, using any figure in an advertisement in the low million range may seem an ill-advised choice for a Jewish audience, although there is some immediate relief that whatever the two million represents, at least it is not referencing the six million Jews of the Holocaust, the iconically powerful number that points to what Oren Stier in chapter 1 of this volume refers to as the uncountable and the unimaginable. If the number is not six million, then one is free to consider an optimistic relationship to a number in the millions, one that is "good for the Jews."[29] A satisfying answer to the seemingly rhetorical question ought to follow, but the one that actually appears makes little sense and appears as a non sequitur: "ArtScroll has a haggadah for everyone."[30] The answer continues, referencing a hodgepodge of numbers not derived from sales figures, as might be expected, but from biblical and midrashic sources:

> There are many numbers that we associate with Pesach: 2010 years of slavery, 10 plagues, 70 Israelites coming into Egypt and 3 million leaving in less than 18 minutes. During the Seder, too, we find many numeric motifs: four cups, four sons, four questions . . . three matzahs . . . and, of course, "who knows one?"[31]

Readers of the advertisement's text, now brought back into the conversation through the authority of numbers in rabbinic literature, are urged to open their imaginative and critical thinking to this stream of biblical and midrashic numbers and to remain as patient as they might be in a homiletical setting for clarity to emerge eventually. How will the matter of what two million represents be resolved? How is ArtScroll tied to Jewish narrative and ritual? At long last, the suspense ends and readers learn the answer: "ArtScroll has another number associated with Pesach. That number is two million—the number of ArtScroll Haggadahs that have graced the Seder table of the Jewish People since the publication of the first ArtScroll Haggadah."[32]

Fusing the references to tradition and sales figures, ArtScroll differentiates itself from other publishing companies with commodities to sell and recontextualizes itself as a presence within the *beit midrash,* the house of sacred text study. The Haggadot the company publishes happen to be comparable in style to their popular Schottenstein edition of the Talmud, offering English translation and copious explanation of the texts and their relevance to a lived Jewish life. And while it may seem unlikely, the Haggadot and Talmud editions are also related to their best-selling line of stylish, informative, and easy-to-follow kosher cookbooks by Susie Fishbein that began with her *Kosher by Design.* The Haggadah, the Talmud in translation, and kosher cookbooks: all of these texts meld a perspective that Orthodox Jews (and others among their readership) would consider authoritative (coming with Orthodox rabbinical approval) in a format accessible to English language Jewish readers. The texts simultaneously satisfy differing levels of curiosity: one can dig more deeply or stay on the surface. The instructions are precise. They can appeal to the most erudite and punctilious of the community as well as to those who want to learn how to comprehend the texts and follow the rules. Jeremy Stolow points to ArtScroll's success in simultaneously cultivating

two audiences: the internal community and those outside of the Orthodox en-
clave, particularly those who can now, with their Haggadah in hand, expand
their repertoire of ritual practices to include Orthodox ones.[33]

Particularly for their core Orthodox customers, ArtScroll's hyperbolic
claim—"That number is two million"—provides good tidings. These numbers
suggest that through ArtScroll's strategically formulated books, Orthodox influence is spreading from the narrow community of insiders to the rest of the
Jewish world. Behind the hyperbole stands a statement that the available means
for spreading Orthodoxy among Jews is not limited to procreation, charismatic
rabbis, or the efficacy of its synagogues and educational institutions. Orthodox
knowledge, practice, and norms—its lifestyle, so to speak, is being disseminated
two-million-fold through ArtScroll's accessible and well-marketed books.

Hyperbolic reckoning about the abundance of Haggadot also appears in
roundup book reviews in Jewish and mainstream sources of the myriad new
Haggadot published in print and online just in time for the holiday. This is when
people are deciding which Haggadot to read before the holiday for pleasure, eru-
dition, and insight; which to present as gifts; and which to purchase in bulk so
as to offer a refreshing, unstained, untorn, and uniform text for all of one's seder
guests. In many such reviews, when a hyperbolic accounting of some aspect of
contemporary Haggadah publishing appears, a nonhyperbolic taking stock of
Haggadot published precedes it, one based on standard bibliographical references.
Bibliography, according to Jeffrey Shandler, represents a kind of Jewish inventory
keeping, a practice that facilitates Jewish diaspora culture. He writes, "Jewish inventories constitute a form of ingathering; they implicitly manifest Jewish solidarity, flouting dispersion and its disparagement."[34] This bibliographic accounting of
Haggadot is intended as evidence based, precise, and empirical. Thus, reviewers
may mention that in 1901, there was Shmuel Wiener's *A Bibliography of the Passover Haggadah* listing 909 publications; Abraham Yaari's *A Bibliography of the
Passover Haggadah* (1960) lists 2700, with an addendum a year later bringing the
number up by 174. Yitzchak Yudlov's *The Haggadah Thesaurus* (1997) accounts for
Haggadot since the beginning of printing to 1960; he counts 4,715 editions.[35]

At this point, hyperbolic reckoning usually appears. Unlike empirical
numbers, the hyperbolic numbers are rounded. For example, more than 5,000
versions of the Haggadah have been published since the invention of printing.
Sometimes 3,000 or 4,000 are the figures cited; in all instances, it is generally
rounded off to the nearest 500. In 1975, Israel Shenker reported in the *New York
Times* that there were 3,500 printed; in 2011, Edward Rothstein, also in the *New
York Times,* offered a particularly graceful updated version:

> Though only read once or twice a year, it has probably had more wine spilled
> on it than any other book ever published. Over the centuries, it has been

paraphrased, abridged, translated, transliterated and transformed. It has been sung, chanted, illustrated and supplanted. And in 5,000 or so editions since the invention of the printing press. . . . [36]

One gets the sense that reviewers conspire to participate in cultivating the vertigo that Haggadah shoppers might anticipate as they stand in a bookstore (or develop carpal tunnel syndrome while surfing the internet), dumbfounded by so many Haggadot to choose from, and unable to select the right edition to be ordered as a single or in bulk (at considerable cost!) for their holiday table. Some reviewers will, at this point, heighten the vertigo, acknowledging uncountable variations of homemade Haggadot and Haggadot that can be patched together, bit by bit from other Haggadot or downloaded from the internet. But targeted readers of the reviews are probably not going to make their own printed Haggadot or they will not ask their guests to bring along smartphones and tablets to display the hosts' or their own exemplars of Haggadah handiwork. These readers want a conventional book with covers, one with commentary that can be appreciated and an appealing visual format, one linked to a Jewish religious denomination or an author/editor/translator with some recognizable Jewish credibility. The latter include Sir Jonathan Sacks, the former British chief rabbi, or Jonathan Safran Foer and Nathan Englander, American Jewish fiction writers. For such readers, relief comes when the reviewer selects only three or four new ones to recommend. It dissipates the chaos of being overwhelmed and assures the possibility of making a well-informed choice. The review indicates which Haggadah is the most suitable for their needs, or how any particular new version is sufficiently different from all previous editions to make it worthy. The review suggests that with or without Judaic literacy, with or without enough spare time for Haggadah study, one can select the right text for the ritual: a text that can be used for a successful seder that transmits the tradition.

In reviews, hyperbolic reckoning appears when the Maxwell House Haggadah is referenced. Its presence, described as "ubiquitous," is quantified, albeit as an estimation: "50 million of these Passover guides have been printed and given away since 1933."[37] The figure is astonishing, and one might think, hard to envision, but it feels affectively verifiable, as there seems to be ample material evidence of abundance close at hand. In one's own cabinets, perhaps in that box in storage, packed away with the Passover dishes, there are stacks of the free-with-a-purchase Maxwell House Haggadot that have been collected or inherited. Also seemingly validating the hyperbolic figure are stacks of Haggadot in display cases next to the jarred borscht and gefilte fish, even in grocery stores of towns with small Jewish populations. What exactly is being given away in such abundant quantities as a premium for the purchase of Maxwell House Coffee? Along with the actual text, it is the tradition of the presence of the iconic Maxwell

House Haggadah itself. It is familiarity, packaged with visual images of a well-dressed multigenerational all-American family at the seder table, all happy beyond measure. The Haggadah in the store, in a storage box, on the table, and the images of the family: it was there last year; it will be there this year, and the next. This object represents a continuity of families observing Passover. It flies in the face of anxieties that just around the corner, desuetude awaits.

What a Big Seder!

Versions of this second example of hyperbolic reckoning materialize just before or right after Passover in Chabad's print and digital descriptions of its large seders. These reports reflect Chabad's state-of-the-art, industrious public relations department and massive and large-scale outreach efforts. When it comes to enormous seders and the particular kind of tall tale they inspire, Chabad stands out. Back in 2001, according to this rounded-off estimation, "almost 9000 public seders" were conducted "in 23 time zones around the world, serving half a million dinner guests."[38] The high figures of Chabad demonstrate a preference for the extraordinary estimate over the mundane literal count. What's more, Chabad's seders are described as coming to pass against all odds and depending upon miraculous intervention.

Here, the apparently hyperbolic figures give evidence of Chabad's success in addressing "vanishing Jews," a term that Maya Balakirsky Katz argues they perceive as a "contemporary demographic, still redeemable, but often displayed as potentially dangerous conduits of assimilation."[39] Hyperbole as a trope affirms Chabad's endurance and singularity in providing hospitality to all Jews. It maintains the success of Chabad's outreach strategies in awakening the spark in each Jewish soul and paving the way for the messiah. It suggests that for every Jew who ventures away from Jewish centers in Israel and abroad, Chabad will dependably provide endless kilograms of matzo. These represent a material symbol of a readily available form of Judaism that can be consumed, one that comes as a gift from Chabad with no strings attached, since Chabad pointedly rarely charges for its hospitality. The discourse of pessimism countered here does not, in this instance, respond overtly to demographic claims, though clearly Chabad is presented as a vast network of institutions that has circumvented bleak statistics. Rather, I suggest that the optimism counters a widely discussed hypothesis that once the Rebbe Menachem Mendel Schneerson, the movement's leader, died in 1994 without leaving an heir, Chabad would cease to flourish.[40]

The legendary quality of reports of Chabad's enormous seders hearkens back to biblical narratives of extravagant postexilic Passover pilgrimages in Jerusalem. The crowd that gathered during King Hezekiah's reign (2 Chronicles 31:1–27) was said to have assembled at the Temple a month late, but their celebration lasted for double the required time, with thousands of bulls and sheep slaughtered. The last time anyone could recall a celebration like this was in the time of Solomon. King Josiah, in his reign (2 Chronicles 35:13), donated an astonishing number of—rounded off—animals for sacrifice: 30,000 lambs and goats for the Passover offerings and 3,000 cattle. Once again, memory is brought in for comparison. Now it is Passover at the time of Samuel that is recalled as the benchmark. Just as these hyperbolic descriptions showed kingly power and the assertion of nationhood in the biblical context, Chabad's seders demonstrate the success of the outreach efforts of any particular shaliach, an emissary of the Rebbe, and create benchmarks for him, his family, and others in the future. With the characteristics of legend from start to finish, Chabad's reported seders share certain elements. They take place in a remote, exotic setting where Jews would be unlikely to be found unless they are on business, on adventures, or are Israelis traveling after their military service, such as Nepal, Thailand, and Iceland. Their guests are not necessarily needy Jews, but Jews who might not otherwise bother observing Passover if not for Chabad's presence and largesse.

A Chabad rabbi has voluntarily assumed a mission to attend to Jewish souls in remote places by establishing a headquarters, called a Chabad House. He and his wife, like the 4,000 or so fellow teams of emissaries worldwide, are described as being extremely devoted to their mission. Accounts laud their piety and "unquestioning mesirat nefesh, that is, self-sacrifice."[41] Their equally devoted family accompanies them to this isolated spot where few Jews live. Unmarried Chabad yeshiva students willing to study and perform voluntary service at the distant outpost assist them, some even arriving, as if dropped from the sky, by helicopter, in time to kasher, chop local (permitted) fruits and vegetables, and pray.[42] Upon the imminent approach of the seder, a crisis looms: political instability, an assassination, a coup d'état, a gas embargo, flood, mudslide, or impending earthquake. A vast-beyond-counting supply of "Kosher for Passover" goods has been ordered and is en route in a container from Israel. But will there be enough time for it to traverse borders and get through customs? When it arrives, will the food still be fresh? Given the few hours of electricity available each day, and that food must be cooked on log ovens improvised by the yeshiva boys, will it be ready for the seders? The anxious rabbi confronts multiple enormous setbacks that stand in the way of his outreach efforts, not to mention uncooperative border guards and greedy hoteliers. As hassles multiply, his faith in the will of God and the protective vision of the Rebbe will keep him optimistic. His seder will succeed; his faith will be rewarded.

Readers of these Chabad narratives may know the rabbi believes in Divine Providence, *hashgacha pratis;* furthermore, they may know he believes that one who is performing a mitzvah (sacred obligation) as someone's agent (in this case, they act on behalf of the Rebbe) is protected from harm along the way by a divine light.[43] The Chabad rabbi has the Rebbe's blessing, which is considered to be as potent now as it was before his death. It is worth noting that during his lifetime, the Rebbe intervened himself from afar in seder preparations, providing materials and what would be understood as the blessings that made the miraculous possible. In 1989, from his headquarters in Brooklyn, the Rebbe, concerned about the seder at the Israeli embassy in Kathmandu for Israeli backpackers, sent three rabbinical students and a quarter of a ton of handmade matzos to Israeli Ambassador Shmuel Moyal. As the narrative of that period went, "Although the provisions were meant to feed 100 people, 500 backpackers showed up . . ." and all were fed.[44]

The Rebbe's Hasidim (faithful followers) understand that the miraculous powers the Rebbe wielded in his lifetime continue even after his death. In this context, his blessing in the seder narratives comes as the timely intervention that produces the dénouement to the plot and leads to an auspicious ending, which has, in fact, been anticipated all along. The Rebbe's prayerful intervention, and just as relevant, the persistently faithful work of his emissaries, makes the miracle of unleavened loaves and enough gefilte fishes for all the Jewish souls possible in Kathmandu or Bangkok. How many Jews attended? The large numbers offered are approximated, reflecting a Jewish resistance to the practice of counting individuals, as if doing so would diminish personhood. Fortunately, by enumerating pieces of gefilte fish served, an approximate census can still be taken.

As in folktales, the emissary shines as a heroic *eved haShem* (servant of the Lord) who receives other-worldly assistance from this-worldly representatives. Not just from fellow Jews, such as Israeli security agents and the random backpacker who just happens to have been a chef in the Israeli army and can set up a field kitchen, but also from unexpected allies of the secular world, including the local police, embassy, and army. Help comes even from animals such as bomb-sniffing dogs, perhaps the biggest surprise of all, given that with the exception of fish, animals rarely figure in Lubavitch stories. Thousands pack the seder; if it is not the largest ever, it is astonishingly large. Someone will have read from the Haggadah for the first time and will offer testimony: the seder opened up a life-changing spiritual awakening. The singular transformation of even a single Jew makes it all worthwhile.

A particularly fine rendition of such a tale chronicles the giant Chabad seder in Kathmandu. That seder, which began in 1989, has become an annual synecdoche for all Chabad's seders worldwide, as well as for its outreach enterprises. This particular report—dateline, Nepal—from Chabad's own website reflects nearly all these set pieces in the stories of enormous seders, and so I cite it at length:

NEPAL—When organizing the largest Passover Seders in the world in an unstable country like Nepal, one must take every scenario in consideration. This year, for instance, wine and matzah were stalled at the Indian border, the hotel manager increased the price for a hall that's supposed to house some 2,000 participants, and additional security forces were required after a terrorist group threatened to attack Jewish targets worldwide.

But for Rabbi Chezky Lifshitz, the Kathmandu-based co-director of Chabad-Lubavitch of Nepal, such hassles are all part of the job. Speaking about the border that has been shut down for the past week and a half—the country's historic elections last month failed to ease political tensions between its monarchy and Maoist Communist groups—the rabbi seemed unfazed about a container of 2,000 bottles of wine, 2,000 pounds of matzah, and 3,000 units of gefilte fish that as of Friday hadn't yet arrived.

"We're not fazed," he stated. "It's happened every year, and we've always succeeded in pulling through."

He added that such headaches pale in comparison to the joy that thousands of Israeli tourists experience at Passover events in Kathmandu. . . .

In the last few days, Lifshitz lobbied government officials to provide 30 extra policemen and bomb-sniffing dogs to guard Kathmandu's Seder, consistently the largest in the world. Israeli intelligence recommended beefing up security at such events in the wake of the Feb. 12 assassination of Imad Mughniyeh, the chief of staff of the Lebanese-based Hizbullah terrorist organization, in Syria. In Nepal, police forces will be assisted by Israel Defense Force soldiers.[45]

Is the size of the crowd and the larder accurate or a wild "guesstimate"? We do not know, but we might suppose that such reporting serves a similar function to the promotional tracts that flooded England in the seventeenth century that boasted about the output of American plantations, the function of the hyperbolic quantification of flocks of fowl and nineteen-inch bass being, in Patricia Cline Cohen's words, "to augment the credibility of the account by making even the most extravagant claims appear highly concrete and objective. . . ."[46] In Chabad's context, hyperbolic imprecision suggests a robust collective that is engaging with the organization.

When Chabad publicizes its large numbers, smaller numbers pertaining to the seder are not relevant. As Cline Cohen observes, "What people choose to count and measure reveals not only what was important to them but what they want to understand and, often, what they wanted to control."[47] Thus, one does not hear that the mega-seder has often been conducted rapidly, anticipating that guests will lose interest before the leader will get through twenty-three pages of Hebrew text of the particularly small 5½" × 7½" Chabad Haggadah used for such seders. One does not learn that rushing through the seder will serve to accommodate a second seder held near midnight. Then the shaliach, his family, and aides-de-camp will hold a seder they consider kosher (i.e., fit and proper) in which there is time to measure the symbolic Passover foodstuffs precisely according to their tradition. Outside the frame of the story occurring in public space, the nature of counting changes: it shifts from hyperbolic pounds of matzo to mere ounces, but ounces that count in a different way. Precision denotes more than just satisfying the will of God. It marks the particularity of the Lubavitch sect when it comes to their own standards of practice and sets their distinctive boundaries as their standards for the least amount of food that can fulfill a commandment different from other Orthodox Jews. For example, while most Orthodox and liberal Jews break off what seems like a reasonable piece of matzo to consume, Lubavitch Jews measure precisely in accordance with their community's norms.[48]

One might anticipate that the optimism evoked by such mass feedings at the seders comes as a vision of secular Jewish participants becoming religious as a result of their Passover experience. According to Elise Berman in her study of Chabad hosting practices, that is but one hoped-for outcome.[49] Feeding guests, on the Sabbath in particular, but on holidays such as Passover as well, forms a central outreach act of the Lubavitch in Chabad Houses around the world. Crowds are anticipated, anyone is welcome, and no one is turned away. Even if it means that the rabbi's wife will need to make a last minute salad by opening up cans of beans and corn in her cupboard and sprinkling it with nuts, there will be an abundance of food for everyone to eat. Berman argues that the "success" of such meals can be defined in two ways. The first way is anticipated: the meal, along with gracious hospitality, prayer, teaching, and model of the rabbi's warm family, makes such a powerful and positive impact on the guests that it initiates change as they become religious themselves, ideally embracing the world of Chabad. But Chabad meals are not about internal proselytizing, recognized as an unrealistic goal. Thus, there is a second, more realistic goal of these meals that Berman describes as an "utterance act," one "unbeknownst to their guests" but understandable to Chabad peers around the world, other emissaries.[50] They aim to perform single acts that effect cosmological change that could bring the messiah and herald a messianic era.[51] The consequence, according to the Chabad website, will be redemption in the form of "the promise of the ingathering of the exiles from the Diaspora, with all Jews settling in their tribal portion of the Holy Land"; eventually, there will be bodily resurrection.[52] This occurs when individual Jews are led to do just one more mitzvah, such as performing the Passover seder rituals, that has cosmic significance. Each individual act of outreach, whatever its limited worldly consequence, is framed as a world-changing engagement in loving kindness, one that deepens the connection between the Lubavitcher Hasid and the Rebbe who has pleaded for such acts. "Each extra act could be the rock that tips the scale."[53] This is a quintessentially optimistic perspective: a tiny act with hyperbolic power, enough to redeem the world.

How Popular Seders Have Become in America!

Our final instance of hyperbolic reckoning involves the claim about how popular the seder has become in America, whether it is held before, during, or after Passover; whether it is held in a home or restaurant; whether it is traditional or not; whether it is kosher or not; whether it lasts thirty minutes or goes late into the night. Against the discourse of pessimism surrounding demographic surveys, here is resoundingly good news about prospects of group survival. Vast numbers of Jews—and their interfaith family and friends—are holding seders or getting themselves invited as guests. This fact is appended to just about any article written in both the secular and Jewish press about any aspect of Passover: suggested menus, seders in restaurants, seders of political or social activism, unusual holiday customs, Passover observance guides, even mini-sermons on themes of the holiday. Writers go beyond claiming that Passover is "one of the most widely celebrated Jewish holidays."[54] To attest to the extent of the holiday's unique popularity, writers offer one precise grand figure or another, the highest being that over 90 percent of American Jews attend a Passover seder. The claim may come with qualification: "of one sort or another." This would, therefore, include all seders, even those that are highly truncated, or fall far outside traditional norms. As in the work of Jacqueline Urla on statistics and Basque nationalists, this figure of over 90 percent can be read as an instance of a counting practice serving to make a minority ethnic group visible and, through what is disclosed and what is disguised, elevating "particular behaviors or characteristics which give status" and constitute a desired social reality.[55] The 90 percent figure of seder attendance suggests, despite other demographics that may attest to disinterest or disenfranchisement, the rallying of Jews on Passover—this annual yearning of individuals to participate and to be, in effect, counted—discloses evidence of ethnic and religious endurance by the group for the group and by the group for outsiders. Connections among Jews and between Jews and some elements of ritual observance endure.

Like the other forms of hyperbolic reckoning, this optimistic perspective potentially could quiet fear of an assimilationist tide. The image of so very many Jews choosing to attend seders provides a radical alternative to the demographers' figures of a lessening interest in Judaism evidenced in declines in synagogue membership, charitable giving to Jewish causes, day school attendance, and financial and ideological support of Israel. Each drop, according to one consultant, "feeds further decline."[56]

But is this figure persuasive enough to work as a hyperbole? Is it "intentional exaggeration, clearly not to be mistaken for empirical evidence or realistic representation" as I defined hyperbole, or is it really a matter of common knowledge or a fact needing corroboration? There may simply be too many different figures that are posited to answer this question. *New York Times* reporter Edward Rothstein turned to the National Jewish Population Survey sponsored by the Jewish Federations of North America when he reported that 79 percent of American Jews, observant or not, attend Passover seders.[57] Other surveys show a range of figures that vary according to locale and, in some instances, over time. Vignettes from the 2001 Jewish population survey show that among part-time residents of the Berkshires, 91 percent "hold or attend a Passover seder all or most of the time." In Cincinnati, Ohio, where Jewish home practice is "average to above average," 76 percent of people attend a Passover seder. In Pittsburgh, Pennsylvania, it is 75 percent, in Hartford, Connecticut, it is 78 percent, and in Middlesex County, New Jersey, it is 83 percent. According to this survey, in Phoenix, Arizona, "where continuity is a concern," the figures, which "decreased from 81 percent in 1983 to 62 percent in 2002," appear to confirm the gravity of the situation.[58]

If there is uncertainty about the figures and an absence of corroboration, there remains an additional matter that could halt the activation of a discourse of optimism readers might otherwise be led to embrace. That is the matter of explanation. Can any high figure of attendance at seders be said to point to broader Jewish commitments? The commitment is so small here, just a one- or two-evenings-a-year gesture. While there is a narrative structure affirming the cosmological significance that discrete acts take in the Chabad religious imaginary, there is none for American figures of seder attendance. It is not clear what factors even account for the large numbers. Is it a rise in spiritual activity in America? A growing desire for ethnic identification? New strategies, by synagogues and families, to welcome Jews and their interfaith spouses and families? An increase in seders hosted by Jewish interfaith families and attended by a broad circle of family and friends, including non-Jews? There are more possibilities still: The appeal of new Haggadot that reflect the political, social, and theological variety in seder-goers. The availability of new Haggadot that get the deed done efficiently in thirty minutes or even less.

I would suggest as well that in places where many American Jews have been inviting their relatives and friends who are non-Jews to join them on Passover, the seder is acquiring some of the qualities of a generic American holiday. It is becoming a social occasion akin to Thanksgiving, one worth marking in celebration of spring and all forms of liberation, no matter one's faith, ethnicity, or extent of religious passion. This growing Americanization of the Passover seder parallels that of other Jewish ritual practices. Those chronicled over past years by the *New York Times* include the use at non-Jewish weddings of the *ketubah* (wedding contract), the *chuppah* (wedding canopy), and the hora dance in which bride and groom are held aloft in chairs.[59] What if the seder's growing popularity stems from its appeal to everyone and anyone? Are more Jews attending seders because it is seen as something Americans do? It remains an open question if optimism

214 | Vanessa L. Ochs

would be the prevailing response to speculation about a hyperbolic reckoning of non-Jews hosting traditional seders.[60] For this last possibility, there is a precedent in biblical narrative worth mentioning, even though it requires a stretch beyond the bounds of conventional hermeneutics. In this account (Exodus 18:1–12), Jethro, the priest of Midian, hears the astonishing story of the Exodus from his son-in-law, Moses, who recounts, in good hyperbolic fashion, "all that the Lord had done to Pharaoh and to the Egyptians for Israel's sake, all the hardships that had befallen them on the way, and how the Lord delivered them."[61] In response Jethro inaugurates what I suggest may be imagined as the first seder sponsored by one who is not a member of the people. Without matzo and bitter herbs, he covers the seder basics: he tells the story of deliverance, blesses God, acknowledges God's greatness, makes a sacrifice for God, and hosts a meal for all the elders of Israel. This meal looks toward the future with optimism, cementing bonds of cooperation.

Conclusion

The spirit of optimism of Passover's hyperbolic reckoning is intended to shape the perspective of the reader in examples such as the ones I have presented. In an optimistic frame of mind, readers may be motivated to do their part in sustaining the Jewish good news by buying new Haggadot, supporting Chabad's far-flung seders, or hosting more seder guests. Small acts, extraordinary consequences. The discourse may well be intended as much for those who articulate it as for those who receive it. This makes sense if we reference a particular unfortunate lonely man imagined by rabbinic literature, the one whose seder table includes no child, no student, and even no wife, and who must, to fulfill the obligation of engaging with the Exodus story, ask himself the four questions and answer them, too. Sacred transmission occurs in this case even when the sender and the recipient of the message are one and the same. In a theological mode, we could understand the discourse in yet another way, as a message dispatched by the one who tells it to God. According to Hasidic lore, God loves stories, and thus, might appreciate hyperbolic reckoning that comes bursting with hopefulness and signifies faith in God and God's power to ameliorate fate. The distinction between the producer and consumer of numerical good cheer is blurred: a community of producers and consumers (including God) are imaginatively created and all are in the same boat.

In literary history, according to Steven H. Webb, "hyperbole has been known as the bad boy of the tropes family, a cunning attempt to manipulate the unsuspecting by claiming or demanding more than the situation permits."[62] When it comes to the religious imagination, however, Webb suggests that this trope may point, at least in a Christian context, toward the gift of grace, God's love, in all its abundance to excess. In the Jewish contexts I have presented, the hyperbolic reckonings of Passover beckon not so much abundant love but an abundance of a hope worth having, a hope that might be fulfilled from single, uncountable seder tables, those carried out by Jews, Jews and their neighbors, and perhaps those generated by their neighbors.

Notes

The source of the title is a direct quote from http://www.jpost.com/Jewish-World/Jewish -News/Holon-Seder-for-1300-Ethiopian-olim-shoots-for-record, describing an attempt by Israel's Immigrant Absorption Ministry to set a Guinness World Record in 2011 by the seder they hosted for 1,300 Ethiopian immigrants in Tel Aviv.

1. Chabad is a Hasidic movement that is also referred to as Lubavitch. While the Chabad seders take place around the world, the headquarters of their organization remains the home of their late spiritual leader in Brooklyn, New York. I refer here to their English-language public relations materials. The seder is the ritual meal conducted, typically at home, on the first and, outside of Israel, on the second eves of Passover. The Haggadah (plural, Haggadot) is the liturgical text that orchestrates the lay-led service, one which includes storytelling, prayer, symbolic foods, a festive meal, and songs.

2. Claudia Claridge, "Of Fox-Sized Mice and a Thousand Men: Hyperbole in Old English," in *Developing Corpus Methodology for Historical Pragmatics*, ed. Carla Suhr and Irma Taavitsainen, Varieng: Studies in Variation, Contacts and Change 11 (2012), http://www.helsinki.fi /varieng/series/volumes/11/claridge/.

3. Claudia Claridge, *Hyperbole in English: A Corpus-Based Study of Exaggeration* (Cambridge: Cambridge University Press, 2010), 247, 253.

4. Peter Childs and Roger Fowler, *The Routledge Dictionary of Literary Terms* (London: Routledge, 2006), 31.

5. Joshua R. Ritter, "Recovering Hyperbole: Re-imagining the Limits of Rhetoric for an Age of Excess" (Ph.D. diss., Georgia State University, 2010), 15.

6. Eugene B. Borowitz, *The Talmud's Theological Language-Game: A Philosophical Discourse Analysis* (Albany: State University of New York Press, 2006), 43.

7. Israeli author Ari Shavit offers his own discourse of pessimism concerning the viability of Jewish life anywhere outside of Israel. Reflecting on the low Jewish birthrate and high intermarriage rate in North America, he concludes about secular young Jews: "They are drifting away from the center of gravity of Jewish identity; they are disappearing into the non-Jewish space." Ari Shavit, *My Promised Land: The Triumph and Tragedy of Israel* (New York: Spiegel and Grau, 2013), 386.

8. See Juliana Ochs, *Security and Suspicion: An Ethnography of Everyday Life in Israel* (Philadelphia: University of Pennsylvania Press, 2011), 68–73.

9. David L. Altheide, *Creating Fear: News and the Construction of Crisis* (New York: Transaction, 2002), 2.

10. Elianna Yolkut, "The Problem with Worrying about 'Jewish Continuity,'" *Ha'aretz*, November 13, 2011, http://www.haaretz.com/jewish-world/the-problem-with-worrying-about -jewish-continuity-1.395277.

11. Pew Research Center, Religion and Public Life Project, "Infographic: Survey of Jewish Americans," December 3, 2013, http://www.pewforum.org/2013/12/03/infographic-survey-of -jewish-americans/.

12. Pew Research Center, Religion and Public Life Project, *A Portrait of Jewish Americans: Findings from a Pew Research Center Study of U.S. Jews* (Washington, DC: Pew Research Center, October 1, 2013), http://www.pewforum.org/files/2013/10/jewish-american-full-report -for-web.pdf.

13. "Reinventing the Synagogue: A Conversation with Allison Fine," *Reform Judaism Online,* Summer 2013, http://reformjudaismmag.org/Articles/index.cfm?id=3263.

14. Laurie Goodstein, "Poll Shows Major Shift in Identity of U.S. Jews," *New York Times,* October 1, 2013, http://www.nytimes.com/2013/10/01/us/poll-shows-major-shift-in-identity -of-us-jews.html.

15. mzjerusalem, "Who Knows Two Million? There's an ArtScroll Haggadah for Everyone!," *blog.ArtScroll.com,* April 2, 2009, http://web.archive.org/web/20090412033011/http:// blog.artscroll.com/2009/04/02/who-knows-two-million-theres-an-artscroll-haggadah-for -everyone/.

16. For example, Elie Wiesel, in his Haggadah offers, "For Rabbi Samson Raphael Hirsch ... the four sons symbolize four generations. The first follows the precepts of the father, the second rebels against them, the third submits without understanding them. As for the last, he doesn't even know that he doesn't know. In other words, there is regression and loss." Wiesel inserts a less despairing interpretation of his own: "It is thanks to the fourth child that we are reading the most important verse of the Seder: 'And you shall tell your son on that day. . . .' This is the essence of our tradition. . . . A Jew must communicate a tradition. Not to do so is to mutilate it." Elie Wiesel, *Hagadah shel pesah = A Passover Haggadah: As Commented upon by Elie Wiesel and Illustrated by Mark Podwal,* ed. Marion Wiesel (New York: Simon and Schuster, 1993), 34–35.

17. Exodus 6:6–8. All biblical citations in this chapter are taken from Jewish Publication Society, *Tanakh* (Philadelphia: Jewish Publication Society, 1985).

18. *Israel* (Jerusalem: Jewish National and University Library–National Sound Archive, 1973), http://jnul.huji.ac.il/dl/music/passover/echad2_eng.html#israel.

19. This text, which entered the Haggadah in the fourteenth century, is based on an eleventh-century poem by Rabbi Joseph Tov Elem. See Nahum N. Glatzer, ed., *The Schocken Passover Haggadah* (New York: Schocken, 1996), 97.

20. Numbers 23:10. Also Psalm 80:16 and Isaiah 35:10, 51:11.

21. For more on the return of Temple ritual practices, see Lawrence Hoffman's commentary in Lawrence A. Hoffman and David Arnow, eds., *My People's Passover Haggadah: Traditional Texts, Modern Commentaries,* vol. 2 (Woodstock, VT: Jewish Lights, 2008). For more on the eschatological vision of Jerusalem, see Neil Gilman's commentary in ibid., 191–194.

22. The holiday inspires even some Jews who do not regularly follow the religious dietary rules to prepare their homes and regulate their diets to exclude leaven as their ancestors might have.

23. "F&W's Ultimate Guide to Passover Recipes," *Food and Wine,* 2014, http://www.foodand wine.com/passover-recipes. "The most prominent trend of new Haggadot is that of marquee names producing marquee products. This year obviously belongs to the aforementioned 'New American Haggadah,' ... with commentaries by Nathaniel Deutsch, Jeffrey Goldberg, Rebecca Newberger Goldstein and Lemony Snicket. That's enough star wattage to light a ner tamid." Jay Michaelson, "'Tis the Season for New Haggadot: Comparing the Best and Biggest Names for Passover," *Jewish Daily Forward,* March 23, 2012, http://forward.com/articles/153440/tis-the -season-for-new-haggadot/.

24. Michael Silverstein and Greg Urban, eds., *Natural Histories of Discourse* (Chicago: University of Chicago Press, 1996), 1.

25. John Austin's term for a speech act that leads to performance of action or change of status. See John L. Austin, *How to Do Things with Words* (Oxford: Oxford University Press, 1975), 5.

26. See the role of illocutionary acts in Paul Connerton, *How Societies Remember* (Cambridge: Cambridge University Press, 1989), 58–61.

27. Jeremy Stolow, *Orthodox by Design: Judaism, Print Politics, and the ArtScroll Revolution* (Berkeley: University of California Press, 2010), 1.

28. According to Susan Stewart, "The twentieth century has signaled the appropriation of the sphere of the gigantic by . . . commercial advertising." Susan Stewart, *On Longing: Narratives of the Miniature, the Gigantic, the Souvenir, the Collection* (Durham, NC: Duke University Press, 1993), 101.

29. In this volume, Oren Stier points to one of the many American Haggadot that was specifically composed to ritualize the memory of Jews who perished in the Holocaust, referring to them as "the six million." As Holocaust Memorial Day events became ubiquitous in America, fewer families used Holocaust Haggadot or the additional Holocaust-related materials created as inserts to the conventional text at their seders.

30. mzjerusalem, "Who Knows Two Million?"

31. Ibid.

32. Ibid.

33. Stolow, *Orthodox by Design*, 31, 72.

34. Jeffrey Shandler, *Keepers of Accounts: The Practice of Inventory in Modern Jewish Life*, vol. 17, *David W. Belin Lecture in American Jewish Affairs* (Ann Arbor: Frankel Center for Judaic Studies, University of Michigan, 2010), 39.

35. Eliezer Brodt, "The Seforim Blog: Rabbi Eliezer Brodt on Haggadah Shel Pesach: Reflections on the Past and Present," *The Seforim Blog: All about Seforim—New and Old, and Jewish Bibliography*, March 27, 2007, http://seforim.blogspot.com/2007/03/rabbi-eliezer-brodt-on -haggadah-shel.html.

36. Edward Rothstein, "Put Yourself in the Story of Passover: The Washington Haggadah at Metropolitan Museum of Art," *New York Times*, April 17, 2011, http://www.nytimes .com/2011/04/18/arts/design/the-washington-haggadah-at-metropolitan-museum-of-art.html.

37. Aaron Howard, "Why Is This Haggadah Different from All Others?," *Jewish Herald-Voice*, March 31, 2011, http://jhvonline.com/why-is-this-haggadah-different-from-all-others -p10812-152.htm.

38. Sue Fishkoff, *The Rebbe's Army: Inside the World of Chabad-Lubavitch* (New York: Schocken, 2009), 209.

39. Maya Balakirsky Katz, *The Visual Culture of Chabad* (Cambridge: Cambridge University Press, 2010), 3.

40. See Samuel C. Heilman and Menachem Friedman, *The Rebbe: The Life and Afterlife of Menachem Mendel Schneerson* (Princeton, NJ: Princeton University Press, 2010).

41. Joshua Runyan, "More Than a Decade since Its Leader's Departure, Chabad-Lubavitch Expands His Call to Better the World," *Chabad.org/News*, June 22, 2007, http://www.chabad .org/news/article_cdo/aid/534279/jewish/Since-its-Leaders-Departure-Chabad-Lubavitch -Expands.htm/r/cache/includerelated/false.

42. Kasher, in this context, means making the area for food preparation ritually acceptable according to Jewish law, including the more stringent requirements for Passover.

43. "A mitzvah protects and rescues while one is engaged in it." Babylonian Talmud, Sotah 21a.

44. Tamar Runyan, "Thousands Share Stories of Transformation at Historic Passover Meal," *Chabad-Lubavitch News,* April 14, 2011, http://www.chabad.org/news/article_cdo/aid/1497338/jewish/Nepal-Seder-Enjoys-Long-History.htm.

45. Yehuda Ceitlin, "Last-Minute Hassles for the World's Largest Seders," *Chabad-Lubavitch News,* April 8, 2008, http://www.chabad.org/news/article_cdo/aid/665935/jewish/Last-Minute-Hassles-For-The-Worlds-Largest-Seders.htm.

46. Patricia Cline Cohen, *A Calculating People: The Spread of Numeracy in Early America* (New York: Routledge, 1999), 50.

47. Ibid., 206.

48. Thus, the first portion of matzo to be consumed is a 5″ × 7″ piece of machine-baked matzo. Less is required for the next portion: this time a 6″ × 4″ piece will suffice. See Rabbi Menachem M. Schneerson, ed., *Haggadah for Pesach* (Brooklyn, NY: Kehot Publication Society, 2007). Note: This Haggadah is not the one used at large Chabad seders and is meant for study and use by the more learned "householders."

49. Elise Berman, "Voices of Outreach: The Construction of Identity and Maintenance of Social Ties among Chabad-Lubavitch Emissaries," *Journal for the Scientific Study of Religion* 48, no. 1 (2009): 69–85.

50. Ibid., 71.

51. Some in Chabad have claimed that the Rabbe Menachem Mendel Schneerson himself is the messiah; others, including the Rebbe himself, have rejected that claim. See Heilman and Friedman, *The Rebbe.*

52. "The Messianic Era—The Basics," *Chabad.org,* http://www.chabad.org/library/moshiach/article_cdo/aid/1128725/jewish/The-Basics.htm.

53. Berman, "Voices of Outreach," 73.

54. Ariela Pelaia, "The Jewish Holiday of Passover (Pesach)," *About.com,* http://judaism.about.com/od/holidays/a/Jewish-Holiday-Passover-Pesach.htm.

55. Jacqueline Urla, "Cultural Politics in an Age of Statistics: Numbers, Nations, and the Making of Basque Identity," *American Ethnologist* 20, no. 4 (1993): 818.

56. Naomi Zeveloff, "What Does Schechter Decline Mean? School Dip Sign of Trouble for Conservative Movement," *Jewish Daily Forward,* January 27, 2012, http://forward.com/articles/149983/what-does-schechter-decline-mean/?p=all&p=all&p=all#ixzz1kHqXrSLG.

57. Rothstein, "Put Yourself in the Story of Passover."

58. Ira Sheskin and Arnold Dashefsky, *Jewish Population in the United States* (Current Jewish Population Reports, Berman Institute–North American Jewish Data Bank, University of Connecticut, 2010), http://www.brandeis.edu/cmjs/conferences/demographyconf/pdfs/Dashefsky_JewishPopulationUS2010.pdf.

59. See Samuel G. Freedman, "Christians Embrace a Jewish Wedding Tradition," *New York Times,* February 11, 2011, http://www.nytimes.com/2011/02/12/us/12religion.html; and Marianne Rohrlich, "Exchanging Vows under a Canopy, No Matter Their Faith," *New York Times,* December 16, 2011, http://www.nytimes.com/2011/12/18/fashion/weddings/more-couples-are-using-a-wedding-canopy-no-matter-their-faith.html.

60. I am not referring here to the many churches that hold Christian adaptations of seders, making an analogy between the Passover seder and the Last Supper of Jesus.

61. Exodus 18:8–9.

62. Stephen H. Webb, "Theological Reflections on the Hyperbolic Imagination," in *Rhetorical Invention and Religious Inquiry: New Perspectives,* ed. Walter Jost and Wendy Olmsted (New Haven, CT: Yale University Press, 2000), 279.

Postscript

Balancing Accounts: Commemoration and Commensuration

Theodore M. Porter

I$_S$ THERE SOMETHING special about the relationship of numbers to Jews and Jewish scholarship? Anyone out there who still reads books from front to back will realize that this one does not make the results of addition depend on culture or religion. It does, however, call attention to limits of comparability that may turn arithmetic results to nonsense. A birth neutralizes a death in the population registers, but morally it is quite another matter. Enumeration in the context of group life may transgress the factual to evoke solidarity or futility, dispassion or melodrama. The focus in these chapters is on the meanings, often symbolic, attributed to numbers, and in this regard Jewish experience in the modern period presents an abundance of distinctive issues and problems, subjects of impassioned discussion and debate. Included among them are the vast and terrifying organized murders and mass emigration of the 1930s and 1940s; the quandaries of assimilation in the postwar world, and a growing uncertainty about what it means to be Jewish; the establishment of a Jewish state of settlers in a diversely peopled region on the eastern shore of the Mediterranean Sea; and an inescapable sense that demographic numbers have implications for political legitimacy as well as power.

Would other religions or cultures, other kinds of human groups, provide material of equal interest and importance for such a study? Quite possibly. But the chapters here make a strong case for this focus on distinctive Jewish cultures of enumeration. They incorporate a density of scholarship that is mainly the achievement of the last few decades and bring it to bear on the human dimensions of numbers. The book has been conceived as an encounter of two quite different areas of research and reflection. One is Jewish studies, with which most of the authors in this volume are associated, and which has grown into a recognized field with many characteristics of a discipline. The other is the historical and cultural investigation of numbers, statistics, and quantification, which also has achieved status since about 1980 as a distinctive topic of study. There had been opponents of quantification before then, but few interpreters or historians, and little sense of a perspective from which to comprehend this fundamental tool of universal science. Meanwhile, beneath the radar of any scholarly attention to cultures of numbers, Jewish groups and the Jewish state were experimenting with new ways of representing themselves numerically.

It is not easy to think of standing outside this numbered world in order to observe it coolly. Behind the numbers, if we are able to imagine lifting this veil, we will usually find more numbers, and these provide hints of the power that supports them. Numbers are expensive, and increasingly so. The so-called era of Big Data is in part a bid to elevate marketing and self-recording over the organized bureaucratic collection and deployment of public numbers. It has turned "data-mining" into a term of praise, and its champions have noisily disdained the formal models and hypothesis testing of academic science. Size is not the principal basis of its distinctiveness. The numbers of official statistics and of business and government accounts have been and remain almost unimaginably big.

The scale of social science rose to a new level in the twentieth century through its embrace of tools of quantification adapted from techniques of official statistics that took off a century earlier. Reflection and critique cost only a pittance by comparison, yet these too required resources. Much, but not all, of the work of interpretation occurred in universities, where, of course, it confronted the Goliath of institutionalized quantification with a frame much smaller than David's. Over the last three or four decades, this topic, or way of thinking, has been spreading through the interstitial spaces of academic life. It grew up in fields such as social history, qualitative sociology, and cultural anthropology, where a few scholars were becoming disenchanted with results of the postwar infatuation with statistics. But it is scarcely an academic field and has none of the institutional trappings of a discipline: no professorships, no programs or departments, no scholarly societies, no journals or book series.[1] It offers a critical perspective appealing as a focus for interdisciplinary seminars and research groups. For such purposes, the difficulty of delimiting it precisely has brought advantages. It provides a space of unusually open intellectual exchange.

The trajectory of my own research is closely tied up with the tools and ambitions that made numbers and statistics into objects of research in the cultural history of science. One founding moment occurred in 1982–1983 at the Center for Interdisciplinary Research of the University of Bielefeld, Germany, with a research group on "the probabilistic revolution." The project was organized by Lorenz Krüger, a philosopher, who was inspired particularly by Thomas Kuhn's theory of scientific revolutions and Ian Hacking's 1975 book *The Emergence of Probability*. The participants, many of them historians or philosophers of science, included statisticians, social historians, and natural and social scientists. But the emphasis, overwhelmingly conceptual, focused on the question of how it became possible within science to think of the world as nondeterministic. The practical tools of data and statistics, and the diverse sites where they have been deployed, were somewhat peripheral to the design of the project, even if they gradually gained prominence within it.[2] Lorraine Daston, for example, was beginning to look at probability calculation in business, medicine, and insurance, while Mary Morgan was reframing her dissertation into a book on the history of economic modeling and econometrics. My dissertation, about chance and quantification, had led me to a fascination with state officials and reformers, gathering and interpreting numbers on poverty, crime, and suicide. Hacking, who had emphasized in his earlier book the place of probability among "low sciences" such as alchemy and medicine, was by then emphasizing the bureaucratic side of statistical data and reasoning. Like Michel Foucault, he looked to highly mundane activities for sources of great conceptual mutations. Metrologists, medical reformers, and census officials are at least as prominent as mathematicians and philosophers in his account of what he called *The Taming of Chance.*[3]

Yet this was nothing like a centrally organized movement. I suspect that some of the authors of the present volume arrived in Ann Arbor for a conference on Jewish numbers with a feeling like that of Molière's Jourdain when he discovered that there was in the world such a things as *prose,* which he had been speaking all his life. I, conversely, was amused and delighted to be invited to participate in a workshop at a Center for Jewish Studies. From my perspective, the widely dispersed character of my research topic has always been a plus, and I have again and again found inspiration in work from an unfamiliar field that I chanced to encounter at a conference or in a footnote. In a great variety of disciplines—including anthropology, sociology, history, literature, art, psychology, education, business, and accounting—numbers, data, or statistics have emerged of late as topics of scholarly inquiry.

There is always cross-disciplinary curiosity as well as misunderstanding among those who take up research on the uses of number and statistics. Some scholars find common ground in the overlapping fields of history of science, history of medicine, or science and technology studies (STS). Many are participants in a shared response to large historical changes of the last few decades, notably to postcolonial themes and a heightened consciousness of globalism, to the ever-changing politics of ethnicity and gender, to "neoliberal" issues of privatization and decentralization, and to administrative strategies worked out in an effort to manage the massive expansion of medicine. The idealization of "evidence-based medicine" and its many analogues, with "evidence" construed overwhelmingly as statistical, has inspired enthusiastic as well as critical reflection from a variety of perspectives. The modern utopia, as envisioned by so many well-placed administrators and philanthropists, is a world governed by benchmarks and indicators, a thinned world that should not require us to look beneath the surface. If, however, our statistics measure the wrong thing, and if people exploit or fall victim to these inaccuracies, numbers can easily lead us astray. A scientist, scholar, or administrator can be enthusiastic about data and numerical reasoning and yet doubt the possibility of theory-free or interpretation-free statistics. An appreciation of the historical and cultural side of numbers may be indispensable to the effective use of quantitative evidence.[4]

The subject matter of the present collection pertains first of all to images, practices, and their circulation, without privileging academic settings or formal structures of information. Some of the chapters, at first glance, do not seem to be about knowledge at all, even in the generous sense of any claim to represent something that happened or that exists (in some measure) in the world. But then we realize that numerical accuracy is somehow at issue in symbolic appropriations of numbers, even as other claims that seem specifically factual prove to be saturated by a rhetorical or moral dimension. In the end, we are not so sure whether and how the rules of arithmetic apply to the things these numbers purport to represent. The entwinement of image and objectivity is what makes this book so fruitful and fascinating.

Grand issues of postcolonialism, globalism, and neoliberalism are not conspicuously present in the volume, which focuses on specifically Jewish themes. These are diverse yet interlinked, first of all, by the experience and memory of the Holocaust. With its six million victims, in round numbers, including the parents or grandparents of so many persons now living, it is ubiquitous in contemporary arts as well as in scholarship. An explicit topic of some papers, it is implicit in most of the rest. As a historical event, it is not ready to be consigned to history but remains present in discussions of the future of Israel and the Jewish people. Its enduring moral resonance does not seem to inhibit its invocation in regard to practical demographic questions that extend well beyond death counts. It is hard to think of anything more sacred on this Earth, yet these millions of victims of organized hate are sometimes treated as commensurable with processes that resemble them only by involving an increase or decrease in numbers of Jews or Israelis. Here, the politics of commensuration is deadly serious.[5]

I proceed in this postscript somewhat counterfactually, citing selectively to draw out dimensions of coherence in the mythical field of number studies as a basis for commenting on its intersections with Jewish studies. But Jewish life is much more than just a slate on which to plot the role played by quantification. Not only its paradoxical commensurations but also the distinctive tensions between individual and collective provide fascinating material for number interpretation. Under the shadow of the Holocaust, anxieties about population have been brought to bear on rates of fertility and of intermarriage. The Holocaust contributes moral urgency to the bibliometry of (mainly) pre-Nazi books in Yiddish, which must be saved even as their owners grow old and die, often far from the lands where they were born. Our thoughts turn silently to the nightmare of anti-Semitism as we examine debates from more than a century ago about statistics of Jewish crime. The Holocaust looms over the contemporary politics of Palestine and Israel, though its appropriateness in this context is bitterly contested. The issues raised are somehow specifically, but by no means uniquely, Jewish ones. They involve the legitimacy, and with it vulnerability, conferred by population numbers, the need to specify criteria of religious or ethnic membership, the temptations of hatred, of ethnic cleansing and ethnic murder. They extend to the historical role of individuals and the moral implications of dissolving them into (numbered) groups. Threats to Israel, as well as its military success, have figured prominently in U.S. and world politics right from its founding in 1948. As I write these lines at the beginning of August 2014, news reports are giving daily updates on the number of deaths in the Israeli invasion of Gaza, including efforts to distinguish children and other noncombatants from soldiers and fighters. Many of the numbers in this book allude in some way to experiences like these.

Yael Zerubavel raises the issue of representation and symbolism in an especially intriguing way in chapter 3 on place names. Hill of the Five could, in principle, have a numerical shape, or bear a star that, in relation to David's, comes up short. Few Israelis could make such a mistake, since they would recognize in the writing an indication of sacredness. The five or three or twelve in these names alludes to so many people who have performed a patriotic act, often at the cost of their lives. The "creative toponym," as she explains, commemorates their heroic self-sacrifice without calling attention to specific individuals. The number provides a name, which is "collective and egalitarian." It creates a "duty to remember," but the memorialization bypasses individuals, extending to the Israeli people or state more generally. The five are barely persons, merely doers of a deed. We sometimes complain of being reduced to a number, but here, by merging identities, the one is amplified even as it is dissolved.

And yet the individual is not quite suppressed but remains a unit on which the greater number depends. We have, in the end, not the *how much* of a fluid medium but the *how many* of atoms or individuals. The numbers that give these places their names do not appear at first to provide more than an evocation of an event and its heroes. And yet, as Zerubavel shows, new information can call a designation into question. Behind the symbolism remains a duty to be factually correct, to omit no one who deserves to be included, however impersonally. She mentions a remarkable case, the twenty-three seafarers who were increased to twenty-four, not on account of new information but because it came to seem necessary to extend this honor to a British officer who had died in the same mission as the twenty-three Israeli ones. Even though the individual members of this group were unknowable from its name, this individual too had earned an anonymous commemoration.

Zerubavel thinks that numbers above about 140 may not be suited to be attached to hills and roads because they are too disturbing. The most prominent and most disturbing of all Jewish numbers, and one that has not been used this way, is six million. In no way can we generalize from this six million, but its singularity exerts a terrible fascination. Oren Stier comments that the figure originated from a very dubious source, the testimony by an SS officer that Adolf Eichmann had told him so in a Budapest apartment eight or nine months before the war, and with it the Nazi Holocaust, was brought to an end. Many figures for the number of victims have been calculated, drawing from a variety of pertinent sources, both old and new. Until recently, some of the most credible estimates were closer to five million than to six. Meanwhile, the figure of six million has maintained its dominance in public discussion, barely responding to sizable fluctuations in scholarly estimates.

An otherwise imperceptible moral principle of approximation may have crept in here, that a round number should in no event diminish the tragedy or the crime. In other respects, the ethics of precision are subtle and complicated. We certainly cannot say that a divergence on the order of five hundred thousand or a million persons is of little consequence. The organized murders of the Roma and Sinta, of the mentally ill, of homosexuals, and of Communists, perhaps on a scale no greater than the uncertainty in the number of Jewish victims, are yet, by any reasonable standard, holocausts in themselves. On the other hand, it would not in the least exculpate the Holocaust deniers who hold forth relentlessly on their internet sites if a number for Jewish deaths closer to five million should come to appear more truthful than six. The moral and historical issues at stake will never be settled by statistics, and yet the numbers are a critically important part of the story. I would not hesitate to call it a duty for historians to achieve as much accuracy on this question as the sources and our methods permit. This is not an alternative, but a complement, to accounts on the level of particular communities, families, and individuals who suffered and died, as well as of the intentions and devices of the perpetrators.

Meanwhile, six million has become an article of faith and not without good reasons. As Stier emphasizes, we are no longer dealing merely with six million, but with "the six million," a collective object rather than a tally of individuals. This figure does much more than merely represent, and so stands somewhat apart from any new calculations. Yet it could, in principle, be called into question if surprising new evidence were to surface. It is decidedly not about precision. The round number serves as a mnemonic, giving a sense, which remains vague and even unimaginable, of the horrifying scale. Yet there are limits to justification by faith. We may discern a curious reversal of accuracy and symbolism in the promise of the Names Recovery Project at Yad Vashem, examined in chapter 2 by Carol Kidron, to identify every one of the six million dead. In practice, of course, this comes down to finding and confirming every victim they can, a goal with wide support. It is on the other hand misleading, not only in supposing that we know a priori how many victims there were but also, and somewhat contradictorily, by implying that the list of names may supply unanswerable evidence of the true number of deaths. It is difficult to imagine that the names could ever constitute the best evidence of the number of victims. So many obstacles exist even to managing the database and combining duplicate records. The most reliable tools for estimating numbers of deaths are likely to remain more impersonal and demographic. Since tallies and registers of individuals were classified by religion in much of continental Europe, the censuses of these lands provide indispensable if imperfect information about the number of Jews before the killing began. Those same records were deployed to organize the killing, which the bureaucratic machinery then documented with chilling quantitative detail. The database at Yad Vashem has no way of counting all those who disappeared with their whole families or are otherwise undocumented. It can, however, give a movingly different form of demonstration that the number is very large, while preserving a sense of the personhood of each unit. Most of the dead show up as somebody's relative.

As with streets of the five or the twenty-three, the relation of the six million to all these individuals is somewhat contradictory. So large a number stands at a great remove from scenes of ordinary life. As Kidron explains, Yad Vashem designed the tools of remembrance to recover and preserve a memory of the victims, but not to pass on stories or to record the feelings of their descendants. This depersonalizing reflects perhaps a taste for hard facts, but with it a preference, once again, for collective over individual commemoration. It is often tempting to interpret this anonymity as a consequence of quantifying technologies or of impersonal bureaucracy. Although numbers can work powerfully to make things uniform, data systems often admit more flexibility than is preserved in their implementation. In the names project at Yad Vashem we detect some element of administrative convenience but mainly a moral choice.

That choice, in a different context, serves as a particular focus of chapter 7 by Josh Friedman on the Yiddish Book Center. A preoccupation with numbers, he explains, implies abstraction from the specificity of context. He writes of the "'thinness' with which numbers describe their objects." Yet this kind of "thin description" offers no escape from morality. The numbers are not cool and value neutral but emotionally laden. Or as Michal Kravel-Tovi puts it, the figures are *wet,* not dry. The choice to deflect attention from individual experience means assigning priority to the collectivity.

We can be more specific. The gauges and test scores and economic measures that normally serve as exemplars of dispassionate objectivity have an instrumental character. They are bound up with specific technologies, deployed to achieve certain ends. The technologies discussed by Kidron and Friedman are more loosely structured and leave open more options. The shift of emphasis away from the commemoration of individuals at Yad Vashem and the Yiddish Book Project, as with Zerubavel's number signs, was deliberate. From the beginning, the census of the dead defined the individual as the unit of record, one page per victim. At first, file space imposed a constraint on the amount of information that could be recorded. But the pages have been converted to electronic form. *All the Names* (if I may allude to José Saramago's wonderful novel) and everything that is likely to be recorded about them could now be held on a normal teenager's cell phone. This "census" is actually a database and could be a repository of all kinds of stories and recollections, submitted by any number of family members and acquaintances. It would in that case be highly unequal since some victims have been survived by neighbors or relatives with rich memories and abundant documents, while for others it is difficult or impossible even to resuscitate a name. The Names Recovery Project has not gone that route but provides little biographies that amount to an identification card in paragraph form. If the data program is constraining, that is by design. Kidron suggests in conclusion that it was set in this mostly impersonal form for the sake of the Israeli state, which welcomes all these victims as posthumous citizens.

The reluctance of the Yiddish Book Center to keep records of how the volumes were used, or even the identities of their donors, seems especially curious. Friedman, as ethnographer, has gathered up moving stories of human attachments to these books, of sacrifices made to buy them, and of the emotional investment of the procurers. Their pitch emphasizes a family legacy as well as a Jewish one, and some of the donors clearly expect the books to be knowable as their own legacy. It would, of course, require cumbersome record keeping to do this, and it would make the Yiddish Book Center exceptional among libraries. University library catalogues, including my own at UCLA, do not individualize books. But my library in most cases does not want multiple copies at all and even refuses donations to its collections until someone has gone through them to cull out duplicates. The Yiddish Book Center was a site of massive redundancy even before it began putting the books online. Preserving something about the original owners of these books, perhaps even how the books mattered for them, would supply a rationale for continued accumulation. We seem to have here an "affective dimension" regarding numbers in place of one regarding persons. Friedman even speaks of the magical aspect of the numbers! The founder of the center, Aaron Lansky, wrote of his achievement as preserver of Yiddish books under the title, *Outwitting History*. He means that Yiddish, at least as the language of books, has survived the Holocaust.

But there are other Jewish number worries and other solutions. Stier mentions the idea of quantified retribution, an eye for an eye and six million for six million. David Ben-Gurion envisioned a sweeter and less gruesome revenge, to replace and in this sense to bring back those who were lost as newborns in the infant nation of Israel. Anat Leibler recalls this politics in her chapter 5 on the demographer Roberto Bachi's population policies in Palestine just before and just after the establishment of the new state. Toward the end of the war, Bachi considered several ideas to ensure a sufficiently powerful position in Palestine for immigrant European Jews. A binational state might work for a while, he supposed, since Jews had the strongest economic position, but it did not appear viable over the long term. Immigration from abroad, similarly, might maintain Jewish dominance for a time, but given comparative birth rates, he calculated that the majority could not last. Partition seemed to him the best option. Leibler shows elsewhere how Israel in 1948 used a census that was also a registration to exclude from this land all who were not present on the census day.[6] Even if the rule had been applied evenhandedly, this worked very much to the disadvantage of the Arab or Palestinian populations. But how long could the Jewish majority endure? Bachi held out some hope for sufficient Jewish reproduction, not by Europeans but by Mizrahi women, the "national womb." He understood all this in terms of the by then widely accepted theory of a second demographic transition. The Mizrahi, being less advanced economically, should maintain high birth rates for some time yet.

There was never any possibility of Jewish majorities in the United States, but the demographic basis for a strong minority population was, for Jewish leaders, a matter of great urgency. Kravel-Tovi studies social scientists who work on Jewish issues. Most of them are Jews themselves, and their passionate anxiety about the Jewish population makes their numbers anything but dry. It looks like nonstate *biopower,* she suggests, invoking a concept promised in one of Foucault's lecture series at the Collège de France and developed only in pieces. What she describes is a bit narrower, focused overwhelmingly on demography. The concerns of Bachi and Ben-Gurion recall the fears that led the French to invent a quantitative science of demography a century earlier.[7] For American Jews, the issue of birth rates was secondary to that of intermarriage, which, predictably, became much more common as Jews achieved full acceptance and equality in the United States. Have the social scientists demonstrated a real threat to Jewish distinctiveness? Kravel-Tovi shows how some were willing to toy with the most disturbing commensuration of all, likening marriages to gentiles to a "silent holocaust."

Seasonal indicators, the topic of Vanessa Ochs's contribution, appear to offer more favorable prospects for Jews as a people. This is the index of matzo, boiled eggs, haroset, and gefilte fish. Unmistakably hyperbolic, it sends Cassandra for a time to the sidelines. We might also speculate in a moment of reflexivity that the capacity of Jewish institutions in America to demarcate a population and carry out a census, this nonstate *demopower,* tells as much about the resilience of Jewishness as any data on outbreeding. Although the mobilization of American interest groups, notably racial and ethnic ones, to demand new questions or revised categories is as old as the census itself, the self-organization of Jewish statistics in central Europe as well as America appears *sui generis*.[8] This is not at all to say that organized private enterprise in the collection of statistical data is something exceptional. Statistical societies that formed in some of the richer countries of Europe and North America in the 1830s and 1840s were interested especially in problems associated with poverty, including labor, poor relief, crime, dirt, and epidemic disease. In our own day, circulation of consumer data among marketers has become the epitome of Big Data.

Mitchell Hart writes about Jewish statisticians who were moved to defend their people against the imputation of bad "racial" characteristics based on questionable statistics. His story focuses on a few episodes from a long-standing discussion of Jewish criminality in Germany. There is a simple pattern that almost anyone could replicate. Some statistics show Jews to be overrepresented in the numbers regarding something undesirable. Somebody says Jews are like that by nature. A closer look by a more sympathetic interpreter, typically a Jewish one, demonstrates that the pattern is not general, that the bad figure admits other interpretations, and that other numbers show Jews in a comparatively favorable light. By the 1880s, when hereditary crime was a hot issue and statistics were abundant, Jewish statisticians had become organized and ready to answer such hostile charges.

We may compare Hart's episodes with a 1913 pamphlet authored by a municipal teacher in Vienna, identified in library catalogues as David Hecht. The anti-Semites, he wrote, accuse Jews of religious murder. But look at the statistics, which show that Jews have the lowest murder rate among religious confessions. There must be some other reason for the charge, a nonrational explanation. Hecht extended the story all the way back to debates in a church council summoned by Constantine to discuss the divinity of Christ. Unable to agree, they turned the discussion to the crucifixion of God's son, which all were happy to blame on the Jews. From calculated rhetoric, this doctrine gradually turned into habit. In humans and animals alike, as Ewald Hering has shown, habits are transformed over time into inherited memories or instincts. It follows, wrote Hecht, that the degenerate ones are not Jews at all, but these Christian anti-Semites. "Anti-Semitism is nothing other than an antipathy for Jews, formed out of religious intolerance and inherited over the course of the centuries." His title summed it up: *Anti-Semitism—A Hereditary Burden, Concisely and Popularly Demonstrated*.[9]

But statistics of Jews were employed not only to defend Jews against attacks by ignorant or unscrupulous outsiders. These numbers were also a way of informing and being informed about a far-flung Jewish community. Sometimes they were intended to stimulate a revision of attitudes or to alter behaviors. In the Jewish state, Jewish statistics have been vital tools of state, while in the United

States and other lands, they have helped to create and sustain a community with a degree of autonomy and self-regulation, though nothing like that of a state. The chapters in this volume illuminate how numbers have been used to defend or reinforce community, even as they reveal anxieties about survival of Jews as a people. Many of them bring out a more pointed worry that Jewish numbers are declining, or, in Israel, that Jews are being swamped. Of course, scholars and social scientists also maintain the number as a basis for taking action. This collection, much more than most works on history of statistics and accounts, brings out the symbolic and passionate dimension of numbers in place of cool logic and detached manipulation. This wider world of numbers, enlivened by emotion and solidarity, has, so far, remained mostly in the shadows. Jews, perhaps, are special, but the perspectives developed here could with advantage be applied, *mutatis mutandis,* to other situations and other groups.

Notes

1. Except, I think, in France, where some of the most important institutions of social science are less sharply defined by disciplinary identity and where *statistique publique,* as the French refer to it, is actively debated. Also, the French national statistical institute, the Institut National de la Statistique et des Études Économiques (INSEE), has a wider remit and a greater public visibility than in many countries. See, for example, Isabelle Bruno, Emmanuel Didier, and Julien Prévieux, *Statactivisme: Comment lutter avec des nombres* (Paris: Découverte, 2014). There is a French online journal on the history of probability and statistics, and there are accounting journals that take more than a passing interest in these questions.

2. Lorenz Krüger, Lorraine J. Daston, and Michael Heidelberger, eds., *The Probabilistic Revolution,* vol. 1, *Ideas in History* (Cambridge, MA: MIT Press, 1987). See also the collectively authored volume by Gerd Gigerenzer, Zeno Swijtink, Theodore Porter, Lorraine Daston, Lorenz Krüger, and John Beatty, *The Empire of Chance: How Probability Changed Science and Everyday Life* (Cambridge: Cambridge University Press, 1989).

3. Ian Hacking, *The Emergence of Probability* (Cambridge: Cambridge University Press, 1975); Lorraine Daston, *Classical Probability in the Enlightenment* (Princeton, NJ: Princeton University Press, 1988); Mary S. Morgan, *The History of Econometric Ideas* (Cambridge: Cambridge University Press, 1990); Theodore M. Porter, *The Rise of Statistical Thinking, 1820–1900* (Princeton, NJ: Princeton University Press, 1986); and Ian Hacking, *The Taming of Chance* (Cambridge: Cambridge University Press, 1990).

4. I reflect on this in Theodore M. Porter, "Thin Description: Surface and Depth in Science and Science Studies," *Osiris* 27, no. 1 (2012): 209–226.

5. See especially Wendy Espeland and Mitchell Stevens, "Commensuration as a Social Process," *Annual Review of Sociology* 24 (1998): 313–343.

6. Anat Leibler and Daniel Breslau, "The Uncounted: Citizenship and Exclusion in the Israeli Census of 1948," *Ethnic and Racial Studies* 28, no. 5 (2005): 880–902; Anat Leibler, "Establishing Scientific Authority—Citizenship and the First Census of Israel," *Tel Aviver Jahrbuch für deutsche Geschichte* 35 (2007): 221–236; and Anat Leibler, "'You Must Know Your Stock': Census as Surveillance Practice in 1948 and 1967," in *Surveillance and Control in Israel*

/Palestine: Population, Territory, and Power, ed. Elia Zureik, David Lyon, and Yasmeen Abu-Laban (London: Routledge, 2011), 239–256.

7. See, for example, Libby Schweber, *Disciplining Statistics: Demography and Vital Statistics in France and England* (Durham, NC: Duke University Press, 2003); and Paul-André Rosental, *L'Intelligence démographique: Sciences et politiques des populations en France (1930–1960)* (Paris: Odile Jacob, 2003).

8. See Paul Schor, *Compter et classer: Histoire des recensements américains* (Paris: École des Hautes Études en Sciences Sociales, 2009) on the census and shaping of ethnic categories in the United States. On Jewish statistics, see Mitchell B. Hart, *Social Science and the Politics of Modern Jewish Identity* (Stanford, CA: Stanford University Press, 2000).

9. See David Hecht, *Antisemitismus—eine erbliche Belastung: Kurzgefasster und volkstümlich gehaltener Nachweis* (Vienna: R. Löwit, 1913).

Bibliography

Almog, Oz. *The Sabra: The Creation of the New Jew.* Berkeley: University of California Press, 2000.

Alonso, William, and Paul Starr, eds. *The Politics of Numbers.* New York: Russell Sage Foundation, 1987.

Altheide, David L. *Creating Fear: News and the Construction of Crisis.* New York: Transaction, 2002.

Ami-Oz, Dr. Moses, and Neri Erelli. "The Twenty-Four Seafarers" [in Hebrew]. http://dl.dropbox.com/u/75665001/%D7%AA%D7%A7%D7%A6%D7%99%D7%A8%20%D7%93%D7%95%D7%97%20%D7%94%D7%9B%D7%92.pdf.

Anders, Edward, and Juris Dubrovskis. "Who Died in the Holocaust? Recovering Names from Official Records." *Holocaust and Genocide Studies* 17, no. 1 (2003): 114–138.

Anders, Gerhard. "The Normativity of Numbers: World Bank and IMF Conditionality." *PoLAR: Political and Legal Anthropology Review* 31, no. 2 (2008): 188–202.

Anderson, Benedict. *Imagined Communities: Reflections on the Origin and Spread of Nationalism.* London: Verso, 2006.

Anderson, Margo J., and Stephen E. Fienberg. *Who Counts? The Politics of Census-Taking in Contemporary America.* New York: Russell Sage Foundation, 1999.

Anonymous. *Der Juden Antheil am Verbrechen, auf Grund der amtlichen Statistik über die Thätigkeit Schwurgerichte, in vergleichender Darstellung mit den christlichen Confessionen.* Berlin, 1881.

——. "Die Kriminalität der Juden in Deutschland." *Im Deutschen Reich* 2, no. 1 (1896): 21–33.

Appadurai, Arjun. *Fear of Small Numbers: An Essay on the Geography of Anger.* Durham, NC: Duke University Press, 2006.

——. "Number in the Colonial Imagination." In *Orientalism and the Postcolonial Predicament: Perspectives on South Asia,* edited by Carol A. Breckenridge and Peter van der Veer, 314–339. Philadelphia: University of Pennsylvania Press, 1993.

——. "Patriotism and Its Futures." *Public Culture* 5, no. 3 (1993): 411–429.

Arad, Roi Chikie. "The Man Who Was on the Boat with the Twenty-Three Seafarers" [in Hebrew]. *Ha'aretz,* February 21, 2013.

Armbrust, Walter. "Egyptian Cinema On Stage and Off." In *Off Stage / On Display: Intimacy and Ethnography in the Age of Public Culture,* edited by Andrew Shryock, 69–98. Stanford, CA: Stanford University Press, 2004.

Asad, Talal. "Ethnographic Representation, Statistics, and Modern Power." *Social Research* 61, no. 1 (1994): 55–88.

Ascher, Marcia. *Ethnomathematics: A Multicultural View of Mathematical Ideas.* London: Chapman and Hall, 1994.

Associated Press. "Pages of 12,000 Yiddish Books Digitally Preserved." *USA Today*, May 6, 2002. http://usatoday30.usatoday.com/tech/news/2002/05/06/digital-yiddish.htm.

Austin, John L. *How to Do Things with Words*. Oxford: Oxford University Press, 1975.

Azaryahu, Maoz. *In Their Death They Commanded: The Architecture of Military Cemeteries in Israel, the Early Years* [in Hebrew]. Tel Aviv: Ministry of Defense Press, 2012.

———. *Namesakes: History and Politics of Street Naming in Israel* [in Hebrew]. Jerusalem: Carmel, 2012.

———. "The Power of Commemorative Street Names." *Environment and Planning D* 14, no. 3 (1996): 311–330.

———. *State Cults: Celebrating Independence and Commemorating the Fallen in Israel, 1948–1956* [in Hebrew]. Sde Boker, Israel: Ben-Gurion Research Center and Ben-Gurion University Press, 1995.

Azaryahu, Maoz, and Aharon Kellerman. "Symbolic Places of National History and Revival." *Transactions* 24, no. 1 (1999): 109–123.

Azoulay, Ariella, and Adi Ophir. *The One-State Condition: Occupation and Democracy in Israel/Palestine*. Stanford, CA: Stanford University Press, 2012.

Bachi, Roberto. *Yehudey Yerushalayim* [Jews of Jerusalem]. Jerusalem: Jewish Agency, 1941.

Badiou, Alain. *Number and Numbers*. Cambridge: Polity, 2008.

Ball, Terence. "The Politics of Social Science in Postwar America." In *Recasting America: Culture and the Politics in the Age of Cold War*, edited by Lary May, 76–92. Chicago: University of Chicago Press, 1989.

Barnes, Barry, and Donald Mackenzie. "On the Role of Interests in Scientific Change." In *On the Margins of Science: The Social Construction of Rejected Knowledge*, edited by Roy Wallis, 49–66. Sociological Review Monograph 27. Keele, UK: University of Keele, 1979.

Bartmanski, Dominik, and Jeffrey C. Alexander. "Introduction: Materiality and Meaning in Social Life: Toward an Iconic Turn in Cultural Sociology." In *Iconic Power: Materiality and Meaning in Social Life*, edited by Jeffrey C. Alexander, Dominik Bartmanski, and Bernhard Giesen, 1–12. New York: Palgrave Macmillan, 2012.

Bartov, Omer. "Chambers of Horrors: Holocaust Museums in Israel and the United States." *Israel Studies* 2, no. 2 (1997): 66–87.

Bauman, Zygmunt. *Modernity and the Holocaust*. Ithaca, NY: Cornell University Press, 2001.

Baumel, Judith Tydor, and Jacob J. Schacter. "The Ninety-Three Bais Yaakov Girls of Cracow: History or Typology?" In *Reverence, Righteousness, and Rahamanut: Essays in Memory of Rabbi Dr. Leo Jung*, edited by Jacob J. Schacter, 93–130. New York: Jason Aronson, 1992.

Bayatrizi, Zohreh. "Counting the Dead and Regulating the Living: Early Modern Statistics and the Formation of the Sociological Imagination (1662–1897)." *British Journal of Sociology* 60, no. 3 (2009): 603–621.

———. "From Fate to Risk: The Quantification of Mortality in Early Modern Statistics." *Theory, Culture and Society* 25, no. 1 (2008): 121–143.

Beaud, Jean-Pierre, and Jean-Guy Prévost. *The Age of Numbers: Statistical Systems and National Traditions* [in French]. Sainte-Foy: Presses de l'Université du Québec, 2000.

Becker, Peter. "Criminological Language and Prose from the Late Eighteenth to the Early Twentieth Century." In *Crime and Culture: An Historical Perspective,* edited by Amy Gilman Srebnick and René Lévy, 23–36. London: Ashgate, 2005.

Beirne, Piers. *Inventing Criminology: Essays on the Rise of "Homo Criminalis."* Albany: State University of New York Press, 1993.

Ben-Gurion, David. *Medinat Yisrael Hamechudeshet* [The Israeli state renewed]. Tel Aviv: Am Oved, 1969.

Benor, Sarah. "Do American Jews Speak a 'Jewish Language'? A Model of Jewish Linguistic Distinctiveness." *Jewish Quarterly Review* 99, no. 2 (2009): 230–269.

Benz, Wolfgang, ed. *Dimension des Völkermords: Die Zahl der jüdischen Opfer des Nationalsozialismus.* Munich: Oldenbourg, 1991.

Bergman, Elihu. "The American Jewish Population Erosion." *Midstream* 23 (October 1977): 9–19.

Berkowitz, Michael. *The Crime of My Very Existence: Nazism and the Myth of Jewish Criminality.* Berkeley: University of California Press, 2007.

——. "A Hidden Theme of Jewish Self-Love? Eric Hobsbawm, Karl Marx, and Cesare Lombroso on 'Jewish Criminality.'" In *The Cesare Lombroso Handbook,* edited by Paul Knepper and Per Jørgen Ystehede, 256–258. London: Routledge, 2012.

——. "Unmasking Counterhistory: An Introductory Exploration of Criminality and the Jewish Question." In *Criminals and Their Scientists,* edited by Peter Becker and Richard F. Wetzel, 61–84. Cambridge: Cambridge University Press, 2006.

Berman, Elise. "Voices of Outreach: The Construction of Identity and Maintenance of Social Ties among Chabad-Lubavitch Emissaries." *Journal for the Scientific Study of Religion* 48, no. 1 (2009): 69–85.

Berman, Lila Corwin. *Speaking of Jews: Rabbis, Intellectuals, and the Creation of an American Public Identity.* Berkeley: University of California Press, 2009.

Bernard-Donals, Michael, and Richard Glejzer. *Between Witness and Testimony: The Holocaust and the Limits of Representation.* Albany: State University of New York Press, 2001.

Blau, Bruno. *Die Kriminalität der Juden.* Berlin, 1906.

Bloom, Etan. "The 'Administrative Knight'—Arthur Ruppin and the Rise of Zionist Statistics." In *Demographie—Demokratie—Geschichte: Deutschland und Israel,* edited by Josef Brunner, 183–203. Göttingen, Germany: Wallstein, 2007.

——. "Zionist Statistics in Light of Jewish Thought." In *The Limits of Quantification: Critical Perspectives on Measuring and Grading People, Their Behaviours and Achievements* [in Hebrew], edited by Yohai Hakak, Lea Kacen, and Michal Krumer-Nevo, 132–172. Be'er Sheva, Israel: Bialik Institute, 2012.

Blum, Alain. "Social History as the History of Measuring Populations: A Post-1987 Renewal." *Kritika: Explorations in Russian and Eurasian History* 2, no. 2 (2001): 279–294.

Borowitz, Eugene B. *The Talmud's Theological Language-Game: A Philosophical Discourse Analysis.* Albany: State University of New York Press, 2006.

Bourguet, Marie-Noëlle. "Décrire, Compter, Calculer: The Debate over Statistics during the Napoleonic Period." In *The Probabilistic Revolution: Ideas in History,* edited by Lorenz Krüger, Lorraine J. Daston, and Michael Heidelberger, 1:305–316. Cambridge, MA: MIT Press, 1987.

Bowker, Geoffrey C., and Susan Leigh Star. *Sorting Things Out: Classification and Its Consequences.* Cambridge, MA: MIT Press, 2000.

Boyarin, Jonathan. *Thinking in Jewish*. Chicago: University of Chicago Press, 1996.

Bridge of Books, A. Directed by Sam Ball. 2001. http://www.yiddishbookcenter.org/our-story.

Bristow, Edward. *Prostitution and Prejudice: The Jewish Fight against White Slavery, 1870–1939*. Oxford: Oxford University Press, 1982.

Brodt, Eliezer. "The Seforim Blog: Rabbi Eliezer Brodt on Haggadah Shel Pesach: Reflections on the Past and Present." *The Seforim Blog: All about Seforim—New and Old, and Jewish Bibliography,* March 27, 2007. http://seforim.blogspot.com/2007/03/rabbi-eliezer-brodt-on-haggadah-shel.html.

Bruno, Isabelle, Emmanuel Didier, Julien Prévieux. *Statactivisme: Comment lutter avec des nombres*. Paris: Découverte, 2014.

Buck, Peter. "People Who Counted: Political Arithmetic in the Eighteenth Century." *Isis* 73, no. 266 (1982): 28–45.

Callon, Michel. "Elements of a Sociology of Translation: Domestication of the Scallops and the Fishermen of St. Brieuc Bay." In *Power, Action and Belief: A New Sociology of Knowledge?,* edited by John Law, 196–233. London: Routledge, 1986.

Callon, Michel, and Bruno Latour. "Unscrewing the Big Leviathan: How Actors Macrostructure Reality and How Sociologists Help Them to Do So." In *Advances in Social Theory and Methodology: Toward an Integration of Micro- and Macro-Sociologies,* edited by Karin Knorr-Cetina and Aaron Cicourel, 277–303. London: Routledge and Kegan Paul, 1981.

Camic, Charles, Neil Gross, and Michèle Lamont. "Introduction: The Study of Social Knowledge Making." In *Social Knowledge in the Making,* edited by Charles Camic, Neil Gross, and Michèle Lamont, 1–40. Chicago: University of Chicago Press, 2011.

Cândea, Virgil. "Icons." In *Encyclopedia of Religion,* edited by Lindsay Jones, 7:4352–4354. 2nd ed. Detroit: Macmillan Reference USA, 2005. *Gale Virtual Reference Library,* April 30, 2014.

Ceitlin, Yehuda. "Last-Minute Hassles for the World's Largest Seders." *Chabad-Lubavitch News,* April 8, 2008. http://www.chabad.org/news/article_cdo/aid/665935/jewish/Last-Minute-Hassles-For-The-Worlds-Largest-Seders.htm.

Chevalier, Louis. *Labouring Classes and Dangerous Classes in Paris in the First Half of the Nineteenth Century*. London: Routledge, 1973.

Childs, Peter, and Roger Fowler. *The Routledge Dictionary of Literary Terms*. London: Routledge, 2006.

Claridge, Claudia. *Hyperbole in English: A Corpus-Based Study of Exaggeration*. Cambridge: Cambridge University Press, 2010.

——. "Of Fox-Sized Mice and a Thousand Men: Hyperbole in Old English." In *Developing Corpus Methodology for Historical Pragmatics,* edited by Carla Suhr and Irma Taavitsainen. Varieng: Studies in Variation, Contacts and Change 11. 2012. http://www.helsinki.fi/varieng/series/volumes/11/claridge/.

Cohen, Hillel. *1929: Year Zero of the Jewish-Arab Conflict* [in Hebrew]. Jerusalem: Keter, 2013.

Cohen, Naomi W. *Not Free to Desist: The American Jewish Committee, 1906–1966*. Philadelphia: Jewish Publication Society, 1972.

Cohen, Patricia Cline. *A Calculating People: The Spread of Numeracy in Early America*. New York: Routledge, 1999.

Cohen, Steven M. "The Demise of the 'Good Jew': Marshall Sklare Award Lecture." *Contemporary Jewry* 32, no. 1 (2012): 85–93.

Cohn, Bernard. *Colonialism and Its Forms of Knowledge: The British in India*. Princeton, NJ: Princeton University Press, 1996.

Cole, Joshua. *The Power of Large Numbers: Population, Politics, and Gender in Nineteenth-Century France*. Ithaca, NY: Cornell University Press, 2000.

Cole, Tim. "Nativization and Nationalization: A Comparative Landscape Study of Holocaust Museums in Israel, the US and the UK." *Journal of Israeli History* 23, no. 1 (2004): 130–145.

Connerton, Paul. *How Societies Remember*. Cambridge: Cambridge University Press, 1989.

Contact: The Journal of Jewish Life Network / Steinhardt Foundation 5, no. 3 (2003).

Contact: The Journal of Jewish Life Network / Steinhardt Foundation 8, no. 4 (2006).

Crump, Thomas. *The Anthropology of Numbers*. Cambridge: Cambridge University Press, 1990.

Curtis, Bruce. *The Politics of Population: State Formation, Statistics, and the Census of Canada, 1840–1875*. Toronto: University of Toronto Press, 2002.

Dan, Joseph. "The Narrative of the Ten Martyrs: Martyrology and Mysticism." In *History of Jewish Mysticism and Esotericism* [in Hebrew], 2:744–776. Jerusalem: Zalman Shazar Center / Historical Society of Israel, 2008.

Daston, Lorraine. *Classical Probability in the Enlightenment*. Princeton, NJ: Princeton University Press, 1988.

De Roos, J. R. B. "Über die Kriminalität der Juden." *Monatsschrift für Kriminalpsychologie* 6 (1909): 10.

Dekel, Irit. "Way of Looking: Observation and Transformation at the Holocaust Memorial, Berlin." *Memory Studies* 2, no. 1 (2009): 71–86.

Deleuze, Gilles, and Félix Guattari. *A Thousand Plateaus: Capitalism and Schizophrenia*. Minneapolis: University of Minnesota Press, 1991.

Della Pergola, Sergio. *World Jewry beyond 2000: The Demographic Prospects*. Oxford: Oxford Centre for Hebrew and Jewish Studies, 1999.

Dershowitz, Alan. *The Vanishing American Jew: In Search of Jewish Identity for the Next Century*. New York: Touchstone, 1997.

Desrosières, Alain. "How to Make Things Which Hold Together: Social Science, Statistics and the State." In *Discourses on Society: The Shaping of the Social Sciences*, edited by Peter Wagner, Bjorn Wittrock, and Richard Whitley, 195–218. Dordrecht: Kluwer, 1991.

———. *The Politics of Large Numbers: A History of Statistical Reasoning*. Cambridge, MA: Harvard University Press, 2002.

De-Vris, David. "Tnuat Hapoalim Beheifa Bashanim 1919–29: Mechkar Bahistoria Shel Poalim Ironiyim Be'eretz Yisrael Hamandatorit [Labor movement in Haifa in the years 1919–29: A historical study of urban workers in the Land of Israel during the British Mandate]." Ph.D. diss., Tel Aviv University, 1992.

Diner, Hasia R. *We Remember with Reverence and Love: American Jews and the Myth of Silence after the Holocaust, 1945–1962*. New York: New York University Press, 2009.

Dobrin, Lise M., Peter K. Austin, and David Nathan. "Dying to Be Counted: The Commodification of Endangered Languages in Documentary Linguistics." In *Proceedings of the Conference on Language Documentation and Linguistic Theory,* edited by Peter K. Austin, Oliver Bond, and David Nathan, 59–68. London: SOAS, 2007.

Donati, Jessica, and Mirwais Harooni. "Last Jew in Afghanistan Faces Ruin as Kebabs Fail to Sell." Reuters, November 12, 2013. http://www.reuters.com/article/2013/11/12/us-afghanistan-jews-idUSBRE9AB0A120131112.

Dotan, Shmuel. *Hama'avak Al Eretz Yisrael* [The struggle over the Land of Israel]. Tel Aviv: Misrad Habitahon, 1981.

Eglash, Ruth. "Holon Seder for 1,300 Ethiopian Olim Shoots for Record." *Jerusalem Post,* April 14, 2011. http://www.jpost.com/Jewish-World/Jewish-News/Holon-Seder-for-1300-Ethiopian-olim-shoots-for-record.

Elazar, Daniel. *Community and Polity: The Organizational Dynamics of American Jewry.* Philadelphia: Jewish Publication Society, 1995.

Eliav, Benjamin. *Hayeshuv Biyemey Habait Haleumi* [The Yishuv in the days of the national home]. Jerusalem: Keter, 1976.

Emsley, Clive. *Crime and Society in England: 1750–1900.* 2nd ed. London: Longman, 1996.

Endelman, Todd. *The Jews of Georgian England, 1714–1830.* 2nd ed. Ann Arbor: University of Michigan Press, 1999.

Engelke, Matthew. "Number and the Imagination of Global Christianity; or, Mediation and Immediacy in the Work of Alain Badiou." *South Atlantic Quarterly* 109, no. 4 (2010): 811–829.

Engelman, Uriah Zvi. "Jewish Statistics in the U.S. Census of Religious Bodies (1850–1936)." *Jewish Social Studies* 9, no. 2 (1947): 127–174.

Espeland, Wendy, and Mitchell Stevens. "Commensuration as a Social Process." *Annual Review of Sociology* 24 (1998): 313–343.

"F&W's Ultimate Guide to Passover Recipes." *Food and Wine,* 2014. http://www.foodandwine.com/passover-recipes.

Falk, Raphael. "The Gene—A Concept in Tension." In *The Concept of the Gene in Development and Evolution,* edited by Peter J. Beurton, Raphael Falk, and Hans-Jörg Rheinberger, 317–348. Cambridge: Cambridge University Press, 2000.

———. *Zionism and the Biology of Jews.* Tel Aviv: Resling, 2006.

Feige, Michael. "The Monument to the Helicopter Disaster and the Paradox of the Privatization of the Commemoration of Fallen Soldiers" [in Hebrew]. *Iyunim Bitkumat Yisrael* 20 (2010): 122–143.

Feldman, Jackie. *Above the Death Pits, Beneath the Flag: Youth Voyages to Holocaust Poland and Israeli National Identity.* New York: Berghahn, 2008.

Fishberg, Maurice. *The Jews: A Study of Race and Environment.* New York: Walter Scott, 1911.

Fishkoff, Sue. *The Rebbe's Army: Inside the World of Chabad-Lubavitch.* New York: Schocken, 2009. http://lib.myilibrary.com?id=454205.

———. "With Flurry of New Local Studies, Jewish Communities Seeing Trends and Making Changes." *JTA,* July 10, 2011. http://www.jta.org/2011/07/10/life-religion/with-flurry-of-new-local-studies-jewish-communities-seeing-trends-and-making-changes.

Foucault, Michel. "Governmentality." In *The Anthropology of the State: A Reader,* edited by Aradhana Sharma and Akhil Gupta, 131–142. Malden, MA: Blackwell, 2006.

——. "Governmentality." In *The Foucault Effect: Studies in Governmentality,* edited by Graham Burchell, Colin Gordon, and Peter Miller, 87–104. Chicago: University of Chicago Press, 1991.

——. *History of Sexuality.* New York: Pantheon, 1978.

——. "Politics and the Study of Discourse." In *The Foucault Effect: Studies in Governmentality,* edited by Graham Burchell, Colin Gordon, and Peter Miller, 53–72. Chicago: University of Chicago Press, 1991.

Frankel, Jonathan. "The 'Yizkor' Book of 1911: A Note on National Myths in the Second Aliya." In *Religion, Ideology, and Nationalism in Europe and America: Essays Presented in Honor of Yehoshua Arieli,* 355–384. Jerusalem: Historical Society of Israel / Zalman Shazar Center, 1986.

Freedman, Samuel G. "Christians Embrace a Jewish Wedding Tradition." *New York Times,* February 11, 2011. http://www.nytimes.com/2011/02/12/us/12religion.html.

Friedlander, Saul. "Memory of the Shoah in Israel." In *The Art of Memory: Holocaust Memorials in History,* edited by James Young, 149–157. Munich: Prestel, 1994.

——. *Probing the Limits of Representation.* Cambridge, MA: Harvard University Press, 1992.

——. "The Shoah between Memory and History." *Jewish Quarterly* 37, no. 1 (1990): 5–11.

Fritzsche, Peter. "Talk of the Town: The Murder of Lucie Berlin and the Production of Local Knowledge." In *Criminals and Their Scientists,* edited by Peter Becker and Richard F. Wetzel, 377–398. Cambridge: Cambridge University Press, 2006.

Fuld, Ludwig. *Das jüdische Verbrechertum: Eine Studie über den Zusammenhang zwischen Religion und Kriminalität.* Leipzig: Theodor Huth, 1885.

Furedi, Frank. *Therapy Culture: Cultivating Vulnerability in an Uncertain Age.* London: Routledge, 2004.

Furet, François, ed. *Unanswered Questions: Nazi Germany and the Genocide of the Jews.* New York: Schocken, 1989.

Geertz, Clifford. "Thick Description: Toward an Interpretive Theory of Culture." In *The Interpretation of Cultures: Selected Essays,* 3–30. New York: Basic Books, 1973.

Geffen-Monson, Rela. "The Sociology of the American Jewish Community." *Modern Judaism* 11, no. 1 (1991): 147–156.

Geller, Jay. "From Mohels to *Mein Kampf:* Syphilis and the Construction of Jewish Identification." In *The Other Jewish Question: Identifying the Jew and Making Sense of Modernity,* 88–131. New York: Fordham University Press, 2011.

Giese, Wilhelm. *Die Juden und die deutsche Kriminalstatistik.* Leipzig, 1892.

Gigerenzer, Gerd, Zeno Swijtink, Theodore Porter, Lorraine Daston, Lorenz Krüger, and John Beatty. *The Empire of Chance: How Probability Changed Science and Everyday Life.* Cambridge: Cambridge University Press, 1989.

Gilbert, Martin. *The Routledge Atlas of the Holocaust.* 3rd ed. New York: Routledge, 2002.

Gilman, Sander. *The Jew's Body.* London: Routledge, 1991.

——. *Smart Jews: The Construction of the Image of Jewish Superior Intelligence.* Lincoln: University of Nebraska Press, 1997.

Glatzer, Nahum N., ed. *The Schocken Passover Haggadah.* New York: Schocken, 1996.

Goldberg, J. J. "America's Vanishing Jews." *Jerusalem Report,* November 5, 1992.

——. "A Jewish Recount." *New York Times,* September 17, 2003.

Goldscheider, Calvin. "Are American Jews Vanishing Again?" *Contexts* 2, no. 1 (2003): 18–24.

——. "Demographic Transformations in Israel: Emerging Themes in Comparative Context." In *Population and Social Change in Israel,* edited by Calvin Goldscheider, 1–36. Boulder, CO: Westview, 1992.

——. "Ethnic Categorizations in Censuses: Comparative Observations from Israel, Canada, and the United States." In *Census and Identity: The Politics of Race, Ethnicity, and Language in National Censuses,* edited by David I. Kertzer and Dominique Arel, 71–91. Cambridge: Cambridge University Press, 2002.

——. *Israel's Changing Society: Population, Ethnicity, and Development.* Boulder, CO: Westview, 2002.

——. *Studying the Jewish Future.* Seattle: University of Washington Press, 2004.

Goldstein, Sidney. "Beyond the 1990 National Jewish Population Survey: A Research Agenda." *Contemporary Jewry* 14, no. 1 (1993): 147–164.

——. "A National Jewish Population Study: Why and How." In *A Handle on the Future: The Potential of the 1990 National Jewish Population Survey,* edited by Barry A. Kosmin, 1–9. 1988. http://www.jewishdatabank.org/studies/details.cfm?Study ID=626.

——. "What of the Future? The New National Jewish Population Study for American Jewry." In *Proceedings of the Rabbinical Assembly,* edited by Rabbi Jules Harlow, 3–13. New York: Rabbinical Assembly, 1992.

Goodstein, Laurie. "Poll Shows Major Shift in Identity of U.S. Jews." *New York Times,* October 1, 2013. http://www.nytimes.com/2013/10/01/us/poll-shows-major-shift-in -identity-of-us-jews.html.

Gordon, Anthony, and Richard Horowitz. "Will Your Grandchildren Be Jews?" *Jewish Spectator* (Fall 1996): 36–38.

Graff, Helmut. *Die deutsche Kriminalstatistik: Geschichte und Gegenwart.* Stuttgart: Ferdinand Enke, 1975.

Greenhalgh, Susan. "Planned Births, Unplanned Persons: 'Population' in the Making of Chinese Modernity." *American Ethnologist* 30, no. 2 (2003): 196–215.

Gubkin, Liora. *You Shall Tell Your Children: Holocaust Memory in American Passover Ritual.* New Brunswick, NJ: Rutgers University Press, 2007.

Guha, Sumit. "The Politics of Identity and Enumeration in India c. 1600–1990." *Comparative Studies in Society and History* 45, no. 1 (2003): 148–167.

Gupta, Akhil. *Red Tape: Bureaucracy, Structural Violence, and Poverty in India.* Durham, NC: Duke University Press, 2012.

Guyer, Jane I., et al. "Introduction: Numbers as Inventive Frontier." *Anthropological Theory* 10, no. 1–2 (2010): 36–61.

Hacking, Ian. "Biopower and the Avalanche of Printed Numbers." *Humanities in Society* 5, no. 3–4 (1982): 279–295.

——. *The Emergence of Probability.* Cambridge: Cambridge University Press, 1975.

——. "Prussian Numbers 1860–1882." In *The Probabilistic Revolution: Ideas in History,* edited by Lorenz Krüger, Lorraine J. Daston, and Michael Heidelberger, 1:377–393. Cambridge, MA: MIT Press, 1987.

——. *The Taming of Chance.* Cambridge: Cambridge University Press, 1990.

Hacohen, Dvora. "Mass Immigration and the Israeli Political System." *Journal of Israeli History* 8, no. 1 (1987): 99–113.

Halbwachs, Maurice. *The Collective Memory.* New York: Harper Colophon Books, 1980.

Hamisrad Haeretz Yisraeli, Shel Hahistadrut Hatzionit, Sfirat Yehuday Eretz Yisrael [World Zionist Organization, Palestine Zionist Office, Enumerating Jews in Palestine], 1918.

Handelman, Don. *Models and Mirrors—Towards an Anthropology of Public Events.* Cambridge: Cambridge University Press, 1990.

———. *Nationalism and the Israeli State: Bureaucratic Logic in Public Events.* Oxford: Berg, 2004.

Hansen-Glucklich, Jennifer. "Evoking the Sacred: Visual Holocaust Narrative in National Holocaust Museums." *Journal of Modern Jewish Studies* 9, no. 2 (2010): 209–232.

Hart, Mitchell B., ed. *Jews and Race: Writings on Identity and Difference, 1880–1940.* Lebanon, NH: Brandeis University Press, 2011.

———. "Jews, Race, and Capitalism in the German-Jewish Context." *Jewish History* 19, no. 1 (2005): 49–63.

———. *Social Science and the Politics of Modern Jewish Identity.* Stanford, CA: Stanford University Press, 2000.

Hasan-Rokem, Galit. "Martyr vs. Martyr—The Sacred Language of Violence." In *A Reader in the Anthropology of Religion,* edited by Michael Lambek, 590–595. Malden, MA: Blackwell, 2008.

Hecht, David. *Antisemitismus—eine erbliche Belastung: Kurzgefasster und volkstümlich gehaltener Nachweis.* Vienna: R. Löwit, 1913.

Heilman, Samuel. "The Sociology of American Jewry: The Last Ten Years." *Annual Review of Sociology* 8 (1982): 135–160.

Heilman, Samuel C., and Menachem Friedman. *The Rebbe: The Life and Afterlife of Menachem Mendel Schneerson.* Princeton, NJ: Princeton University Press, 2010.

Heilman, Uriel. "NJPS 2000–01: A Lost Cause?" *Jerusalem Post,* December 17, 2003.

Hermann, Tamar. "The Bi-national Idea in Israel/Palestine: Past and Present." *Nations and Nationalism* 11, no. 3 (2005): 381–401.

Herring, Hayim. "How the 1990 National Jewish Population Survey Was Used by Federation Professionals for Jewish Continuity Purposes." *Journal of Jewish Communal Service* 76, no. 3 (2000): 216–227.

Hess, Aaron, and Art Herbig. "Recalling the Ghosts of 9/11: Convergent Memorializing at the Opening of the National 9/11 Memorial." *International Journal of Communication* 7 (2013): 2207–2230.

Hess, Jonathan. *Germans, Jews, and the Claims of Modernity.* New Haven, CT: Yale University Press, 2002.

———. "Johann David Michaelis and the Colonial Imaginary: Orientalism and the Emergence of Racial Antisemitism in Eighteenth-Century Germany." *Jewish Social Studies,* n.s., 6, no. 2 (2000): 56–101.

Hilberg, Raul. *The Destruction of the European Jews.* Rev. and definitive ed. New York: Holmes and Meier, 1985.

———. *The Destruction of the European Jews.* 3rd ed. New Haven, CT: Yale University Press, 2003.

———. "The Statistic." In *Unanswered Questions: Nazi Germany and the Genocide of the Jews,* edited by François Furet, 155–171. New York: Schocken, 1989.

Hilgartner, Stephen. *Science on Stage: Expert Advice as Public Drama.* Stanford, CA: Stanford University Press, 2000.

Hill, Jane H. "'Expert Rhetorics' in Advocacy for Endangered Languages: Who Is Listening, and What Do They Hear?" *Journal of Linguistic Anthropology* 12, no. 2 (2002): 119–133.

Hillier, Bill, and Kali Tzorati. "Space Syntax: The Language of Museum Space." In *A Companion to Museum Studies*, edited by Sharon Macdonald, 282–301. Oxford: Wiley-Blackwell, 2011.

Hoffman, Lawrence A., and David Arnow, eds. *My People's Passover Haggadah: Traditional Texts, Modern Commentaries.* Woodstock, VT: Jewish Lights, 2008.

"Hope Was Lost" [in Hebrew]. *Davar,* January 13, 1961.

Horowitz, Bethamie. "Stop Worrying: Details Follow." *The Forward,* December 22, 2006.

Houri, Jackie. "Nahariya's Municipality Is Changing Street Names" [in Hebrew]. *Ha'aretz,* October 26, 2010.

Howard, Aaron. "Why Is This Haggadah Different from All Others?" *Jewish Herald -Voice,* March 31, 2011. http://jhvonline.com/why-is-this-haggadah-different-from -all-others-p10812-152.htm.

Hull, Matthew S. "Documents and Bureaucracy." *Annual Review of Anthropology* 41 (2012): 251–267.

Huyssen, Andreas. *Twilight Memories: Marking Time in a Culture of Amnesia.* London: Routledge, 1995.

If Eighty, It Is Not a Legend: Herzliya's 80th Anniversary [in Hebrew]. Herzliya, Israel: Herzliya Municipality, 2004.

Igo, Sarah. *The Averaged American: Surveys, Citizens, and the Making of a Mass Public.* Cambridge, MA: Harvard University Press, 2007.

———. "Subjects of Persuasion: Survey Research as a Solicitous Science, or, The Public Relations of the Polls." In *Social Knowledge in the Making*, edited by Charles Camic, Neil Gross, and Michèle Lamont, 285–306. Chicago: University of Chicago Press, 2011.

"In Memory of the 140" [in Hebrew]. *Davar,* April 30, 1946.

Inda, Jonathan Xavier. *Targeting Immigrants: Government, Technology, and Ethics.* Malden, MA: Blackwell, 2006.

Israel. Jerusalem: Jewish National and University Library–National Sound Archive, 1973. http://jnul.huji.ac.il/dl/music/passover/echad2_eng.html#israel.

Jackson, John L. *Thin Description: Ethnography and the African Hebrew Israelites of Jerusalem.* Cambridge, MA: Harvard University Press, 2013.

Jaffe, A. J. "The Use of Death Records to Determine Jewish Population Characteristics." *Jewish Social Studies* 1, no. 2 (1939): 143–168.

Jaggar, Allison. "Love and Knowledge: Emotion in Feminist Epistemology." In *Gender/ Body/Knowledge: Feminist Reconstructions of Being and Knowing*, edited by Allison Jaggar and Susan Bordo, 145–171. New Brunswick, NJ: Rutgers University Press, 1989.

Jasanoff, Sheila. *The Fifth Branch: Science Advisers as Policymakers.* Cambridge, MA: Harvard University Press, 1990.

Jewish Publication Society. *Tanakh.* Philadelphia: Jewish Publication Society, 1985.

Kadosh, Ruti. "The Heroines Who Did Not Exist" [in Hebrew]. *Ma'ariv,* April 21, 2009.

Kalpagam, U. "The Colonial State and Statistical Knowledge." *History of the Human Sciences* 13, no. 2 (2000): 37–55.

Kapferer, Bruce. "Ritual Dynamics and Virtual Practice: Beyond Representation and Meaning." *Social Analysis* 48, no. 2 (2004): 33–54.

Katriel, Tamar. "*Gibush:* The Crystallization Metaphor in Israeli Cultural Semantics." In *Communal Webs: Communication, Culture, and Acculturation in Contemporary Israel,* 11–34. Albany: State University of New York Press, 1991.

Katz, Maya Balakirsky. *The Visual Culture of Chabad.* Cambridge: Cambridge University Press, 2010.

Kaviraj, Sudipta. *The Imaginary Institution of India: Politics and Ideas.* New York: Columbia University Press, 2010.

Kawall, Mariana, and Leal Ferreira. "When 1 + 1 ≠ 2: Making Mathematics in Central Brazil." *American Ethnologist* 24, no. 1 (1997): 132–147.

Kelner, Shaul. "In Its Own Image: Independent Philanthropy and the Cultivation of Young Jewish Leadership." In *The New Jewish Leaders: Reshaping the American Jewish Landscape,* edited by Jack Wertheimer, 261–321. Hanover, NH: University Press of New England, 2011.

——. *Tours That Bind: Diaspora, Pilgrimage, and Israeli Birthright Tourism.* New York: New York University Press, 2010.

Kemp, Adriana. "Labour Migration and Racialisation: Labour Market Mechanisms and Labour Migration Control Policies in Israel." *Social Identities* 10, no. 2 (2004): 267–292.

Kertzer, David I., and Dominique Arel, eds. *Census and Identity: The Politics of Race, Ethnicity, and Language in National Censuses.* Cambridge: Cambridge University Press, 2002.

Kidron, Carol A. "Embracing the Lived Memory of Genocide: Holocaust Survivor and Descendant Renegade Memory Work at the House of Being." *American Ethnologist* 37, no. 3 (2010): 429–451.

Kirshenblatt-Gimblett, Barbara. *Destination Culture: Tourism, Museums, Heritage.* Berkeley: University of California Press, 1998.

Kosmin, Barry. "An Appreciation of the Contribution of Egon Mayer to Jewish Populations, Community, and Family Studies." *Contemporary Jewry* 26, no. 1 (2006): 159–168.

Kosmin, Barry, et al. *Highlights of the CJF 1990 National Jewish Population Survey.* New York: Council of Jewish Federations, 1991.

Krampf, Arie. "The Metaphysics of the Fact: The Social Measurement in Historical and Comparative Perspective." In *The Limits of Quantification: Critical Perspectives on Measuring and Grading People, Their Behaviours and Achievements* [in Hebrew], edited by Yohai Hakak, Lea Kacen, and Michal Krumer-Nevo, 103–131. Be'er Sheva, Israel: Bialik Institute, 2012.

Kravel-Tovi, Michal, and Yoram Bilu. "The Work of the Present: Constructing Messianic Temporality in the Wake of Failed Prophecy among Chabad Hasidim." *American Ethnologist* 35, no. 1 (2008): 64–80.

Krüger, Lorenz, Lorraine J. Daston, and Michael Heidelberger, eds. Vol. 1 of *The Probabilistic Revolution: Ideas in History.* Cambridge, MA: MIT Press, 1987.

Krüger, Lorenz, Gerd Gigerenzer, and Mary S. Morgan, eds. Vol. 2 of *The Probabilistic Revolution: Ideas in the Sciences.* Cambridge MA: MIT Press, 1987.

Kula, Witold. *Measures and Men.* Princeton, NJ: Princeton University Press, 1986.

Kuznitz, Cecile. *YIVO and the Making of Modern Jewish Culture: Scholarship for the Yiddish Nation.* Cambridge: Cambridge University Press, 2014.

Lambek, Michael, and Paul Antze. "Introduction: Forecasting Memory." In *Tense Past: Cultural Essays in Trauma and Memory,* ed. Paul Antze and Michael Lambek, xi–xxxviii. New York: Routledge, 1996.

Lang, Berel. "Holocaust Memory and Revenge: The Presence of the Past." *Jewish Social Studies,* n.s., 2, no. 2 (1996): 1–20.

Lansky, Aaron. "Flip Side." *Book Peddler* (Summer 2011): 20–25.

——. "Just between Us." *Book Peddler* (Winter 1985): 2–5.

——. *Outwitting History: The Amazing Adventures of a Man Who Rescued a Million Yiddish Books.* Chapel Hill, NC: Algonquin, 2004.

——. "Road Map." *Book Peddler* (Fall 2011): 16–23.

"Last Journey of the Lamed-Hei Heroes of Israel" [in Hebrew]. *Ha'tsofe,* January 20, 1948.

Latour, Bruno. *Science in Action: How to Follow Engineers and Scientists through Society.* Cambridge, MA: Harvard University Press, 1987.

Lave, Jean. *Cognition in Practice: Mind, Mathematics and Culture in Everyday Life.* Cambridge: Cambridge University Press, 1988.

Lazarsfeld, Paul F. "Notes on the History of Quantification in Sociology—Trends, Sources and Problems." *Isis* 52, no. 2 (1961): 277–333.

Legaspi, Michael C. *The Death of Scripture and the Rise of Biblical Studies.* Oxford: Oxford University Press, 2010.

Leibler, Anat. "Disciplining Ethnicity: Social Sorting Intersects with Political Demography in Israel's Pre-state Period." *Social Studies of Science* 44, no. 2 (2014): 271–292.

——. "Establishing Scientific Authority—Citizenship and the First Census of Israel." *Tel Aviver Jahrbuch für deutsche Geschichte* 35 (2007): 221–236.

——. "Statisticians' Ambition: Governmentality, Modernity and National Legibility." *Israel Studies* 9, no. 2 (2004): 121–149.

——. "'You Must Know Your Stock': Census as Surveillance Practice in 1948 and 1967." In *Surveillance and Control in Israel/Palestine: Population, Territory, and Power,* edited by Elia Zureik, David Lyon, and Yasmeen Abu-Laban, 239–256. London: Routledge, 2011.

Leibler, Anat, and Daniel Breslau. "The Uncounted: Citizenship and Exclusion in the Israeli Census of 1948." *Ethnic and Racial Studies* 28, no. 5 (2005): 880–902.

Lemke, Thomas. *Bio-politics: An Advanced Introduction.* New York: New York University Press, 2010.

Levi, Primo. *The Drowned and the Saved.* Translated by Raymond Rosenthal. New York: Summit, 1988.

Leykin, Inna. "'Population Prescriptions': State, Morality, and Population Politics in Contemporary Russia." Ph.D. diss., Brown University, 2013.

Liebman, Charles S., and Eli'ezer Don-Yiḥya. *Civil Religion in Israel: Traditional Judaism and Political Culture in the Jewish State.* Berkeley: University of California Press, 1983.

Lipstadt, Deborah E. *The Eichmann Trial.* New York: Nextbook/Schocken, 2011.

Lutz, Catherine. "Emotion, Thought, and Estrangement: Emotion as a Cultural Category." *Cultural Anthropology* 1, no. 3 (1986): 287–309.

Macdonald, Sharon. "Enchantment and Its Dilemmas: The Museum as a Ritual Site." In *Science, Magic and Religion: The Ritual Processes of Museum Magic,* edited by Mary Bouquet and Nuno Porto, 209–227. Oxford: Berghahn, 2005.

Magilow, Daniel H. "Counting to Six Million: Collecting Projects and Holocaust Memorialization." *Jewish Social Studies,* n.s., 14, no. 1 (2007): 23–39.

Marcus, Jacob Rader. *To Count a People: American Jewish Population Data 1585–1984.* Washington, DC: University Press of America, 1990.

Marx, Karl, Friedrich Engels, and David Borisovich Goldendach. *The Communist Manifesto of Karl Marx and Friedrich Engels.* New York: Russell and Russell, 1963.

Mayer, Egon. *A Demographic Revolution in American Jewry.* Vol. 1, *David W. Belin Lecture in American Jewish Affairs.* Ann Arbor: Frankel Center for Judaic Studies, University of Michigan, 1992.

Melamed, Shoham. "Motherhood, Fertility, and the Construction of the 'Demographic Threat' in the Marital Age Law." *Theory and Criticism* 25 (2004): 69–96.

Mendelsohn, Daniel. *The Lost: A Search for Six of Six Million.* New York: HarperCollins, 2006.

Mendelssohn, Moses. "Remarks Concerning Michaelis' Response to Dohm (1783)." In *The Jew in the Modern World: A Documentary History,* edited by Paul Mendes-Flohr and Jehuda Reinharz, 48. Oxford: Oxford University Press, 1995.

"The Messianic Era—The Basics." *Chabad.org.* http://www.chabad.org/library/moshiach/article_cdo/aid/1128725/jewish/The-Basics.htm.

Metz, Karl H. "Paupers and Numbers: The Statistical Argument for Social Reform in Britain during the Period of Industrialization." In *The Probabilistic Revolution: Ideas in the Sciences,* edited by Lorenz Krüger, Gerd Gigerenzer, and Mary S. Morgan, 2:337–350. Cambridge, MA: MIT Press, 1987.

Michaelis, Johann David. "Arguments against Dohm (1782)." In *The Jew in the Modern World: A Documentary History,* edited by Paul Mendes-Flohr and Jehuda Reinharz, 31. Oxford: Oxford University Press, 1995.

Michaelson, Jay. "'Tis the Season for New Haggadot: Comparing the Best and Biggest Names for Passover." *Jewish Daily Forward,* March 23, 2012. http://forward.com/articles/153440/tis-the-season-for-new-haggadot/.

Miller, Peter. "Governing by Numbers: Why Calculative Practices Matter." *Social Research* 68, no. 2 (2001): 379–396.

Milton, Gordon. *Assimilation in American Life: The Role of Race, Religion and National Origins.* Oxford: Oxford University Press, 1964.

"A Monument Was Unveiled to Those Who Died at the Bombing of the Akhziv Bridge" [in Hebrew]. *Ma'ariv,* June 5, 1969.

Moore, MacDonald. "The Neodox: Prophets of Spreadsheet Tribalism." Unpublished manuscript.

Morgan, Mary S. *The History of Econometric Ideas.* Cambridge: Cambridge University Press, 1990.

Mosse, George. *Fallen Soldiers: Reshaping the Memory of the World Wars.* New York: Oxford University Press, 1990.

Muehlmann, Shaylih. "Rhizomes and Other Uncountables." *American Ethnologist* 39, no. 2 (2012): 339–352.

"Mystery of the Burial of the Thirteen Solved Twenty Years Later" [in Hebrew]. *Davar,* May 22, 1966.

mzjerusalem. "Who Knows Two Million? There's an ArtScroll Haggadah for Everyone!" *blog.ArtScroll.com,* April 2, 2009. http://web.archive.org/web/20090412033011 /http://blog.artscroll.com/2009/04/02/who-knows-two-million-theres-an-artscroll -haggadah-for-everyone/.

Nerel, Gershon. "Yad Ha'Shemona: A Unique Moshav of Finns and Israelis in the Judean Hills" [in Hebrew]. *Ariel* 168 (December 2004): 100–111.

Niewyk, Donald L., and Francis R. Nicosia. *The Columbia Guide to the Holocaust.* New York: Columbia University Press, 2000.

Nobles, Melissa. *Shades of Citizenship: Race and the Census in Modern Politics.* Stanford, CA: Stanford University Press, 2000.

Nora, Pierre. "Between Memory and History: Les Lieux de Mémoire." *Representations* 26 (Spring 1989): 7–25.

——. *Les Lieux de mémoire.* Vol. 1, *La République.* Paris: Gallimard, 1984.

Norden, Edward. "Counting the Jews." *Commentary* 92, no. 4 (1991): 36–43.

Oberschall, Anthony. *Empirical Social Research in Germany 1848–1914.* Paris: Mouton, 1965.

Ochs, Juliana. *Security and Suspicion: An Ethnography of Everyday Life in Israel.* Philadelphia: University of Pennsylvania Press, 2011.

Paley, Julia. "Making Democracy Count: Opinion Polls and Market Surveys in the Chilean Political Transition." *Cultural Anthropology* 16, no. 2 (2001): 135–164.

Patriarca, Silvana. *Numbers and Nationhood: Writing Statistics in Nineteenth-Century Italy.* Cambridge: Cambridge University Press, 1996.

Paul-Schiff, Maximilian. "Zur Statistik der Kriminalität der Juden." *Zeitschrift für Demographie und Statistik der Juden* 5, no. 5 (1909): 70–75.

Pelaia, Ariela. "The Jewish Holiday of Passover (Pesach)." *About.com.* http://judaism .about.com/od/holidays/a/Jewish-Holiday-Passover-Pesach.htm.

Peled, Yoav. "Ethnic Democracy and the Legal Construction of Citizenship: Arab Citizens of the Jewish State." *American Political Science Review* 86, no. 2 (1992): 432–443.

Penslar, Derek J. *Shylock's Children: Economics and Jewish Identity in Modern Europe.* Berkeley: University of California Press, 2001.

——. *Zionism and Technocracy: The Engineering of Jewish Settlement in Palestine, 1870–1918.* Bloomington: Indiana University Press, 1991.

Peterson, Brian. "Quantifying Conversion: A Note on the Colonial Census and Religious Change in Postwar Southern Mali." *History in Africa* 29 (2002): 381–392.

Pew Research Center, Religion and Public Life Project. "Infographic: Survey of Jewish Americans." December 3, 2013. http://www.pewforum.org/2013/12/03/infographic -survey-of-jewish-americans/.

——. *A Portrait of Jewish Americans: Findings from a Pew Research Center Study of U.S. Jews.* Washington, DC: Pew Research Center, October 1, 2013. http://www.pew forum.org/files/2013/10/jewish-american-full-report-for-web.pdf.

Pinchevski, Amit, and Efraim Torgovnik. "Signifying Passages: The Signs of Change in Israeli Street Names." *Media, Culture and Society* 24, no. 3 (2002): 365–388.

Porter, Theodore M. "Lawless Society: Social Science and the Reinterpretation of Statistics in Germany, 1850–1880." In *The Probabilistic Revolution: Ideas in History,* edited by Lorenz Krüger, Lorraine J. Daston, and Michael Heidelberger, 1:351–376. Cambridge, MA: MIT Press, 1987.

———. *The Rise of Statistical Thinking, 1820–1900.* Princeton, NJ: Princeton University Press, 1986.

———. "Statistical and Social Facts from Quetelet to Durkheim." *Sociological Perspectives* 38, no. 1 (1995): 15–26.

———. "Thin Description: Surface and Depth in Science and Science Studies." *Osiris* 27, no. 1 (2012): 209–226.

———. *Trust in Numbers: The Pursuit of Objectivity in Science and Public Life.* Princeton, NJ: Princeton University Press, 1995.

Portugese, Jacqueline. *Fertility Policy in Israel: The Politics of Religion, Gender, and Nation.* Westport, CT: Praeger, 1998.

Posner, Richard. *Public Intellectuals: A Study of Decline.* Cambridge, MA: Harvard University Press, 2001.

Prakash, Gyan. *Another Reason: Science and the Imagination of Modern India.* Princeton, NJ: Princeton University Press, 1999.

"A Project [in Memory] of *Hannah Szenes*" [in Hebrew]. *Davar,* April 21, 1946.

Putnam, Robert D. "Bowling Alone: America's Declining Social Capital." *Journal of Democracy* 6, no. 1 (1995): 65–78.

Rabinovitch, Lara, Shiri Goren, and Hannah S. Pressman, eds. *Choosing Yiddish: New Frontiers of Language and Culture.* Detroit: Wayne State University Press, 2013.

Rabinow, Paul. *French Modern: Norms and Forms of the Social Environment.* Cambridge, MA: MIT Press, 1989.

Raved, Ahiya. "Haifa Central Station Named after Those Killed by the Katyusha Rocket" [in Hebrew]. *Ynet,* July 9, 2007.

Ravidowicz, Simon. *Israel: The Ever-Dying People and Other Essays.* Madison, NJ: Fairleigh Dickinson University Press, 1986.

Reinke, Herbert. "Die 'Liason' Strafrechts mit der Statistik." *Zeitschrift für neuere Rechtsgeschichte* 12, no. 1 (1990): 169–179.

"Reinventing the Synagogue: A Conversation with Allison Fine." *Reform Judaism Online.* http://reformjudaismmag.org/Articles/index.cfm?id=3263.

Reisman, Bernard. "The Leadership Implications of the National Jewish Population Survey." *Journal of Jewish Communal Service* 68, no. 4 (1991): 350–356.

———. "Reflections on the 1990 National Jewish Population Survey." *Contemporary Jewry* 14, no. 1 (1993): 165–172.

Reuveni, Yaakov. *Mimshal Hamandat Be'eretz Yisrael, 1929–1948: Nituach History-Medini* [The mandatory government in the Land of Israel, 1929–1948]. Ramat Gan, Israel: Bar-Ilan University Press, 1993.

Ritter, Joshua R. "Recovering Hyperbole: Re-imagining the Limits of Rhetoric for an Age of Excess." Ph.D. diss., Georgia State University, 2010.

Ritterband, Paul, Barry Kosmin, and Jeffrey Scheckner. "Counting Jewish Populations: Methods and Problems." *American Jewish Year Book* (1988): 204–221.

Rohrlich, Marianne. "Exchanging Vows under a Canopy, No Matter Their Faith." *New York Times,* December 16, 2011. http://www.nytimes.com/2011/12/18/fashion/weddings/more-couples-are-using-a-wedding-canopy-no-matter-their-faith.html.

Rose, Nikolas. *Numbers, Powers of Freedom: Reframing Political Thought.* Cambridge: Cambridge University Press, 1999.

Rosental, Paul-André. *L'Intelligence démographique: Sciences et politiques des populations en France (1930–1960).* Paris: Odile Jacob, 2003.

Rose-Redwood, Reuben, Derek Alderman, and Maoz Azaryahu. "Geographies of Top-onymic Inscription: New Directions in Critical Place-Name Studies." *Progress in Human Geography* 34, no. 4 (2010): 453–470.

Rothstein, Edward. "Put Yourself in the Story of Passover: The Washington Haggadah at Metropolitan Museum of Art." *New York Times,* April 17, 2011. http://www .nytimes.com/2011/04/18/arts/design/the-washington-haggadah-at-metropolitan -museum-of-art.html.

Rudoren, Jodi. "Holocaust Told in One Word, 6 Million Times." *New York Times,* January 26, 2014, 1.

Runyan, Joshua. "More Than a Decade since Its Leader's Departure, Chabad-Lubavitch Expands His Call to Better the World." *Chabad.org/News,* June 22, 2007. http:// www.chabad.org/news/article_cdo/aid/534279/jewish/Since-its-Leaders-Departure -Chabad-Lubavitch-Expands.htm/r/cache/includerelated/false.

Runyan, Tamar. "Thousands Share Stories of Transformation at Historic Passover Meal." *Chabad-Lubavitch News,* April 14, 2011. http://www.chabad.org/news/article _cdo/aid/1497338/jewish/Nepal-Seder-Enjoys-Long-History.htm.

Ruppin, Arthur. *Die Juden der Gegenwart.* Berlin, 1904, rev. 1911.

——. "Die Kriminalität der Christen und Juden in Deutschland 1899–1902." *Zeitschrift für Demographie und Statistik der Juden* 1, no. 1 (1905): 6–9.

——. "Die sozialen Verhältnisse der Juden in Preussen und Deutschland." *Jahrbücher für Nationalökonomie und Statistik* 23 (1902): 781–784.

Sarna, Jonathan. "The Secret of Jewish Continuity." *Commentary* 98, no. 4 (1994): 55–58.

Savage, Rowan. "'Disease Incarnate': Biopolitical Discourse and Genocidal Dehuman-isation in the Age of Modernity." *Journal of Historical Sociology* 20, no. 3 (2007): 404–440.

Saxe, Leonard. "Counting American Jewry." *Sh'ma* 41, no. 673 (2010): 14–15.

Saxe, Leonard, and Charles Kadushin. "The Arithmetic of U.S. Jewry." *Jerusalem Post,* November 17, 2003, 135.

Schneerson, Rabbi Menachem M., ed. *Haggadah for Pesach.* Brooklyn, NY: Kehot Publi-cation Society, 2007.

Scholem, Gershom. "The Thirty-Six Hidden Righteous Men in Jewish Tradition." In *Scholem's Studies of Hasidism* [in Hebrew], edited by David Assaf and Esther Liebes, 316–320. Jerusalem: Magnes, 2008.

Schor, Paul. *Compter et classer: Histoire des recensements américains.* Paris: École des Hautes Études en Sciences Sociales, 2009.

Schroeder, Peter W., and Dagmar Schroeder-Hildebrand. *Six Million Paper Clips: The Making of a Children's Holocaust Memorial.* Minneapolis: Kar-Ben, 2004.

Schudson, Michael. "Dynamics of Distortion in Collective Memory." In *How Minds, Brains and Societies Reconstruct the Past,* edited by D. L. Schacter, J. T. Coyle, G. D. Fischbach, M. M. Mesulam, and L. E. Sullivan, 346–364. Cambridge, MA: Harvard University Press, 1995.

Schultz, Kevin. "Religion as Identity in Postwar America: The Last Serious Attempt to Put a Question on Religion in the United States." *Journal of American History* 93, no. 2 (2006): 359–384.

Schweber, Libby. *Disciplining Statistics: Demography and Vital Statistics in France and England.* Durham, NC: Duke University Press, 2003.

——. "Styles of Statistical Reasoning: The French Liberal Tradition Reconsidered." In *The Age of Numbers: Statistical Systems and National Traditions* [in French], edited by Jean-Pierre Beaud and Jean-Guy Prévost, 299–324. Sainte-Foy: Presses de l'Université du Québec, 2000.

Schwenken, Carl Philipp Theodor. *Notizen über die berüchtigsten jüdischen Gauner und Spitzbuben.* Marburg u. Cassel: Johann Christian Krieger, 1820.

Scott, James. *Seeing like a State: How Certain Schemes to Improve the Human Condition Have Failed.* New Haven, CT: Yale University Press, 1998.

Seabra Lopes, Daniel. "Making Oneself at Home with Numbers: Financial Reporting from an Ethnographic Perspective." *Social Anthropology* 19, no. 4 (2011): 463–476.

Segev, Tom. *The Seventh Million.* Translated by Haim Watzman. New York: Hill and Wang, 1993.

Sekula, Allan. "The Body and the Archive." *October* 39 (Winter 1986): 3–64.

Seltzer, William, and Margo Anderson. "The Dark Side of Numbers: The Role of Population Data Systems in Human Rights Abuses." *Social Research* 68, no. 2 (2001): 481–515.

Shafir, Gershon. "Capitalist Binationalism in Mandatory Palestine." *International Journal of Middle East Studies* 43, no. 4 (2011): 611–633.

Shafir, Gershon, and Yoav Peled. *Being Israeli: The Dynamics of Multiple Citizenship.* Cambridge: Cambridge University Press, 2002.

Shamir, Ilana. *Commemoration and Remembrance: Israel's Way of Shaping Its Mnemonic Landscape* [in Hebrew]. Tel Aviv: Am Oved, 1996.

Shandler, Jeffrey. *Adventures in Yiddishland: Postvernacular Language and Culture.* Berkeley: University of California Press, 2006.

——. *Keepers of Accounts: The Practice of Inventory in Modern Jewish Life.* Vol. 17, *David W. Belin Lecture in American Jewish Affairs.* Ann Arbor: Frankel Center for Judaic Studies, University of Michigan, 2010.

Shapiro, Ann-Louise. *Breaking the Codes: Female Criminality in Fin-de-Siècle Paris.* Stanford, CA: Stanford University Press, 1996.

Shapiro, Edward. *A Time for Healing: American Jewry since World War II.* Baltimore: Johns Hopkins University Press, 1992.

Shavit, Ari. *My Promised Land: The Triumph and Tragedy of Israel.* New York: Spiegel and Grau, 2013.

Sheskin, Ira. "Comparisons between Local Jewish Community Studies and the 2000–01 National Jewish Population Survey." *Contemporary Jewry* 25, no. 1 (2005): 158–192.

——. "Local Jewish Population Studies: Still Necessary after All These Years." *Contemporary Jewry* 15, no. 1 (1994): 26–38.

Sheskin, Ira, and Arnold Dashefsky. *Jewish Population in the United States.* Current Jewish Population Reports. Berman Institute–North American Jewish Data Bank, University of Connecticut. 2010. http://www.brandeis.edu/cmjs/conferences /demographyconf/pdfs/Dash efsky_JewishPopulationUS2010.pdf.

Sh'ma 41, no. 673 (2010).

Shryock, Andrew. "In the Double Remoteness of Arab Detroit: Reflections on Ethnography, Culture Work, and the Intimate Disciplines of Americanization." In *Off Stage / On Display: Intimacy and Ethnography in the Age of Public Culture,* edited by Andrew Shryock, 279–314. Stanford, CA: Stanford University Press, 2004.

Siddur Kol Yaakov / The Complete ArtScroll Siddur, Nusach Ashkenaz. 3rd ed. Edited and translated by Rabbi Nosson Scherman, co-edited by Rabbi Meir Zlotowitz. New York: Mesorah, 1990.

Silverstein, Michael, and Greg Urban, eds. *Natural Histories of Discourse.* Chicago: University of Chicago Press, 1996.

Simmel, Georg. *The Sociology of Georg Simmel.* Translated and edited by Kurt H. Wolff. New York: Free Press, 1950.

Skal, Moshe. "The Events That Transformed the Relationship between Arabs and Jews" [in Hebrew]. Review of *Tarpat,* by Hillel Cohen. *Ha'aretz Sefarim,* December 27, 2013, 8–9.

Spyer, Patricia. "Serial Conversion / Conversion to Seriality: Religion, State, and Number in Aru, Eastern Indonesia." In *Conversion to Modernities: The Globalization of Christianity,* edited by Peter van der Veer, 171–189. New York: Routledge, 1996.

Starr, Paul. "The Sociology of Official Statistics." In *The Politics of Numbers,* edited by William Alonso and Paul Starr, 7–57. New York: Russell Sage Foundation, 1987.

Steinhardt, Michael. "On the Question of Crisis." *Contact: The Journal of Jewish Life Network* 5, no. 3 (2003): 9–10.

Stewart, Susan. *On Longing: Narratives of the Miniature, the Gigantic, the Souvenir, the Collection.* Durham, NC: Duke University Press, 1993.

Stier, Oren Baruch. *Committed to Memory: Cultural Mediations of the Holocaust.* Amherst: University of Massachusetts Press, 2003.

Stigler, Stephen. *The History of Statistics: The Measurement of Uncertainty before 1900.* Cambridge, MA: Belknap, 1990.

——. "The Measurement of Uncertainty in Nineteenth-Century Social Science." In *The Probabilistic Revolution: Ideas in History,* edited by Lorenz Krüger, Lorraine J. Daston, and Michael Heidelberger, 1:287–293. Cambridge, MA: MIT Press, 1987.

Stolow, Jeremy. *Orthodox by Design: Judaism, Print Politics, and the ArtScroll Revolution.* Berkeley: University of California Press, 2010. http://public.eblib.com/EBL Public/PublicView.do?ptiID=547598.

"Street of the Four" [in Hebrew]. *Davar,* February 24, 1946.

Stypinska, Justyna. "Jewish Majority and Arab Minority in Israel's Demographic Struggle." *Polish Sociological Review* 1, no. 157 (2007): 105–120.

Svonkin, Stuart. *Jews against Prejudice: American Jews and the Fight for Civil Liberties.* New York: Columbia University Press, 1999.

Tenenbaum, Shelly. "Good or Bad for the Jews? Moving Beyond the Continuity Debate." *Contemporary Jewry* 21, no. 1 (2000): 91–97.

Thiele, A. F. *Die jüdischen Gauner in Deutschland: ihre Taktik, ihre Eigentümlichkeiten, und ihre Sprache.* Berlin, 1840.

"Thirty-Five Fighters Sent as Reinforcement" [in Hebrew]. *Ha'tsofe,* January 20, 1948.

"Thirty-Five Hagana Members Were Killed by an Ambush" [in Hebrew]. *Ha'aretz,* January 18, 1948.

Tidhar, David. *Encyclopedia of the Founders and Builders of Israel.* 2012. http://www .tidhar.tourolib.org/.

Timmermans, Stefan, and Steven Epstein. "A World of Standards but Not a Standard World: Toward a Sociology of Standards and Standardization." *Annual Review of Sociology* 36 (2010): 69–89.

Trial of the Major War Criminals before the International Military Tribunal, Nuremberg, 14 November 1945–1 October 1946. Vol. 3. Nuremberg, Germany: International Military Tribunal, 1947. http://www.loc.gov/rr/frd/Military_Law/pdf/NT_Vol-III .pdf.

Trial of the Major War Criminals before the International Military Tribunal, Nuremberg, 14 November 1945–1 October 1946. Vol. 19. Nuremberg, Germany: International Military Tribunal, 1947. http://www.loc.gov/rr/frd/Military_Law/pdf/NT_Vol-XIX .pdf.

Trial of the Major War Criminals before the International Military Tribunal, Nuremberg, 14 November 1945–1 October 1946. Vol. 31. Nuremberg, Germany: International Military Tribunal, 1947. http://www.loc.gov/rr/frd/Military_Law/pdf/NT_Vol-XXXI .pdf.

Trumbower, Jeffrey A. *Rescue for the Dead: The Posthumous Salvation of Non-Christians in Early Christianity.* Oxford: Oxford University Press, 2001.

Twain, Mark. *Chapters from My Autobiography.* Project Gutenberg, 2006. http://www .gutenberg.org.

Uehling, Greta. "The First Independent Ukrainian Census in the Crimea: Myths, Miscoding and Missed Opportunities." *Ethnic and Racial Studies* 27, no. 1 (2004): 149–170.

Ulbricht, Otto. "Criminality and Punishment of the Jews in the Early Modern Period." In *In and Out of the Ghetto: Jewish-Gentile Relations in Late Medieval and Early Modern Germany,* edited by R. Po-Chia Hsia and Hartmut Lehmann, 49–70. Cambridge: Cambridge University Press, 1995.

Urla, Jacqueline. "Cultural Politics in an Age of Statistics: Numbers, Nations, and the Making of Basque Identity." *American Ethnologist* 20, no. 4 (1993): 818–843.

Verein zur Abwehr des Antisemitisums. *Die Kriminalität der Juden in Deutschland.* Berlin: Mitteilungen des Vereins zur Abwehr des Antisemitismus, 1896.

Violi, Patrizia. "Trauma Site Museums and Politics of Memory: Tuol Sleng, Villa Grimaldi and the Bologna Ustica Museum." *Theory, Culture and Society* 29, no. 1 (2012): 36–75.

Vollmer, Hendrik. "How to Do More with Numbers: Elementary Stakes, Framing, Keying, and the Three-Dimensional Character of Numerical Signs." *Accounting, Organizations and Society* 32, no. 6 (2007): 577–600.

Von Liszt, Franz. *Das Problem der Kriminalität der Juden.* Giessen, Germany: Alfred Töpelmann, 1907.

Vyleta, Daniel M. *Crime, Jews and News: Vienna 1895–1914.* New York: Berghahn, 2007.

——. "Jewish Crimes and Misdemeanors: In Search of Jewish Criminality (Germany and Austria, 1890–1914)." *European History Quarterly* 35, no. 2 (2005): 299–325.

Wagner, Peter. "'An Entirely New Object of Consciousness, of Volition, of Thought': The Coming into Being and (Almost) Passing Away of 'Society' as a Scientific Object." In *Biographies of Scientific Objects,* edited by Lorraine Daston, 132–157. Chicago: University of Chicago Press, 2000.

Wassermann, Rudolf. "Ist die Kriminalität der Juden Rassenkriminalität?" *Zeitschrift für Demographie und Statistik der Juden* 7, no. 3 (1911): 36–39.

Webb, Stephen H. "Theological Reflections on the Hyperbolic Imagination." In *Rhetorical Invention and Religious Inquiry: New Perspectives,* edited by Walter Jost and Wendy Olmsted, 279–299. New Haven, CT: Yale University Press, 2000.

Weinreich, Max. *Hitler's Professors: The Part of Scholarship in Germany's Crimes against the Jewish People.* 2nd ed. New Haven, CT: Yale University Press, 1999.

Welner, Alter. *Armed in Front of the Camp: The Story of a Religious Unit* [in Hebrew]. Tel Aviv: Defense Ministry Press, 1984.

Wertheimer, Jack. "Family Values and the Jews." *Commentary* 97, no. 1 (1994): 30–34.

Wertheimer, Jack, Charles Liebman, and Steven Cohen. "How to Save American Jews." *Commentary* 101, no. 1 (1996): 47–51.

White, Geoffrey M. "National Subjects: September 11 and Pearl Harbor." *American Ethnologist* 31, no. 3 (2008): 293–310.

Wiesel, Elie. *Hagadah shel pesah = A Passover Haggadah: As Commented upon by Elie Wiesel and Illustrated by Mark Podwal,* edited by Marion Wiesel. New York: Simon and Schuster, 1993.

Winter, Jay. *Sites of Memory, Sites of Mourning: The Great War in European Cultural History.* Cambridge: Cambridge University Press, 1995.

Wistrich, Robert. "Do the Jews Have a Future?" *Commentary* 98, no. 1 (1994): 23–26.

Woocher, Jonathan S. *Sacred Survival: The Civil Religion of American Jews.* Bloomington: Indiana University Press, 1986.

Yadin-Israel, Azzan. "A Measure of Beauty." *Jewish Review of Books* 3 (Fall 2010): 44–45.

Yerushalmi, Yosef Hayim. *Zakhor: Jewish History and Jewish Memory.* Seattle: University of Washington Press, 1982.

Yiftachel, Oren. "'Ethnocracy': The Politics of Judaizing Israel/Palestine." *Constellations* 6, no. 3 (1999): 364–390.

Yolkut, Elianna. "The Problem with Worrying about 'Jewish Continuity.'" *Ha'aretz,* November 13, 2011. http://www.haaretz.com/jewish-world/the-problem-with -worrying-about-jewish-continuity-1.395277.

Young, James Edward. *Writing and Rewriting the Holocaust: Narrative and the Consequences of Interpretation.* Bloomington: Indiana University Press, 1988.

Yuval-Davis, Nira. *Woman-Nation-State.* Basingstoke, UK: Macmillan, 1989.

Zakim, Michael. "Statistics-for-Profit." In *Measuring Everything* [in Hebrew], 73–86. Be'er Sheva, Israel: Ben-Gurion University Press, 2010.

Zaloom, Caitlin. "Ambiguous Numbers: Trading Technologies and Interpretation in Financial Markets." *American Ethnologist* 30, no. 2 (2003): 1–15.

———. "Trading Technologies and Interpretation." *Financial Markets* 30, no. 2 (2003): 1–15.

Zandberg, Esther. "Garden of Eden Made by Man" [in Hebrew]. *Ha'aretz,* April 6, 2001.

Zarrow, Sarah Ellen. "'Holy Sacred Collection Work': The Relationship between YIVO and Its Zamlers." In *Going to the People: Jews and the Ethnographic Impulse,* edited by Jeffrey Veidlinger. Bloomington: Indiana University Press, forthcoming.

Zelizer, Barbie. *Remembering to Forget: Holocaust Memory through the Camera's Eye.* Chicago: University of Chicago Press, 1998.

Zerubavel, Eviatar. "Calendars and History: A Comparative Study of the Social Organization of National Memory." In *States of Memory: Continuities, Conflicts, and Transformations in National Retrospection,* edited by Jeffrey K. Olick, 315–337. Durham, NC: Duke University Press, 2003.

———. "Social Memories." In *Social Mindscapes: An Invitation to Cognitive Sociology,* 87. Cambridge, MA: Harvard University Press, 1997.

Zerubavel, Yael. "The Historical, the Legendary, and the Incredible: Invented Tradition and Collective Memory in Israel." In *Commemorations: The Politics of National Identity,* edited by John R. Gillis, 105–123. Princeton, NJ: Princeton University Press, 1994.

——. "'Numerical Commemoration' and the Challenges of Collective Remembrance in Israel." *History and Memory* 26, no. 1 (2014): 5–38.

——. "Patriotic Sacrifice and the Burden of Memory in Israeli Secular National Hebrew Culture." In *Memory and Violence in the Middle East and North Africa,* edited by Ussama Makdisi and Paul A. Silverstein, 77–100. Bloomington: Indiana University Press, 2006.

——. *Recovered Roots: Collective Memory and the Making of Israeli National Tradition.* Chicago: University of Chicago Press, 1995.

Zeveloff, Naomi. "What Does Schechter Decline Mean? School Dip Sign of Trouble for Conservative Movement." *Jewish Daily Forward,* January 27, 2012. http://forward.com/articles/149983/what-does-schechter-decline-mean/?p=all&p=all&p=all#ixzz1kHqXrSLG.

Ziv, Yehuda. *A Moment in Situ: Stories behind Place Names* [in Hebrew]. Jerusalem: Tsivonim, 2005.

Zubrzycki, Geneviève. *The Crosses of Auschwitz: Nationalism and Religion in Post-Communist Poland.* Chicago: University of Chicago Press, 2006.

Websites

"Beit Sturman." http://www.beit-shturman.co.il/he/ [in Hebrew].

"Bnei Brak." http://www.bnei-brak.muni.il/Pages/default.aspx [in Hebrew].

Burstein, Lior. "Misparim." http://www.hebrewsongs.com/?song=misparim.

"Children's Holocaust Memorial and Paper Clip Project." http://www.whitwellmiddleschool.org/?PageName=bc&n=69258.

"Givat Ha'Shelosha." http://www.ptarchive.co.il/he/ArchiveItem.aspx?t=1&p=1&iid=15 [in Hebrew].

"Hadag Nahash Misparim Lyrics." http://www.lyrics46.com/HADAG-NAHASH-MISPARIM-LYRICS/177493/.

"Haifa Street Guide." http://www.haifa-streets.co.il/Lists/List1/DispForm.aspx?ID=5895 [in Hebrew].

"In the Footsteps of 1947." http://www.merchavim.org.il/cgi-webaxy/item?41 [in Hebrew].

"Kibbutz Givat Three." http://www.dsharon.org.il/597/ [in Hebrew].

"Kiryat Shemona." http://www.k-8.co.il/AboutUs/history/Pages/default.aspx [in Hebrew].

"Ma'ale Ha'Hamisha." http://www.maale5.com//Default.aspx [in Hebrew].

"Maoz." http://www.maoz.org.il/ [in Hebrew].

"Medal Act of 1993." http://www.israelmint.com/?section=449&product=2520&lineItem=419 [in Hebrew].

"Milestones in History." http://ramat-hasharon.muni.il/%D7%90%D7%91%D7%A0%D7%99-%D7%93%D7%A8%D7%9A%D7%91%D7%94%D7%99%D7%A1%D7%98%D7%95%D7%A8%D7%99%D7%94/ [in Hebrew].

"Mishmar Ha'Shelosha." http://tnuathaavoda.info/places/home/places/1155802705.html [in Hebrew].

Muggia, Gal. "Ani Ma'amin." https://vimeo.com/41743115.
"Ness Ziona." http://www.masa.co.il/article/6450/%D7%92%D7%9F-%D7%94-73-%D7%91%D7%A0%D7%A1-%D7%A6%D7%99%D7%95%D7%A0%D7%94/ [in Hebrew].
"Netiv Ha'Asara." http://www.netiv-10.co.il/12432/%D7%94%D7%99%D7%A1%D7%98%D7%95%D7%A 8%D7%99%D7%94 [in Hebrew].
"Nir Hen." http://www.homee.co.il/%D7%9F%D7%A0%D7%99%D7%A8-%D7%97/ [in Hebrew].
"Pa'amei Tashaz." http://www.merchavim.org.il/cgi-webaxy/item?41 [in Hebrew].
"Ramat Gan." http://www.tm-it.co.il/krinizi-ramat-gan/show_item.asp?levelId=65011)/ [in Hebrew].
"Rehov Ha'Arba'a." http://www.ezy.co.il/memoSite.asp?memorial_id=41 and http://www.ezy.co.il/memoSite.asp?memorial_id=113 [in Hebrew].
"Rehov Kam." http://www.haifa-streets.co.il/Lists/List1/DispForm.aspx?ID=5448 [in Hebrew].
"The Shoah Victims' Names Recovery Project." *Yad Vashem, the Holocaust Martyrs' and Heroes' Remembrance Authority.* http://www.yadvashem.org/yv/en/remembrance/names/.
"Tel Aviv Street Guide." http://www.tel-aviv.gov.il/thecity/pages/streetsguide.aspx?tm [in Hebrew].
"Today: Opening of New Permanent Exhibition SHOAH in Block 27 at Auschwitz-Birkenau Curated by Yad Vashem." *Yad Vashem, the Holocaust Martyrs' and Heroes' Remembrance Authority.* http://www.yadvashem.org/yv/en/pressroom/pressreleases/pr_d etails.asp?cid=795.
"Tourism in the Valley." http://www.bikathayarden.co.il/index/%D7%90%D7%A0%D7%93%D7%98%D7%AA-%D7%94%D7%A0%D7%93 [in Hebrew].

Contributors

Coeditor **Deborah Dash Moore** is Frederick G. L. Huetwell Professor of History at the University of Michigan and former director of the Jean and Samuel Frankel Center for Judaic Studies. A historian of American Jews, she focuses on the twentieth-century experience. She is author of a trilogy: *At Home in America: Second Generation New York Jews* (1981), *GI Jews: How World War II Changed a Generation* (2004), and *To the Golden Cities: Pursuing the American Jewish Dream in Miami and L.A.* (1994).

Joshua B. Friedman is Adjunct Assistant Professor in the Department of Anthropology at Brooklyn College. His doctoral research focused on the instrumentalization of Yiddish language and culture within the American Jewish nonprofit sector. The project was supported by the National Science Foundation, the University of Michigan's Institute for the Humanities, and the Frankel Center for Judaic Studies at the University of Michigan.

Mitchell B. Hart holds the Alexander Grass Chair in Jewish History at the University of Florida. He is author of *Social Science and the Politics of Modern Jewish Identity* (2000) and *The Healthy Jew* (2007); he has edited *Jews and Race: Writings on Identity and Difference, 1880–1940* (2011) and *Jewish Blood: Metaphor and Reality in Jewish History, Religion, and Culture* (2009). He is co-editor, with Tony Michels, of the *Cambridge History of Judaism: The Modern World*, which will appear in 2016.

Carol A. Kidron is Senior Lecturer (Associate Professor) in the Department of Sociology and Anthropology at the University of Haifa. Her research interests include personal, communal, and collective Holocaust and genocide commemoration and the ways in which therapeutic discourse and particularly trauma constructs have informed contemporary subjectivities. She has published in leading journals, including *Current Anthropology* and *American Ethnologist*.

Michal Kravel-Tovi is Lecturer (Assistant Professor) of Anthropology in the Department of Sociology and Anthropology at Tel Aviv University. Her work focuses on contemporary Jewish life, including messianism among Chabad-Lubavitch Hasidim, state-run Jewish conversion in Israel, and sociodemographic statistics among American Jewry. Her work has been published in *American*

Ethnologist, Religion, Ethnic and Racial Studies, and *Journal of the Royal Anthropological Institute.*

Anat Leibler is a lecturer in the Science, Technology and Society Graduate Program, Bar-Ilan University. Her interests focus on population management, census, demographic classifications, and globalization of economic statistics. Her work has been published in *Social Studies of Science, Racial and Ethnic Studies,* and *Israel Studies.* She is preparing for publication her book, *Landscape of Numbers: Political Demography in the Making of the Israeli Nation-State.*

Vanessa L. Ochs is Professor of Religious Studies at the University of Virginia and the author of *Inventing Jewish Ritual,* winner of a 2007 National Jewish Book Award. Her other books include *Sarah Laughed, The Jewish Dream Book* (with Elizabeth Ochs), *The Book of Jewish Sacred Practices* (edited with Irwin Kula), *Words on Fire: One Woman's Journey into the Sacred,* and *Safe and Sound: Protecting Your Child in an Unpredictable World.* For her writing, she was awarded a Creative Writing Fellowship by the National Endowment for the Arts.

Theodore M. Porter is Professor of History at UCLA and author of books and many articles focusing mainly on history of statistics and quantification and history of the social and human sciences. The best known book is *Trust in Numbers* (1995), which won the Ludwik Fleck Prize after publication, and has now been published in Japanese translation, with a French translation in the works. His next book, appearing soon, will be *The Unknown History of Human Heredity.*

Oren Baruch Stier is Associate Professor of Religious Studies at Florida International University. He directs FIU's Holocaust Studies Initiative as well as its Jewish Studies Certificate Program. He is the author of *Holocaust Icons: Symbolizing the Shoah in History and Memory* (2015) and *Committed to Memory: Cultural Mediations of the Holocaust* (2003) and co-editor of *Religion, Violence, Memory, and Place* (2006). He has published articles in the *Journal of the American Academy of Religion, Prooftexts, Jewish Social Studies,* and *Numen,* among others. He has been a Center for Advanced Holocaust Studies fellow at the United States Holocaust Memorial Museum and has served as co-chair of the Religion, Holocaust and Genocide Group of the American Academy of Religion. In spring 2013, he was the guest curator for the exhibition "Race and Visual Culture under National Socialism" at the Wolfsonian Teaching Gallery at FIU's Frost Art Museum.

Yael Zerubavel is Founding Director of the Allen and Joan Bildner Center for the Study of Jewish Life and Professor of Jewish Studies and History at Rutgers University. She has published *Recovered Roots: Collective Memory and the Making* *of Israeli National Tradition* (1995) and numerous articles on collective memory and identity, Israeli national myths, war and trauma, and symbolic landscapes. She is currently completing *Desert in the Promised Land: Memory, Space, and the Counterplace in Israeli Culture* and is working on a new book project on biblical representations and the performance of antiquity in Israeli culture.

Index

Page numbers in italics refer to figures.